The Beginning of
the Great Game in Asia
1828-1834

The Beginning of the Great Game in Asia 1828-1834

BY

EDWARD INGRAM

Associate Professor in History
at Simon Fraser University

Clarendon Press · Oxford
1979

Oxford University Press, Walton Street, Oxford OX2 6DP

OXFORD LONDON GLASGOW NEW YORK
TORONTO MELBOURNE WELLINGTON CAPE TOWN
NAIROBI DAR ES SALAAM HONG KONG TOKYO
KUALA LUMPUR SINGAPORE JAKARTA
DELHI BOMBAY CALCUTTA MADRAS KARACHI

Published in the United States by
Oxford University Press, New York

British Library Cataloguing in Publication Data

Ingram, Edward
   The beginning of the great game in Asia, 1828–1834.
   1. Asia – Foreign relations – Great Britain
   2. Great Britain – Foreign relations – Asia
   I. Title.
327.41′05   DS33.4.G7   78–40078

ISBN 0–19–822470–2

Printed in Great Britain by
Western Printing Services Ltd., Bristol

to
Mrs. David Fraser Jenkins

in memory of youth

Ignorance is a delicate exotic fruit;
touch it and the bloom is gone.

LADY BRACKNELL,
The Importance of Being Earnest,
Act I

Preface

As a child I lived in a beautiful garden with high walls, iron gates, and armed guards, outside Calcutta. Sometimes I was allowed out; driven in a large old American car to visit another beautiful garden to play with other English children. We never travelled for pleasure, only taking the train to Darjeeling to escape the heat, or to Bombay to catch the P & O steamer when going on leave. India was a blurred glimpse through a carriage window. Whether from the burning sun or the pelting rain mattered little; what could be seen could not be understood.

I strayed many years later into a similar garden with similar inhabitants: the wall was a high hedge, the Indians outside were Frenchmen, of a sort, the place Drummondville, Quebec. Continuing across the vast Canadian prairie, to stand in the ruin of the imperial cable station at Bamfield, British Columbia, and gaze westwards across the Pacific, I sighed at having been born too late to serve the empire on which the sun was never to have set. Instead I must write of it. These tales of Englishmen in the near east are offered as a tiny tribute to those who knew that effortless countrymen were meant to win superior prizes.

Diplomatic histories are too often accounts of the origins of wars. This is true of the Eastern Question. Good books have been written about the Greek War for Independence, the First Afghan War, and the Second Mahomet Ali Crisis. There is no similar book about the period between 1828 and 1833, after the treaties of Turkmanchay and Adrianople and before the treaties of Münchengrätz, when the Duke of Wellington and Earl Grey were Prime Minister. Those were the crucial years when the Great Game in Asia began.

The period has a second significance. The Eastern Question is usually divided geographically: one follows the British as far as Damascus or beyond Basra. Turkey is part of, or becomes part of, the concert of Europe; Afghanistan is an outwork, or is to be turned into an outwork, of British India; Persia strays between them. So eminent a scholar as Sir Charles Webster dismissed the First Afghan War as irrelevant to his study of British foreign policy.

The division reflected a faulty understanding of Britain's power and vital interests. Between 1828 and 1834 British policy throughout the near east was the result of debating how to defend India from Russia. The Great Game in Asia was the result.

The history of the young Englishmen, who braved danger and hardship to provide detailed information of the geography, trade, and political systems of the near-eastern states, is not repeated here. James and Alexander Burnes, Arthur Conolly, James Baillie Fraser, Joseph Wolff, Francis Chesney, and Robert Urquhart, need no introduction, and their own accounts of their travels are better reading than any of the books written about them. I have tried to explain why they were sent and what was the result. Too often forgotten are their elders, Claude Wade in the Punjab, Henry Pottinger in Sind, John McNeill in Persia, and Robert Taylor at Baghdad, who worked equally hard if less dramatically to safeguard British India. Finally this book is about two men whose work has always and unfairly been criticized; if it has heroes, they are Edward, Lord Ellenborough, and Sir Henry Ellis.

One of the more fashionable and tiresome private vocabularies belongs to theorists of modernization, or development and under-development as they sometimes call it. The controversies that rage amongst them rarely illumine and never entertain. Each theory represents an affection or contempt for civilized society, and this was so in the nineteenth century. Late Georgian Englishmen were interested in others when eager to change themselves; when eager to change others they were narcissistic. Comprehension was less valued by them than self-confidence. Forgetting that Utopia was not supposed to come about, they proved at the beginning of the Great Game in Asia that reform caused paralysis or upheaval. This need not, I hope, be called inducing under-development.

This book owes its existence to two distinguished scholars, Elie Kedourie, Professor of Politics in the University of London, whom I have only recently been privileged to meet, but who told me to begin, and Rose Louise Greaves, Professor of History in the University of Kansas, who arrived unannounced one day from the United States and told me to finish. I hope they will now enjoy reading what they encouraged me to write. Anyone who is bored should not hold them responsible.

Acknowledgements are due to the following: to the Controller of Her Majesty's Stationery Office for Crown-copyright material in the Public Record Office; to Her Majesty's Secretary of State for Foreign and Commonwealth Affairs for Crown-copyright material in the India Office Library and India Office records; to R. J. Bingle, Assistant Keeper, and Martin Moir, Deputy Archivist, at the India Office Library for their kindness and help; to the Department of Paleography and Diplomatic in the University of Durham, the Trustees of the British Museum and of the Broadlands Manuscripts, the National Library of Scotland, the National Library of Wales, the Bodleian Library, the University of Nottingham Library, and the University of Edinburgh Library, for material from their collections; to the President's Research Grants' Committee at Simon Fraser University and their Chairman, Professor Klaus Rieckhoff, for their generosity each year; and to the Canada Council for paying my way to Pakistan.

Writers often thank their colleagues for their help. Mine have given none. Many of them appear not to value diplomatic history; to share with E. H. Carr a belief that history as a discipline has progressed beyond it into more sophisticated analysis of ideas and economics. Perhaps they are right, but too many of the books they like might have been written about anywhere at any time. Historians, unlike political scientists or sociologists, should tell stories. I have tried.

Writers often thank their typists. I thank mine. Mrs. George L. Cook is not a particularly good typist, but her spelling and grammar are good. The responsibility for any mistakes is mine, but the fault is hers. Finally, writers too often thank their wives. I have no wife. Instead I thank four friends, Megan Nelson and Geoffrey Thompson, who compiled the index, and Eileen Warrell and Richard Crockford, but for the company of whom, occasionally delightful, always exasperating, this book might have been written five years ago.

The Empress Hotel,
Victoria Day, 1976   E. R. I. E.

Contents

List of Maps

Notes on references

ABBREVIATIONS

Add. MSS.	British Library, Additional Manuscripts
B.T.	Public Record Office, Board of Trade Records
cd	court of directors of the East India Company
E.U.L.	University of Edinburgh Library
Film. MSS.	Microfilmed Manuscripts
F.O.	Public Record Office, Foreign Office Records
ggic	governor-general in council
gicB	governor in council at Bombay
I.O.	India Office Library, India Office Records
I.O.L.	India Office Library
MSS. Eur.	India Office Library, European Manuscripts
P.R.O.	Public Record Office Manuscripts
sc	secret committee of the East India Company
W.O.	Public Record Office, War Office Records

THE INDIA OFFICE RECORDS

The India Office Records are being rearranged with new titles. Whenever possible these are used in references. When not, the old long titles are abbreviated. The abbreviations are explained in the bibliography.

SPELLING AND DATES

Because this is a study of British policy, written from British sources for British and American readers, a parade of foreign names and titles would be pretentious. To see in similar works a grand vizier called a *ṣadr-i a'ẓem* and Oudh spelt Avadh irritates me. Places and persons are here spelt according to common English usage. All dates are given according to the Gregorian calendar. The Julian calendar, in use in Russia, was twelve days behind.

I

Introduction

Fanatics have their dreams, wherewith they weave
A paradise for a sect; . . .

KEATS,

The Fall of Hyperion, I. 1–2

EVERY NEW STUDENT of British foreign policy in the early nineteenth century should be warned against Webster and Temperley. The giants of diplomatic history in England, they divided the period into six long misleading books: reading them bewitches one. Their spell may not work on foreigners, but it appeals to an Englishman's most primitive political instinct. Utrecht, Vienna, and Versailles, were the equivalent for Webster and Temperley of the Glorious Revolution, the loss of the American colonies, and the Great Reform Act, for Macaulay and Trevelyan. At the end of the First World War, who could resist the idea that at the beginning of every century, the British, their general will personified in Marlborough, Wellington, and Haig, marched into Europe, as they marched between times into Bengal, or Ashanti, or Egypt, sorted everything out for a hundred years, and then went about their business? Louis XIV and Wilhelm II were not Surajah Dowlah and Arabi Bey, but they were not unlike. Each time the British intervened they had better ideas; at Versailles Webster himself had suggested how to improve them. The treaties were landmarks in a history of progress, and the 1930s were humiliating, because the British appeared at Versailles to have made a mistake.

The British and their diplomatic historians suffer from a variety of a complaint named by Toynbee the lunatic hallucination of whigs: for them, unlike Macaulay, history had not come to an end, but the British role in it was fixed. The First World War, therefore, was not, as for certain American historians, to end all wars; the balance of power would periodically require adjustment, but the British, led by Neville Chamberlain reading Temperley on

Canning during the Munich Crisis, would always manage to adjust it. The Second World War did not destroy this illusion, because the British, who had always relied on others to fight on their behalf, assumed that the Americans, like Blücher at Waterloo, had merely arrived late, and Stalingrad to be a diversion from el-Alamein. Nor was the illusion destroyed by the Iron Curtain and the European Union. Naturally the British did not join: after the Napoleonic Wars they had soon abandoned the Congress System and denounced the Holy Alliance. They continued to go about their imperial and world-wide business, until their spell was broken by the Suez Crisis. If they could not put down Nasser, and those who raged against trying were really taken by surprise at having to, how were they to cope again with Hitler? Sir Anthony Eden was right to see one as the other,[1] because the dilemma of Britain as great power had been her need since the mid-eighteenth century to defend her European and imperial interests at the same time, without, by using all her energy, power, and available funds, in defence of one, having to choose between the two.

After 1784, Great Britain as great power was Britain and British India: she had to appear both a powerful European and a powerful Asiatic state, or she could be neither. Both were illusions, able to be cherished by the British and deceiving others, only as long as favourable circumstances meant that the British need not defend their claims. Survival depended on a belief in a glorious past, warranting a belief in an equally glorious future, provided the British could avoid at any moment coming to terms with the present.[2] A. J. P. Taylor often reminds us that by 1939 a choice had to be made between Germany and Russia, but this was reason enough to postpone it: disaster had followed Grey's choice between Germany and France. What happened when the British preferred the present to the future was shown by Churchill in the Second World War. The conservatives were ousted in 1945, partly because in a flash of realism the British sensed how badly they had been tricked; their heritage squandered and their future jeopardized for a moment of excitement in a wrong cause. Because peripheral

---

[1] *The Memoirs of the Rt. Hon. Sir Anthony Eden: Full Circle* (London, 1960), pp. 430–2; Hugh Thomas, *Suez* (New York, 1967), pp. 52, 57.

[2] In 1939 Neville Chamberlain believed, that if the British stood perfectly still, the prospect of a world war would disappear, because Hitler would realize that Germany could not win. See R. A. C. Parker, 'Britain, France, and Scandinavia, 1939–40', *History*, lxi (1976), 369–87.

states cannot fight total wars without destroying themselves, fighting unnecessary and ineffective campaigns on the fringes of Europe had destroyed British India. With it went Great Britain. The Raj, as a military conquest depending for its existence on will and strength, could have survived the fall of Greece, even the fall of France, more easily than the surrender of Singapore. Wavell, Auchinleck, and the Mediterranean fleet who were needed in the China Sea, won great victories in north Africa, but at greater cost; Montgomery did not even win.

Since Robinson and Gallagher and R. L. Greaves explained, nearly twenty years ago, how far Britain's policy in the partition of Africa and the near east was influenced by her Indian interests,[1] the importance of India to Britain has become unquestioned, and the needs of Indian defence and its effects on Britain in Europe between 1882 and 1939 have been studied in detail.[2] In earlier periods, when firstly as a source of tribute, then as an export market for British manufactures and surplus capital, India was economically most valuable to Britain, playing a decisive role in the Industrial Revolution, British India is treated as a separate state, hardly rating mention in the standard histories of British foreign policy.[3] Perhaps the ties with India seem to have been more evident in the early twentieth century, because cabinet ministers and even foreign secretaries, Lansdowne, Curzon, Halifax, and Sir John Anderson, amongst them, had trained at Calcutta or New Delhi. A century earlier they might have done the same at the board of control.

Diplomatic historians have come to terms with Austria–Hungary, two states sometimes with one foreign policy; Great Britain in the early nineteenth century was one state sometimes with two. The second foreign office was housed not at Fort William, as governors-general often liked to pretend, nor at the East India Company, who supplied soldiers and civil servants but

---

[1] R. Robinson and J. Gallagher, *Africa and the Victorians: The Official Mind of Imperialism* (London, 1962); R. L. Greaves, *Persia and the Defence of India, 1884–1892* (London, 1959).

[2] For a review of recent work see E. Ingram, 'The Defence of India, 1874–1914: A Strategic Dilemma', *Militärgeschichtliche Mitteilungen* (1974), 215–24.

[3] See, e.g., K. Bourne, *The Foreign Policy of Victorian England, 1830–1902* (Oxford, 1970), and R. W. Seton-Watson, *Britain in Europe, 1789–1914: A Survey of Foreign Policy* (Cambridge, 1945). There is one useful chapter about the defence of India in the 1880s in C. J. Lowe, *The Reluctant Imperialists: British Foreign Policy, 1878–1902* (London, 1967).

had lost their influence over policy, but at the board of control, where the president, who was responsible for the tranquillity and security of British India, had, whenever he could not persuade the foreign secretary to act, to take decisions in his place. The problem of how to ensure the security of British India did not begin when the British occupied Egypt in 1882, which is when many histories take up the subject, but upon the French occupation in 1798, and affected or threatened to affect British policy in Europe as early as during and immediately after the Napoleonic Wars.

During this period, also, the problem changed. As long as British India was only one state amongst many, the British feared invasion or coalition; after 1818, when they became the paramount power, they feared rebellion and expense. India, perhaps because it should not be thought of as a colony, is the exception to all the rules of Victorian colonial history. Deprived Indians did not become depraved in the 1870s and 1880s, like Robinson and Gallagher's Egyptians, nor had they been transformed in English eyes by the Mutiny: that excited only people who had never before thought of India. Englishmen who had wanted to assimilate Indians had given up trying in the 1840s, and many Englishmen had never tried.[1] A constant war was waged between conservatives, the romantic imperialists as they are called, and utilitarian and evangelical reformers; and it as powerfully affected the government of India's defence and foreign as their legal and economic policies.

This assumption, that India and the defence of India were as important to Britain in the early as in the late nineteenth century, provides standards of measurement for British foreign secretaries different from the ones established by Webster, Temperley, and Seton-Watson, and some odd results. The most censured foreign secretary is Wellesley, whereas his predecessor, Canning, and his successor, Castlereagh, are both just as highly praised. The praise is undeserved, because vain, over-sexed, idle Wellesley, in trying simultaneously to destroy the French empire in Europe and prevent the creation of a Russian empire in the near east, showed the better understanding of Britain's most vital interests. Before Castlereagh went to the foreign office, he had failed at the board of

---

[1] See F. G. Hutchins, *The Illusion of Permanence: British Rule in India* (Princeton, 1967), and G. D. Bearce, *British Attitudes towards India, 1783–1858* (London, 1961).

control; Canning, determined in the 1820s not to allow the defence of India to affect the balance of power in Europe, jeopardized both. Palmerston keeps his customary high place, but not for the customary reason. Every foreign secretary in the first half of the nineteenth century must be asked how well he co-operated with his colleagues at the board of control. Although Canning fails, Palmerston, and equally significantly Aberdeen in his relations with Ellenborough, succeed. Between 1835 and 1841 Palmerston worked closely and equably with Hobhouse. Their policy in the near east may appear to have been set out by Palmerston, the result of his nightmares over the treaty of Unkiar Skelessi.[1] This was not the case. Palmerston's policy had been supplied between 1831 and 1834 by the board of control, where Charles Grant had it explained to him by Henry Ellis.

The obvious place to look for connections between Britain's interests as a European and Asiatic state is the near east. Elizabeth Monroe, in a perceptive phrase, described the British view of the near east as of a desert with two edges, one the business of the foreign office, the other of the government of India.[2] This was true only until the war of the Second Coalition, when Bonaparte in Egypt and Paul in Georgia jumped dramatically into the middle. Miss Monroe might have been describing the work of British historians, who often write about the Straits, Syria, and Egypt, from the records of the foreign office, or about the North-West Frontier and the Persian Gulf from those at the India office. Lost between the two are Persia and Baghdad, one bounced between them, the other often ignored by both: finding out what happened there is thus made more difficult. Because the near east has been mapped for the British by cataloguers, the Eastern Question (the effect of the decline of Turkey on the balance of power in Europe), and the steps taken in the near east by the British in an attempt to increase the security and stability of British India, known since the 1830s as the Great Game in Asia, are usually studied separately, whereas the most important task for a historian of Great Britain as great power is to find the connections between the two. How to defend British India puzzled the British throughout the nineteenth

---

[1] See, e.g., F. E. Bailey, *British Policy and the Turkish Reform Movement: A Study in Anglo-Turkish Relations, 1826–1853* (Cambridge, Mass., 1942), p. 29.

[2] E. Monroe, *Britain's Moment in the Middle East, 1914–1956* (London, 1963), p. 12.

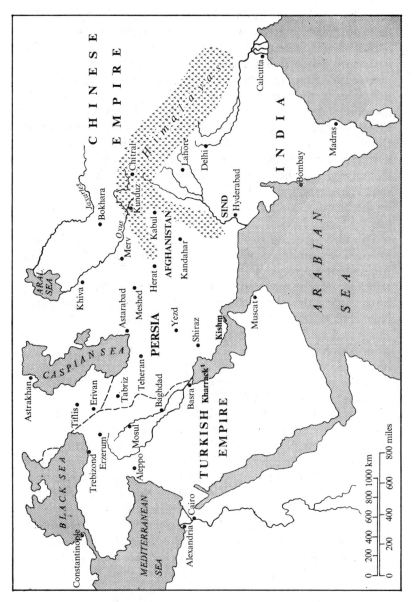

The Near East and India

century, and must qualify everything said about their activities in the near east.

In histories of British foreign policy, problems of security are too often ignored, as if wealth were power, or the balance of power in Europe were security enough. This reflects the behaviour of many British diplomatists, mesmerized by continental politics: even those, who had to serve time in America and Asia, on returning to Europe promptly forgot about them, and also forgot that however attractive the social life of a European capital, and however far world politics were a series of bargains between European states, the interests bargained were not always European.[1] For Britain, a peripheral and insular state, whose navy, however poor an offensive weapon, could prevent invasion, this may not have mattered, although by the twentieth century the forgotten world more and more often burst in upon the British, but the history of British India, where the intrusion was always expected, cannot be explained except in relation to defence and foreign policy. This study of a few important years in the 1820s and 1830s tries to explain why the British began to play the Great Game in Asia, and what they hoped to achieve.

II

The Great Game in Asia offers an alternative explanation to the Imperialism of Free Trade of Britain's interests in the near east; the circumstances in which, and the methods by which, the British government could act; and a test of the arguments put forward in the debate carried on in the *Economic History Review* for the twenty-five years since this classic phrase was coined. Gallagher and Robinson meant it to summarize their attack on the traditional assumptions that the mid-Victorians were anti-imperialist, distrusted forward policies, and did not much care what happened to Britain's colonies; arguing instead, that in a century of continuous expansion in all forms, the British government worked towards paramountcy by whatever means seemed locally most suitable: 'Refusals to annex are no proof of reluctance to control.'[2] This

---

[1] See, for an excellent example, M. Gilbert, *Sir Horace Rumbold: Portrait of a Diplomat* (London, 1973).

[2] J. Gallagher and R. Robinson, 'The Imperialism of Free Trade', *Economic History Review*, 2nd series, vi (1953–4), 3.

policy reflected the determination of British industrialists and merchants to extend their influence throughout the world, by sub-ordinating local handicrafts to British manufactures and local raw materials to British investment. 'The usual summing up of the policy of the free-trade empire as "trade not rule" ', they said, 'should read "trade with informal control if possible; trade with rule when necessary".'[1]

This argument was first attacked by Oliver MacDonagh, who said that free trade must be distinguished from freedom to trade, because the ark of the free-trade covenant, *laissez-faire*, was incompatible with Gallagher and Robinson's definition of imperialism as the political steps necessary to integrate new regions into the expanding economy.[2] MacDonagh was himself attacked by R. J. Moore, who showed that the Manchester School, with Mac-Donagh's paragon of free traders, Richard Cobden, at their head, exploiting India as a source of cotton, their vital raw material, and as a field of guaranteed investment for finance capital secured against the public revenues, created a clan of bondholders with a fixed interest in a permanent imperial connection.[3] India is usually treated as the exception proving the rules of imperial history, and was so this time, strangely enough by the most outspoken critic of Gallagher and Robinson, D. C. M. Platt.

Platt criticized the role given by Gallagher and Robinson to the British Government. All British statesmen, he agreed, however aristocratic, and however interested in the political power brought by wealth, 'appreciated that the answer lay in trade'.[4] Despite this, early and mid-Victorian governments did little to help overseas trade. They refused to help individuals, partly because they saw their responsibility to be the general interest, partly because noble-men, bored by and ignorant of trade, and despising anyone who did commercial not political work, particularly in Europe where the two could usually be separated, used the slogans *laissez-faire* and free trade as an excuse for doing nothing. Victorians, who con-

---

[1] Ibid., p. 13.

[2] O. MacDonagh, 'The Anti-Imperialism of Free Trade', *Economic History Review*, 2nd series, xiv (1961–2), 489–501.

[3] R. J. Moore, 'Imperialism and "Free Trade" Policy in India, 1853–4', *Economic History Review*, 2nd series, xvii (1964–5), 135–45.

[4] D. C. M. Platt, *Finance, Trade, and Politics in British Foreign Policy, 1815–1914* (Oxford, 1968), p. 1. The title of this book is misleading. The treatment of the first half of the nineteenth century is slight.

demned monopolies, restricted their policies to opening up world markets for international trade on equal terms.

The object of official negotiations was usually a commercial treaty. Once it was signed, traders had to look after themselves in fair competition with rivals; the foreign office would only protect them against local injustice or evasion of the agreed terms. Platt's most closely argued example was south America. The occasional intervention in south America, taken by Gallagher and Robinson to be a sign of Britain's determination to obtain paramount influence throughout the world, Platt proved to be exceptions to a general rule of continuing Canning's policy: a refusal to try to end the political turbulence in south America, because perpetual meddling was bound to be the result.[1] Platt is himself equally misleading, when he implies that Britain would have tolerated all political changes in south America. Canning would not have tolerated the reimposition of Spanish rule. Nor was south America unstable, merely disordered. South Americans quarrelled by permission of the British, because, whatever the effect on Britain's trade, as long as no other great European power intervened, their quarrels did not affect Britain's security.

Platt later was equally critical both of Gallagher and Robinson's 'fanciful picture' of the expectations of British manufacturers and merchants,[2] and of Bernard Semmel's claim that they were 'determined if possible, to extend their influence throughout the world'.[3] To see the early nineteenth century as a period of uninterrupted expansion is false: short booms were followed by alarming slumps, followed in turn by long slow periods, building up to another boom, and another cycle. The effect was most marked in areas of least economic importance. During the railway boom better return on capital could be made at home; traders knew that their market in south America, China, and Turkey was limited. They could find nothing to buy: to sell they had to compete against local handicraft industries, which had cheap labour, knew local tastes, and did not have to pay customs duties. As long as the home and colonial market absorbed the available investment capital, raw materials

[1] D. C. M. Platt, 'The Imperialism of Free Trade: Some Reservations', *Economic History Review*, 2nd series, xxi (1968), 298–300.

[2] D. C. M. Platt, 'Further Objections to an "Imperialism of Free Trade", 1830–60', *Economic History Review*, 2nd series, xxvi (1973), 80.

[3] B. Semmel, *The Rise of Free Trade Imperialism: Classical Political Economy, The Empire of Free Trade, and Imperialism, 1750–1850* (Cambridge, 1970), p. 12.

could not provide the necessary return for British manufactures. 'No rapid, sustained, and dramatic increase', concluded Platt, 'could be anticipated for areas in which the purchasing power of the population was so low, the return trade so restricted, and the internal market . . . so self-sufficient.'[1]

Both Gallagher and Robinson and Platt were both wrong and right. All of them were wrong about the near east, because they ignored the government of India. British India was more than the exception to prove the rules of Victorian economic policy, and a fact to be disregarded by economic historians: the Raj was half of Great Britain. Platt criticized F. E. Bailey for arguing that Britain's interests in the near east were economic not political,[2] but Platt himself did not explain what the political interests were. Nor did Sir Charles Webster, who saw that 'those in charge of policy were more concerned with strategy and politics than with the economic consequences of their actions', but thought that 'the heart of the problem was the Straits'.[3] It was not: the security of British India was equally important. This has nothing, very little anyway, to do with control of the routes to the east, a fascinating by-way down which H. L. Hoskins led so many diplomatic historians.[4] The true explanation is a conundrum.

Like most explanations of complicated questions in history, this one appears deceptively simple: whenever the function of stability was security for property, it depended upon order. This is why south America and China cannot be listed with Turkey. The formula, which governed life in British India, did not affect Britain's interest in south America or China, where upheaval did not affect Britain's security: the British argued about how far it should influence their policy in the near east. Turkey, Persia, and Afghanistan, were not just another area of marginal economic interest, one of the 'long' trades Platt rightly argues that early Victorians, who bothered to try, found so hard to expand and make profitable; they were the field for the Great Game in Asia.

'I cannot help the big wigs you bring forward,' said Lord Goderich to Wilmot Horton about the political economists'

---

[1] Platt, 'Further Objections', p. 84.

[2] F. E. Bailey, 'The Economics of British Foreign Policy, 1825–1850', *Journal of Modern History*, xii (1940), 455–6.

[3] Sir Charles Webster, *The Foreign Policy of Palmerston, 1830–1841* (London, 1951), i. 85.

[4] H. L. Hoskins, *British Routes to India* (London 1928).

theories of emigration policy in 1826. 'They look at it solely in the abstract.'[1] British politicians were traditionally sceptical of theoreticians and intellectuals, but, provided their schemes would cost nothing, they were occasionally allowed to experiment overseas. The near east at the beginning of the Great Game in Asia was one area of experiment, because Britain's reasons for seeking paramount influence there, or for deciding not to, stemmed not only from self-confidence and hope, but also from awareness of weakness and danger. The arguments of both Gallagher and Robinson and Platt are inapplicable to the near east, because, whenever they think about Victorian foreign policy there, they are thinking about the wrong sort of state.

This is unfair to Gallagher and Robinson; when they turned their names around they saw more clearly. The assumption underlying *Africa and the Victorians*, that the security of British India determined British policy in the scramble for Africa, applies throughout the nineteenth century to British policy in the near east, where Robinson and Gallagher's frontier between trade and empire is drawn too late. The British had turned from one to the other at the end of the eighteenth century, because as soon as British India was transformed from a trading company into a political and military power, the British recognized that it was more important to keep everyone out of the near east than to develop the area themselves. Robinson and Gallagher meant their frontier to signify only a change of method, in response to changing circumstances; strategy, whatever form it took, was always planned in defence of economic interests. This is not true: strategy in the near east did help to protect economic interests elsewhere, but that was not its only justification. The biggest fault in the theory of an imperialism of free trade is that in claiming to explain everything it may explain nothing.

Gallagher and Robinson argued that throughout the nineteenth century the British exerted whatever political and military leverage was necessary to obtain the conditions for sustained economic expansion; that their interest was investment and trade. According to Platt, this was false, because there was little investment and the government rarely acted on behalf of trade. When applied to the

---

[1] Quoted in H. J. M. Johnston, *British Emigration Policy, 1815–1830* (Oxford, 1972), p. 149.

near east, both arguments are false. The government of India were willing to threaten force to open up areas to trade; but to increase their security not their wealth. Strategy was not planned in the defence of economic interests, trade was encouraged as the cheapest method of defence. This is easily explained, as long as the government of India and the British government are compared in terms of Henry Kissinger's distinction between continental and peripheral states.[1]

Kissinger, who was distinguishing between the priorities of Austria and Britain after the Napoleonic Wars, might just as well have distinguished between the government of India and the British government, whose outlook was affected by their different military, political, and geographical situations. British policy in the near east had always to try to reconcile the two. Britain, as an island militarily secure behind a strong navy, was worried about international aggression, the result of a change in the foreign policy of states: the government of India, militarily exposed in central Asia, tried to prevent changes in the governments of other states which might lead to changes in foreign policy. Britain, confident that her political institutions would not be threatened by rebellion, could develop the doctrine of non-interference, because political revolution in other states would not affect her: the government of India, in constant fear of rebellion, demanded the right of general interference in allied and neighbouring states to prevent dangerous examples.

Finally, Britain, as an island, threatened only if the continent of Europe were dominated by a single state (the France of Louis XIV or Napoleon), and confident in a general war of being the last to be attacked, advocated the balance of power as the best way to keep the peace. Because the balance of power limits but does not prevent aggression, in an attempt to deter it the government of India conjured a common threat. The common threat perceived by Prince Metternich in Europe was liberalism and nationalism, always described as the Revolution; in the near east the government of India tried in their relations with other states to make Russian expansion serve the same purpose.

The government of India were in a weaker position than Metter-

---

[1] H. A. Kissinger, *A World Restored* (Universal Library Edition, New York, 1964), pp. 5–6. Kissinger described Britain as insular, but he must have meant peripheral: one could make similar statements about Russia.

nich. If Russia, whose power threatened Austria as much as the Revolution did, or nearly so, could be persuaded to accept his definition of their common interest, he would paralyse both his enemies at once, rather, in turning the power of Russia against the Revolution, they would paralyse one another. The dilemma of the British in the near east was the difficulty of persuading the Russians that their expansion was the only threat to peace. As a result, the state of affairs in the near east could never be legitimized by an acceptance of shared obligations in the face of shared danger; it merely represented a balance of tension. Between 1828 and 1907 the Great Game in Asia was Britain's search for a method of preventing the power of Russia from endangering British India.

In the seventeenth and eighteenth centuries, during the decline of Turkey and Persia, until the East India Company turned themselves into an Indian state, and the Russians began to turn formerly Turkish and Persian protectorates in the Caucasus into Russian ones, the international systems of Europe, the near east, and India, could be treated as separate. When, after 1798, this was no longer possible, the British had to decide how they could prevent the transformation of the near east into a component of the European balance of power, and, as a result, the creation of a lever against Britain in Europe in the form of threats against British India. Naturally the British tried to reproduce in the near east the conditions giving them security in Europe. Because the geography of Asia prevented their finding a geographical equivalent to the Channel, they looked for a political equivalent; alternatively they looked for two devices used to maintain the balance of power in Europe, the Burgundian Circle, and its successor, to which in Europe they were usually opposed, the Holy Alliance. The Great Game in Asia was partly a mirror reflecting all three.

As the Hindu Kush could not provide a satisfactory frontier, the British tried to find an alternative at one of two places beyond them. The first, until 1828, when it was annexed by Russia, was the river Arras and the fortresses of Erivan and Nakitchevan; the second was the fortress of Herat. These fortresses were not thought of primarily as barriers against invasion, although the British hoped that in an emergency they might serve that purpose, but as a means to prevent or limit the expansion of Russian territory, or, and equally threatening to British India, French and Russian influence. Unfortunately, the first frontier, depending for its stability upon a

British protectorate over Persia, was likely to appear offensive not defensive, whereas the second, depending on a protectorate over Afghanistan, might, by offending the Sikhs, lead to war along the military frontier of British India.

Because British India was a continental not a peripheral state, her political frontier had to be set up as far beyond her military frontier as possible, but still in Asia. If the British could hold back France and Russia, they might never have to fight them, and this had to be done in Asia, because having to retaliate in Europe would itself have been the lever against their security as a dual monarchy they were trying to forestall. When, after the resignation of Wellesley in 1812, they stopped trying to turn Persia into a protectorate, they tried to replace it by an Asiatic equivalent to the Burgundian Circle. If they could construct a zone of buffer states, stretching from Turkey, through Persia, to Khiva and Bokhara, with agreed frontiers, recognized by Russia as independent, and preserved by British pressure equal to Russian, the European and Indian political systems might be separated, avoiding both the incorporation into the European system of the near east, and, which would have been equally dangerous to Great Britain, its partition between them.

Paradoxically, this zone could be created only by applying in the near east the canons of European diplomacy as practised by the British, who understood the Vienna Settlement to be a balance of power represented by stable frontiers drawn on maps, and the Congress System to be a method of dealing with aggression. To Britain aggression meant invasion; to British India, as to Metternich, aggression was a function of rapid or violent change. If the buffer zone were to be stable, and behind it the British were to construct both a stable political frontier at the Arras and a stable military frontier at the Indus, change in Persia and Turkestan had to be treated as unrest, and Afghanistan, the Punjab, and Sind, treated as protectorates, whose rulers ruled by permission of the British, not as in Persia and Bokhara owing to equal pressure from Britain and Russia. This attempt to prevent change, either by rapidly assimilating the natives, as utilitarian and evangelical reformers proposed, or by petrifying the existing political and social structure, in response to the conservatives' claim that assimilation would cause upheaval, resembled in the near east the attempt to forestall the contagion of the Revolution, that was the purpose of the Holy Alliance, to which the British were so hostile, and of whose architect, Prince Metternich, they were impatient and suspicious.

Equally paradoxically, these devices for ensuring the stability of British India themselves extended the European political system into the near east, but in an odd way. The aim of British policy was to keep out, not to move in. Peripheral states cannot fight total wars; their existence depends upon limiting their liabilities. Continental states have to prevent war, because all war is likely to become total, and defeat will destroy the state. To enable Great Britain to prosper as both, and as both a European and Asiatic state, the British had to prevent themselves being weakened as both, by attacks upon one meant to injure the other, or by having to choose which to defend. Although Great Britain in Europe as a peripheral state existed only yesterday and tomorrow, whereas Great Britain in Asia, a continental state like the Thousand Year Reich, existed only today, every day the inhabitants of both being good Englishmen played games. In the Home Counties they played cricket, in the Upper Provinces of India they played polo, and, for a hundred and fifty years, between Delhi and Constantinople they played the Great Game in Asia.

II

The Persian Connection 1801-1828

> The degree of a nation's civilization
> is marked by its disregard for the
> necessities of existence.
>
> THORNTON CLAY,
> *Our Betters*,
> Act I

IN OLDEN DAYS, examiners of the Joint Board of the General
Certificate of Education at the Ordinary Level liked to ask candidates to compare and contrast the foreign policies of Castlereagh
and Canning. Everyone knew how to answer this question, but
only fools did so; the chances of individuality or distinction were
minute. One contrasted their tastes, methods, attitudes to public
opinion and reform; one suggested, at least in my day one was told
to suggest, that Canning acted upon Castlereagh's assumptions:
Castlereagh used the Congress System to check revolution,
Canning the Monroe Doctrine to check reaction. Their ideas of
the balance of power might be left out, because, as long as Mac-
millan played his Greek to Eisenhower's Roman, Englishmen were
still brought up to believe that the world was a pleasure garden for
their entertainment.

The English are fond of continuity in foreign policy. Russell
echoed Palmerston, Rosebery echoed Salisbury, or so one is to
believe, and Eyre Crowe explained his suspicions of Germany by
quoting the younger Pitt. Disraeli stands apart: nobody pretends
he was Gladstone in disguise. In the early nineteenth century, when
for twenty years the foreign secretary was Anglo-Irish, continuity
might reasonably have been expected, were it not more significant
that for three years he was also Anglo-Indian. The answers would
have been more interesting, had the examiners of the Joint Board
asked candidates to compare Castlereagh with Wellesley, and the
beginning of the Great Game in Asia might by now have been
better understood.

II

The Great Game was Britain's response after 1829 to the treaties of Turkmanchay and Adrianople, a watershed in Anglo-Russian relations, because they forced the British to ask how they could defend India from Russia. Long before, in the war of the Spanish Succession, Swift had warned them not to fight themselves, but to look for someone to fight on their behalf.[1] This had led during the eighteenth century to continual quarrels between the partisans of Austria and Prussia, copied in the nineteenth century between partisans of Afghanistan and Persia. Occasionally, when both factions were disappointed, they looked for a third champion to the Turkish governor of Baghdad. The agony of Paris could not compare with the difficulty of choosing between these three: after seventy years spent hesitating, the British could still not decide. The alternative was an alliance with Germany; which partly explains why the Germans in the 1890s would not agree to one, unless Britain would join the Triple Alliance.[2]

The British began the game under the handicap of having practised against the French.

The fact . . . is [it was said in 1829], that those who ridicule the idea of the danger from Russia, are persons who have long been accustomed to look to France . . . and, having made up their minds that France cannot attack our Indian empire, they save themselves the trouble of thinking, . . . merely substituting in their minds the word 'Russia'.[3]

This was foolish, because, although both states might try to provoke rebellion in India, compelling the British to defend India as far away as possible, very different strategies would be needed.[4] France, who had to threaten an invasion, posed a military problem; Russia, who had merely to expand, a political one. The effect on the

[1] 'Upon the Conduct of the Allies', *The Prose Works of Jonathan Swift*, ed. H. Davis (Oxford, 1939–74), vi. 3–69.
[2] J. A. S. Grenville, *Lord Salisbury and Foreign Policy: The Close of the Nineteenth Century* (London, 1964), pp. 292–6.
[3] G. de Lacy Evans, *On the Practicability of an Invasion of India* (London, 1829), p. 36. As late as 1843 Wellington and Ellenborough were worried about the possibility of a French invasion of India. So hard, claims J. L. Morison, 'From Alexander Burnes to Frederick Roberts: A Survey of Imperial Frontier Policy', *Proceedings of the British Academy*, xxii (1936), 180, do diplomatic fallacies die.
[4] The only survey, unfortunately too short, is P. C. M. S. Braun, *Die Verteidigung Indiens 1800–1906: Das Problem der Vorwärtsstrategie* (Cologne, 1968).

security of British India of treating Russia as if she were France can best be illustrated by the history of the Persian Connection during and immediately after the Napoleonic Wars.

Britain was officially connected to Persia by two treaties which caused confusion and resentment. The first was negotiated in 1800–1 by John Malcolm, at the end of a legendary, and equally costly, mission to Teheran, which was meant principally to help Lord Wellesley, the governor-general of India, deceive the East India Company and the board of control. To hide his attempt to succeed the Mogul Empire as the paramount power, Wellesley had to portray British India as threatened by invasion, by Bonaparte in Egypt, by Zeman Shah, by Tipu Sultan. A connection with Persia was to appear to divert Zeman Shah from the invasion of British India he had neither the inclination nor the means to undertake.[1]

Malcolm's treaty, he assured Wellesley, was intended to present 'an equitable appearance [rather] than to burden the British government with any serious engagements'.[2] By pledging Persia to help the British defeat a French or Afghan invasion, the treaty was meant to be merely an unnecessary defence against an imaginary danger.[3] To Fath Ali Shah, a notorious miser, such extravagance meant that the Persian Connection was to strengthen the defence of British India, that the British had an interest in developments in Persia, and in particular, as Persia had been fighting Russia over Georgia for forty years, that they would join in any future dispute over the Russo-Persian frontier in the Caucasus. In 1804, when the Russians invaded Azerbaijan, the shah asked for British help. He was echoed for three years by the British residents at Basra and Baghdad, who were more frightened than either the government of India or the foreign office by the south-eastward expansion of Russia. They thought only of invasion, and believed that neither France nor Russia could march on India; that should either try,

---

[1] E. Ingram, 'The Defence of British India—III: Wellesley's Provocation of the Fourth Mysore War', *Journal of Indian History*, Golden Jubilee Volume (1973), 595–622.

[2] Malcolm to Wellesley, 20 Jan. 1801, I.O. G/29/22.

[3] The treaty guarded against neither an Afghan invasion of only Sikh or Maratha territory, nor French penetration into inland Persia. It secured only Oudh and the Persian Gulf. It is printed in *A Collection of Treaties, Engagements, and Sanads relating to India and Neighbouring Countries*, ed. Sir C. U. Aitchison (Calcutta, 1862), vii. 108.

Persia could not be expected to bar the way. Without strengthening the defence of British India, a connection with Persia would make it more difficult to negotiate a European coalition against France.

Georgia and the Mahometan Khanates in 1801

Napoleon could not legitimize his empire, without forcing Britain to become a colonial state and Russia an Asiatic one; to withstand him, the two states had to co-operate. The foreign office, who realized this, ignored all appeals to step between Turkey or Persia and Russia, until, in the spring of 1807, it seemed likely that in alliance with France they would divert the tsar from the decisive battles due to be fought against Napoleon in Poland. When the British decided to mediate between Russia and Persia, and to trace their frontier in the Caucasus, they hoped to oblige not Fath Ali but the tsar, and were trying to preserve the European balance of power. They were too late: the treaty of Finkenstein was shortly followed by the treaty of Tilsit. As soon as the

Third Coalition fell apart, the foreign office lost interest in Persia.[1] Unfortunately, the ambassador at Vienna, Sir Robert Adair, remembered that the coalition had been defeated, partly because Austria had felt as threatened by Russian advances in Turkey as by French advances in Germany and Poland. As a result, in a rash moment two years later, the British tried to set Persia against the Franco-Russian alliance.

Chatham supposedly once rebuked an ambassador at Vienna for not writing often enough. The ambassador protested that as little was happening he had little to say, which was precisely, said Chatham, what he wished to be regularly told. The foreign office should have paid attention to this story. As long as they were busy negotiating and salvaging coalitions, they might have forestalled a demand of Canning, by telling British agents in the near east, that their instructions were 'comprised in a few short words, *to be quiet*',[2] because nothing they could do would help. Left without instructions they tried. 'O!', lamented Canning later, 'that people would learn that doing nothing is as often *a measure* . . . as the most diligent activity; and that clever people could . . . own that they have no instructions, when they really have none.'[3]

The cleverest and worst-timed plan to help was Adair's, who had moved meanwhile from Vienna to Constantinople. His instructions had prepared him for everything which might have happened, except what happened in 1809, when Austria alone declared war on France.[4] Because the Austrians might have hesitated to risk a decisive battle in the west, as long as a Russian army menaced their eastern frontier in Galicia, Adair tried to draw off the Russians, by persuading the Turks to attack them from Moldavia.[5] He also told the British envoy at Teheran to encourage the Persians to carry on fighting in the Caucasus.[6] This coalition against France's ally was intended only to strengthen Britain's. Unfortunately, it also meant admitting for the first time that the British had an interest in Persia: equally unfortunately, as it

---

[1] E. Ingram, 'An Aspiring Buffer State: Anglo-Persian Relations in the Third Coalition, 1804–1807', *Historical Journal*, xvi (1973), 509–33.

[2] Canning to Strangford, no. 13, 31 Dec. 1825, F.O. 181/65.

[3] Canning to Granville, private no. 2, 10 Jan. 1826, P.R.O. 30/29/8/9, no. 412.

[4] Canning to Adair, nos. 1–4, 26 Jan. 1808, F.O. 7/60.

[5] Adair to Canning, no. 12, 19 Mar. 1809, Sir Robert Adair, *Negotiations for the Peace of the Dardanelles in 1808–1809* (London, 1845), i. 143.

[6] Adair to Jones, 20 July, 13 Aug. 1809, Kentchurch Court MSS. 8635–6.

entangled Persia in European international politics, it was not their true interest.

Being responsible for the safety of British India, the board of control were more frightened than the foreign office by the signs of Franco-Russian co-operation in the east. In the autumn of 1807 they had sent Sir Harford Jones to Persia, to challenge the influence of General Gardane and the French military mission, and to persuade the shah to break the treaty of Finkenstein.[1] Credentials were supplied by the foreign office, instructions by the board of control: the object was to strengthen British India against the probable effects of a French or Russian feint at invasion. This proved to be easily done, because the French in attacking India, like the British in defending it, had to make an impossible choice. On the way to their goal were three mutually hostile states. The French might expect help from Russia, or from Turkey or Persia, the British from Afghanistan or from Persia and the Sikhs: neither could expect help from all three. As the choice was impossible, the British would not choose; the government of India behaved as if every near-eastern state were as interested as they were in resisting the French.[2] Seemingly foolish, this behaviour was actually shrewd. Any other terms for an alliance would have entangled the British in insolvable local quarrels, which would not otherwise have affected them. Their experience over Ochakoff in 1791 had taught them to look for allies who would offer not need help.

The government of India, hypnotized in 1808 by Jones's rival to speak for Britain in the near east, Sir John Malcolm, calculated that if Persia would not co-operate with Britain she could be made to.[3] This was true only as long as Britain's rival was France and not Russia. States not trading overseas are impossible to blockade, and the Kajars, who needed the support of tribes living around the Caspian and in Azerbaijan, feared a Russian invasion from Georgia more than a British invasion from the Persian Gulf.

The quarrel between Harford Jones and the government of India in 1808–9, about the value of a connection with Persia, affected Anglo-Persian relations for thirty years. Jones knew that

[1] The best account of Franco–Persian relations is V. J. Puryear, *Napoleon and the Dardanelles* (Berkeley/Los Angeles, 1951), *passim*.

[2] E. Ingram, 'The Defence of British India—II: A Further Examination of the Mission of Mountstuart Elphinstone to Kabul', *Journal of Indian History*, xlix (1971), 66–8.

[3] Malcolm to Minto, private, 15 Apr., 5 June 1808, Minto MSS. M/182.

Britain's interest in Persia was defensive. As soon as General Gardane had been driven out, ending the threat from France, the best way to have forestalled a threat from Russia would have been to mediate between Russia and Persia, and to stabilize their frontier in the Caucasus.[1] This might both have encouraged Russia to fight France in Poland, and, by separating the affairs of Persia from the affairs of Europe, have helped Britain hold back Russia in the near east. By co-operating with Adair, in return for his help against the government of India, Jones turned the Persian Connection into an offensive alliance. Not only did this prove an expensive and tiresome charade, it clashed with Canning's strategy of carrying on the fight against France, without, as far as could be avoided, fighting Russia.[2]

One barrier to a satisfactory connection with Persia during the Napoleonic Wars was the instability of British governments. Whenever the Persians tried to act on a British policy, they learnt that it had been changed. The government of India were often equally puzzled, uncertain whatever the policy whether they were to carry it out. The changes were reflected in the status of the Persian mission, bounced at intervals as in a game of catch between the foreign office, the government of India, and the board of control. From the beginning it had been obvious that Persia might be a less valuable ally than Afghanistan, because more difficult to separate from the balance of power in Europe. When Bonaparte invaded Egypt in 1798, the foreign office would not accept the responsibility of defending British India; the board of control, who were responsible, would not defend India in alliance with Persia. Until 1807 Anglo-Persian relations had been carried on by the government of India. The apparent political advantage, that the British government might ignore the Russo-Persian war, was also costly, because the shah of Persia demanded heavy bribes for treating the governor-general as his equal.

Harford Jones's credentials from George III were supposed only to lower the cost of negotiating with Persia, by giving him equal rank to General Gardane. Instead they enabled Jones to ignore instructions from the government of India to end the Persian Connection and leave Persia, while he negotiated in the new year

[1] Jones to Canning, no. 17, 28 Aug. 1809, F.O. 60/2.
[2] Canning to Leveson Gower, private, 29 Sept., 2 Oct. 1807, P.R.O. 30/29/8/4, nos. 180, 182.

of 1809 a preliminary treaty of alliance, known as the treaty of
Teheran. Misled by Adair, Jones offered the shah a subsidy for
breaking the treaty of Finkenstein and carrying on the fight against
Russia, and a military mission to train in Persia a force of regular
infantry.[1] The foreign office, who had failed to prop up the Third
Coalition in Europe, were being led towards the mirage of an
Asiatic substitute.

III

Before the military mission arrived, their purpose had been
changed. The preliminary treaty reached London in the autumn
of 1809, to find Wellesley just moved in at Downing Street, the
only foreign secretary before Palmerston interested in Persia, and
who planned, by transferring the Persian mission to the foreign
office, and by turning the Persian Connection into a subsidiary
alliance, to continue the policy for which he had been brought
home from India. Persia was not to be an ally in the European war,
nor the farthest outpost of India against European invasion. This
had never frightened Wellesley,[2] who taught his brother Wellington and Ellenborough, that whereas France was only a temporary
military threat to India, the threat from Russia, although political
and apparently more distant, was permanent and demanded a
permanent defence. Persia was needed as the protectorate of an
expanding Indian empire, because the best defence of India, and
the best way to make sure it stayed calm, was order beyond its
frontiers.

The Grand Llama, who often disagreed with his colleagues, was
in the right more often than is usually supposed. This time he
ignored the policy not only of the foreign office, anxious for
coalitions, and of the board of control, anxious to prevent invasion,
but of the government of India. Wellesley had rejected their
policy when John Malcolm had first suggested it in 1800. For
thirty years, from his first mission to Persia until his resignation
in 1830 as governor of Bombay, Malcolm argued that weak unruly
near-eastern states strengthened British India. By guerrilla attacks
upon outposts and lines of supply, they could delay a European
army marching eastwards, until the British could attack them in the

---

[1] Jones to Canning, no. 4, 16 Mar. 1809, with encls., F.O. 60/2.
[2] E. Ingram, 'The Defence of British India—I: The Invasion Scare of 1798',
Journal of Indian History, xlviii (1970), 581-2.

flank. This strategy would depend upon one initiative; the British were to build an island fortress in the Persian Gulf, ideally with Malcolm in command, whence they could police the seas, control neighbouring rulers, and march against a European invader.[1] Then a connection with Persia would become merely an unnecessary infringement of Britain's independence.

Persia and Turkestan

Here, in Wellesley's answer to Malcolm that in the near east disorder could not be ignored lest it lead to instability, is one origin of the Great Game in Asia. While weak and unruly, Persia might throw back a French invasion from Anatolia or Baghdad, but could

[1] Malcolm to Wellesley, 26 Feb. 1800, I.O. G/29/22.

not prevent creeping Russian expansion towards Azerbaijan or Khiva. Only if the Persian government were both strengthened, particularly their control over the frontier provinces, and at the same time persuaded to renounce their claim to Georgia, declared in 1801 a protectorate of Russia, could border clashes be prevented, which would otherwise lead to Russian expansion in search of a secure frontier. Wellesley's alterations in 1810 to the terms of Jones's preliminary treaty implied, that the best way to safeguard British India would be to stabilize the balance of power in the near east; responding to the Russian protectorate over Georgia by a British protectorate over Persia.

Because British India was not a neighbour of Persia, this would have to be done cautiously: too obvious an interest might appear offensive not defensive, and might provoke the Russian counter-attack Wellesley's aid was meant eventually to prevent. Wellesley doubled the subsidy Jones had offered as payment for a force of regular infantry, and enlarged the military mission to be sent to train them. Although the Persians would have preferred Indian troops to a subsidy, standard practice in India, and wanted Britain to promise she would not make peace until the Russians had been driven from Georgia, Wellesley turned down these requests as provocative. He also would not send British naval officers to train the Persian navy on the Caspian, offering instead shipwrights and carpenters, who would be less noticeable. Finally, Wellesley told Jones's successor at Teheran to negotiate a new commercial treaty, and to decide where to open factories and consulates.[1]

Wellesley, like Gardane, wanted to reorganize the Persian army, to supplement the irregular cavalry by a corps of infantry, who were not to drive the Russians from Georgia, as the French had promised at Finkenstein, nor to defend Azerbaijan against invasion. Their function, like the Indian Army's, was to be paramilitary; to increase the influence of the dynasty over the tribes, and of the British over the dynasty. Because the shah divided his time between treasure and concubines, the Kajars, unfortunately, were legion. 'Although in the vigour of his age,' remarked a Russian diplomatist, the shah '. . . is incapable, unambitious, and without energy. He is abandoned to sensuality, and having a disgust for everything like business, has entirely resigned the conduct

---

[1] Wellesley to Ouseley, 13 July 1810, F.O. 60/4.

of political and military affairs.'[1] His deputy for foreign affairs was his second son, Abbas Mirza, governor of Azerbaijan, but it was never certain, that if he decided upon a course of action the shah would supply the necessary funds, nor that he would finally obtain the throne. For twenty-five years before Abbas Mirza's son succeeded his grandfather in 1834, the British had to be prepared for civil war in Persia.

Early Kajar Persia was an empire. The principal provinces and towns were governed by sons of the shah, who, provided they sent annually to Teheran suitable sums in tribute, were left to govern as they pleased. Owing to its likely effect on the balance of power at the byzantine Kajar court, any suggestion of military reform could be expected to cause violent disagreement. Fath Ali Shah, who preferred negotiation to fighting, had always hoped to appease the Russians in the Caucasus; his priorities resembled Wellesley's, British help in stabilizing Persia's north-west frontier. This preference was shared by Persia's most able minister, who knew that a static society could not easily resist a developing one, but too much of whose energy and ability were exhausted maintaining himself in office. Useless in foreign affairs, and unsettling at home, the British offer might endanger not strengthen the dynasty by slighting Abbas Mirza's greatest rival, the governor of Kermanshah, who was popular with the tribes and an inspired leader of the traditional irregular cavalry. Wellesley's assumption, that a stronger imperial government was necessary to create a stable balance of power, was likely to increase the disorder in Persia by provoking civil war.

Abbas Mirza was as eager as everyone else was hesitant. His pre-eminence depended upon holding back Russia, and possessing an army capable of defeating his brothers whenever their father should die. Unfortunately, 'accustomed to have all his wishes accomplished the moment they were expressed, [he] conceived that a disciplined army could be created by his evincing a disposition to have one'.[2] Understanding the advantages of discipline,

---

[1] W. von Freygang, *Letters from the Caucasus and Georgia* (London, 1823), p. 314. J. B. Fraser, *Narrative of a Journey into Khorasan in the Years 1821 and 1822* (London, 1825), p. 203, calculated that the shah had at least fifty sons and one hundred daughters, and that fourteen sons and four grandsons were governing provinces or cities.

[2] Malcolm to Minto, 22 July 1810, I.O. Bengal/SPC/231, 22 Sept. 1810, no. 59.

he did not understand its dependence upon good training, tactics, and supply.[1] To have turned his regular infantry into a useful weapon would have required more thorough political and social reform than he could accept. Without it, they became a liability not an asset, and he survived only because they also became a symbol of the determination of both Britain and Russia to support him. Their history is a good example of why the government of India had argued, that British policy in the near east, and any plans for the defence of British India, should avoid entanglement in local politics.

Wellesley had hoped to do so, by the introduction of what became a classic British device: Persia was to be reformed by example, by the properties of British manufactures. Given a little time, a closer connection followed by a military mission and increased trade might preserve order in Persia, without entangling the British in local politics, and create a balance of power in the Caucasus. While the Kajar dynasty consolidated their hold on Azerbaijan, Ghilan, and Mazenderan, the mountain tribesmen in the Mahometan Khanates beyond Persia's north-west frontier might keep the Russians at bay. That the Russians might prefer to advance immediately to the Arras, the only strategically satisfactory barrier between the Caucasus and Azerbaijan, would have to be risked. The policy prophesied Ellenborough's famous attempt twenty years later to open the Indus to British merchants in order to flood Turkestan with cheap ironware. Neither Wellesley nor Ellenborough was interested in profit: trade, as war to Clausewitz, was an extension of diplomacy.

The assumption disregarded the existing pattern of trade in the near east. Wellesley understood the political disadvantages resulting from the victory in the late eighteenth century of the Kajars over the Zands, whose power had been based in Fars, and who were consequently more receptive to British suggestions; he ignored the Persian custom of buying British goods from Russians, who sent them overland to Azerbaijan more cheaply than the British could ship them to Bushire. Here was the dilemma of all free-trading imperialists: how much pressure should they bring, what local responsibilities should they accept, or what inducements offer, to persuade a foreign state to agree to more favourable terms of trade. Wellesley hoped that his effort to stabilize the Russo-Persian

[1] James Morier's journal, Add. MSS. 33482, fos. 42–3.

frontier in the Caucasus would tempt the shah, and to tempt Abbas Mirza by promising him the throne.

There was no alternative to accommodating Abbas Mirza. Had the governor of Fars been named the shah's deputy for foreign affairs, the British might have had more influence for less money, but civil war in Persia would have been certain: Abbas Mirza would have asked for Russian help. To prevent this, the British might try to negotiate with Russia a joint guarantee of his succession, or they might try to outbid Russia for his goodwill. 'That government will be most acceptable to him', remarked the British resident at Teheran in 1830, 'which will assist him to mount the throne . . . He would rather wear . . . [the crown] in dependence than run any risk of not wearing it at all.'[1] By then there was a danger that the British were becoming more his dependant than he theirs; or worse, that he might buy security as a protectorate of Russia.

Playing the Great Game in Asia was hazardous. Some who played risked death; a few were killed; many went home in disgrace. This happened to three successive envoys at Teheran, Sir Harford Jones, Sir Gore Ouseley, and Sir Henry Willock, who all fell foul of Sir John Malcolm. Jones had never been forgiven by Wellesley and Malcolm for arguing in 1799, that if the government of India wished to become the paramount power in India, and to find an ally capable of defending them against European invasion, Afghanistan would be a better ally than Persia.[2] The offence was twofold: Wellesley did not expect subordinates to express opinions, nor to reveal the policy he tried hard to disguise. The Persian Connection was supposed to be valuable because the shah could prevent the Afghans from invading India.

Wellesley had tried to stop the appointment of Jones in 1807. Three years later he brought him home, sending to Teheran instead Sir Gore Ouseley, an Anglo-Indian adventurer, who had earned this reward by persuading the nawab-vizier to give in to Wellesley's threats in 1800 to annex Oudh, without calling attention to them by abdicating. Ouseley knew that British policy in Persia would have to be equally well disguised. His success at it did him no good. In 1812 Wellesley was replaced at the foreign office by

---

[1] Encl. in Campbell to sc, 30 July 1830, I.O. Persia/45.
[2] E. Ingram, 'A Preview of the Great Game in Asia—II: The Project of an Alliance with Afghanistan, 1798–1800', *Middle Eastern Studies*, ix (1973), 164–9.

Castlereagh, who recalled Ouseley from Teheran as he had previously recalled Wellesley from Fort William.

To carry out foreign policy in the east in wartime proved impossible: instructions travelled more slowly than Napoleon. Ouseley, who had taken the usual leisurely passage around the Cape of Good Hope, was overtaken at Teheran by the invasion of Russia. The foreign office, eager to negotiate a Russian alliance, having offered to pay Persia for carrying on the war, in 1813 offered payment for stopping. Given the shah's notorious avarice—he is supposed to have charged his concubines for his favours—[1] the payment asked was small. Ouseley, perhaps because his avarice was equally notorious, was better liked by the shah than Malcolm and Jones, and was permitted in 1813 to negotiate for Persia the treaty of Gulistan, on terms that even the Russians, who were delighted, admitted to have given away more to them than was necessary.[2] In return, Ouseley promised that Britain would support Persia in her negotiations with Russia to trace their frontier in the Caucasus, continue paying the subsidy until this had been done, and recognize Abbas Mirza as heir apparent.[3]

Ouseley saw no contradiction between these terms. Wellesley, who wished to separate the Persian Connection from the balance of power in Europe, had never intended the subsidiary infantry to fight Russia. Because, by the terms of the treaty of Gulistan, Persia still controlled the strategic passes from the Caucasus into Azerbaijan, as far as diplomatic practice could, tracing her northwest frontier would protect her territory. Trade, the British military mission, and an agreed succession, would then strengthen the Persian government and increase their control over the provinces along the frontier.

In India Wellesley had expected his allies to pay for British troops, whose avowed purpose was to overawe them: 'A body of our own troops', he remarked of the nizam of Hyderabad,' . . . would tend to strengthen him for *our* purposes only.'[4] In Persia the government of India must pay, until replaced by the profits from

[1] Fraser, *Journey into Khorasan*, pp. 196–7.
[2] Cathcart to Castlereagh, no. 135, 31 Dec. 1813, F.O. 65/87.
[3] Morier and Ellis to Castlereagh, nos. 1 and 5, 21 Aug., 30 Nov. 1814, F.O. 60/9.
[4] Wellesley to Dundas, private no. 1, 23 Feb. 1798, *Two Views of British India: The Private Correspondence of Mr. Dundas and Lord Wellesley, 1798–1801*, ed. E. Ingram (Bath, 1970), p. 21.

trade, but the object was the same: reform to Wellesley meant dependence. Persia was to become a protectorate; British India was to be defended at the Arras; and the Mahometan Khanates between Georgia and Azerbaijan were to act as a buffer between the European and Indian political systems.

The policy soon affected the Kajar dynasty as Wellesley had hoped. The subsidiary infantry looked to India for equipment and to their British officers for leadership; as soon as the Persians were left to fight by themselves, they were defeated. The effect was equally marked on Abbas Mirza and the shah. Abbas, who had failed to back up his claims by victory over the Russians, would rely increasingly upon his foreign connections. The treaty of Teheran guaranteed him the throne, and the British subsidy paid him a third of his income.[1] It was so important to him, that Ouseley feared he might hinder the frontier negotiations with Russia, in an attempt to prolong it.

This danger was offset by an astonishing offer from the shah. Tiresomely, accepting it would have revealed the policy Wellesley had tried to hide. When Ouseley repeated in 1813 Britain's traditional request for permission to fortify an island in the Persian Gulf, the shah replied[2] that

he had determined to place himself entirely in the hands of England—that he would empower and permit the English to build forts for the defence of his country wherever it should seem the most fitting and that they should garrison them with their own troops—that he would provide 200,000 men in forty days after they should express a wish for them, which they might dispose of as they choose, drilling and paying them themselves;—that they might send for as many of their troops from India, and that to sum up the whole, he would place the whole of his country into their hands.

Not until the arrival of de Reuter would the British again be invited to take over Persia.

The visions of Wellesley, who in 1805 had left the government of India's credit exhausted and much of the Indian Army unpaid, took no account of costs. He forgot that British India had to be defended not only far away but cheaply. Harford Jones had warned him in 1809, that the British would not be able to expand their

---

[1] Ouseley to Castlereagh, no. 35, 29 Dec. 1812, F.O. 60/7; James Morier's Journal, Add. MSS. 33843, fos. 25–7.
[2] Ibid., fos. 120–2; Ouseley to Castlereagh, no. 1, 16 Jan. 1813, F.O. 60/8.

trade with Persia: until they developed the route through Trebizond and Erzerum after 1830, British goods from Bushire never
challenged Russian goods from Tiflis. An attempt made in 1799
to increase the sale of woollens by granting generous terms of
credit had glutted the market.

Nor had the British anything to buy. The goods they had
bought in the eighteenth century had become increasingly scarce,
owing to the disorder in Persia during the civil wars, and by 1800
the British had stopped looking for them. As a result British trade
could not settle Persia nor replace the subsidy.[1] Instead the subsidy was destroying the only value of the trade. The Persians,
because they had little to sell, had paid for what they bought in
specie, providing the government of Bombay, who were short of
revenue from land, with an alternative source of funds. After 1809
these went towards the subsidy. Instead of the political and strategic advantages brought by trade, the Persian Connection was
causing financial stress.

IV

Monetary calculations might alarm the East India Company,
who had to pay the subsidy: the foreign office ignored them.
Castlereagh criticized Wellesley's Persian policy, and again
amended the treaty of Teheran, because he also criticized Wellesley's definition of Britain's vital interests. Castlereagh agreed with
Wellesley that the defence of British India must be separated from
the balance of power in Europe, but not that the two were equally
important. A British attempt to turn Persia into a protectorate
might divert Russia from the grand alliance firstly against Napoleon, then the Revolution. To prevent this, in 1814 Castlereagh
ended the subsidy,[2] lowered the rank of the British envoy, withdrew the military mission, and refused to take any part in tracing
the Russo-Persian frontier in the Caucasus. The concert of
Europe, like the coalitions against Napoleon, would depend upon

---

[1] 'Memorandum [by Harford Jones] Respecting the Trade with Persia', in
Jones to sc, 13 April 1809, I.O. G/29/30. For details of Anglo-Persian trade in
the eighteenth century see A. A. Amin, *British Interests in the Persian Gulf*
(Leiden, 1967).
[2] Castlereagh to Ouseley, separate, 23 Sept. 1814, F.O. 60/9; same to Morier,
separate, 9 Jan. 1815, F.O. 60/10. The definitive version of the treaty of Teheran
is printed in *Diplomacy in the Near and Middle East: A Documentary Record,
1535–1914*, ed. J. C. Hurewitz (Princeton, 1956), i. 86.

ignoring eastern questions, lest they turn necessary allies into enemies.

The difference between Wellesley and Castlereagh, which showed in Europe as well as Asia, was most obvious in the Mediterranean. Wellesley imagined Italians, like Persians, to be Indians; he treated the king of Naples as a troublesome subsidiary ally, as if he were the nawab-vizier of Oudh, and planned to rule Sicily as a British colony. The Italians saw this: the British, remarked the king of Sardinia, 'consider me and all the rulers of Mediterranean islands as mere Indians and nabobs'.[1] Castlereagh, who was shocked by Wellesley's assumptions, reversed his policy in the Mediterranean as he reversed it in Persia. This did not help the Persians.

Whereas Wellesley had seized the Persian mission in 1810 for the foreign office, Castlereagh wanted to pretend it did not exist. He continued until his suicide the policy he had formulated at Vienna: the defence of British India was not to interfere with the Congress System. In 1814, Ouseley had promised the shah, that as a prelude to stabilizing the frontier, Britain would persuade Russia to return part of the territory ceded at Gulistan. Every year for five years, the British ambassador reminded the tsar of this promise; but he was not expected to listen. Castlereagh told him at Aix-la-Chapelle that the Persian Connection was defensive, and that Britain would use her influence at Teheran to hold back the Persians in the Caucasus. Perhaps Castlereagh and Canning therefore are rightly linked. One is used to thinking of Canning as foreign secretary applying principles formulated by Castlereagh, but one might as reasonably turn them around. Castlereagh in 1818, following Canning in 1807, thought that mediating between Russia and Persia meant persuading the Persians to do as the Russians asked.[2]

The particular cause of this invitation to Russian obstinacy was the approach of a Persian ambassador, who had been sent to persuade the British, either to honour Ouseley's promises, or to pay the shah to be freed from them.[3] Castlereagh had hoped to avoid

---

[1] J. Rosselli, *Lord William Bentinck: The Making of a Liberal Imperialist* (London, 1974), pp. 147–51, 168.

[2] Castlereagh to Cathcart, nos. 1 and 3, secret, 2 Feb. 1819, with encls., F.O. 181/17.

[3] 'Memorandum [by Joseph Planta] upon the Probable Objects of the Persian

both, but had to compromise. He agreed to pay—or to make the East India Company pay, who would make the government of India pay—100,000 tomauns as a final payment of the subsidy; but he also warned the ambassador that only Britain's need to defend India far away gave her any interest in Persia, who could best preserve her independence by friendly relations with Russia, and by tracing their frontier in the Caucasus. The shah had always been willing to trace the frontier, and had no fixed ideas about where it should be, as long as the British would promise to make the Russians respect it. This was why he had agreed to the treaty of Gulistan. Castlereagh offered no support, only the veiled threat that Britain would not permit Persia to attack or to become dependent upon Russia.[1] As long as the Congress System worked, there was no danger of Russian expansion in the east; by provoking Russia, a close connection with Persia might create the problem it was meant to solve.

One of the oddities of the Great Game in Asia was that most men, who played, played more than once, confusing policy and strategy by the regular reintroduction of earlier arguments. Castlereagh's near-eastern policy was affected by the board of control's having fallen briefly under John Malcolm's influence. Malcolm was not a member himself, but the president from 1812 to 1816, the earl of Buckinghamshire, had been his mentor at Madras, and Buckinghamshire's bastard and private secretary, Henry Ellis, a protégé of Malcolm and his wholehearted supporter in his quarrels with Harford Jones, had gone with him on his second mission to Persia in 1808, and had later gone with another of his admirers on a mission to Sind. When Ellis returned to England in 1811, Malcolm gave him glowing testimonials; in return at the board of control he paid attention to Malcolm's opinions. Henry Ellis was the most important player at the beginning of the Great Game, because he played for the third time as a member of the board of control in Grey's administration, and for the fourth as ambassador at Teheran during Melbourne's, when he had as decisive an influence over Palmerston's near-eastern

Mission', [1819], *The Memoranda and Correspondence of Robert Stewart, Viscount Castlereagh*, ed. marquess of Londonderry (London, 1848–54), xii. 113.

[1] 'Records of Conferences between Castlereagh and Abul Hassan Khan', 20 June, 29 July 1819, F.O. 60/18.

policy as he had had previously over Castlereagh's. Fortunately, in the meantime he had found the answer to his puzzle.

When Castlereagh sent Ellis to Persia in 1814 to negotiate the amendments to the treaty of Teheran, he followed Malcolm in arguing that entangling Britain in the internal affairs of Persia, as Wellesley had planned, was unnecessary: order in Persia was not the prerequisite of security in India. To ignore Persia would be equally unwise. Ellis expected Abbas Mirza to oppose Castlereagh's amendments, because they removed from the treaty the article, matching an article in the treaty of Gulistan, which promised him the throne. This might endanger British India, were Abbas left to depend upon Russian help, which

can only be obtained by further cessions of territory, which he will not hesitate to grant, until Persia becomes a mere province of Russia. That such a state of things would in case of war with the latter power, disturb the security of British India, might I think be shown, and it would perhaps be of some use if Government were to decide how far they intend to interest themselves in the independence of Persia.

I find that Abbas Mirza's prospect of succession [said Ellis] is by no means certain, and that consequently he can rely only upon his present superior influence with the King and his connections with Russia and England. Adherence therefore to the policy of non-interference in the affairs of the succession, already adopted by Government, becomes the more apparent and necessary.[1]

Ellis had revealed the dilemma in which Castlereagh would place everyone responsible for the security of India. 'Any increase of the territory or even of the influence of Russia in the quarter of Persia', said Ellis, 'may be eventually dangerous to the interests of our Indian empire.' Although Britain did not need to turn Persia into a protectorate, she did need her as a buffer, and must find a way to hold back Russia, which 'did not disturb the more important relations with the court of St. Petersburg in Europe'.[2]

Although Ellis had spotted the weakness in Malcolm's argument, that unrest in Persia and the weakness of the Persian government would defend India against France but not Russia, the distinction escaped Castlereagh. In 1817 Sir Gore Ouseley, who

[1] Ellis to Buckinghamshire, 22 Aug. 1814, I.O.L. Film. MSS. 764.
[2] 'Memorandum [by Henry Ellis] on the Extent of the British Mediation between Persia and Russia for the Restoration of Territory to the Former', 28 Mar. 1815, F.O. 60/10.

had tried to recruit British officers on half pay for the Persian army, was sharply rebuked by the foreign office for disturbing 'the delicate situation of affairs between Russia and that country'.[1] Training had been ended with the subsidy. Unfortunately, while disentangling Britain from the Persian Connection, lest it endanger the Vienna Settlement, Castlereagh did nothing to guard against the alternative danger that the Kajars might become dependent upon Russia.

Castlereagh sometimes forgot, that even when kings were friends, dynastic diplomacy did not rely upon friendship for security. In his attempt to subordinate the defence of India to the Congress System he, too, ignored the likely effect of the dynastic rivalry in Persia. Although the shah had permitted Ouseley to negotiate for Persia at Gulistan, he had been opposed by Abbas Mirza. Similarly, although Alexander's attention might be diverted from the Caucasus to the Revolution, despite the death in 1821 of the governor of Kermanshah, Abbas Mirza's greatest rival, only victory over Russia or continuing tension in Russo-Persian affairs would sustain his pre-eminence in Persia. After 1819 the British chargé d'affaires at Teheran, Henry Willock, repeatedly warned the Persians that Britain would not again intervene at St. Petersburg on their behalf, nor would Russia permit it. Willock also reminded Castlereagh of the danger. Until Persia and Russia had traced their frontier, and negotiated a definitive peace, Britain would have to pay subsidies, should Russia invade Azerbaijan.[2]

War became more and more likely in the 1820s, because Abbas Mirza's was not the only vested interest. One strategically satisfactory barrier existed between Georgia and Azerbaijan, the river Arras and the fortress towns of Erivan and Nakitchevan, which command the important routes both north to south and east to west. This barrier was in Persia. Unless the British, by persuading the Russians to stabilize the frontier farther north, helped the Persians to keep it, the Russian government of Georgia would not rest until they had captured it.[3] As soon as they had, to prevent the Kajars' becoming dependent upon Russia would be difficult. Castlereagh, who thought of the Vienna Settlement geographically,

[1] Planta to Ouseley, 30 Oct. 1817, F.O. 60/12.
[2] Willock to Canning, no. 19, 4 Sept. 1825, F.O. 60/25; same to Castlereagh, no. 32, 4 Aug. 1820, F.O. 60/18.
[3] Walpole to Morier, 15 May 1815, F.O. 65/98; J. F. Baddeley, *The Russian Conquest of the Caucasus* (London, 1908), pp. 99–105.

as a balance between frontiers drawn on maps, in the near east ignored most important facts of geography.

Castlereagh was equally uninterested in tracing the frontier between Persia and Afghanistan. In his determination not only to rid the foreign office of the Persian Connection, in practice if not in fact, but to ignore the problem of the defence of British India, in 1814 he left in the treaty of Teheran the most dangerous article of all, article nine, which stipulated that Britain would not step between Persia and Afghanistan. As long as Persia was to be treated as a British protectorate, and the Mahometan Khanates as a buffer between the European and Indian political systems, as Wellesley had planned, quarrels between Afghanistan and Persia would not affect the British, because they would take place within a system over which the British were, or might become, the paramount power. Were the foreign office to ignore Persia, and the Persian pacification of Khorassan to cause a collision with the Afghans, the government of India might find themselves unable to construct an alternative system of defence in Afghanistan: were the Persians to capture Herat, the frontier between the European and Indian political systems would move dangerously far east.

In the 1820s this became more likely, because Castlereagh's successor at the foreign office, George Canning, anxious to prove his individuality by his 'love of undoing',[1] was determined to be rid of the Persian Connection. As long as the foreign office were responsible for it, it might adversely affect the European balance of power. Since 1817, the Persians had been demanding British support in a dispute with Turkey, the first sign that they would seek territorial compensation for their losses in the Caucasus in areas where it would threaten British interests. When war broke out in 1821, if their commander had not died, a Persian army would have captured Baghdad. Although Abbas Mirza, who had expected Russian support, was denied it, and the unsuccessful campaigns in Anatolia became unpopular in Persia, they distracted the sultan at a moment when the British wanted him to act decisively against the rebellions in the Principalities and Greece.

The war between Persia and Turkey also revived the squabble about Britain's commitments to Persia under the treaty of Teheran. Persia's demands for payment of the arrears of subsidy, which

---

[1] *The Journal of Mrs. Arbuthnot, 1820–1832*, eds. F. Bamford and duke of Wellington (London, 1950), i. 328.

Castlereagh had promised but the government of India not paid, became so nasty, that in 1822 Henry Willock, threatened with the loss of his head, went home to London, shortly followed by an envoy from the shah. Canning, who greeted Willock's arrival with the question, 'Henry Willock? I know a man of that name at Teheran, but certainly not in London',[1] then seized the chance to solve Henry Ellis's puzzle, of how to hold back Russia in Asia without complicating Anglo-Russian relations in Europe, by giving back control of the Persian mission to the government of India.

Anglo-Persian relations were regularly complicated by quarrels about rank. During the Napoleonic Wars, the British had assumed the shah would treat the governor-general of India as his equal: the shah had often expected British agents to negotiate with Abbas Mirza or the governor of Fars. Both sides were willing to abandon their pretensions, the British for action and the shah for money; how readily each did so depended upon his momentary interest in the connection. Usually, as happened after 1822, they went opposite ways at the same time. Abbas Mirza, Willock told Canning,[2]

is incensed at the present moment to spurn the yoke of Russia. He looks around and finds that England is the only power which can at all assist him. He is disposed to resume the strict relations which formerly existed with her, and he may possibly for a short time cultivate them. But the weight of Russia presses upon him. She has during the last seven years consolidated her authority in Georgia; he has neglected his army and finds himself daily more weak.

This analysis only confirmed Canning's opinion, that the Persian Connection would not defend but endanger Britain's vital interests.

Canning's arguments in 1822 and 1823 were deliberately deceptive, and give a good example of why so many men found it hard to trust him. He told Abbas Mirza that the mission would be placed 'on a higher footing';[3] he also told the board of control and the East India Company. His reason for transferring as well as enlarging the mission was, that

the objects of the intercourse with Persia are principally, if not purely Asiatic . . .

Whether Russia herself may not have adopted and may not hereafter

[1] Sir H. Rawlinson, *England and Russia in the East* (London, 1875), p. 38, fn.
[2] Willock to Canning, no. 9, 14 June 1825, F.O. 60/25.
[3] Canning to Abbas Mirza, 27 May 1823, F,O. 60/23.

attempt to put into practice the designs which Bonaparte entertained and abandoned, it is not now necessary to discuss. It seems to be sufficient for the present that it is with a view to India chiefly that a good understanding with Persia is a matter of importance; and it seems to follow that an Asiatic mission to an Asiatic court would, for objects essentially Asiatic, be more expedient than the maintenance of a chargé d'affaires from London in competition with a Russian minister of higher rank and allowances.

Parliament would not permit him the alternative of sending a minister of higher rank from the Crown, because the function of the Persian Connection was 'the defence of an empire in which the British public conceive the immediate government of the East to have the immediate interest'.[1]

This decision, which was opposed by both the board of control and the government of India, who realized that to threaten British India Russia did not need to emulate Bonaparte, provoked another argument about the value of the Persian Connection. Canning, echoing Castlereagh, argued that as Britain's only interest in Persia was the defence of British India, it could and must be separated from European international politics. The government of India countered in 1825 that it could not.[2] They had better memories than the foreign office: Wellesley had proved that trying to turn Persia into a protectorate would be costly and difficult. The best defence policy was to treat Persia as a buffer, preserved by pressure whenever necessary at St. Petersburg, where the government of India could not replace the foreign office, because they could not 'assume a tone calculated to provoke [a] direct rupture'.[3]

The East India Company, who also misunderstood Canning's remarks about the defence of British India, had at first thought he wanted them to increase their influence in Persia, and had offered the post of resident to Sir John Malcolm. He refused it, because he thought that Wellesley's policy of turning the Persian Connection into an Indian subsidiary alliance also could be carried out only by the foreign office.[4] Canning had also not meant to revive Welles-

---

[1] Canning to Wynn, confidential, 19 Dec. 1822, F.O. 60/21.

[2] Amherst to Canning, private, 23 Mar. 1825, F.O. 60/26; ggic to sc, 25 Mar. 1826, I.O. L/PS/5/4.

[3] Swinton to Macdonald, 18 Mar. 1825, I.O. Bengal/SPC/329, 18 Mar. 1825, no. 29.

[4] Minute of Malcolm, 28 Sept. 1826, F.O. 60/29.

ley's policy; the government of India were not 'to aim at a preponderant influence over the counsels of Persia, but to keep open a
friendly communication and maintain a channel of information'.[1]
The treaty of Teheran was the unfortunate result of passing
circumstances on the continent during the Napoleonic Wars, and
the British should break it, before it restricted their freedom of
action in Europe.

Preventing the conquest of Persia by Russia might be attempted,

if there were no other political questions in the world . . . but it is quite
another question whether a war with Russia would be a proper price to
pay for this system of early precautions . . . The government of India
[said Canning] should distinctly know that the transference of the
Persian mission from England to India was intended not to strengthen,
but to relax the bonds of a most inconvenient compact.[2]

In the nineteenth century a tradition grew up that Britain, as a
peripheral and naval power, did not negotiate alliances in time of
peace. The government of India were a continental and military
power: exposed and insecure, and valuing freedom of action less
than freedom from invasion and revolt, they thought the foreign
office should undertake to protect them.

The shah saw as clearly as the government of India, that as a
result of the transfer Persia would get no help from Britain in her
frontier negotiations with Russia.[3] He refused at first to admit the
British resident, Sir John Macdonald, who did not reach Teheran
until September 1826, and after the outbreak of the second Russo-
Persian war. The delay suited Canning. He had avoided, and had
prevented the government of India's being entangled. The delay
also suited the Russians. They had time to outwit Abbas Mirza,
who had hindered the commission set up to trace the Russo-
Persian frontier as revised by the treaty of Gulistan,[4] because he
hoped tense Russo-Persian relations would help him extract

[1] 'Memorandum Relative to the Persian Mission', 1830, I.O. L/PS/3/1,
p. 180.

[2] Canning to Wynn, private, 24 Oct. 1826, F.O. 60/29; M. E. Yapp, 'The
Control of the Persian Mission, 1822–1836', *University of Birmingham Historical
Journal*, vii (1959–60), 162–79.

[3] Willock to Canning, no. 10, 30 Dec. 1823, F.O. 60/22; same to Howard de
Walden, 22 Sept. 1824, F.O. 60/24.

[4] Willock to Canning, no. 8, 27 Dec. 1823, F.O. 60/22. For details of the origins
of the war see P. Avery, 'An Enquiry into the Outbreak of the Second Russo-
Persian War, 1826–28', *Iran and Islam: Essays in Memory of the Late Vladimir
Minorsky*, ed. C. E. Bosworth (Edinburgh, 1971), pp. 17–45.

money from his father and the British. He had to increase his revenue somehow, to pay an army which would appear capable of defending Islam and recapturing the territory lost by previous defeats.

Abbas Mirza did not, however, as Willock believed, stir up religious fanaticism in Persia because he wanted to fight: he was trapped by it. If he can be said to have had any consistent policy after the death of his ablest minister in 1821, it was to hover close to war. When in November 1825 the Russians occupied Gokcha, recognized by Russia in 1819 as belonging to Persia under the treaty of Gulistan, Abbas took fright at the dangers his own behaviour had created. The shah refused to take charge of Russo-Persian relations, which Abbas Mirza had controlled for twenty years, whereas the religious classes, who had always criticized his army reforms, now forced him to fight by proclaiming a holy war.[1]

Although in 1826 Abbas Mirza attacked first, Macdonald and the board of control both argued that the Russians had behaved so provocatively as to warrant treating them as the aggressors.[2] This would have entitled Persia, by the treaty of Teheran, to subsidies and British mediation. Canning refused to pay a subsidy. Whether or not Russia were substantially the aggressor, Britain could not finance the enemies of her European allies: the Napoleonic Wars had proved that supporting weak states against strong ones merely bought defeat expensively. In 1827 his colleagues eventually forced Canning to offer British mediation. As soon as he learnt that Russia, as he had expected, disliked the idea, he did nothing.[3] 'Mr. Canning,' said the duke of Wellington, 'appears . . . most anxious to shake off Persia.'[4]

If 'these incredibly foolish treaties', as Canning called the treaty of Teheran,[5] were allowed to affect Anglo-Russian relations, Britain would suffer in Europe. In 1826 and 1827 Canning was trying to use 'every engine short of war . . . to save Greece through

---

[1] Willock to Canning, no. 24, 28 Nov. 1825, F.O. 60/25; same to same, no. 20, 23 Aug. 1826, with encl., F.O. 60/27; H. Algar, *Religion and State in Iran 1785–1906* (Berkeley/Los Angeles, 1969), pp. 76–9, 83–93.

[2] Macdonald to sc, 19 Sept. 1826, I.O. Persia/39; Wynn to Canning, 2 Oct. 1826, F.O. 60/29.

[3] Disbrowe to Dudley, nos. 12 and 14, 22 Mar., 4 Apr. 1827, F.O. 65/164; Dudley to Disbrowe, no. 5, 27 June 1827, F.O. 65/163.

[4] Wellington to Malcolm, private, 12 Dec. 1826, Sir J. W. Kaye, *Life and Correspondence of Major-General Sir John Malcolm* (London, 1856), ii. 454.

[5] Canning to Wynn, 9 Oct. 1826, F.O. 60/29.

the agency of the Russian name upon the fears of Turkey'.[1] His under-secretary doubted whether Canning would succeed in controlling Russia, and he himself admitted that he was 'not *quite* satisfied with our co-operation: but it was worth the trial, and it affords the only *chance* of bringing things to a conclusion in the East without a war'.[2] This difficult attempt was not to be endangered by the demands of Persia. When Canning's successor and disciple offered British good offices during the peace negotiations at Turkmanchay, he meant, as Castlereagh had meant at Aix-la-Chapelle, that Britain would encourage Persia to give in to the Russian demands. The only help offered Persia was one payment of the subsidy, to be spent on paying off part of her indemnity, and in return for removing the subsidiary articles from the treaty.[3]

'We have too much sacrificed our interests on the side of India', complained the president of the board of control in 1828, 'to a weakness in favour of Russia. All our exertions at Teheran have been for Russian interests.'[4] Wellington argued that Canning should have tried to hold back both Persia and Russia. Had the Russians ignored him, they should have been warned that Britain would claim her right as a great power to be consulted about the terms of peace.[5] Canning was busy fighting a different war, for liberalism against the Holy Alliance. He had made the choice Castlereagh would have made, but had struggled and been lucky to escape, that the balance of power in Europe mattered more to Britain than the security of British India.

Castlereagh and Canning had assumed that Britain did not need

---

[1] Canning to S. Canning, private and confidential, 5 Sept. 1826, F.O. 352/13/1, fo. 162; same to Granville, private and confidential no. 4, 13 Jan. 1826, P.R.O. 30/29/8/9, no. 417.

[2] Canning to S. Canning, private, 3 July 1826, F.O. 352/13/1, fo. 146.

[3] Sc to ggic, 14 Sept. 1827, I.O. L/PS/5/543; Macdonald to sc, 12 Oct. 1827, I.O. Persia/41. Canning had followed the advice of Henry Ellis, except that too little had been done and too late. Ellis had argued that Britain could never fight for Persia, nor allow her to treat a dispute over an unsettled frontier as a ground for war; but he had also stated that Britain must offer Persia a sufficiently large subsidy, to enable her to pay a sufficiently large indemnity, to escape the alternative of the surrender of Erivan. Memorandums by Ellis, 5 Oct., 5 and 19 Dec. 1826, F.O. 60/29.

[4] Ellenborough's diary, 25 Sept. 1828, Lord Ellenborough, *A Political Diary, 1828–1830*, ed. Lord Colchester (London, 1881), i. 224.

[5] Wellington to Ellenborough, 9 Oct. 1828, *Despatches, Correspondence, and Memoranda of Field-Marshal, Arthur, Duke of Wellington*, ed. duke of Wellington (London, 1867–78), v. 117.

a connection with Persia: it would weaken her in Europe and do nothing to strengthen British India. As far as Persia could fight Russia, she would fight on her own behalf, and supporting her would be merely a waste of public money. As long as the defence of India was seen as a military problem, defence against invasion, as it had been against Napoleon, the foreign office believed that Persia was not the right place to fight. The British navy should attack in the Mediterranean or the Black Sea, the army in India defend at the Indus. Provided Britain remained friendly with Turkey and the Sikhs, she might connect the defence of British India with the balance of power in Europe, or separate them, as it suited her.

In 1828, after Persia and Russia had signed the treaty of Turkmanchay, these assumptions about Persia proved false. Canning, who had in 1822 'acknowledged [the] hopelessness of interfering with effect between Russia and Persia for the amelioration of the conditions of peace imposed by the emperor upon the shah',[1] forgot that they had been negotiated on behalf of Persia by Sir Gore Ouseley. He also ignored the vital question: Persia did not need more territory, she needed a stable north-west frontier. By annexing Erivan and Nakitchevan, Russia at Turkmanchay took from Persia the one strategically satisfactory barrier between the Caucasus and Azerbaijan. She also confirmed her exclusive right to sail warships on the Caspian; was given extra-territorial rights for Russian residents, the pattern for European capitulations in the nineteenth century; and was also given the right to station consuls wherever in Persia Russian merchants might need their help.

Finally, in a dramatic change of policy, by recognizing Abbas Mirza as heir apparent, and by demanding a large indemnity and then going without part of it, the Russians implied that they planned to turn Persia into a protectorate.[2] British policy changed equally dramatically after the death of Canning and the resignation of Goderich, when the duke of Wellington became prime minister, and in September 1828 appointed Lord Ellenborough president of the board of control. They saw at once, that as the frontier question between Persia and Russia was settled, Russia would threaten British India by befriending not enmity towards Persia.

The new governor-general of India in 1828, Lord William

[1] Canning to Wynn, confidential, 19 Dec. 1822, F.O. 60/21.
[2] The treaty is printed in Hurewitz, *Near and Middle East*, i. 96.

Bentinck, also saw this, and argued that as a result the British government must take back the control of the Persian mission.

The fact is [he told Malcolm, who agreed with him], that Persia is now little better, if so good, as a Maratha power, and equally unable to cope with Russia, as the latter was with us . . . She is completely at the mercy of Russia; and if Russia should take it into her head to invade India, she will begin, not by the invasion of Persia, but, as Bonaparte should have acted towards Poland, by a close alliance.[1]

Russia might then encourage Persia to expand towards Baghdad, Bahrein, or Herat, all threatening the tranquillity which was Britain's most vital interest in the near east.

The causes of the bitterness and recrimination between Persia and Britain in 1828 began in the mistake made by the Persians in 1801, who saw substance in Malcolm's shadow of a treaty, and had been aggravated after 1807, when the British had firstly suited their policy in Persia to their European alliances, and had then realized the ineffectiveness and the dangers of so doing: by trying to exert an Asiatic lever on European politics, Britain was inviting European states to exert an Asiatic lever against her. France would have to threaten an invasion, Russia would have merely to expand; both might persuade the Indian states to attack the British. Wellesley, who never feared the French, but wanted to forestall the Russians, tried in 1810 to safeguard the empire in India he had tried to create, and was certain would soon be created, by turning Persia into a protectorate. If the European and Indian political systems could be separated by a frontier in the Mahometan Khanates, or, even should they be annexed by Russia, if the Russo-Persian frontier could be stabilized, Persia would be separated from Europe, Perso-Afghan quarrels could be ignored as local, and the British would have found in Persia the ally for whom Swift had told them to seek.

Castlereagh and Canning, lacking Wellesley's vision and so able to see only one thing at a time, both ignored a problem they could not comprehend. By trying to break Britain's connection with Persia, and by their refusal to support the shah's attempts to stabilize his north-west frontier, they permitted Persia to be forced into dependence upon Russia. Far from freeing their European policy from the effects of Asiatic entanglements, Castlereagh's

[1] Bentinck to Malcolm, private, 25 Sept. 1828, Portland MSS. PwJf/1400.

behaviour at Aix-la-Chapelle, and Canning's during the Russo-Persian war, proved how closely the two had become connected. The repercussions for British India were dramatic. The terms of the treaty of Turkmanchay moved the frontier between the European and Indian political systems from the Mahometan Khanates to Khorassan, and, as a result, the problem of locating Persia's eastern frontier became as urgent as had been the partition of the Caucasus for the security of British India.

The history of the Persian Connection between 1800 and 1828 had revealed, firstly the folly of treating the danger to British India from Russia as if she were France, and secondly, that even if the British preferred to avoid the expense and entanglement of turning Persia into a protectorate, they had to try to preserve her as a buffer state. By 1830, Ellenborough, who realized this, planned to struggle unceasingly at St. Petersburg to hold back Russia, and at Teheran to regain a hold over Persia. Simultaneously, he planned an offensive in Afghanistan and Turkestan, in an attempt to forestall the Russians as Wellesley had planned to forestall them in Persia. Because the foreign office might be embarrassed, and the government of India powerless, the board of control should take over the direction of British policy in the near east. Between 1828 and 1834 they gradually did. The result, an attempt to find an alternative to the Persian Connection, was the Great Game in Asia.

III

The Summons to Play 1828-1830

One should always play fairly . . .
when one has the winning cards.

MRS. CHEVELEY,
An Ideal Husband,
Act I

THE AUTHOR OF the most delightful text for children on European affairs published in England in the nineteenth century, counselling her readers to

. . . thank the goodness and the grace
Which on my birth have smiled
And made me in these Christian days
A happy English child.[1]

then guided them rapidly eastwards on a tour revealing the dilemma faced by nineteenth-century English statesmen, who made policy for the near east.

Russia was depraved: 'There are many rich lords in Russia who are very cruel to the poor people. They treat them like slaves . . . and take away their things whenever they please.' The ruler of Russia was a tyrant, who 'does what he likes. He can put people in prison whenever he is displeased.' If Russia were bad, Turkey was worse,

because it has such a bad religion. It is not the Roman Catholic religion —that is a sort of Christian religion; the religion of Turkey is not a Christian religion; it is called Mohammedanism. There was once a wicked man called Mahomet, and he pretended that God sent him to teach people; but he was a false prophet, and he taught people lies and wickedness.

The King of Turkey is called the Grand Seignior. He does whatever he pleases. He has a great many wives. He lives in a beautiful palace. He keeps a number of deaf and dumb men in his palace as servants.

---

[1] *Near Home; or the Countries of Europe Described,* by the author of *The Peep of Day, Far Off,* etc. (63rd Thousand, London, 1870), p. 5.

They cannot disturb him by talking, and they cannot hear what he says. He also has dwarfs and black men in his palace. The servants he likes best are black dwarfs, who are deaf and dumb.[1]

Russia denied an Englishman's belief in civil liberty, equality of opportunity, and private property; Turkey denied his belief in self-restraint, frugality, and the need to avoid superstition. Only the Great Game in Asia made it necessary if not easy to choose between them.

The xenophobia of an island people did not always affect British foreign policy: foreign secretaries had to decide how far and why Britain should tie herself to other states, and when necessary arouse public support. What set Great Britain apart was being the first world power. Other states had interests outside Europe, but the European balance of power was known to be their most vital interest; the Great Game in Asia was one of many British debates about priorities. In the middle of the eighteenth century, the British had debated whether fighting in the colonies or on the continent was the better way to preserve their security. The alternatives were more apparent than real: as long as three other European states were naval and colonial powers, naval wars fought in the colonies helped to preserve the balance of power on the continent.

In the early nineteenth century the situation was turned about. The fulcrum of the balance of power had moved eastwards from the Burgundian Circle to the Holy Alliance, and sea power had little effect on it. Instead, as soon as the British became in 1818 the paramount power in India, the European balance of power affected the stability of the empire. Except possibly at the Dardanelles, British India could not be defended at sea. In the nineteenth century, both in Europe and Asia, the British had to assume, that whenever their interests were threatened, another state could always be found, equally threatened and willing to help. One object of the Great Game in Asia was to find the ally who would defend British India.

The search was forced on the British by the consequences of the Greek rebellion. Paradoxically, the British replaced the Mogul Empire the same year as the congress of Aix-la-Chapelle. The balance of power in Europe and India appeared to have been

[1] Ibid., pp. 24–5.

stabilized, and might have been had the British included Turkey in the Vienna Settlement. Castlereagh, who had tried to include her in the Final Act at Vienna recognizing the new frontiers of states, had also suggested that everyone should promise to fight on behalf of the settlement. The tsar promised to fight, but would not include Turkey: if Russia were to remain free to attack Turkey, Britain would not fight for Russia in Poland. As both proposals were set aside, the balance of power in the near east remained unstable at a time when the British had begun to realize, that their most vital interest in the area was to persuade everyone to ignore it. During the Greek rebellion the British tried in vain to find convincing arguments.

Castlereagh and Canning both believed states should intervene in areas vital to their interests: Austria might intervene in Naples, so might Britain in Portugal, as an ally of the king. They did not believe, as they explained when denouncing the protocol of Troppau, in joint intervention to prevent all political and social change. The Greek rebellion revealed the dangers of this distinction. Castlereagh and Canning objected to joint intervention in principle, and denied the Russian claim to intervene in defence of vital interests, hoping that if nobody intervened the Turks would put down the rebellion. They then explained that this policy would help to stabilize the European balance of power; to which the tsar replied that the balance of power would be more effectively stabilized by appeasing the Greeks.[1]

The British, whose aims in the near east were usually shared by Prince Metternich, although rarely would either admit it, and never at the same time, managed to hold back the tsar: the sultan failed to put down rebellion, until the Egyptian troops he used, and the stories of massacre which followed them, harmed him politically in Europe as much as they helped him win victories in Greece. After 1825, when a new tsar seemed more and more determined to help the Greeks, Canning tried to hold him back by working with him. Although Canning died in 1827 confident that 'Greece [is] thus disposed of',[2] the result was the battle of Navarino and the Russo-

---

[1] Sir C. Webster, *The Congress of Vienna, 1814-1815* (London, 1963); Kissinger, *World Restored*; F. H. Hinsley, *Power and the Pursuit of Peace* (Cambridge, 1963).

[2] Canning to Granville, private and confidential, 13 July 1827, P.R.O. 30/29/8/12, no. 564. This was Canning's last letter about politics. For his Greek

Turkish war. According to C. W. Crawley, Wellington, appalled by Navarino, tried to make amends to the Turks by deriving no benefit. Had Britain, France and Russia continued to co-operate in 1828, by threatening the sultan with a blockade of the Dardanelles, the Greek question might have been solved. Instead the lack of a British policy was one reason why the sultan would not give way, and one cause of the Russo-Turkish war.[1]

The traditional criticism of Wellington cannot thus be justified. The difference between Wellington and Canning was the same as the difference between Castlereagh and Wellesley: the Wellesley brothers shared an Anglo-Indian conception of Britain's vital interests. Wendy Hinde suggests that Canning, 'like Castlereagh had inherited from Pitt a strong belief in the importance of preserving the Ottoman Empire as a bastion against a possible Russian threat . . . to the British position in India'.[2] There is no sign that any of them thought this, but the Wellesleys did. Although Canning listed amongst his reasons in 1826 for avoiding a war against Turkey over Greece, the effect of a 'war of the mitre against the turban . . . [on our] 100 millions of Mahometan and unchristian subjects in Asia',[3] this was a more compelling argument for Wellington. At the time Canning was supposedly estimating the effect in India of his Greek policy, he was ignoring the likely effects of his policy in Persia.

The Persian Connection was sacrificed to Canning's attack on the Holy Alliance in Europe; the Greeks were sacrificed to Wellington's anxiety about the security of British India. Persia was the key to Wellington's dilemma in Greece. Using force against Turkey might have caused unrest in India; weakening Turkey would endanger India's security in the future; threatening Russia would have looked too much like helping the Turks, for which the public were not yet ready, would in Wellington's opinion have been merely bluff, and might have provoked Russian retaliation in Asia. If the Russians were stopped in Greece, they might push on in Persia; because Canning had not stopped them in Persia, they

policy, see H. W. V. Temperley, *The Foreign Policy of Canning* (2nd edition, London, 1966), pp. 348–55.

[1] C. W. Crawley, *The Question of Greek Independence: A Study of British Policy in the Near East, 1821–1833* (London, 1930), pp. 94–112.

[2] W. Hinde, *George Canning* (London, 1973), p. 384.

[3] Canning to Granville, private, no. 32, 2 June 1826, P.R.O. 30/29/8/10, no. 479.

were more difficult to hold back in Greece. The Eastern Question and the defence of British India could not be separated. As soon as the Greek question was seen in 1828 to be Asiatic as well as European, British policy would be hesitant for the reason Austrian near-eastern policy always was, because, unless Britain had a continental ally, she could not appear openly and directly opposed to Russia.

Wellington had to wait until the wars in the east were over in 1829, and then devise a method of creating a new near-eastern balance of power. One method, suggested by the foreign secretary, the earl of Aberdeen, was to enlarge Greece. The Greeks were helped, and were seen as successors to the Turks, by men who thought historically; in return a new Greek empire, more Hellenistic than Attic, might help Britain by becoming powerful and stable enough to discourage European expansion in the eastern Mediterranean while encouraging British trade. Greece, however, could not defend British India. As soon as Ellenborough, at the board of control, began to challenge Aberdeen for influence over Wellington, Greece lost her charm. The security of British India, if not the balance of power in Europe, depended upon preserving Turkey. The method chosen, which the British also expected to create a balance of power in the near east, was the Great Game in Asia.

When the treaty of Adrianople followed in 1829 the treaty of Turkmanchay, the British realized their danger. 'We are certainly in a bad way,' said Wellington. 'We have made the greatest sacrifices . . . to our allies. In return, they have not performed their promises.'[1] Russia had helped the Greeks only because she wished to attack Turkey. 'We have been the tools of Russia', added Ellenborough, 'and have been duped with our eyes open.'[2] He meant that the Russians would not be duped; that they would not subordinate their interests in the near east to Austria's in checking the Revolution and Britain's in checking France. Both had tried to draw the attention of Russia to western Europe. During the Greek rebellion both failed, because neither of the dangers threatening them, the power of France Britain, and liberalism and nationalism Austria, directly endangered Russia. Metternich, who had always argued that these two movements were contagious,

[1] Wellington to Aberdeen, 25 Aug. 1829, Add. MSS. 43057, fo. 298.
[2] 29 Apr. 1829, Ellenborough's *Diary*, ii. 25.

hoped to use the Polish rebellion to prove his point. The treaties of Münchengrätz seemed to show that by 1833 he had succeeded. The British misunderstood Russian policy in the near east between Adrianople and Münchengrätz. Nicholas was following the alternative Russian policy begun by Paul; willing to preserve Turkey and Persia as weak states on his southern frontier, as long as they remained more susceptible to Russian pressure than either British or French. The British often feared a partition; sometimes they even feared that Metternich had agreed to one. Their mistake, although huge, was unimportant: because the aim of both Russian policies was paramount Russian influence throughout the near east, and both were equally threatening to British India, British policy remained the same even when they understood. The Great Game in Asia was an attempt begun during the winter and spring of 1829-30 to devise a counterweight. Had the Dardanelles and Persia fallen to Russia, the British hoped to make a stand in Turkestan and Baghdad.

II

The Russians took little territory from Persia and Turkey at Turkmanchay and Adrianople, but it was very valuable. Turkey lost Anapa and Poti on the east coast of the Black Sea; Persia lost Erivan and Nakitchevan and control of the passes from the Caucasus to Azerbaijan. Crawley, who said that Russia's 'gains in Asiatic Turkey were not of immediate significance',[1] did not see that, added to what she had taken from Persia, they endangered British India by weakening the frontiers of both states. As a result of the Russian victories, lamented the British resident at Teheran, in August 1829, 'the vast tract of territories extending on one side from the Araxes to the Halys, and on the other from the Euxine to Basra, may now be considered as prostrate at the feet of the Great Lord of the North'.[2] Russia could now 'control at pleasure the destiny of Asia Minor', echoed Aberdeen, '. . . and whether she may be disposed to extend her conquests to the east or to the west, no serious obstacle can arrest her progress.'[3]

As a result of Castlereagh's and Canning's determination to

---

[1] Crawley, *Greek Independence*, p. 169.
[2] Macdonald to Ellenborough, 18 Aug. 1829, E.U.L. MSS. Dk/2/37, fo. 69.
[3] Aberdeen to Heytesbury, no. 22, 31 Oct. 1829, F.O. 181/78; printed in Bourne, *Foreign Policy of Victorian England*, p. 210.

ignore the near east, Persia had been turned into a component of the European balance of power, and the frontier between the European and Indian political systems had been moved eastwards from the Caucasus to Khorassan. Not everyone saw this as endangering British India. Britain's 'mere Russian'[1] ambassador at St. Petersburg, Lord Heytesbury, thought the tsar knew Russia to be too weak to attempt an invasion. 'I consider this country,' he said, 'colossal as is its mass, and formidable as are the obstacles it presents to an invader, to possess fewer and less formidable means of aggression than any other of the Great Powers of Europe.'[2] Here he prophesied a famous quarrel six years later, when Lord Ponsonby at Constantinople, seeing the Turks to be too weak to resist a Russian invasion, and Lord Durham at St. Petersburg, seeing the Russians to be too weak to attempt one, each bombarded Palmerston with letters abusing the other.

Heytesbury was unpopular with the board of control and the foreign office, because for ten years after the treaty of Adrianople few officials in England but he and Durham believed anything said by the Russians. Perhaps this was wise; Aberdeen, who later was willing to believe them, misunderstood what they said, causing confusion and resentment. It was better, said Palmerston, 'to go by the general rule and believe that when Russian agents are employed there must be an intrigue on foot'.[3]

Ellenborough, who wholeheartedly agreed, wanted to warn Russia in October 1829, that 'any attempt . . . to extend her conquests in Persia . . . would be considered . . . as an unfriendly act to His Majesty as an Asiatic power'.[4] Because the expansion of Russia endangered British India, it must stop. Canning had wanted the government of India to carry on Anglo-Persian relations, although he had planned to tell them what to do, in the hope of avoiding a quarrel with Russia; Ellenborough, fearing it might be soon too late, wanted to provoke one. This warning was not sent, however, partly because the Russians made no more demands on Persia, partly because Ellenborough's cabinet colleagues did not see how Britain, short of a European war, could back it up.

After he became president of the board of control in September

[1] 29 Aug. 1829, Ellenborough's *Diary*, ii. 88.
[2] Heytesbury to Aberdeen, separate and secret, 29 June 1829, F.O. 65/180.
[3] Palmerston to Ponsonby, private, 17 Feb. 1833, Broadlands MSS. GC/PO/655.
[4] Ellenborough to Wellington, 15 Oct. 1829, *Wellington*, vi. 227.

1828, Ellenborough began to play the Great Game in Asia as a less noticeable way of hemming in Russia. Able, ambitious, and fidgety, and kept in the cabinet mostly because Wellington and Peel feared 'he would be very disagreeable in opposition',[1] in preparation for taking over from Aberdeen, of whom he thought little, Ellenborough set out to turn the board into a second foreign office. He

seems to give all his attention to oriental subjects [said a member of the British mission at Teheran], and to make his presidency of the board of control something more than a sinecure. I am glad to see someone among the ministers thinks it his duty to take charge of national interests in the east.[2]

Ellenborough's policy was clear and simple. 'I would in Persia and everywhere,' he said, 'endeavour to create the means of throwing the whole world in arms upon Russia at the first convenient time.'[3] If Britain could not hold back Russia herself, she must find help; only a bold offensive, with Aberdeen rallying Europe and Ellenborough Asia, could earn the board of control the fame Ellenborough was seeking.

Wellington and Aberdeen were more cautious, refusing to rally Europe and doubtful whether Ellenborough could rally Asia. Persia would be of no use as an ally; her many defeats had proved that the Persian army could never hold back Russia. With proper training they might act as a police force, and by keeping order in Azerbaijan deny Russia the opportunity to make new demands. As Wellesley in 1810 had been the first to realize, the geographical position of both Persia and Turkey, as neighbours to Russia but not to Britain nor British India, meant that asking more of them, or trying to turn them into protectorates, might cause to happen what the British were trying to prevent. 'We must take care', said Wellington in reply to Ellenborough's demand for an ultimatum, 'that while peace is our object and policy . . . we are not accused, as

[1] Wellington to Peel, 16 Aug. 1828, *Wellington*, iv. 615; Peel to Wellington, 18 Aug. 1828, ibid., p. 632.

[2] McNeill to Wilson, [1830], *Memoir of the Rt. Hon. Sir John McNeill, G.C.B., and of his Second Wife Elizabeth Wilson*, by their grand-daughter (London, 1910), p. 132.

[3] 10 Oct. 1828, Ellenborough's *Diary*, i. 238. Ellenborough is so outspoken in his diary that one wonders whether to believe him. Discount the flamboyant phrases, and the opinions are accurately reflected in his private letters and despatches.

the Persians were two years ago, and the Turks more recently, of exciting wars against the emperor on his eastern frontiers.'[1]

This awareness, that Britain could not defend British India in alliance with Persia, was the result of Castlereagh's and Canning's policy since the Napoleonic Wars. The British had always supposed that near-eastern states, above all Persia, would prefer a connection with Britain to one with France or Russia, because Britain unlike the others would never threaten them. 'This country', said Sir John Macdonald of Persia as late as 1829, 'is . . . prepared and eager to embrace us with all the warmth and sincerity of friendship on the slightest manifestation of reciprocity on our side.'[2] This had once been true, but, as soon as she lost Erivan and Nakitchevan, Persia was bound to pay more attention to Russia than Britain. This might endanger British India, should Russia make amends to Persia for her losses in the Caucasus by helping her to capture Baghdad or Herat. The British had to forbid both. Soon after the treaties of Turkmanchay and Adrianople, the British conquered their fear that Russia would demand more territory; they were still frightened that Russia might use Persia and Turkey, as Wellington had told Ellenborough not to use them, as weapons of indirect assault.

'Persia ruled on our Indian system', said Macdonald, 'might in a short time be made equal to any struggle against an invader.'[3] Were this true, it was a pity; even Wellesley had admitted that Britain could not rule Persia in this way, but Russia might try. The state of affairs was best described by Heytesbury. 'The Turkish sultan will probably be as submissive hereafter to the tsar', he said, 'as any of the princes of India to the [East India] Company.'[4] 'Henceforth', said Aberdeen in November 1829, 'it is incontestable that the sultan will reign only by the sufferance of Russia.'[5] What was true of Turkey was true of Persia: unless the British could think of a way to match Russia, and to keep them as buffer states, they would soon become her protectorates. 'It must

---

[1] Wellington to Ellenborough, 9 Oct. 1828, *Wellington*, v. 117; Aberdeen to Ellenborough, private, 20 Oct. 1829, Add. MSS. 43058, fo. 19. J. A. Norris, *The First Afghan War, 1838–1842* (Cambridge, 1967), p. 21, exaggerates the extent to which Wellington agreed with Ellenborough.

[2] Macdonald to Malcolm, 15 Dec. 1829, E.U.L. MSS. Dk/2/37, fo. 107.

[3] Macdonald to Ellenborough, 12 Dec. 1829, ibid., fo. 106.

[4] Heytesbury to Aberdeen, private, 30 Sept. 1829, Add. MSS. 41558, fo. 241.

[5] Aberdeen to Gordon, no. 28, 10 Nov. 1829, F.O. 78/179.

now be admitted', echoed the British ambassador at Constantinople, 'that both these nations are perfectly subdued and at the mercy of Russia.'[1]

Whether or not Russia was strong enough to invade India did not matter. Trying to match Russian influence in Turkey and Persia would turn the defence of British India into a political not a military problem, and the Russians,

having the desire . . . to mix themselves up as principals in every concern, and having a real interest in none, I am not quite certain [the duke told Aberdeen] that they are not the most inconvenient for us to deal with in friendly terms of any power in Europe.[2]

Ellenborough, who agreed, knew why: whatever Heytesbury might say, 'that Russia will attempt, by conquest or by influence, to secure Persia as a road to the Indus I have the most intimate conviction. It is evident that the latter and surer mode, that of influence, is the one she now selects.'[3] Russia might have no choice. Heytesbury's opinions irritated Ellenborough, because in India the British had had no choice, or so they said: their dealings with the Pindaris and the Marathas had proved, that when a territorial state tried to live beside nomads and marauders, it was bound to expand.

The British began to play the Great Game in Asia in December 1829, less to prevent the invasion of India than bankruptcy and rebellion. Had the Russians invaded, the British would have beaten them, as they knew that they would at length have beaten the French, had Bonaparte invaded from Egypt. They worried whether they would win quickly enough. Should anyone invade, said the commander-in-chief, India, in 1808, 'it must be of extreme importance to put an immediate and decisive end to the contest by the complete defeat of the enemy, for it is impossible to calculate the effects which a reverse might produce on the minds and conduct of the natives.'[4] Anglo-Indians who worried about rebel-

---

[1] Gordon to Macdonald, 19 Oct. 1829, I.O. Bengal/SPC/72, 10 Mar. 1830, no. 2. According to Gordon, the commercial stipulations of the treaty of Adrianople 'in many respects denied to the Porte the exercise of those rights which essentially belong to an independent government'. Gordon to Aberdeen, no. 48, 19 Sept. 1829, F.O. 78/181.

[2] Wellington to Aberdeen, 14 July 1829, *Wellington*, vi. 13.

[3] Ellenborough to Wellington, 18 Oct. 1829, *Wellington*, vi. 238.

[4] Minute of Hewett, 15 Feb. 1808, I.O. Bengal/SPC/205, 15 Feb. 1808, no. 1.

lion, believed, like Metternich in Europe, that in Asia unrest would spread. Russian expansion was bound to cause unrest in the near-eastern states, Russian influence wars between them and unrest in India. As a result, the British dreaded 'not so much actual invasion by Russia as the moral effect which would be produced amongst our own subjects in India . . . by the continued apprehension of that event'.[1]

Fear of rebellion haunted the government of India, fear of bankruptcy the board of control. Should the Russians ever approach near enough to Afghanistan, or gain an influence as 'practically [to] place the resources of Persia at the disposal of Russia', they might, 'without any ultimate intention to attempt actual invasion . . . take up a menacing position which would occasion an expenditure in India ruinous to our finances',[2] by using up the credit of the government of India. British public finance in the nineteenth century tried to please the rich, who were sure to invest profitably everything they did not have to pay in taxes. British India was supposed to pay tribute, then dividends, not to need subsidies.

To calm fears of rebellion and bankruptcy, British India should ideally be defended far away and cheaply, but still in Asia. Not keeping the European and Indian political systems apart would 'operate in a material degree as a check upon our policy in Europe':[3] trying to limit the extension of Russian power in Poland or the Balkans would lead to threats against British India. Both the defence of British India and the balance of power in Europe would benefit, could the British check Russian influence throughout the near east, and without being tied down themselves.

In the heady atmosphere of the early nineteenth century, during the second phase of the Industrial Revolution, the British believed that in a fight for influence in the near east they had one great asset, the quality and variety of their manufactures. Trade in the near east, like Christianity in India, was to serve the empire. The idea that Russian manufactures might serve their empire seemed absurd.[4] Unfortunately, the British did little trade with the near

---

[1] Sc to ggic, 12 Jan. 1830, I.O. L/PS/5/543.

[2] Sc to ggic, 2 Dec. 1828, I.O. L/PS/5/543; Ellenborough to Macdonald, private and confidential, 23 Dec. 1829, P.R.O. 30/9/4 pt. 1/4. Macdonald thought similarly. Macdonald to Gordon, 28 Nov. 1829, E.U.L. MSS. Dk/2/37, fo. 98.

[3] Sc to ggic, 12 Jan. 1830, I.O. L/PS/5/543.

[4] 1 Feb. 1830, Ellenborough's *Diary*, ii. 181.

east, certainly not enough and not where they needed it. Ellen-borough and Aberdeen set out to expand it. To beat the Russians to Turkestan, Ellenborough planned in 1830 to open a new trade-route up the Indus; to challenge them in Turkey and Persia, Aberdeen sent a British consul to Trebizond, who was to develop the existing route through Erzerum into Azerbaijan. Should he succeed, the Great Game in Asia would be played by merchants, and the battle for influence in the near east won with cooking pots and cotton goods, as cheaply and as far from India as possible.

This decision showed how dramatically the British had changed their attitude to the Turks. Since 1791, the British had resented it, whenever the Turks had come to terms with France or Russia. Not that they were ever offered help: they were expected, like the Persians, to defend the interests of Britain, remaining too weak to act as an agent of French imperialism, while strong enough not to become dependent upon Russia. Instead, also like the Persians, they had been disastrously defeated. 'This clumsy fabric of bar-barous power', muttered Aberdeen to his brother after the treaty of Adrianople, 'will speedily crumble into pieces from its own inherent causes of decay.'[1] Momentarily, while the British toyed with the idea of enlarging Greece, this need not have endangered Britain's interests in Europe, but, unless Mahomet Ali of Egypt were allowed simultaneously to annex Syria, and replace the sultan as Britain's indispensable Asiatic ally, it was bound to endanger British India.

The ambassador at Constantinople, Aberdeen's brother Sir Robert Gordon, who had begun his career under Gore Ouseley in Persia, and understood the importance of a balance of power in the near east to the safety of British India, replied that 'means as well as arguments are not wanting to uphold the Ottoman Empire'.[2] Rebellions would never destroy the dynasty, unless the Russians took advantage of them to make further demands, which could always be prevented by sending the British fleet to the Black Sea. Gordon, a believer in naval power, had wanted to summon the fleet to the sea of Marmora when the Russian army reached Adrianople.[3] Aberdeen, tutored by Wellington, whose friend Charles Arbuthnot had never forgotten the failure of the Dar-

[1] Aberdeen to Gordon, no. 28, 10 Nov. 1829, F.O. 78/179.
[2] Gordon to Aberdeen, no. 84, 15 Dec. 1829, F.O. 78/181.
[3] Gordon to Aberdeen, private, 6 Jan. 1830, Add. MSS. 43210, fo. 202.

danelles Expedition in 1807, replied that the effect of sea power as an offensive weapon at the Straits was an illusion. Sending them into the sea of Marmora would 'have placed our fleet in a *rat trap* and would have made us cut a ridiculous figure'.[1]

To be effective in any crisis, the fleet must enter the Black Sea soon enough to prevent the Russian army from crossing the Balkan Mountains. This would mean a European war, which it was the aim of British policy to avoid. The expansion of trade might prevent such crises by increasing order in Turkey: 'We should readily co-operate', Aberdeen told Gordon, 'in any practicable and rational means which might be devised for giving additional security to its existence.'[2] Whether Turkey should crumble or revive, whether as an eastern equivalent to Greece, or as an Asiatic buttress against India, one other means of adding to her security, or preparing for her collapse, seemed available: the government of India were told to seek a closer connection with the governor of Baghdad. The British had a similar chance to guard against the collapse of Persia; they could forestall the Russians in Turkestan. Visions of the future of Turkestan were the immediate origin of the Great Game in Asia.

III

One sometimes wonders which is worse for British politicians, travelling or reading. Disraeli's travels merely illustrated his daydreams, whereas Wellington's Indian experience misled him, and also misled Ellenborough: they both paid too much attention to Sir John Malcolm. Unfortunately Ellenborough also liked to read. He read Fraser's travels in Khorassan, Meyendorff's in Bokhara, and Gamba's in the Caucasus,[3] all because at the end of October 1829 he happened to read Colonel George de Lacy Evans.

Lacy Evans, like Hobson writing on imperialism at the end of the Boer War, published two books on the problems of invading India, neither novel nor alarmist, but coming out after the treaties of Turkmanchay and Adrianople at a suitable moment, and an important influence on British policy. Their arguments are worth

---

[1] Aberdeen to Gordon, private, 3 Oct., 8 Dec. 1829, ibid., fos. 114, 193.

[2] Aberdeen to Gordon, no. 9, 26 Feb. 1830, F.O. 78/188.

[3] Fraser, *Journey into Khorasan*; Baron Georg von Meyendorff, *Voyage d'Orenbourg à Bokhara fait en 1820* (Paris, 1826); J. F. Gamba, *Voyage dans la Russie méridionale, et particulièrement dans les provinces situées au dela du Caucase, fait depuis 1820 jusqu'en 1824* (Paris, 1826).

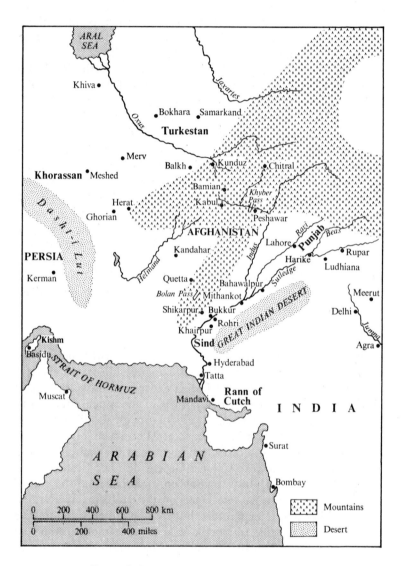

Beyond the North-West Frontier in 1820

more detailed attention than they usually receive, because they both crystallized the fears of government, and explained how British India might be defended. They also spurred Ellenborough's ambition. The strategy put forward was free from the two traditional objections to British moves in Asia, Castlereagh's and Canning's to disturbing the balance of power in Europe, and Wellesley's and Wellington's to offending Russia by causing unrest along her southern frontier. Instead India was to be defended in Turkestan. Ellenborough began the Great Game in Asia: Evans summoned him to play.

The assumption from which Evans began was the decisive change in the European balance of power since the Napoleonic Wars: Russia had become more powerful and more threatening than France. Whereas Britain had previously ignored Russian expansion in Asia in order to hold back France, holding back Russia in the near east had now become a vital British interest, were Britain and France to be able to limit Russian power in Europe. Britain's failure to counteract Russia's rights in Turkey under the treaty of Kutchuk-Kainardji, by including her in the Vienna Settlement, meant that Russia 'can never be at a loss for plausible, if not unanswerable, pretexts for engaging in hostilities whenever it shall perfectly accord with her position to do so'. 'Persia [too] is now in a very dependent situation,' said Evans. '. . . Commanding position on the frontiers, and a completely over-awing influence in its political conduct, are obviously sought for.'[1]

This situation endangered the balance of power, because once Poland had been partitioned, the only lever Britain and France had against Russia was to threaten an attack in the Black Sea. Should Russia obtain control of the Bosporus and the Dardanelles, and should she, by opening a trade route from Trebizond through Mosul to Basra, obtain an influence in the Persian Gulf, 'it should, perhaps, require a very onerous series of efforts on the part of both those powers, in conjunction, to restrain the other within any reasonable limitation of its pretensions'.[2] Here was prophesied the cause of the Crimean War.

Because Russia's commanding influence would act as a lever against Great Britain, by threatening British India, Britain's

---

[1] G. de Lacy Evans, *On the Designs of Russia* (London, 1828), p. 78.
[2] Ibid., p. 17.

dilemma was a double one. The Russian traveller, Baron Meyendorff, had claimed for Russia the right to develop and civilize the
states of Turkestan.[1] This claim, of course denied by most Englishmen, caused Evans, following James Baillie Fraser,[2] to choose
Khiva as the most strategically vital point in central Asia. The
Russian conquest of Khiva, claimed another Russian traveller,
would draw the trade of India, Afghanistan, and Turkestan,
north-westwards towards the Caspian and the Volga.[3] Any better
conditions for trade which might result would not benefit Britain
commercially, because the Russians would immediately set up
tariff barriers against British goods, and politically would be
threatening: 'There can be no doubt', said Evans, 'that the mere
appearance of a Russian force upon the eastern shore of the
Caspian would alone be calculated to unsettle and disturb, in a most
inconvenient manner, the general feeling of the people of India.'[4]

According to Evans, if the Russians wished to invade India,
they would march not from Azerbaijan across Persia towards
Herat, because the British based in the Persian Gulf might then
attack them in the flank, but from the east coast of the Caspian to
Khiva, then sail up the Oxus to Balkh or Kunduz, and cross the
Hindu Kush to Kabul. Evans expected this march to take two
campaigns, the first spent between the Caspian and Balkh, the
second crossing the Hindu Kush and the Khyber Pass to Attock.
Although he did not realize how difficult it was to cross the Hindu
Kush, Evans dealt with the problems of transport and supply
between Astrakhan and Balkh; providing food and water between
the Caspian and Khiva would be no more difficult for the Russians
than the British had found marching from Kosseir to the Nile
during their expedition to Egypt in 1801, and the terrain was no
more barren. Evans claimed that fishing boats used on the Aral
Sea would do for transport on the Oxus, and, if anyone criticized
his argument for leaving out the great distances involved, he replied that a British army had marched 2,200 miles in seven months
during the Maratha Wars, and that the Russians on the east coast
of the Caspian were no farther from Kabul than the British on the
Sutledge from Calcutta. In Evans's opinion, those who thought

[1] Meyendorff, *Voyage à Bokhara*, p. 303.
[2] Fraser, *Journey into Khorasan*, pp. 238–40.
[3] Count N. N. Mouraviev, *Voyage en Turcomanie et à Khiva fait en 1819 et
1820* (Paris, 1823), p. 333.
[4] Evans, *Invasion of India*, pp. 92–3.

distance a sufficient defence against invasion, showed how ignorant they were of the logistics of continental warfare.

The Russians would choose the route through Khiva and up the Oxus, because they knew Britain would have difficulty in finding a suitable defence. Bokhara and Khiva were 'totally incapable of resistance'; Persia was less likely to hold up Russia than to join her in invading Afghanistan. Somewhere in central Asia a bastion must be found: 'The defence of dependencies held by the sword rather than by the affection of the inhabitants, can only be advantageously made in advance of their frontiers.'[1] The necessary Asiatic ally, concluded Evans, would have to be Afghanistan.

The defence recommended by Evans in his second book, published in 1829 after Britain's choices had been reduced by the defeat of Persia and Turkey, was very different from his first. In 1828 he suggested combined operations in the Black Sea; sending units of Indian infantry to fight in Persia, to force the Russians to concentrate, when the Persian cavalry could surround them; and cutting Russia's communications with Khiva by combined operations on the Caspian from a base at Astarabad. Because of the terms of the treaty of Turkmanchay and Russia's overwhelming influence over the sultan following the treaty of Adrianople, this offensive in Turkey and Persia would prove impracticable. Instead the defence of British India must be shifted both eastwards and westwards. The government of India should send agents to Bokhara, Kabul, and Peshawar, who could send detailed reports of what the Russians were doing, and should intervene between rival princes to unify Afghanistan. When this had been done, a detached corps of the army in India should be sent forward to the Hindu Kush north of Kabul.

At the same time as the government of India were to begin this forward policy in Afghanistan, the foreign office must try to hold back the Russians by counter-action in Europe. The only way to do this, if the sultan would not or could not help, was to resurrect the Polish question. That had been the bargain offered by Castlereagh at Vienna; Russian rule over Poland in return for leaving alone Turkey. If the Russians would not leave Turkey alone, they should not rule Poland. The choice of Poland as the necessary ally may seem foolish; in the 1930s, when Poland was needed as a great power, it showed how desperate Britain was. A century

[1] Evans, *Designs of Russia*, pp. 169, 23.

earlier Evans, as a good radical, saw Poland as a principle; as
Metternich also saw, only resurrecting the Polish question would
convince the tsar that the principles of the Holy Alliance, as
Metternich defined them, were to be applied to the near east,
because only a rebellion in Poland would convince him that
Russia was directly threatened by the Revolution. Both radicals
and conservatives saw the fate of Poland as the key to the balance
of power in Europe: their arguments about what that fate should
be depended upon whether they wished to buttress or overturn
the existing political and social structure.

The self-confidence of Englishmen has matched their exaggerated ideas about Britain's power. Utilitarians, who lamented
the backwardness and idolatry of Indians, were certain they could
instantly transform them. Imperialists, fearing the impossibility
of defending British India, were equally certain at bottom they
knew how: Englishmen, as Kipling said, had only to behave as
Englishmen.

Even if our moral force alone, with at least a very moderate physical aid
[said Evans], were heartily brought into play, what terror might not be
scattered, even to the headquarters of those, who would seem even now
to be leaguing themselves against the independence of nations.[1]

Ellenborough was one of the first to spot the most suitable physical
aid: Britain's moral force was to be hidden in manufactures.

Reading Evans confirmed Ellenborough's fears of a Russian
offensive throughout Asia. 'I feel that we shall have to fight the
Russians on the Indus,' he said, 'and I have long had a great
presentiment that I should meet them there and gain a great
battle.'[2] Evans had expected the Russians to reach the Indus in
two campaigns. Ellenborough thought they would need three,
but doubted whether his colleagues would try to stop them, even
when they were as far east as Kabul. The best way to stop them,
as Evans had recommended, would be to send 60,000 troops to
Kabul, so closing the passes across the Hindu Kush, as soon as
the Russians occupied Khiva. With 40,000 troops in reserve at
Lahore and Delhi, the North-West Frontier of India would be
secure. Ellenborough realized that the army in India might defeat

[1] Evans, *Invasion of India*, p. 90.
[2] 3 Sept. 1829, Ellenborough's *Diary*, ii. 92.

a Russian invasion at the Sutledge, still the British North-West Frontier in Hindustan, but, were the Russians to advance no farther than Kabul, they might cause constant upheaval and ruinous expense without the risk of battle.[1] The British not the Russians would need to force the decision, and as far beyond their frontier as possible. Unfortunately this might mean choosing between the Afghans and the Sikhs, who were hereditary enemies. Ellenborough's embryo strategy, based on Evans, was likely to antagonize both. The British were often to find that forward policies, and plans to fight in the near east, instead of defending British India, were likely to provoke frontier wars.

His reading also strengthened Ellenborough's belief that Russia would not 'suddenly cease to be ambitious, or cease to use perfidy for the purpose of obtaining her ambitious ends',[2] merely because the treaties of Turkmanchay and Adrianople had given her a strategically satisfactory frontier in the Caucasus. Ellenborough had planned to counter the Russian offensive by a British offensive everywhere in the near east. 'Let us constantly look', he had urged his colleagues, 'to the restraining of Russian encroachments and the diminution of Russian power as the true and legitimate object of our policy.'[3] Wellington thought this too dangerous; the Persian Connection was to be restored, after the damage done to it by Canning, only as far as might help to strengthen the Kajar dynasty, so denying Russia another chance to intervene in their affairs.

In Afghanistan Wellington, hectored by Ellenborough, was willing to be bolder; he had no doubt the British could throw back a Russian invasion of India, but he agreed with Ellenborough that they must somehow force a decision. Ellenborough would have allowed the government of India to deal with Afghanistan as if they were a separate Asiatic state. This was too bold: they might not send troops, nor negotiate an alliance, but Wellington would let them try subsidies, a standard British device, costly and ineffective throughout the Napoleonic Wars. Finally, in contrast with his policy of keeping Persia out of Anglo-Russian relations, Wellington agreed in December to demand at St. Petersburg an

---

[1] 30 Oct. 1829, ibid., p. 123.

[2] Ellenborough to Aberdeen, 20 Oct. 1829, P.R.O. 30/9/4 pt. 5/7. Ellenborough even suspected the Russians of planning to buy Manila from Spain.

[3] 'Memorandum [by Ellenborough] on the State of the Greek Affair and General Policy with regard to Russia', 14 Sept. 1828, *Wellington*, v. 55.

explanation of any Russian expansion towards Khiva.[1] One reason why the British, at the beginning of the Great Game in Asia, tried to defend India in Turkestan, was their assumption that as long as the Russians had not crossed the Caspian, the affairs of Khiva and Bokhara could be separated from the international politics of Europe, and, as they were at a distance from Russia as well as British India, the Russians could not claim, as they did in Turkey and Persia, that their being neighbours gave them a better claim than the British to influence over the sultan and the shah.

Ellenborough had Wellington in a vice. He had been given an active department in place of the privy seal, because he had threatened otherwise to join the opposition, and active he would be. He was not going to commit in Asia what he expected from Aberdeen in Europe, 'a number of little errors which will let down the character of our diplomacy and materially injure us'.[2] Ellenborough was ambitious and bold. If the government of India were not to behave as a separate state, which would actually have infuriated Ellenborough, who wanted more not less control over them, the board of control were to behave as a separate foreign office for Asia: 'I told the Chairs distinctly', he recorded in 1830, 'that I intended to take upon the King's Government the whole responsibility of the foreign policy of India.'[3] As the board knew regrettably little about Asia, Ellenborough decided to find out more. For information about the invasion routes, and what the Russians were doing, in December 1829 he turned to Lord Heytesbury at St. Petersburg, Sir John Macdonald at Teheran, Macdonald's brother-in-law, Sir John Malcolm, at Bombay, and the governor-general of India, Lord William Bentinck.

In addition to an assessment of the likelihood of Russian invasion, and how it could be prevented, in order to decide how to defend India against the equally unsettling effects of Russian expansion, the board of control wanted information about six subjects: firstly, the tonnage of vessels in the ports on the Caspian, the size of the Russian navy on the Caspian, and the volume of trade with Russia; secondly, the route and time taken by caravans from Orenburg to Bokhara, the size of caravans and the

---

[1] 16 Dec. 1829, Ellenborough's *Diary*, ii. 148; Ellenborough to Malcolm, private, 18 Dec. 1829, P.R.O. 30/9/4 pt. 5/2.

[2] 22 Aug. 1828, Ellenborough's *Diary*, i. 201.

[3] 2 July 1830, ibid. ii. 297.

number each year, and what the land was like; thirdly, details of Russian settlements on the east coast of the Caspian; fourthly, details of Russian moves towards the Aral Sea; fifthly, the military and political state of Khiva, Bokhara and Kokand; and sixthly, annual returns of the trade of central Asia, to be estimated for as many years back as feasible, and to be submitted in future each December.[1] To obtain some of this information locally, Ellenborough sent a young cavalry officer in the Indian Army, who had been home on leave, overland from St. Petersburg to Teheran, hoping he could find out about the most vital subject, what the Russians were doing on the east coast of the Caspian. More will be heard of Arthur Conolly; his influence on the Great Game in Asia was considerable.

The first to reply, in January 1830, unquestionably the most perceptive and sensible British diplomatist of the period, despite the exaggerated claims made on behalf of Stratford Canning, was Lord Heytesbury. His quiet tone was free from the bombast with which Englishmen usually treated the subjects of Russian influence in central Asia, and the possibility of Russia's invading India. Aberdeen had recently warned Heytesbury that he was not suspicious enough of Russia to suit the government.[2] One can see why they were cross. When Heytesbury rejoiced in the summer of 1829 at 'very satisfactory accounts from the theatre of war', he meant Russian not Turkish victories, which '. . . will it is hoped incline the sultan to more pacific measures'.[3] The extent of Russia's victory by the treaty of Adrianople never frightened Heytesbury, although he did not underestimate it, because he understood that the Russians planned to preserve not partition Turkey.[4] As nobody in London believed him, he went on ignoring warnings from the foreign office, who misunderstood Russian policy, which he thought likely to cause unnecessary collisions.

Heytesbury treated a Russian invasion of India as a chimera. The Russians, whose field army had been almost annihilated in the Turkish war, had 'too thorough a consciousness of the real weakness of the country to entertain for an instant a serious threat of

---

[1] Encl. no. 2 in sc to Macdonald, 18 Dec. 1829, F.O. 248/60; Aberdeen to Heytesbury, no. 33, secret and confidential, 23 Dec. 1829, F.O. 65/178.

[2] Aberdeen to Heytesbury, private, 13 Dec. 1829, Add. MSS. 43089, fo. 125.

[3] Heytesbury to Macdonald, 1 July 1829, E.U.L. MSS. Dk/2/37, fo. 63.

[4] Heytesbury to Aberdeen, private and confidential, 15 Oct. 1829, Add. MSS. 43089, fo. 104.

ever embarking on so gigantic an enterprise as the invasion of India'. Russia's only interest in central Asia was trade, and posed Britain a political not a military problem. As Russian trade with central Asia was growing, and Russia had never hidden her aim to draw the trade of Afghanistan and Turkestan north-westwards, although there were no signs of an expedition against Khiva, one might be planned. This would endanger Britain, only if Russian agents, 'who invariably outstrip the orders of their government', stirred up 'a sort of ill-will towards Great Britain' amongst the tribes beyond British India's North-West Frontier and any of her own discontented subjects.[1]

This could be prevented, if the government of India sent agents to Bokhara and Kabul, to counter Russian influence at Khiva, and if the foreign office, as the best way to obtain accurate information, set up a consulate at Tiflis, where the French already had one. Here, in however mild a form, was one of the illusions characteristic of the Great Game in Asia. Heytesbury thought that Russian influence in central Asia need not be threatening, because easily matched; his analysis, although unintentionally, served by backing up Evans as a second summons to Ellenborough. Unfortunately the rulers of Bokhara and Kabul did not govern the territories which the British, seeing states on maps, supposed they must.

Sir John Malcolm and Sir John Macdonald had been sent copies of Evans's books to read. In the spring and summer of 1830, they replied to Ellenborough in harmony, Malcolm descanting upon Macdonald's arguments, that Evans had foretold the wrong danger in the wrong place. They also lied. Malcolm and Macdonald, who were brothers-in-law, had grown used during thirty years to thinking of the government of India's policy in the near east as a family heirloom, and were fighting to reorganize the Persian mission to suit two other members of the family who were members of it. Their family interests were one cause of what H. W. C. Davis has called the two schools of defence and frontier policy, the Bombay and the Ludhiana.[2] The Bombay School wanted to defend India in Persia, or, if Persia should have to be

---

[1] Heytesbury to Aberdeen, no. 9, secret and confidential, 18 Jan. 1830 F.O. 65/185.
[2] H. W. C. Davis, 'The Great Game in Asia, 1800–1844', *Proceedings of the British Academy*, xii (1926), 239–40.

abandoned, in Sind. This explains their choice amongst the possible invasion routes. Were the Russians to advance from the Caspian towards Khiva, or from Orenburg towards Bokhara, and then alongside the Oxus towards Afghanistan, India would be defended at Kabul or in alliance with the Sikhs, and by the resident at Delhi and his assistant at Ludhiana. The Persian mission would be left out.

Macdonald had warned Sir Robert Gordon the previous year that the Russians would easily conquer Transcaspia, and that as soon as they had captured Bokhara, 'the way is short and easy from the Oxus to the Indus. The Russians themselves would be astonished at the facility of their conquests.'[1] In answering Ellenborough he turned this about. Both supplies and a decisive victory would be more difficult to find than Evans had suggested, because the Turcomans would avoid defeat by retreating. The same would happen in Afghanistan: its division 'renders that unhappy kingdom equally unfit to resist, as unable to facilitate, the progress of a foreign invader'.[2] The danger from this to the Russians was their need of quick victories to ensure success. They would need them for the reason the British did; because any setback would cause trouble in areas already pacified.

This, too, had been turned about. Macdonald had previously praised the Russians' success in pacifying the territories they conquered, and had used this to explain why Persia was the obvious route to India, and the necessary Russian ally. Persians, he said,[3]

managed as are our sepoys are in India . . . might be made (both cavalry and infantry) as faithful and efficient as any soldiers in the world; and in this the danger lies if a European state should at any time acquire dominion in Persia. The invasion of India, if ever contemplated, can only be undertaken with a hope of success by Persian troops formed and led by European officers.

Because Persia would help, should Russia offer to share the spoils, a Russian protectorate over Persia would be the greatest danger to British India; and Britain's most vital interest was to counteract Russia in Persia, by making sure that Abbas Mirza

[1] Macdonald to Gordon, 28 Nov. 1829, E.U.L. MSS. Dk/2/37, fo. 110.

[2] Macdonald to Ellenborough, [12–30] Jan. 1830, ibid., fo. 110.

[3] Macdonald to Ellenborough, 16 Sept. 1829, ibid., fo. 85.

would not have to fight a war for the succession.[1] Macdonald knew, although he did not tell Ellenborough, how difficult this would be. 'If Russia be determined to exercise the ascendancy she possesses from her power, and position,' he told his brother-in-law, 'it is not here but in Europe that we can hope to arrest her progress.'[2]

According to G. J. Alder, until Arthur Conolly, continuing his overland journey from England through Afghanistan to India, reached Herat in September 1830, nobody responsible for the defence of India was aware of its strategic importance.[3] This is not true. Criticizing Evans's choice of the Oxus route, and replacing it by the route through Khorassan, made Herat, as both Macdonald and Malcolm knew, 'the key of Afghanistan'.[4] The role of Herat in the defence of British India began not, as Alder suggests, when Conolly published the story of his travels, nor when he wrote a series of papers for the government of India in 1831, but two years earlier when Macdonald and Malcolm tried to seize the initiative in the Great Game in Asia.

They claimed that the dangers to Britain in India from Russia were indirect, as Heytesbury had said, but in Persia not Turkestan. Malcolm had warned Wellington four years earlier, that Canning's refusal to intervene in the Russo-Persian war would lead to the permanent loss of British influence at Teheran. The consequence was the one foreseen by Macdonald, that Russia might overawe the shah of Persia and use him as a tool. Malcolm assumed the Russians would never waste effort in trying to invade India themselves, because they knew that paramount power in India depended on command of the sea; they would threaten disturbances whenever it might suit them in Europe. This placed Malcolm in a quandary: opposite policies were needed to prevent invasion and Russian expansion. Against invasion the best defence was the very weakness and turbulence of the near-eastern states.

The power of Asiatic countries to resist the invasion of a regular army [said Malcolm] depends less upon their riches than their poverty, the

---

[1] 'Remarks [by Sir John Macdonald] on Lieut.-Col. Evans's Late Work', 1 Mar. 1830, I.O. Bengal/SPC/358, 8 July 1830, no. 8.

[2] Macdonald to Malcolm, 17 June 1829, E.U.L. MSS. Dk/2/37, fo. 98.

[3] G. J. Alder, 'The Key to India?: Britain and the Herat Problem, 1830–1863—Part I', *Middle Eastern Studies*, x (1974), 186–8.

[4] Macdonald to Ellenborough, [12–30] Jan. 1830, E.U.L. MSS. Dk/2/37, fo. 110.

want of resources of their country, the unsettled habits of the inhabitants, and their being in fact intangible to the attack of regular
force. They yield like a reed to the storm, but are not broken.[1]

Trying to strengthen Kabul or Bokhara would increase not lessen
the danger of invasion: the more settled they became, the more
likely were they to give in to Russia, particularly as the Russians
did not immediately foist on colonies their own customs and
officials. Because Persia was already more settled, she was more
easily overawed. Throughout his career Malcolm had opposed
policies of reform.

There were military as well as political reasons for concentrating
upon Persia not Turkestan. Evans was ignorant of geography. He
had every reason to be: Ellenborough could not provide Wellington with an accurate map of Cutch. According to Malcolm, a
regular army could not cross the Hindu Kush; they must turn it
by the capture of Herat, and the shah of Persia might be willing to
try. Expansion eastwards might compensate for his dependence
upon Russia, and in 1826 the ruler of Herat had seized Ghorian,
the most eastern town in what the Persians claimed to be their
province of Khorassan. Malcolm was adamant that the fall of
Herat must not be permitted: if it were, a Russo-Persian army, or
a Persian army instructed by Russians, might be at the Indus in
two campaigns. The best way to defend Herat, however, was not
to fight Russia for influence over Persia, but to hold her back by
threatening to retaliate in Europe. 'I am quite satisfied', said
Malcolm, 'that the safety of not only India from attack but of those
Asiatic monarchs it is our policy to protect, is our power to destroy
the commerce and arrest the progress of this Empire in Europe.'[2]
Malcolm evidently did not apply in Europe his prescription for
Asia, that primitive states are more difficult than developed ones
to overawe.

Malcolm saw only one reason for paying attention to Turkestan:
a connection with the Tekke-Turcomans might help the Russians
to overawe Persia. Here Malcolm had spotted the vital rectangle
for Britain in central Asia, bounded by Meshed, Bokhara, Kunduz,
and Herat. Malcolm did not expect the Russians to expand from

[1] 'Notes [by Sir John Malcolm] on the Invasion of India by Russia' in Malcolm
to Ellenborough, private, 1 July 1830, P.R.O. 30/9/4, pt. 5/7; see also minute of
Malcolm, 4 July 1830, I.O. Bengal/SPC/358, 20 Aug. 1830, no. 3.
[2] Ibid.

Orenburg to Bokhara, because their spectacular victories had been won in the Caucasus and on the Caspian. Should they continue south-eastwards, they might be stopped between Bokhara and Herat. This suggestion revealed to Ellenborough the flaw in Malcolm's argument. Turbulence might be the best defence against invasion: it was no barrier to gradual but equally threatening Russian conquest. Nor was protecting Persia by threatening to retaliate in Europe, as long as Wellington and Aberdeen would not agree, the navy could not promise to force the Straits, and Austria would support Russia over Poland. The alternative was an offensive in Turkestan, intended to create the stable barrier to Russian expansion Heytesbury had implied could best be done, by turning the tribal kingdoms of Afghanistan and Turkestan into territorial states. As Lacy Evans had also suggested, to forestall the Russians in this vital rectangle should be the object of the Great Game in Asia.

IV

Between 1828 and 1830, at the beginning of the Great Game in Asia, British policy in the near east was worked out by the board of control and the government of Bombay. The government of India were hardly involved; their advice was asked, but ignored. Partly this was a clash of personalities. Whereas Sir John Malcolm was an old friend of Wellington from the days at the turn of the century when Wellington had been making his reputation in India as a soldier and Malcolm his as a diplomatist, the governor-general of India, Lord William Bentinck, had incurred 'the lasting hostility of Wellington'[1] during the Spanish and Mediterranean campaigns at the end of the Napoleonic Wars, when Bentinck tried to copy in Italy Wellington's achievements in Spain. Time and again Wellington had opposed Bentinck's nomination to succeed Earl Amherst, and Bentinck, who had long sought the post, was appointed in 1827 only because Canning had to fill it, and the first five men he asked would not accept.[2] Bentinck, said Wellington,[3] 'did everything with the best of intentions; but he was a *wrong-headed man*, and if he went wrong he would continue in the wrong line. Other men might go wrong and find it

---

[1] Rosselli, *Bentinck*, p. 68.
[2] Philips, *East India Company*, pp. 260–1.
[3] 17 June 1829, Ellenborough's *Diary*, ii. 51.

out, and go back; but if he went wrong he would either not find it out, or, if he did, he would not go back.' This sketch was accepted by Ellenborough, despite his doubts about Wellington's judgement, as a sufficient reason for ignoring Bentinck's unpalatable advice.

Bentinck's influence was further weakened because he seemed to be friendly with the junior but most able member of his council, Sir Charles Metcalfe. They were not friends, they often disagreed, although Bentinck's defence and frontier policies owed more to Metcalfe than is usually thought, but Bentinck often sent on to London papers by Metcalfe outspokenly criticizing the board's policies. Wellington and Ellenborough claimed to admire Metcalfe's ability but to doubt his judgement: 'I a little fear Sir Charles Metcalfe,' said Ellenborough. 'He is rather too vehement. I doubt whether he would be a safe man.'[1] When the government clashed with Bentinck, Ellenborough talked of fettering him by naming Malcolm, not Metcalfe, his provisional successor, and was held back only because Wellington feared, that as Malcolm's health was failing, he would die if he went to Calcutta. Sir John Kaye, whose biography of Metcalfe is notorious, was not alone in thinking him unsuited to be the model Anglo-Indian; but he was no more unsuited than Bentinck.

The difference between Bentinck backed by Metcalfe and Ellenborough backed by Malcolm over Britain's interests in the near east may be simply stated and was obvious from the start: Bentinck and Metcalfe wanted to consolidate not to expand. In India, where so few Englishmen lived at the mercy of so many natives, the Indian Army could not be relied upon to protect the imperial government; they must be backed up by settlers. Bentinck wanted to copy the Russian practice of military colonies,[2] Metcalfe to allow Englishmen to own land in India as the best way to attract their capital. No tax concessions were to be made to them, however: the economy was to be run on behalf of political stability. Similarly, Englishmen were to obey the laws governing Indians.[3] Metcalfe never feared a repeat of the American rebellion,

[1] 29 Dec. 1829, ibid., p. 154; Clare to Bentinck, private, 13 Jan. 1832, Portland MSS. PwJf/630.

[2] Bentinck to Ellenborough, private, 25 Aug. 1830, P.R.O. 30/9/4 pt. 5/1.

[3] Memorandum by Metcalfe, 11 Oct. 1829, ibid., pt. 2/2; minute of Bentinck, 1 Sept. 1829, I.O. L/E/3/30, p. 483. When the directors of the East India Company learnt that Bentinck supported Metcalfe's plans for settlement, they

because the settlers would remain a small minority, who would not forget that the imperial connection was needed to ensure their safety.[1]

The board of control's traditional objections to settlement, formulated at the end of the eighteenth century by Henry Dundas, were based upon Portuguese not American precedents. Bentinck and Metcalfe thought they could prevent what later happened, as the board had predicted, that settlers would demand to be treated as Englishmen not as subjects, and that all Englishmen would band together to tyrannize all Indians. If the British planned to conciliate Indians, settlers should be discouraged because their behaviour would cause unrest; if the Indians were to be assimilated, settlers would not be needed. The board traditionally had a second objection. Convinced by Montesquieu of the enervating effect of the tropical climate, they believed that settlers would grow lazy, and mine the empire from within.[2] Far from providing security, they would become a burden. Instead, each generation of officials should set out young and healthy from England, or better still Scotland.

This is one of the issues separating Metcalfe, and maybe Bentinck, from both utilitarian reformers and imperialists who preferred to conciliate Indian customs.

Some say [said Metcalfe] that our empire in India rests upon opinion, others on main force. It in fact depends upon both. We could not keep the country by opinion if we had not a considerable force, and no force that we could pay would be sufficient, if it were not aided by the opinion of our invincibility. Our force does not operate so much by its actual strength as by the impression which it produces, and that impression is the opinion by which we hold India.[3]

Metcalfe agreed with Malcolm, for example, that Englishmen must appear superior: they disagreed about how appearances could be most easily and effectively kept up.

As important as settlement to Bentinck and Metcalfe was the stability of the British North-West Frontier; they were interested

secretly planned his immediate recall. Walker to Bentinck, 2 Oct. 1829, Portland MSS. PwJf/2170.

[1] Memorandum by Metcalfe, 13 Dec 1829, I.O. L/E/3/31, p. 79.

[2] F. G. Hutchins, *The Illusion of Permanence: British Rule in India* (Princeton 1967), pp. 60–70.

[3] Quoted in D. C. Boulger, *Lord William Bentinck* (Oxford, 1892), p. 175.

in the Great Game in Asia only if it could help. Because the government of India would find it as difficult to defend the frontier against Turcomans and Afghans as the Russians would to conquer them, turbulence in central Asia, which Malcolm thought the best defence against European invasion, might also cause permanent unrest in India.[1] Wellington was angered when Bentinck in 1829 moved the government of India to Meerut, where they might be attacked by Afghan raiding parties; a border was no barrier to such a shadowy menace. Bentinck hoped, by moving the capital to the Upper Provinces as the prelude to their reform, to stabilize the frontier, and to strengthen the Indian Army: the martial races might leaven the Bengalis, as in the Napoleonic Wars the French had the Neopolitans and the British the Portuguese. So far Bentinck and Metcalfe agreed; they disagreed about the type of frontier needed. Bentinck wanted to create a stable balance of power amongst the states immediately beyond it, Metcalfe to make sure that they could safely be ignored.

The idea of a stable North-West Frontier depended upon an enthusiasm for steam.[2] There was no other way sufficiently to improve communications; the Ganges, flowing too fast in the wet season, and too shallow for sail boats in the dry, could be used only by steamers. Bentinck, who moved the government's steamers in Assam to the Ganges, had started by the time he left India in 1835 a three-weekly service, hoping that his successor could quickly reinforce the North-West Frontier from Allahabad. There was an alternative route. Steam navigation on the Indus and the Sutledge was to be Bentinck's greatest interest in Sind.

A rumour spread in 1830 that in Grey's administration Wellesley would take over from Ellenborough at the board of control. What, one wonders, might have happened then? From the beginning, the ruined career of Wellesley, as shadowy a menace as an Afghan invasion, hovered over the Great Game in Asia, a portent to Ellenborough of the ruin to come. Malcolm at Bombay and Metcalfe at Fort William had both trained under Wellesley in the dizzying days when Britain's most magnificent satrap, hating anyone senior enough to question, had surrounded himself by a group of eager, energetic, and able boys. Each was heir to half Wellesley's inheritance. Metcalfe shared his determination to turn

---

[1] Minute of Bentinck, 29 June 1832, I.O. Bengal/SPC/367, 6 Aug. 1832, no. 3.
[2] Bentinck to Loch, 17 Aug. 1828, Portland MSS. PwJf/135.

British India into a successor to the Mogul Empire;[1] Malcolm
knew that Wellesley had planned to push British influence beyond
the North-West Frontier, not as a defence against invasion, which
had never frightened him, but to create a frontier in depth. The
value of the Persian Connection, for example, lay in helping to
control the Afghans.

Rehearsing in Persia for the Great Game in Asia had been the
most exciting and successful moments in Malcolm's career;
Metcalfe's rehearsal in the Punjab in 1808 had been his most
humiliating. Dragged from camp to camp by Ranjit Singh,
without the means to influence or coerce him, he doubted ever
afterwards whether it was possible to negotiate with natives: one
could never convince them that their interests were identical with
one's own. Sind and the Punjab, left untouched as buffer states,
were the best frontier of India available against Afghans and Turcomans; the Russians Metcalfe ignored. 'Twenty years ago', he
said, 'the writer of this minute was employed to negotiate an
alliance against a French invasion, with a native state beyond our
north-western frontier. A French invasion was our bugbear then
as a Russian one is now.'[2] Bentinck, who had also in his youth
worked with Wellesley as governor of Madras, and Metcalfe, as his
most influential adviser on foreign policy, did not see how they
could more easily defend or police India by playing the Great
Game in Asia. Unfortunately, however sensible Metcalfe's and
Bentinck's preoccupation with increasing the control of the
imperial government in India, they missed Ellenborough's point
that the Russians should not be expected, like the French, to
threaten invasion, except perhaps by encouraging others, but to
cause unrest and so expense. His object was political not military;
to create conditions in the near east themselves capable of forestalling threats to the security of British India bound otherwise
to follow from the expansion of Russia.

Bentinck, who later, as he refused to read a report on central
Asia, said that 'civilization alone interests me, and I would rather
see the improvement and happiness of America than all the rest
of the world beyond the limits of Europe',[3] in 1830 left to Malcolm

---

[1] Minute of Metcalfe, 24 June 1832, I.O. L/PS/5/123, 6 Aug. 1832, no. 84.
[2] Minute of Metcalfe, 25 Oct. 1830, Sir J. W. Kaye, *Selections from the
Papers of Lord Metcalfe* (London, 1855), p. 151.
[3] Bentinck to Metcalfe, [1832], Portland MSS. PwJf/1779.

the task of sending Ellenborough the information about central Asia for which he had asked. Malcolm, who had criticized Lacy Evans, told his aide-de-camp, Captain Bonamy, to write a more reliable report of what was known. Of the three traditional invasion routes, Bonamy rejected two. Alexander's route along the coast of Makran could be blocked from the sea; the Bolan Pass led to the Great Indian Desert. The point of danger to the British was the Khyber Pass. Bonamy chose the Khyber because he feared rebellion almost as much as Bentinck did. To prevent Russian expansion in central Asia from threatening the tranquillity of India, Bonamy wanted to negotiate closer connections with Persia and the Sikhs, and to add a connection with Dost Mahomet Khan at Kabul. This grand alliance resembled Minto's efforts in 1808 to guard against the likely effects of the treaties of Finkenstein and Tilsit. Minto had not then realized that the treaties contradicted one another; nor that the British could not expect the friendship of all the near-eastern states at once.

If such a policy were to succeed, argued Bonamy, the British must find out more about the routes across central Asia, and about the Indus. If this river could be opened to British ships, the British might counter the Russians by drawing the trade of Turkestan away from the Caspian Sea. The river would be equally useful for defence: troops deployed on the Indus might cut an enemy's line of advance, and, by fast communication overland to London, policy on the North-West Frontier could be matched with the work of the foreign office in Europe.[1] Here again was enthusiasm for steamers, admired by Malcolm as much as by Bentinck. Here also was a forward policy. As Mountstuart Elphinstone had argued twenty years before, during his mission to Shah Shuja at Peshawar,[2] if the British planned to counter the Russians in central Asia, they must move the military frontier of British India to the Indus.

V

How far north-west to move the British frontier was the most contentious decision needed at the beginning of the Great Game in

---

[1] 'Memorandum [by J. Bonamy] on the North-West Frontier of British India and on the Importance of the River Indus as Connected with its Defence', 1830, I.O. Bengal/SPC/358, 14 Oct. 1830, no. 7.

[2] Elphinstone to Minto, 23 and 28 Mar. 1809, I.O. H/657, pp. 283, 367.

Asia. Ellenborough was perfectly aware of this; equally aware that to mention it would cause an uproar in the cabinet, the East India Company, and at Fort William. Bonamy's recommendations were exactly what Ellenborough was planning. Although he knew he needed more detailed information, he was too impatient to wait for replies to the questions he asked; instead he used information collected at the board of control, and Heytesbury's reports, which he said backed up Evans's. Ellenborough's confederate at the board was the assistant secretary in charge of the secret department, Benjamin Jones, who had begun his career there fifteen years earlier, as private secretary to Robert Dundas, second Viscount Melville. Both Dundas and his more famous father, Henry Dundas, had believed India could be invaded overland from Europe. Jones shared their belief, and believed forward policies in India as well as the near east to be the best defence. He wanted the government of India to work for more direct control over their subsidiary allies, as the best way to guard against rebellion, and for indirect control over states beyond the North-West Frontier, as the best and cheapest defence.[1]

The frontier itself was to be moved forward to the Indus. Early in December 1829, Jones told Ellenborough that boats of 200 tons could sail up the Indus to Lahore in twelve days. Here was the answer to defending India against both the Russians and the tribes of central Asia; here, too, was Ellenborough's call to greatness. 'No British flag', he hymned, 'has ever floated upon the waters of this river. Please God it shall, and in triumph, to the source of all its tributary streams.'[2]

Ellenborough had no doubt that Britain could supply Kabul, Bokhara, and the Turcomans, better and more cheaply with every-thing they bought from Russia. He did sometimes wonder what they could supply in return, 'except turquoises, lapis lazuli, and . . . ducats'.[3] There was to be a similar barrier to expanding Britain's trade with Persia through Trebizond. Undaunted, Ellenborough set out to persuade Wellington and the East India Company to send a trial shipment of goods to Afghanistan, and to survey the Indus under cover of sending a present of horses to

[1] Philips, *East India Company*, pp. 268, 271-2.
[2] 9 Dec. 1829, Ellenborough's *Diary*, ii. 144.
[3] 20 Dec. 1829, ibid., p. 153.

Ranjit Singh. His aim, he admitted, was political, but he claimed his method to be exclusively commercial, 'repelling the Russian commerce from Kabul and Bokhara by carrying our goods directly up the Indus'.[1]

The secret committee, 'thinking to humbug and bully me', as Ellenborough put it,[2] had already quarrelled with him the previous year about the cost of forward policies. They had tried to escape paying for the military missions Ellenborough wanted to train the armies of Persia and Baghdad. This time Ellenborough promised, that as the purpose of trading with central Asia was political, the government would make good the company's losses.[3] Because Ellenborough hoped to persuade Ranjit Singh to reopen an old canal between the Sutledge and the Jumna, a short time might see a profit; if the Ganges and Indus basins could be joined together, trade would flow more easily from east to west across northern India.[4] So might troops. Ellenborough was as keen on steamers as Bentinck and Malcolm. On the Ganges and Indus they would be the best means of policing the whole of northern India, as they were to pacify and police Baghdad.

Ellenborough did not forget that by his bargain with Aberdeen and Wellington, provided the British held back at Teheran and Constantinople, they might move forward at Baghdad as well as in Turkestan. The governor of Baghdad had for some years been asking the government of Bombay to send him arms, steamers, and a military mission to train his troops. This had brought on a quarrel in 1828 between Bombay and Fort William, prophesying quarrels about policy in Persia and in Sind. Should the governor ask again, Ellenborough was eager to agree.[5] At Baghdad there need be no contradiction between the new British policy of trying to buttress Turkey, and the government of India's old policy of

---

[1] Ellenborough to Wellington, 19 Dec. 1829, *Wellington*, vi. 327. Rosselli, *Bentinck*, p. 266 and A. H. Bilgrami, *Afghanistan and British India, 1793–1907* (New Delhi, 1972), pp. 62–3, are wrong to state that the principal reason for seeking to trade on the Indus was economic.

[2] 26 Sept. 1829, Ellenborough's *Diary*, ii. 101.

[3] Loch to Ellenborough, private, 15 Sept. 1829, I.O. L/PS/3/1, p. 174; Ellenborough to Loch, 15 Jan. 1830, P.R.O. 30/9/4 pt. 1/4. Ellenborough thought that cheap ironmongery would sell best.

[4] Ellenborough to Jones, 27 Dec. 1829, ibid., pt. 5/2; same to Bentinck, private, 22 May 1830, Portland MSS. PwJf/941.

[5] Ellenborough to Malcolm, private, 27 Oct. 1829, P.R.O. 30/9/4 pt. 5/2. For details, see Ch. VI, pp. 147–53.

being ready to turn Baghdad into a protectorate, should Turkey be partitioned.

Baghdad was also to be shielded by British influence in Anatolia and Azerbaijan. In Persia, a military mission, for which the East India Company had reluctantly agreed in 1829 to pay, were to forestall the likely reasons for future Russian intervention, by training a force of infantry capable of policing the frontier provinces, and making sure Abbas Mirza mounted the throne. In Anatolia the British had to act even more cautiously: the purpose of the consulate opened at Trebizond in 1830 was to help maintain order along the Russo-Turkish frontier, as the military mission were to do in Azerbaijan, and so forestall any crisis that might lead to the annexation by Russia of Erzerum.[1] As long as the Turks kept Erzerum, the British hoped that Turkey and Persia might defend British India by turning into a near-eastern Burgundian Circle, a buffer zone between the British on the Indus and in Afghanistan and the Russians in the Caucasus and on the Black Sea.

'We shall have the missions to Sind and Lahore,' said Ellenborough on 18 December 1829, 'and the commercial venture up the Indus, and the instruction to [Sir John] Macdonald. In short all I want.'[2] Turkey and Persia were to be held defensively, while the offensive in the Great Game in Asia began in Sind and Afghanistan. The game was also to be played at two levels, diplomatic and commercial; the second was supposed quickly to take over from the first. Ellenborough was determined to beat the Russians to the vital rectangle in Turkestan. They should be temporarily held back by pressure at St. Petersburg and subsidies paid to the near-eastern states; soon Britain's influence would be kept up by trade not subsidies, making pressure at St. Petersburg less necessary. In January 1830, Ellenborough told Bentinck to send either a diplomatic mission to Kabul and Bokhara, or an Englishman disguised as a merchant, who could collect more detailed information about Turkestan. Bentinck was also to send samples of British goods to Bokhara to find out what would best sell. If subsidies seemed the only way to open up the market, and to make it safer for British traders, he might pay them, but he was not to negotiate alliances without consulting London.[3]

---

[1] For details, see Ch. VII, pp. 193–6.
[2] 18 Dec. 1829, Ellenborough's *Diary*, ii. 151.
[3] Sc to ggic, 12 Jan. 1830, I.O. L/PS/5/543.

From here on Ellenborough hid what he had in mind. Bentinck was to do all this without alarming Ranjit Singh and the amirs of Sind. If the British were to trade up the Indus, they would need commercial treaties with the states along its banks, which might provide the chance to negotiate a closer connection with Ranjit Singh, and to find out, in as much detail 'as that which would be obtained by a military reconnaissance', the strength of the Sikh army and what would be likely to happen when Ranjit died.[1] Ellenborough wanted to turn the Punjab into a protectorate, and to secure its lapse to the British; in the meantime he wanted to use Ranjit against the amirs of Sind. Shielded by the desert, they had always tried to stay in isolation. This had previously suited the British. It was in Sind that the most dramatic change in policy could be expected.

The British border with Sind was a good example of the difficulty of finding a satisfactory North-West Frontier. The Rann of Cutch would hold up a European army, but not Baluchi raiding parties; it defended the British against invasion, but they could not police it. They had always refused to police Cutch jointly with Sind, because then

we are drawn into the system of the states on the right [bank] of the Indus and the Sutledge . . . It is with this view of its ultimate consequences that we are desirous of withdrawing ourselves from all connection with the country bordering Sind. We wish to maintain that country as an impassable barrier between us, and Sind, between the domestic Indian system of alliances, and the political system of states beyond our frontier.[2]

This distinction was being given up by Ellenborough. His new defence policy would require a new frontier policy: to suit the British the amirs of Sind must now come out of isolation. 'We cannot permit any jealous feeling on their parts to close the navigation of the Indus,' said Ellenborough, 'should it appear to offer results not only commercially but politically important.'[3] If the amirs would not trade, Ranjit Singh must make them. Hidden in Ellenborough's instructions to Bentinck, however well disguised, was the threat of force.

For Ellenborough the Great Game in Asia was to solve three

[1] Sc to ggic, 2 Mar. 1830, I.O.L/PS/5/543.
[2] Sc to ggic, 9 Jan. 1829, ibid.   [3] Sc to ggic, 12 Jan. 1830, ibid.

entangled problems. The British had to decide where to defeat a Russian invasion. This danger, perhaps chimerical, was less so when indirect. Their second need was to create a stable balance of power in central Asia, to guard against the effects of gradual Russian expansion, and ideally to forestall it. All Ellenborough's schemes for trading were directed to this political object.

I do not apprehend that any movement of the Russians of which the ultimate object may be India [said Ellenborough] will from the first assume the character of a great enterprise, and be of a nature to spread general alarm in central Asia, while it would afford England just ground for decisive intervention in Europe. I expect rather that the ultimate object will be disguised with the utmost art, that nothing will be done in a hurry, that the *éclat* of brilliant and rapid success will be sacrificed to the more solid advantage to be derived from slow and sure progress. Neither do I think that the Russians will at first look to the actual invasion of India, they will rather desire to occupy the countries from which former conquerors of India have in a campaign marched to Delhi; and, certain of the ultimate possession of their prey, mature all the means of aggression in a position in which their mere presence will excite doubts and apprehensions in the minds of all our subjects and ruin our finances by the expense of constant preparation of war. It is on this account that the correct information is necessary to us. It must be our object to prevent the sowing of the seed, not to wait till it has become a tree beyond our means to remove.[1]

The policy to be carried out beyond the frontier depended on where the frontier was and the form it took; trade needed access, and might need support, or the possibility of it. Similarly, if the British were to assume that they could defeat a Russian invasion, or an invasion organized by Russia, at their North-West Frontier, and police the frontier effectively, at a time when steamers had captured the imagination, the Indus seemed more suitable than the Sutledge. Ellenborough had no time to solve these problems. He might have, but in leaving the whigs for Wellington, he had joined the wrong group at the wrong time. In November 1830 he went out of office.

Between 1828 and 1842, one high point of the Great Game in Asia, two parallel decisions were being prepared; whether annexation followed from not interfering in the internal affairs of allied

---

[1] Ellenborough to Macdonald, private, 15 May 1830, P.R.O. 30/9/4 pt. 1/5; same to Malcolm, private, 18 Dec. 1829, ibid., pt. 5/2.

states in India, and whether moving firstly the military then the political frontier of British India forward to the Indus followed from deciding to try to create a stable balance of power amongst the states immediately beyond the North-West Frontier, or of having failed to. These were choices, and most Englishmen, knowing that such choices are not asked of the self-confident and secure, instinctively postponed them. Ellenborough, with a realistic grasp of Britain's political position, based on Wellington's and Aberdeen's grasp of her relative military weakness, began the Great Game on the assumption that if nasty choices were to be avoided, nasty circumstances must be forestalled. This determination to forestall developments, and not merely to react to them, shows how far Wellesley's and Ellenborough's Great Game, not Castlereagh's Congress System, was based on the truer perception of the needs of a continental state, which had to create satisfactory circumstances, on the assumption that left untended they might endanger and not protect.

In Europe, even in moments of grave peril, as in 1801 when fighting France and the League of Armed Neutrality, the British could rely upon geography and as a result the navy to protect them. In India there was no equivalent barrier: neither the Hindu Kush, the Himalayas, nor the Indus, could stand in for the Channel. One might argue, of course, that in 1801 as after Tilsit, because the continental states were more suspicious of one another than of Britain, the British were protected by the balance of power. However true later in the century, when Imperial Germany might, although she would not, have defended British India, this was not so earlier, when Austria and Prussia depended upon Russian support; they could not threaten her. The scarcity in Europe of allies who were able to help, even if they might wish to, compelled the British to look for an alternative in Asia.

The expansion of Russia to the Arras in 1828, and of British India to the Indus, which was accepted as bound to happen upon the death of Ranjit Singh, meant that the area between the two could no longer be treated as a political system independent of the European and Indian political systems; the balance of power between the three had changed too decisively. Either the area must be occupied by the British to forestall the Russians, it must be partitioned between them, or it must be turned into a buffer zone. At the beginning of the Great Game in Asia, the British hoped to forestall the Russians, and to occupy the area without actually doing so, by the creation of a stable balance of power between Turkomans, Afghans, and Sikhs. If their hope seems absurd, and their fears imaginary, remember Minto's answer to objections similar to Metcalfe's in similar circumstances twenty years earlier: 'Our measures must be calculated to meet . . . an emergency, because if we should be wrong in disbelieving the accounts [of impending danger] . . . and they should in the event prove true, the error would be irreparable.'[1] Britain, rich, secure behind her navy, and politically stable, was militarily impregnable; British India, poor, politically turbulent, and with a frontier to defend, had to forestall threats not wait to parry them. As the Channel was missing, Ellenborough and Wellington hoped an Asiatic Burgundian Circle could be created, and behind it, although neither they nor their successors in India, the utilitarians, would have admitted it, an Asiatic Holy Alliance.

[1] Minto to Barlow, private and secret, 1 Feb. 1808, Minto MSS. M/159.

IV

A Mirage in Central Asia 1830-1833

Little Indian, Sioux or Crow,
Little frosty Eskimo,
Little Turk or Japanee,
O! Don't you wish that you were me?
ROBERT LOUIS STEVENSON,
A Child's Garden of Verses

ONE OF THE oddities of the second British empire is that whigs
and liberals, to their embarrassment, annexed as much territory as
tories and conservatives, who might have rejoiced; and one reason
for it was their badly controlled and narrow-minded charity, by
which they were led repeatedly into scrapes. The whigs, with a
passion for civil liberties, and evangelicals and utilitarians, with
one for equal opportunity of salvation and self-help, wanted to
reform foreigners as they wanted to reform their countrymen. In
the 1830s they were often encouraged to try on foreigners what
their countrymen preferred to go without: Lord Durham was sent
off to St. Petersburg then to Canada. All of them hated force and
believed in persuasion; the validity of their beliefs being obvious,
force would never be necessary. Maybe they were right, and maybe
foreigners were foolish not to share their optimism, but they had
one tiny fault: they were prone to disappointment.

Robinson and Gallagher have described how natives went from
under-privilege to delinquency.[1] Their sequence should be
changed. Indians were delinquent before the Mutiny, from which
Englishmen merely learnt what Anglo-Indians already knew. In
the near east the English were more patient; few had visited, fewer
had lived there, and ignorance and inexperience often make
Englishmen tolerant and understanding. Conservative Englishmen
that is. With an instinctive relish for oddity and extravagance,
conservatives were less dismayed by poverty, oppression, and
superstition. Others were not expected to agree with them; those

---

[1] Robinson and Gallagher, *African and the Victorians*, p. 467.

whom they could not persuade they happily and guiltlessly coerced. In the 1830s the difference between these attitudes was exemplified in the use to be made of trade in the defence of British India.

In his famous instructions to the government of India in January 1830, telling them to open the Indus to British trade with central Asia, as the cheapest way to hem in Russia, Ellenborough admitted that this demand to trade might have to be backed by force. Ellenborough wanted to run steamers on the Indus: to find out whether its upper tributaries were navigable, a gift of horses was to be sent to Ranjit Singh. The amirs of Sind, who ruled the southern half of the river, were notoriously suspicious of Englishmen, 'but we cannot permit', said Ellenborough, 'any jealous feeling on their parts to close the navigation of the Indus'.[1] Sind was in reach of British troops; how he meant to gain access to Afghanistan and Bokhara, Ellenborough did not say. His policy, however, was clear: British goods were to be given diplomatic, and when unavoidable military protection, and the military frontier of British India was to be moved forward to the Indus. Ellenborough, who could not risk appearing too aggressive, or he would have frightened Aberdeen and Wellington, chose the Indus route to central Asia as the principal defence of India to be less fettered by his hesitant cabinet colleagues. Anywhere farther west he might have needed the foreign office or the British army.

However rarely in the history of British foreign policy one sees a new policy stated in principle, at the beginning of the Great Game in Asia one can see two. Ellenborough in the autumn and winter of 1829, and his successor at the board of control, Charles Grant, in the spring and summer of 1831, explained to British agents, from Anatolia and Baghdad in the west as far as Sind and the Punjab in the east, precisely how they were to treat the princes in whose states they worked. Grant, and his most influential adviser on foreign policy at the board of control, Henry Ellis, were trying to decide how to hold back Russia without breaking Canning's rule, that the defence of British India should be kept separate from the balance of power in Europe. The way they looked at the amirs of Sind, the governor of Baghdad, and the prince royal of Persia, was the way Palmerston would look at Mahomet Ali.

Ellenborough, who had an equally good reason for being vague, had pursued the opposite policy. Believing the defence of British

[1] Sc to ggic, 12 Jan. 1830, I.O. L/PS/5/543.

India to be in danger of entanglement with the balance of power in Europe, Wellington and Aberdeen, anxious to postpone the crisis Ellenborough was equally anxious to hasten, had expected him to plan a strategy that would not give offence to Russia. Ellenborough's answer was to split the near east. At Constantinople and Teheran the British might act as cautiously as Wellington wished: the sultan and the shah should only be warned against giving the Russians any excuse again to meddle. In Baghdad and Turkestan, however, the Russians might be forestalled. 'There is good Mahometan and anti-Russian feeling in the countries to the east of the Euphrates,' said Ellenborough in October 1829, after the treaty of Adrianople, 'and if any mischief happens there it will be our own fault.'[1]

In Sind and Baghdad, backed up if necessary from a base in the Persian Gulf, trade would open the way for steamers, steamers for trade, political and when unavoidable military pressure, and paramount British influence. From Baghdad into Anatolia and Azerbaijan, from Sind into Afghanistan and Turkestan, Britain's influence would spread northwards, hidden in trade, but backed by power. Successful states hint at but do not exercise their power; yet Ellenborough knew that trade could not manage without support. Nor might the near east be left, as Sir John Malcolm had suggested, to disorder and decay, because they spread: the British would have to be ready to act when necessary. Ellenborough wanted the governor of Baghdad to employ British soldiers and to buy British steamers. He was as anxious to see steamers on the Indus. Steamers served conservatives, as their principle of equal opportunity utilitarians, and strategic bombers contemporary American warlords; as a way to bring western enlightenment to natives without being soiled by daily contact.

Ellenborough and Grant chose different symbols because they saw India differently. How to defend British India would always worry conservatives, Ellenborough amongst them, because they knew that the Raj was one in a row of military conquests, and would last as long as they had the strength or will to uphold it. Grant shared the utilitarian and evangelical self-confidence: as soon as privilege and superstition were done away, the two most serious obstacles to the safety of British India, the chances of rebellion and bankruptcy, would be overcome. Anglicized India

[1] Ellenborough to Wellington, 18 Oct. 1829, *Wellington*, vi. 227.

would be rich and happy; its only necessary defence a group of buffer states, preserved by European diplomatic practice, and behaving better as they copied the behaviour of Indians. Then the principles underlying the Poor Law Amendment Act would defend British India.

All the utilitarians thought they needed in the 1830s, to make British India safe, and to win the Great Game in Asia almost without trying, was a little time. Paramount political influence would not be needed: trade following commercial treaties might work alone, and steamers on the Indus and Euphrates were to carry only letters and manufactures. The proper diplomatic attitude towards the near-eastern states, treating them with the scrupulous restraint of one independent state to another, would persuade them to behave similarly, and the Russians to copy them; Turks, Persians, and Afghans, would be happy to take up the British practice of non-intervention, along with the other advantages of civilization the British offered. 'It will require no great diplomatic skill', said Henry Ellis in 1832, 'to convince the governments of Afghanistan and Turkestan . . . that while Russia may include the annihilation of their independence within her schemes of conquest, Great Britain can have no such intention.'[1]

However well meaning its aim, such a policy could succeed only if the near-eastern monarchies were territorial states. They were not; abandoning nomadic for sedentary habits was to be one of their improvements. Nor, as the British understood the term, were they sovereign states. Although other European states might be persuaded to treat them as if they were, they were unlikely so to treat one another. Unless they could be persuaded to, the balance of power in the near east could not be stabilized.

Reformers have short memories. What happened in the past does not matter to them. The most dedicated have the narrowest minds; perhaps a fixed purpose demands them. Anyone planning strategy for the defence of British India ignored at his peril the history of the Persian Connection in the Napoleonic Wars. In the summer of 1831, when Grant and Ellis changed Ellenborough's policy in Sind, and gave the resident at Baghdad new instructions about how to treat the governor, implying for the first time that the Turkish Empire was to be only an agreed territory on the map, they also set out more precisely Britain's relationship to Persia.

[1] Memorandum by Ellis, 14 June 1832, I.O. Persia/48.

Palmerston's reaction in 1833 to Mahomet Ali's conquest of Syria is supposed to have been the beginning of a policy of reforming Turkey. This had previously been tried in Persia, and had proved too difficult; it was now to be tried in Sind and Turkestan. As a result of these experiments, the British, guided by Ellenborough and Henry Ellis, adopted an idiosyncratic notion of reform.

II

Lord William Bentinck, one of the most able, and the most enigmatic governor-general of India, has until recently been ignored by historians, who have ignored everyone who preferred fair administration to 'a taste for conquest and aggrandizement'.[1] His great rival for oblivion is Sir John Shore. Bentinck had worked hard for his appointment, his father the duke of Portland had first suggested it in 1804, but nobody in England or India knew for certain why he was there. Perhaps he wished to blot out his recall from Madras in 1807; perhaps to pay his debts; perhaps to put into practice some ideas of the utilitarians, with whom he was increasingly in sympathy. He told James Mill, on behalf of the movement, that 'I am going to India, but I shall not be governor-general . . . you will'.[2]

Because this remark was supposed for a long time to have been made to Bentham himself, and because Bentinck is now known to have been less friendly with the Benthamites than with the leading evangelicals, it is fashionable to overlook his utilitarianism, to see in the evangelical revival alone the source of his zeal for reform.[3] This is foolish. Bentinck is a problem, because as soon as one notices his zeal, its limitations are obvious. Playing the Great Game in Asia is supposed to have been one: his policies, said his recent biographer, 'prepared the way for the annexation of Sind and the First Afghan War'.[4] This opinion, however common, rests upon

---

[1] The phrase was used about Wellesley. Ricketts to Hawkesbury, 6 Nov. 1801, Add. MSS. 38237, fo. 172.

[2] Bentham to Young, 28 Dec. 1828, *The Works of Jeremy Bentham*, ed. J. Bowring (London, 1838–43), x. 576.

[3] See J. Clive, *Macaulay: The Shaping of an Historian* (New York, 1973), p. 317; and Rosselli, *Bentinck*, pp. 84–6. J. Rosselli, 'Lord William Bentinck and his Age', *Bengal: Past and Present*, xcvi (1975), 79, claims that Bentinck's utilitarianism was only the equivalent to the marxist colour given to all present-day thought. This will not do: utilitarianism was much closer to nineteenth-century liberalism than marxism to twentieth-century social democracy.

[4] Rosselli, *Bentinck*, p. 225; see also Norris, *Afghan War*, p. 50.

two mistakes; failing to distinguish between frontier and defence policy, and between utilitarian and imperialist assumptions. Whatever game Bentinck played on the frontier, it was not the one Ellenborough had in mind: its aim was the security of British India as a property, the most valuable Englishmen owned.

Utilitarians had a passion for equality of opportunity, but equally for the security of private property, even inherited wealth. If this is not stressed, the social conflict in England in the 1820s and 1830s is seen as a struggle between two types of wealth, instead of between riches and poverty.

> In consulting the grand principle of security, [asked Bentham] what ought the legislator to decree respecting the mass of property already existing? He ought [came the ready answer] to maintain the distribution as it is already established . . . When security and equality are in conflict, it will not do to hesitate a moment, equality must yield.[1]

There was no conflict in India between the reformer's demand for civil liberty but belief in despotic government.[2] Bentinck believed that one put up the structure in which the other might be enjoyed.

Fort William in the early nineteenth century was so perilous a place, that Bentinck was one of two governors-general between the Napoleonic Wars and the Indian Mutiny to return with his reputation undamaged. This was partly because he belonged to one of the most famous and powerful political families. Wellington, who did not share Bentinck's zeal, distrusted him, but warned Ellenborough that 'Lord William was a great card, and we must not do anything to offend unnecessarily him and his connection'.[3] The advantages of such a position were negative. Sir John Malcolm complained that Bentinck always appeared hesitant.[4] Because his policies were unpopular in turn with the government, the directors, and the Indian Army, he may be forgiven for being slow to make up his mind about things which seemed to him unimportant. This explains his reply to Ellenborough's summons to play the Great Game in Asia.

---

[1] 'Principles of the Civil Code', *Bentham*, i. 311.

[2] Compare Rosselli, *Bentinck*, p. 333. Bentinck, for example, openly supported the employment of army officers in civilian posts, and the replacement in India of the civilian by a military system of government.

[3] 16 and 23 June 1829, Ellenborough's *Diary*, ii. 55, 148.

[4] Malcolm to Stuart, 9 July 1830, I.O. H/734, fo. 308. See also G. D. Bearce, 'Lord William Bentinck: The Application of Liberalism to India', *Journal of Modern History*, xxviii (1956), 234-46.

Bentinck ignored his instructions to send an embassy to Bokhara. The embassy to Lahore would have to take place; Ellenborough had sent the horses, supposed to be a gift to Ranjit Singh, actually an excuse for a survey, which would tell whether the Indus could be opened up for trade. In June 1830 Bentinck warned Ellenborough in his elusive manner that little but trouble would come of it. 'I doubt very much the practicability of sending a steamship up the Indus', he said, 'and I should doubt also, if it were practicable, whether Ranjit Singh's authority is sufficiently established over the tribes in the desert to ensure protection and security to mercantile intercourse in that direction.' Ranjit Singh, who was already suspicious of the British, would probably not help; if he did, he had no influence, and no claim to influence, over the amirs of Sind, who were traditionally more suspicious. Because demands for the protection of trade would lead to demands for intervention, the scheme would merely stir up trouble on the North-West Frontier. As for the horses, his predecessor had sent Ranjit Singh some bad horses from Calcutta; the drays Ellenborough had sent he would 'probably look upon . . . as elephants'.[1]

At Bombay 'Boy' Malcolm, still as keen on jaunts as he had always been, thought Ellenborough's horses a great lark. To make sure the amirs of Sind could not send them overland, in August 1830 he added a heavy carriage.[2] Bombay's interest in Sind matched Ellenborough's new strategy. Throughout his career Malcolm had argued that the best forward defence of British India would be an island fortress in the Persian Gulf. The expedition to Kishm in 1821 had proved one of his two islands uninhabitable: the climate was vile, the supply of water inadequate, food had to be shipped from Bombay. If an alternative site could be found on the Indus, the British would keep their strategic flexibility, supposedly the advantage of naval power. Bombay was potentially the best naval base in India; defending India from Sind and the Persian Gulf would make its government more important. It might also end their continual financial crises. For fifty years they had been short of land revenue, relying on loans from private traders, paid back

[1] Bentinck to Ellenborough, private, 1 June 1830, P.R.O. 30/9/4 pt. 2/2.
[2] Minute of Malcolm, 9 Aug. 1830, I.O. Bengal/SPC/358, 14 Oct. 1830, no. 4. This had first been suggested by the resident at Cutch. Both men forgot that twenty years earlier the governor-general had sent Ranjit Singh a carriage overland; but it had arrived rather battered.

by subsidies from Bengal. Sind might give them what they needed.

No team of Great Gamesmen could be made up without a surgeon. Malcolm's attention had been drawn to Sind by Dr. James Burnes, who had been sent in 1827 to treat the amirs at Hyderabad.

It is scarcely possible [Burnes had said] to conceive a more easy, or as far as the people generally are concerned, a more willing conquest . . . there is no district which would better repay management than Sind . . . Then the River Indus might once more become the channel of communication and wealth, between the interior of Asia and the peninsula of India.[1]

Although Burnes's report was criticized as 'most unsatisfactory and meagre',[2] it held up a tantalizing vision of greatness for Bombay. Thirty years earlier the danger of invasion had helped the presidency to survive Wellesley's attempt to abolish it. They still had a vested interest, as Malcolm saw, in taking over from Bengal the plans for a steamer service to England and for a new frontier policy.

A steamer service to Suez and up the Indus would expand trade at Bombay. Sind might also increase their land revenue. 'I shall hope some demonstration on the part of Russia will make men alive to the value of this presidency,' said Malcolm to Wellington in September, 'and that circumstances may admit of our settling on the Indus. The revenues of Sind would go far to meet our deficit.'[3] Whereas Bentinck was busy reducing the costs of administration and of the Indian Army, in order to avoid a deficit that after 1833, when the East India Company's trading privileges would be taken away, could not be made up from the profits on trade with China, Malcolm, who had been taught by Wellesley to believe that the best way to avoid deficits was to annex more territory, saw in the Great Game in Asia a perfect opportunity.

At Fort William Sir Charles Metcalfe, knowing Malcolm of old, and knowing what he and Ellenborough meant to do, challenged them in October with one of his classic statements of the opposite

---

[1] Dr. James Burnes, *Narrative of a Visit to the Court of . . . the Ameers of Sind* (Bombay, 1829), pp. 120–1.
[2] Pottinger to Malcolm, private, 8 July 1830, F.O. 705/23.
[3] Enclosure in Malcolm to Wellington, 1 Sept. 1830, *Wellington*, vii. 225.

policy. Meddling with other people led to war: the assumption that they were looking forward to British guidance was false. To survey the Indus under cover of sending a present to Ranjit Singh Metcalfe thought to be highly objectionable. 'It is a trick,' he said, 'in my opinion unworthy of our government, which cannot fail, when detected, as most probably it will be, to excite the jealousy and indignation of the powers on whom we play it . . . It is not impossible that it will lead to war.'

Because the states beyond the British North-West Frontier, who had seen that friendship with the British led eventually to annexation or a protectorate, would resent any closer connection, Ellenborough's defence policy in central Asia would lead to costly and unnecessary frontier wars. If the British wanted to escape the effects of unrest beyond the Hindu Kush, Metcalfe went on,[1]

the only certain thing is, that we ought not wantonly to offend intermediate states, by acts calculated to rouse hostile feelings against us, but rather to cultivate friendly dispositions.

We could not do better than by avoiding forced intimacy, for, either our character is so bad, or weaker states are naturally so jealous of the stronger . . . [that] we cannot oblige our neighbours more than by desisting from seeking intercourse with them.

The best defence against attacks from central Asia, and the best available North-West Frontier, was to leave Sind, the Punjab, and Afghanistan, undisturbed.

For the British Sind became temporarily a family affair. In December 1830, Malcolm picked as escort for Ranjit's horses, and to survey the Indus on the way, the temporary assistant to the resident at Cutch, James Burnes's younger brother, Lieutenant Alexander Burnes. Burnes had been sent to Cutch to map the area beyond the British frontier. Map-making was always politically explosive and had always to be disguised; supposedly he had been sent to protest to the chiefs of Parkar about raids into British territory, and had been told not to go into Sind.[2] This disguise was kept up during his mission to Lahore. Surveying the Indus was so sensitive a project that one disguise was to be disguised by another: Burnes was to talk to the amirs of Sind about the problems of policing their British frontier.[3] His work in Cutch, and his brother's

[1] Minute of Metcalfe, 25 Oct. 1830, I.O. L/PS/5/120, 30 Oct. 1830, no. 113.
[2] GicB to cd, 1 Sept. 1830, I.O. L/PS/6/184.
[3] Pottinger to Burnes, 18 Jan. 1831, I.O. L/PS/5/120, 6 May 1831, no. 13.

earlier work in Sind, made Burnes the obvious choice. So did his character. Energetic, brash, able, and ruthlessly ambitious, he was a copy of Sir John Malcolm in his youth. Such men were briefly admired in the 1830s; as comets they blazed with light and then exploded. Burnes's great rivals were Robert Urquhart and Francis Chesney.

On 21 January 1831 Burnes set out for Lahore. The amirs of Sind, trying to force him to travel overland, twice refused to let him up the Indus. They claimed, which to the British was merely an excuse, the river to be too shallow, and to be unable to protect the expedition from bandits.[1] Twice Burnes had to return to Mandavi. His commanding officer, Colonel Henry Pottinger, the resident in Cutch, wanted to tell 'that government that we consider it as an enemy', and hoped the navy would 'be *ordered* to blockade all the ports of Sind and ruin their trade . . . [which] should bring these insolent barbarians to their senses'.[2] From the start it was clear that the amirs of Sind would give way only to the threat of force.

Bentinck, who was still not enthusiastic, was willing to postpone the mission for a year until the next cold weather, and told the resident at Ludhiana to 'explain the *contretemps* to Ranjit Singh the best way you can'.[3] Instead the resident persuaded Ranjit to threaten the amirs with invasion. In February they gave way, after Ranjit's troops in Derajat had feinted towards Shikarpur.[4] Despite Bentinck's scepticism, Ranjit had a passion for horses, but his interest was a warning of trouble to come: he was as determined as Ellenborough to turn Sind into a protectorate. On 10 March for the third time Burnes set sail from Mandavi. Without misfortune, and charting the course of the Indus as carefully as he could, he reached Hyderabad on 18 April. Three months later he handed over the horses to Ranjit Singh.

Burnes's report to Bentinck, written in September after his return from Lahore, echoed his brother and Malcolm. As the people of Sind, he said, were longing for the progress and enlight-

[1] Pottinger to Norris, 27 Feb. 1831, ibid., no. 25; R. A. Huttenback, *British Relations with Sind, 1799–1843* (Berkeley/Los Angeles, 1962), pp. 22–4.

[2] Pottinger to Norris, private, 24 and 26 Feb. 1831, F.O. 705/23.

[3] C. M. Wade, *A Narrative of Services, Military and Political, 1801–1844* (Ryde, 1847), pp. 15–16.

[4] Wade to Prinsep, 21 May 1831, I.O. L/PS/5/120, 5 Aug. 1831, no. 62.

enment only the British could provide,[1] trading up the Indus was the obvious way to satisfy them. 'There is an uninterrupted navigation from the sea to Lahore,' said Burnes, because below the junction with the Sutledge, even in the dry season, the water never fell below fourteen feet and the current was always moderate.[2] The conclusion to be drawn was obvious: the Indus was ideal for steamers. Any barriers to trade would be political. The amirs at Khairpur were friendly and would encourage trade; their cousins at Hyderabad, anxious to stay isolated, were equally against it. This, equally obviously, could not now be tolerated.

Burnes had spotted a chance to back up Malcolm's argument that island fortresses beyond the frontier were the best way to defend British India, and to combine this with Ellenborough's plans for creating a stable balance of power in central Asia. In the autumn of 1831 a marriage was being arranged between the amirs of Hyderabad and Persia. Although the British resident at Teheran thought the idea 'quite erroneous',[3] given Ellenborough's and Malcolm's fear that Russia might turn Persia into a protectorate, this marriage meant the possibility of Russian influence in Sind. The British would then find it harder to control the amirs, at the moment when the Indus and Ravi had proved navigable, and shown that the Bolan Pass could no longer be ignored as an invasion route.

Having neatly sketched the danger, Burnes produced an equally neat defence. An island fortress in the Indus opposite Bukkur would serve the same purpose as one at Kishm. It would symbolize Britain's paramount influence in Sind and northwards to Peshawar, be a good base from which to police the Indus and protect British traders, and, lying near the invasion routes from Afghanistan, would enable the British to attack an enemy's flank. Burnes had tried hard to prove Ellenborough's hypothesis, that the best way to forestall Russia in central Asia would be to move the military frontier of British India forward to the Indus.

[1] Alexander Burnes, *Travels into Bokhara; being an Account of a Journey from India to Kabul, Tartary, and Persia; also a Narrative of a Voyage on the Indus . . in the Years 1831, 1832 and 1833* (London, 1834), iii. 37–8
[2] 'A Geographical and Military Memoir [by Alexander Burnes] of the Indus and its Tributary Rivers from the Sea to Lahore', 12 Sept. 1831, I.O. Bengal/ SPC/363, 25 Nov. 1831, no. 22.
[3] Campbell to Prinsep, 4 Dec. 1831, I.O. Persia/46.

The best-educated Englishmen, infinitely pragmatic, are expected to become civil servants. They have been educated, and prove they are educated, by answering examination questions, in which what one says in answer depends upon how the examiners phrase the question. H. W. C. Davis long ago remarked that British agents were never asked to tell what they had seen in the near east; they were told what to look for, and merely asked whether they had found it. Russian activity was one of the things to be looked for, and, as Englishmen are healthy, energetic, and enjoy games, naturally it was found.[1] Burnes had written his report for Malcolm and Ellenborough. In the English system the men who tutor candidates are not usually permitted to mark the examinations. Before Burnes came back from Lahore, Malcolm had gone home to England and Ellenborough into opposition, leaving Burnes's work to be judged by Bentinck and Charles Grant.

The influence of Alexander Burnes upon Anglo-Indian policy in the near east has always been over-estimated. His report convinced Bentinck, he courteously remarked, 'that the advantage offered by the river Indus political and military, if the occasion should ever arise for providing for the defence of India against invasion . . . as commercial in the facilities for navigation and for the transport of goods . . . had in no way been exaggerated'.[2] This may have been true, because steam navigation was a talisman to Bentinck, but his aims, both political and commercial, were different from Ellenborough's and Malcolm's; being less interested in a new military frontier at the Indus, more interested in trade. Bentinck shared Metcalfe's assumption that the British should not meddle in the states beyond their North-West Frontier: unlike Metcalfe he meant to make sure they stayed as they were, and thought he knew how to manage it. He changed his policy in the summer of 1831, and began belatedly to play the Great Game, not because of Burnes, nor Ranjit Singh,[3] but under the influence of the man he considered 'the ablest . . . in the service, and the most noble-minded . . . he had ever seen', Charles Trevelyan.

Charles Trevelyan is a forgotten figure in the Great Game in Asia. In 1831 he was twenty-four and had been out in India for five years, most of the time as assistant to the commissioner at Delhi.

[1] Davis, 'Great Game in Asia', pp. 237–8.
[2] Ggic to sc, 19 Nov. 1831, I.O. L/PS/5/42.
[3] As is claimed by Rosselli, *Bentinck*, p. 233.

In Trevelyan 'the fusion of evangelical and radical outlook was most completely realized'.[1]

He is quite at the head of that active party among the younger servants of the Company who take the side of improvement [said his brother-in-law, Macaulay, three years later] . . . He has no small talk. His mind is full of schemes of moral and political improvement, and his zeal boils over in all his talk. His topics, even in courtship, are steam navigation, the education of the natives, [and] the equalization of the sugar duties.[2]

Bentinck, who was childless, had during his life gained and returned the affection of a number of bright young men at the start of promising careers, who treated him like a father. Trevelyan was the last and closest: 'Lord William, a man who makes no favourites, has always given to Trevelyan the strongest marks, not of a blind partiality, but of a thoroughly well grounded and discriminating esteem.'[3]

Trevelyan in India is best known for the part he played in the controversy about whether to educate Indians in English. In 1838, at the end of his famous pamphlet on education, quoting Macaulay's more famous minute, he explained how future revolution might be prevented by reform.[4]

The only means at our disposal for preventing the one and securing the other . . . is, to set the natives on a process of European improvement, to which they are already sufficiently inclined . . . The natives will not rise against us, we shall stoop to raise them . . . and we shall exchange profitable subjects for still more profitable allies . . . Trained by us to happiness and independence, and endowed with our learning and political institutions, India will remain the proudest monument to British benevolence; and we shall long continue to reap, in the affectionate attachment of the people, and in a great commercial intercourse with their splendid country, the fruit of that liberal and enlightened policy which suggested to us this line of conduct.

These words might as well have described Trevelyan's view of central Asia, and his policy for creating a stable balance of power

---

[1] E. Stokes, *The English Utilitarians and India* (Oxford, 1963), p. 46.

[2] Macaulay to his sister, 7 Dec. 1834, Sir G. O. Trevelyan, *The Life and Letters of Lord Macaulay* ('Silver Library' Edition, London, 1908), p. 279.

[3] Ibid. See also Rosselli, *Bentinck*, pp. 58–60.

[4] C. E. Trevelyan, *On the Education of the People of India* (London, 1838) pp. 192–5. For Trevelyan's role in the controversy over education see J. F. Hilliker, 'Charles Edward Trevelyan as an Educational Reformer in India', *Canadian Journal of History*, ix (1974), 275–92.

beyond the North-West Frontier. When Bentinck arrived at
Delhi in April 1831, Trevelyan's views on foreign policy not
reform first captured his attention, and explain why the governor-
general overcame his previous hesitation.

In the spring of 1831, while Burnes was surveying the Indus as
best he could, and taking Ellenborough's horses to Ranjit Singh,
Trevelyan at Delhi was gathering the most recent information
about central Asia. His most useful source was an exact contemporary, the Bengal cavalry officer, who had been sent out overland
from England to Persia through Russia by Ellenborough, had then
tried to reach Khiva, and when that proved impossible had gone
on overland to India through Afghanistan, encouraged by the
resident at Teheran.[1] Arthur Conolly, whose taste for adventure
led to his death in a dungeon at Bokhara, matched Trevelyan's
exuberance by a deep religious conviction. Their blend of the
utilitarian with the evangelical provided one half of Bentinck's
ambivalent frontier policy.

Conolly examined central Asian politics, Trevelyan trade; both
then suggested how they might be combined. The start of Conolly's
argument was the common assumption that the British could not
defend India against Russia in central Asia by fighting: sepoys
would be beaten, British troops too expensive and too few. What
Britain needed, as Jonathan Swift had long before explained, was
an ally; a central Asian state must be found with interests similar
to Britain's and willing and able to defend them. The choice for
Conolly was easy: because Persia was and would remain a Russian
puppet, 'our defence must be the strength of the Afghans and our
friendship with them'.[2] The choice was also reflected in Conolly's
selection of the most strategically vital point in the near east. At
different times since 1798, Perim, Baghdad, Kharrack or Kishm,
Kandahar, and Bukkur, had all competed to become the forward
point at which British India might be most successfully defended.
Conolly reminded Bentinck of the strategic importance of Herat.

[1] Campbell to Prinsep, 3 Aug. 1831, I.O. Persia/46. The court of directors,
even at their most parsimonious, agreed to repay Conolly, because his journey
served a 'purpose which has certainly been satisfactorily fulfilled'. Cd to ggic,
25 Mar. 1834, I.O. L/PS/6/479. For details see A. Conolly, *Journey to the North
of India, Overland from England, through Russia, Persia and Afghanistan* (London,
1834).
[2] 'Report Commercial and Military upon the Countries between the Caspian
and the Indus by C. E. Trevelyan . . . and Arthur Conolly', [15–30] Mar. 1831,
I.O. Bengal/SPC/363, 25 Nov. 1831, no. 8.

Unlike the government of Bombay, Conolly did not ignore the possibility of invasion from Khiva up the Oxus, but he thought it more likely that Russia would march through Persia towards Herat, as the easiest way to turn the Hindu Kush. As the last battle for India would be fought at the Indus, because the British could retreat no farther, Conolly was as eager as Burnes for an island fortress at Bukkur. Defensive strategy, however, as Metternich in redefining the Holy Alliance had argued, was of no use to continental states who could not draw upon popular support; they needed a method of taking the offensive. Conolly, like Evans and Ellenborough, wanted a connection with the Afghans, who might then allow the British to station troops at Kandahar and Kabul. This demand was one cause of two disastrous Afghan Wars. Conolly and Trevelyan could not foresee this. They expected their soldiers to be welcomed.

'Instead of discussing how we are to fight the Russians when they arrive,' said Trevelyan, who even planned against a coalition between Nicholas I, the Manchu Emperor, and the Dalai Lama, 'we ought to make the most of our present advantages to check their further approach, which will be tantamount to preventing their coming altogether.'[1] The British already traded with Afghanistan. This trade must be encouraged and expanded from the factory to be built at Bukkur, as the obvious way to create, by economic and social reform in the near east, a group of stable buffer states between the Indus and the Caspian Sea, which would not only solve the problem of defence against Russia, but create a stable balance of power beyond the British North-West Frontier. Sind, the Punjab, and Afghanistan, were to be treated as separate territorial states, all connected with the British. There was only one complication: even if they could be treated as states, Afghanistan was not one state but three. Because, as long as this continued, one would always help Russia whenever another helped the British, the aim of British policy in central Asia should be to unify Afghanistan.

This was not a new idea, but the choice of prince was new: owing to the city's strategic importance, Afghanistan was to be united under Kamran Khan, the Sadozai ruler of Herat. A few subsidies would be needed at the start, to help Kamran defeat his enemies, but the benefits would well repay the outlay. 'As the

[1] Trevelyan to Bentinck, 15 Mar. 1831, ibid., no. 7.

Afghans are situated upon our frontier,' said Conolly, 'an alliance with them can never be productive of the embarrassment which has attended our alliance with the Persians, and the dilemma can never occur where we have to choose between abandoning our ally or engaging in a distant and ruinous war.' Afghanistan was not, of course, a neighbouring state; she would become one only were Sind turned into a British protectorate.

The policy had a second attraction: because British friendship would prove Kamran's greatest asset in the struggle, Conolly and Trevelyan said it would be cheap. The Afghans, like the Sindians and the inhabitants of British India, were anxiously awaiting the benefits of progress, to follow from adopting British habits.

In our negotiations with the Afghans [added Trevelyan] we shall have everything to offer them and nothing to require . . . We shall offer them peace, security and independence, the increase of trade and an im-provided [sic] condition of social life, and, in return for these advantages we require only their friendship and goodwill . . .

A connection therefore which enables us to hold out the most important advantages while no sacrifice is require[d] cannot fail to be as easily formed as, when formed, it can be productive of nothing but friendship and goodwill . . .

They now see that their weakness lies in disunion . . . Both nobles and people feel themselves degraded . . . and they would accept with feelings of gratitude any assistance we could give them in restoring the integrity of their nation.[1]

Utilitarians and evangelicals never saw foreign sin and degradation as incurable. The natives were retarded but not depraved: they stood like the poor in need of stimulant. Then reform would lead to order, order to a stable balance of power in the near east, stability to the effortless defence of India. Foreigners thought so too. 'Il faut avoir voyagé dans le Pendjab', remarked a touring Frenchman, 'pour connaître quel immense bienfait c'est pour l'humanité, que la domination des Anglais dans l'Inde.'[2] This was true; nevertheless Trevelyan had himself revealed the difficulty of extending such benefits beyond the Khyber Pass. The policy

---

[1] 'Report . . . by Trevelyan . . . and Conolly', ibid., no. 8.

[2] Jacquemont to his father, 25 Apr. 1831, *Correspondance de Victor Jacquemont . . . pendant son voyage dans l'Inde (1828–1832)* (4th edit., Paris, 1846), ii. 45.

meant to create friendship and goodwill actually depended on them.

Conolly and Trevelyan, working at Delhi, had judged more shrewdly than Burnes how to answer. Their policy seemed not to need continuous diplomatic initiatives at the risk of frontier wars, nor would continuous effort be needed. As soon as Sind, the Punjab, and Afghanistan, had recognized one another as independent states with agreed frontiers, the effects of trade would defend India permanently, against rebellion as well as European invasion. Meanwhile the government of India might remain detached, busy with the reform of law and education. It was a vision so grand as to make Ellenborough's appear tawdry.

The prophecy was followed by the arrival from England in the autumn of new instructions. Charles Grant, who had succeeded Ellenborough at the board of control, was the son of a famous and able chairman of the East India Company, who had the same name, and both were lifelong evangelicals. Grant worked hard at the board of control, against the opposition of the Company and the civil service, to set up the Anglican church in India. Similarly, he named his friend Macaulay, firstly to the board of control, then to the Bengal council, because they both believed the English language, as the English church, would help to legitimize British rule in India. Evangelicals brought social order by destroying superstition, utilitarians salvation by providing equal opportunity and security for the just rewards of labour. Although one promised rewards in the next world, and the other in this, they demanded the same virtues; both also believed in instantaneous conversion. Because the evangelical Grant and the somewhat utilitarian Bentinck were as well matched as had been Ellenborough and Malcolm, the initiative in the Great Game in Asia moved from Bombay to Fort William.

Grant said he agreed with Metcalfe's criticism of Ellenborough and Malcolm, which showed only that he understood their policy better than Metcalfe's objections to it. Metcalfe did not distinguish between good and bad actions beyond the frontier: he called both provocative. Grant, who could not believe that the poor and downtrodden, whether in the slums of London, Calcutta, or Hyderabad, would not seize the chance to improve themselves, wanted to know more about the Indus basin, confident that Sind, which he imagined fertile and ideally suited to economic and social reform, no longer suspicious, would grasp that 'our motive is to extend our commerce and *only* our commerce', and that everything would be done 'on a footing only of the most friendly equality'.

If, on the other hand [Grant warned Bentinck in July] it should be found impossible thus to extend our commercial relations, and to acquire the free use of the Indus, through the fair influence of persuasion, in the manner described . . . we have to desire that you will abstain from a resort to any other means.

This warning was given because Grant knew that in the past 'the chances of war and conquest . . . seem[ed] almost invariably to follow the extension of our commercial intercourse in the East'.[1] Grant also knew that past experience was no guide to future conduct—to Utopians it never is—because the past had not reasoned rightly. This time the advantages of being turned into Englishmen by trade would surely be too obvious to be denied.

III

British trade, sent to take the benefits of civilization to the backward, as the best way to increase order, and so create a stable balance of power, instead caused trouble. This was soon obvious on the North-West Frontier of India. Grant, by separating trade from politics, had changed Ellenborough's defence policy but ignored the frontier. Bentinck knew that this could not be done: every defence policy implied a frontier policy. In the autumn of 1831, Bentinck, who was ready to continue the search for more detailed and accurate information about central Asia, was also ready to begin negotiating with the amirs of Sind and Ranjit Singh the commercial treaties needed to open the Indus to British trade. Because he had learned how powerful were the Sikhs, the order of these negotiations was turned about.

Since the agent at Ludhiana had paid in 1827 the first official visit to the Punjab to follow Charles Metcalfe's mission to negotiate an anti-French alliance in 1808, Ranjit Singh had been trying to find out how the British would react, when, having annexed western Bahawalpur, he invaded Sind, in order to capture the commercially and strategically valuable town of Shikarpur, which controls the road from the Indus through the Bolan Pass to Quetta.[2] Bentinck had at first not believed Ranjit strong enough to threaten

---

[1] Sc to ggic, 29 July 1831, I.O. L/PS/5/544.
[2] Wade to Metcalfe, 1 Aug. 1827, I.O. Bengal/SPC/348, 12 Oct. 1827, no. 3. As long as Metcalfe was commissioner at Delhi, he refused to give any answer.

Sind. As soon as he forced the amirs to admit Burnes, Bentinck changed his mind; a commercial treaty with Ranjit, followed by joint threats against the amirs, would be the quickest way to force them to open the Indus to British ships. Such methods, which would not have upset Ellenborough, were forbidden by Grant. They might also encourage the Sikhs to invade Sind. This had to be prevented, because Trevelyan, who thought the Sikhs already too powerful, wanted simultaneously to cherish and check them. 'In 1809 the rising power of the Sikhs was considered so formidable', he explained, 'that it was deemed necessary to place a check upon its further progress . . . If therefore we open to the Sikhs the door to . . . Sind, their power must rise to an inconvenient height.'[1] In 1809 Ranjit Singh had been forbidden by Minto the states east of the Sutledge; Bentinck, trying to create a stable balance of power beyond the British North-West Frontier, now wanted to forbid him Sind.

The difference between utilitarians and evangelicals is that utilitarians do not expect to work by faith alone: conversion requires effort. Bentinck warned Grant that if the British wished to act 'as protectors and mediators' upon the Indus, the threat of force could not be avoided.[2] He was careful, however, always to act in a manner implying that he was not threatening, but might if unreasonably resisted. To create a situation in which force might be threatened, but might be balanced by inducement, in the summer of 1831 Bentinck prised out of Ranjit Singh an invitation to meet him in October at Rupar. The purpose of the meeting was to set out Bentinck's frontier policy.

The agent at Ludhiana, Captain Claude Wade, who at their first meeting had dealt surprisingly well with Ranjit Singh, thought that the obvious way to defend India against Russia was to turn the Punjab into a protectorate, and Afghanistan into a buffer state. It would be

a question for the Government to consider [he said in August] whether its best line of policy would not consist in taking advantage of our connection with the Maharajah Ranjit Singh to counteract Russian diplomacy; we possess the same ascendancy in the counsels of his Highness

[1] Quoted in K. Singh. *A History of the Sikhs* (Princeton, 1963), i. 275, fn.; ggic to sc, 19 Nov. 1831, I.O. L/PS/5/42.

[2] Bentinck to Grant, private, 17 Dec. 1831, 1 May 1832, Portland MSS. PwJf/2594/1.

that Russia does in those of Persia, and a power to establish a paramount influence in Afghanistan is as open to us through the agency of the maharajah, as to Russia through that of the king of Persia.[1]

Ranjit Singh, however, was just as determined that the talks should be only a sign of friendship, to buttress his power in the Punjab, not an opportunity for changing the terms of the Anglo-Sikh connection.[2] He undoubtedly feared what Wade was suggesting, an offensive and defensive alliance similar to the one offered in 1808 by Minto against France. Both Wade and Ranjit were mistaken in thinking that Bentinck was formulating a new defence policy. His policy was offensive; but all he asked of Ranjit was to do nothing.

Bentinck did not tell Ranjit Singh that he was about to negotiate a commercial treaty with Sind, lest Ranjit should either encourage the amirs to resist, or offer in return for Shikarpur to force them to give way. If the amirs, whom Bentinck expected to resist, could be overawed by this show of Anglo-Sikh friendship, they might more willingly agree to trade. Bentinck had acted just in time. While at Rupar in October he learnt that a Sikh army had occupied south-western Bahawalpur and were stationed at the frontier of Sind. Ranjit Singh had acted just too late. Bentinck made his point at Rupar, that neither the British nor the Sikhs were to annex Sind, which, as Ranjit realized, meant accepting a new definition of the British North-West Frontier. The British would not interfere with their neighbours, except to offer them opportunities of social and economic reform, but they would no longer allow them to interfere with one another; they were all to behave as independent states with agreed frontiers. To the British this was virtue, to the natives perhaps ruin. A famous British traveller, asking Ranjit Singh shortly afterwards how he believed one might approach God, was given this sibylline reply: 'One can come nigh unto God by making an alliance with the British government, as I lately did . . . at Rupar.'[3]

---

[1] Wade to Prinsep, 5 Aug. 1831, I.O. Bengal/SPC/362, 9 Sept. 1831, no. 8.

[2] Wade to Prinsep, 1 June 1831, I.O. Bengal/SPC/361, 29 July 1831, no. 29; V. Jacquemont, *État politique et social de l'Inde du Nord en 1830: Extraits de son journal de voyage* (Paris, 1933), pp. 386–7.

[3] Revd. J. Wolff, *Travels and Adventures* (London, 1861), p. 375. The statement agreed between Bentinck and Ranjit Singh was printed in Aitchison, *Treaties*, ii. 239.

This policy was also to be carried out in Sind; British relations with Sind were to serve the needs of trade not strategy. These were not, of course, alternatives, nor did the policy require a choice: the expansion of trade was to be the defence of India. Similarly the commercial treaty was not to imply that Britain would protect Sind. Bentinck refused to take advantage of the rivalries between the amirs to turn Sind into a protectorate;[1] he would settle neither the succession in Sind, nor disputes between Sind and her neighbours. Sind was needed like the Punjab as one of a group of states with agreed frontiers: Bentinck would not interfere, he would not permit the Sikhs to interfere, but he would not promise to defend Sind if they did. If the amirs thought that the British had a strategic interest in protecting their independence, they would never agree to trade, and defence would be sacrificed to frontier policy.

Bentinck's aims in October were out of Ellenborough by Grant:

to obtain the free navigation of the Indus with a view to the advantages that might result from substituting our own influence for that derived by Russia, through her commercial intercourse with Bokhara, in the countries lying between Hindustan and the Caspian Sea, as well as because of the great facilities afforded by the river for the disposal of produce and manufactures of the British dominions both in Europe and in India.[2]

The method was negative, as opposed to Ellenborough's positive methods, but still meant a forward frontier policy. Only if the states beyond the British North-West Frontier also respected each other's frontiers, could the expansion and increasing profitability of British trade forestall the Russians in central Asia, and create a stable balance of power, by symbolizing the utilitarian and evangelical values which were the prerequisite of economic and social order. Utopians are fortunate in not being asked to choose between what suits them and what is right: 'The laws of God', hymned Trevelyan, 'are so happily adjusted that in benefiting the natives, we benefit ourselves.'[3]

---

[1] Prinsep to Norris, 30 May 1831, I.O. Bengal/SPC/361, 17 June 1831, no. 3.
[2] Prinsep to Pottinger, 22 Oct. 1831, I.O. Bengal/SPC/363, 25 Nov. 1831, no. 27.
[3] Quoted in Rosselli, *Bentinck*, p. 183.

Such assumptions paid too little attention to the way in which Asiatic states were organized. The expansion of trade was more likely to undermine than buttress, for example, the amirs. Since 1783 Sind had been divided between three branches of a Baluchi tribe, the Talpuras: one appeared to rule lower Sind from Hyderabad, another upper Sind from Khairpur, the third, and least powerful, the north-east corner from Mirpur. These divisions were misleading. The amirs thought of Sind as a family fief. As far as it was a state, it was not, like Afghanistan, three states but one; all three branches of the family had estates throughout Sind, and they were all mixed up. The amirs sometimes acted separately, sometimes together: they had gained a precarious independence from Afghanistan; were anxious not to lose it to the British or the Sikhs; and the British, who appeared less threatening, they knew to be more. Because the Baluchi chiefs were autonomous, even when the amirs acted together, like the sultan of Turkey they only ruled, they did not govern. They governed only their family estates, carrying on foreign policy and collecting dues together.[1] While left alone Sind although disordered was stable. Here was the contradiction bound to cause a quarrel with the British: trying to increase order would cause instability. The amirs could negotiate a treaty with the British, they could not enforce it in Sind: the British were demanding what they could not perform. When they said that they could not promise to protect Alexander Burnes on his way to Lahore, they were right. Trade would need protection. The amirs, who had every reason to doubt whether they could give it, knew that, were they to fail, the British would be bound to intervene.

The amirs of Sind did not lack a British champion. Charles Trevelyan's certainties might overwhelm Lord William Bentinck at Delhi, but when Metcalfe at Calcutta learnt of Bentinck's plans, he protested bitterly in the autumn of 1831, that in foreign politics faith was no substitute for knowledge. Metcalfe, echoing Bentinck's comments to Ellenborough the year before, did not believe trade could bring order: it would instead cause instability. The government of India would be more and more tempted to intervene, both to make the near-eastern states respect one another's

---

[1] For descriptions of Sind, see in addition to James Burnes, Crow to Duncan, 3 Oct. 1799, Add. MSS. 13698, fo. 216; memorandum by Henry Ellis, 1809, I.O. H/591, p. 414; and memoir by W. Pottinger on Sind, [1832], F.O. 705/18.

frontiers, and to provide the political order within them necessary for uninterrupted trade. All this was to be risked in defending India against an imaginary danger.

If . . . I were asked what is best to be done with a view to a Russian invasion [said Metcalfe], I should say that it is best to do nothing until time shall show us what we ought to do, because there is nothing that we can do in our present blind state that would be any certain benefit.[1]

If Metcalfe was uncertain what should be done, he was equally certain what was to be avoided. 'Every step by which we approximate ourselves to the Russians', he added, 'appears to me to be playing their game for them. The only manner in which they could be formidable to our power in India, is by shortening the distance between us.' A forward policy would weaken not strengthen the defence of British India.

The policy would also create unrest along the British North-West Frontier. Metcalfe, too, saw no need to choose between defence and frontier policy; both would be jeopardized.

I am exceedingly sorry to learn [he added] that Your Lordship is about to embark on negotiations about the Indus. I see that no one is proof against the temptation of extension. It seems to be contrary to our nature to remain quiet and contented with what we have got. In my mind, this move on the Indus is the forerunner of perilous wars and ruinous expenditure . . . [The amirs of Sind] will see in Your Lordship's proposals the confirmation of their fears. They will not agree to them willingly. The next step according to our usual policy is to compel them. We are too overbearing to be thwarted, and thus we advance crushing the independence of every state that we come near. We profess moderation, and nevertheless show by our continual restlessness that there is no safety in our neighbourhood.[2]

Demanding to trade by way of the Indus with Afghanistan and Bokhara would lead, Metcalfe repeated time and time again, to frontier wars and annexation.

Placing Sir Charles Metcalfe in any of the groups, who vied to impose their principles upon the government of India in the early nineteenth century, is difficult. Eric Stokes placed him amongst the

---

[1] Quoted in E. Thompson, *The Life of Charles, Lord Metcalfe* (London, 1937), p. 283.

[2] Metcalfe to Bentinck, private, 9 Oct. 1831, Portland MSS. PwJf/1606.

romantic imperialists, with Malcolm, Munro, and Elphinstone, men who rejected the universal application of abstract principles.[1] Although Munro and Metcalfe disagreed with Malcolm and Elphinstone about whether the Indian privileged classes should be buttressed or destroyed, all three opposed policies of assimilation. D. N. Panigrahi has challenged this description, placing Metcalfe amongst the evangelical and utilitarian associates of Bentinck.[2] Although Metcalfe possessed one hallmark of this group, belief in the value of education in English, he lacked two others: the system of communal land tenure he preferred[3] denied both the whig and utilitarian assumption that protection of private property was needed for social order, and the classical economists' assumption that self-help was needed for economic growth.

Metcalfe's increasing isolation within the government of India was partly over questions of timing: he also denied the evangelical belief in instantaneous conversion. Until 1818, following Wellesley, Metcalfe had treated territorial expansion as inevitable.[4] Thereafter he argued that the boundaries of British India should be fixed. Inside the remaining native states should be annexed, outside they should be left alone.[5] Reform required time: otherwise, as Burke would have agreed, it caused more damage than could be calculated. In opposing Bentinck's policy in central Asia and on the North-West Frontier, Metcalfe was echoing Munro.

The ruling vice of our government [he once said] is innovation . . . it is time that we should learn that neither the face of the country, its property, nor its society, are things that can be suddenly improved by any contrivance of ours, though they may be greatly injured by what we mean for their good.[6]

Bentinck's policy, concluded Metcalfe, would destroy the states beyond the British North-West Frontier, amongst which it was meant to create a stable balance of power.

[1] Stokes, *Utilitarians and India*, pp. 16–18.

[2] D. N. Panigrahi, *Charles Metcalfe in India: Ideas and Administration, 1806–1835* (Delhi, 1968), pp. 11–23.

[3] The villagers held their land in common and engaged for the payment of land tax by the village as a unity.

[4] Metcalfe to Jenkins, private, 3 Nov. 1814, Sir J. W. Kaye, *Life and Correspondence of Charles, Lord Metcalfe* (London, 1854), i. 394.

[5] Memorandum by Metcalfe, 7 Sept. 1820, *Metcalfe Papers*, p. 151.

[6] Minute of Munro, 31 Dec. 1824, G. R. Gleig, *Life of Major General Sir Thomas Munro, Bart.* (London, 1830), ii. 381.

The policy was likely to cause equal disruption in the civil service. The Great Game in Asia was noisy and uproarious: the Englishmen who played quarrelled more often and heatedly with one another than with the Russians. Four years were wasted in choosing between the two families who wanted to represent Britain in Persia; two more while it was realized that the wrong one had been chosen. The problem was not new, and while so many depart-ments of government were involved it could hardly have been avoided. In the 1830s it became more severe.

The energetic young men with good health, who were needed to collect information about central Asia, seemed to gain too easily too great an influence over policy. Their seniors, used to relying on native news writers, feared that their advice would be ignored and their careers ruined. Englishmen—more often younger sons of impoverished Scots—had traditionally gone out to India to make their fortune, planning to return home to set up in society. This was becoming more difficult, because the methods of making a fortune were no longer tolerated; instead one was paid a higher salary, enough to live on, provided one were regularly promoted. From the evangelical revival dates the Anglo-Indian's insoluble dilemma. Official British India was a totalitarian state within a state; everything was determined by official rank, and the higher one's rank the greater one's prestige. Ironically, however high one's rank, it was not transferable: in England it meant nothing. Anglo-Indians were so competitive within their system, because they knew that life would be meaningless when they had to leave.

Not the least poignant quarrel broke out between Alexander Burnes and his superior at Mandavi, Henry Pottinger. They had staying power, these older men, because they held regular appoint-ments. Conservatives can afford to make mistakes: because they do not claim to possess a talisman, they are not discredited when the spell appears broken. One such was Pottinger. Burnes died at Kabul, his policy turned down; Pottinger lived to become gover-nor of Madras, and to this day his portrait hangs in Whitehall. While Burnes was sent on missions of inquiry, firstly up the Indus then to Bokhara, Pottinger was chosen to negotiate the commercial treaty with Sind. He did not expect much to come of it, because he sensed that all the talk about the possibilities of trade was exag-gerated. 'I *do* differ', he had warned the government of Bombay in July 1831, 'from many of the facts and opinions stated by . . .

Burnes.'[1] Pottinger also sensed that not Burnes's information but their own Utopianism had misled the government of India and the board of control. His repeated efforts to base British policy on Ellenborough's more wordly calculations were repeatedly rebuffed.

Henry Pottinger, like Henry Ellis, was a 'Malcolmite', a supporter of Sir John Malcolm in his famous quarrel with Sir Harford Jones between 1808 and 1810 about how the British should treat the shah of Persia. He had begun his diplomatic career as a member of the British mission to Sind in 1809. Afterwards he had travelled through Baluchistan and Persia, one of a number of junior officers sent by the government of India to obtain more detailed information about the overland invasion routes. The account he published in 1816 showed how similar to Malcolm's was his attitude to the natives. The Sindians, he claimed,[2]

are avaricious, full of deceit, cruel, ungrateful, and strangers to veracity; but, in extenuation of their vices, it is to be recollected, that the present generation has grown up under a government, whose extortion, ignorance, and tyranny is possibly unequalled in the world; and that the debasement of the public mind, is consequent to the infamy of its rulers, seems to be an acknowledged fact in all countries. I do not, however, wish it to be inferred, that I ascribe the gross defects I have stated in the Sindian character to that cause alone, because I am more disposed to attribute the majority of them to that moral turpitude which may almost be pronounced, to pervade in a greater or lesser degree, the population and society of every nation in Asia.

Malcolm and Pottinger agreed with evangelicals and utilitarians about the condition of Asiatics; they lacked their confidence in the prospects of reform.

Upon returning to Bombay, Pottinger had served on the staff of the governor, then in the revenue branch, which he disliked. Always bored by the routine of administration, he enjoyed a crisis when he might strut and hector, characteristics of Anglo-Indian diplomacy. The negotiations with Sind were an ideal opportunity to forward his career. Pottinger, said the governor of Bombay, 'tho' not a brilliant man . . . succeeds better than most in managing

[1] Pottinger to Norris, 7 July 1831, I.O. Bengal/SPC/363, 25 Nov. 1831, no. 25.
[2] H. Pottinger, *Travels in Beloochistan and Sind* (London, 1816), p. 376.

natives'.[1] What was meant by management confirms Pottinger's similarity to Malcolm.

All . . . Asiatics [said Pottinger] . . . estimate their successful policy by the impositions they can put upon foreigners, regarding punctilious ceremonies, which it should be peculiarly the aim of every person acting in a public capacity to crush by the most explicit and immoveable measures; otherwise he may calculate, not merely on entailing himself the derision of the court he is employed at, but that his future negotiations will be cramped and interrupted by every series of litigious etiquette that can be devised; and possibly, from that very circumstance, prove in the end equally unavailing and derogatory.[2]

In Pottinger the amirs of Sind were to receive the threat they had expected and feared. His attitudes were their justification for wishing to keep the British at a distance.

Although Pottinger received his instructions in October 1831, he did not reach Hyderabad until January the following year. The negotiations had not gone as Bentinck had planned. Burnes had claimed the amirs at Khairpur to be friendly, that the traditional hostility to the British was felt only by their cousins at Hyderabad. Bentinck had therefore hoped, if Pottinger negotiated with the different branches of the Talpura family separately, starting at Khaipur, to force the amirs at Hyderabad to agree to the same terms. The amirs at Khairpur were as willing to open the Indus to navigation as had been predicted. Nearer to the Punjab, they saw the value of a connection with the British; they also wanted to make certain it would not lead to annexation. The best insurance was unity. Khairpur told Pottinger that no treaty with them was necessary. They would only offer to carry out in their territory whatever terms were agreed at Hyderabad.[3]

Bentinck had given Pottinger the usual mixture of arguments, any one of which was supposed to convince the amirs of the opportunities being offered them. To have threatened the amirs would have offended the board of control; it was also forbidden by Bentinck's bargain with Ranjit Singh. Bentinck was trying to negotiate separately with the two states on the British North-West

[1] Clare to Bentinck, private, 5 Jan. 1832, Portland MSS. PwJf/624; K. Ballhatchet, *Social Policy and Social Change in Western India, 1817–1830* (London, 1957), pp. 23–4.
[2] Pottinger, *Travels in Sind*, p. 365.
[3] Pottinger to Prinsep, 6 Apr. 1832, F.O. 705/12, p. 161.

Frontier, as the best way to preserve their independence and their existing frontiers. He had not told Ranjit Singh that he was about to negotiate with Sind, and was equally careful not to tell the amirs what had been agreed with Ranjit at Rupar: if the amirs expected a Sikh invasion, they might more easily give way. Bentinck, like Grant, had higher hopes from the appeal of self-improvement. Pottinger was to explain to the amirs that Vattel's law forbade the closure of straits to others by the controlling power.[1] Whether the Indus might reasonably be described as a strait mattered less than persuading the amirs, and after them the rulers of Afghanistan and Bokhara, to obey the canons of European diplomatic practice. This was essential were the Asiatic monarchies to abandon nomadic for settled habits, and to treat one another as independent states with agreed frontiers.

'It is utterly impossible', Pottinger warned Bentinck in February 1832, 'that I can ever give an adequate idea of the suspicions and fears of the government [of Sind] in my despatches, and this is all mixed up with sickening vanity.'[2] One thing, however, was clear to the amirs: if a British connection was to be worth the risk, it must include a defensive alliance against Ranjit Singh. Pottinger agreed, because he wanted Sind to become a British protectorate, but Bentinck turned it down. Their connection with the Sikhs was still the government of India's best defence, not against European invasion, but against the disturbance and debt which would be caused by wars along the North-West Frontier. The Sikhs, although checked, were to be cherished; like Ellenborough, Bentinck hoped that if the connection were kept up, the Punjab would lapse to the British when Ranjit died.[3] By then British trade would have brought order to the area beyond the North-West Frontier; meanwhile the tranquillity of the Upper Provinces was not to be endangered by concessions to the amirs which might offend the Sikhs.

Refused this concession to the amirs, the terms of the agreement Pottinger negotiated at Hyderabad were unsatisfactory. By a

[1] Prinsep to Pottinger, 22 Oct. 1831, I.O. Bengal/SPC/363, 25 Nov. 1831, no. 27.

[2] Pottinger to Bentinck, private, 5 Feb. 1832, F.O. 705/12, p. 89. Pottinger's despatches to Prinsep and McNaghten, the governor-general's secretaries, bound together in this volume, give a detailed description of his negotiations with the amirs.

[3] McNaghten to Bentinck, private, 26 Dec. 1831, Portland MSS. PwJf/1354

treaty signed on 20 April 1832, the amirs agreed to open the Indus to British trade, subject to three restrictions: no armaments might be shipped through Sind, by road or river; British vessels on the Indus might not be armed; and no Englishman might live in Sind.[1] By a supplementary treaty the amirs agreed to help the British and Jodhpur police their common frontiers in the Rann of Cutch and the Great Indian Desert.[2] To a utilitarian like Bentinck it mattered less, but Pottinger thought, as Ellenborough would have, that the treaty was blemished, because the amirs would not allow British residents to be stationed at Khairpur and Hyderabad. He had tried to convince the amirs that the British residents would help them to hold back the Sikhs, to be told that a defensive alliance would be of greater help.[3] As long as British agents were not to be stationed in Sind, British trade must rely upon the amirs' proving able to govern their territories more effectively than ever they had; at Mandavi Pottinger would be too far away to give any help. Naturally this most worried the government of Bombay, who were most interested in the success of trade on the Indus. 'Without some British officer on the spot to settle disputes,' said the governor in March, 'our traders will be exposed to endless difficulties.'[4]

Sir John Malcolm's wish to annex Sind continued to influence attitudes at Bombay during the administration between 1830 and 1834 of his successor, an Anglo-Irish nobleman, the earl of Clare, 'un grand seigneur anglais . . . homme de sens, d'un goût cultivé et de parfaites manières'.[5] Clare, the only man in India who might treat Bentinck as his equal, and whose letters to him are full of social and political gossip hot from London, was outspoken in his comments upon frontier policy. Although he admitted that Pottinger, in suggesting that the British should guarantee to defend Sind and the Talpura dynasty, which would turn a commercial treaty into a protectorate, had exceeded his instructions, Clare was just as eager to find some way to obtain political control. 'What barbarians the amirs are!' he told Bentinck. 'You really must adopt the course recommended by Ellenborough and tumble them.'[6]

[1] Aitchison, *Treaties*, vii. 37–8.
[2] Ibid., p. 40.
[3] Ggic to sc, 2 July 1832, I.O. L/PS/5/43.
[4] Clare to Bentinck, private, 10 Mar. 1832, Portland MSS. PwJf/646.
[5] Jacquemont to Dunoyer, 6 July 1832, *Jacquemont*, ii. 311.
[6] Clare to Bentinck, private, 8 Jan. 1832, Portland MSS. PwJf/626.

Clare shared Sir Charles Metcalfe's view of the situation beyond the North-West Frontier; but he wished to carry out the opposite policy. The obvious method of overawing the amirs, as Ellenborough had suggested, was joint threats from the governor-general and Ranjit Singh, as Clare could not believe 'the amirs will be so mad as to resist you both'. Because Ranjit would undoubtedly see even a commercial treaty as a symbol of British paramountcy, the government of India should realize, that paramount influence in Sind would depend upon similar influence at Lahore. Both states should be turned into protectorates, because, however restricted the connection, 'a blow up hereafter in either state will infallibly involve us in the quarrel'.

The object of placing at our command the resources of . . . [Sind] is no doubt very great [said Clare], but it is to me very questionable that we shall ever be able to do so by indirect means . . . [The treaty] will probably end in our semi-barbarous ally breaking it, and in our being obliged to take position [possession] of his country.[1]

Choosing not to would destroy British trade, and endanger their defence policy against Russia. Any connection with Sind, concluded Clare, in January 1832, 'must lead to our establishing a permanent influence from Lahore to the sea and if we do not . . . someone else will'.[2] Here is the language of Wellesley in 1798, except that Wellesley had not believed it.

Most Great Gamesmen were soldiers. By 1827 the government of India's preference for employing soldiers as diplomatists had become so marked, that the board of control told them not to appoint any more.[3] One exception was permitted: the strategic calculations underlying the expansion of trade were shown when the government of India continued to employ soldiers in the near east. Pottinger could open only the southern stretches of the Indus to British trade; the frontier north from Shikarpur came under the agent at Ludhiana, Captain Claude Wade. Wade, who in 1831 was thirty-seven, had seen no action since the campaign against the Pindaris in 1819, after which he had made his mark, like Alexander Burnes, because he could draw good maps. Map-making, as medicine, started many hopeful diplomatists on successful careers.

[1] Minute of Clare, 28 Apr. 1831, I.O. Bombay/SP/74, 18 May 1831, no. 89.
[2] Clare to Bentinck, private, 11 Jan. 1832, Portland MSS. PwJf/629.
[3] Wynn to Bentinck, 3 Oct. 1827, Portland MSS. PwJf/2369.

Late in December 1831, as Pottinger was about to set out for Hyderabad, Bentinck sent Wade to Ranjit Singh, to explain the negotiations and how opening the Punjab to similar trade would increase his revenues.[1] Wade's reception was not friendly, because Ranjit knew that the commercial treaties were Bentinck's way of putting into practice the principles they had agreed to at Rupar. Ranjit would have preferred Ellenborough's plan, to help the British, as he had in 1830, by threatening the amirs of Sind: then as a reward he might have been allowed to annex Shikarpur. He agreed not to oppose the negotiations with Sind, and to negotiate a similar treaty for the Punjab, only because his British connection helped him maintain his leadership of the Sikh Confederation. He was in a difficult position: the amirs of Sind wished to keep the British at a distance, Ranjit needed their connection, although he knew that these commercial developments might reduce its political value.[2]

Anglo-Indian diplomatists habitually exceeded their instructions. Wade, as exuberant as Burnes and as masterful as Pottinger, alarmed the Sikhs by asking for navigation rights on all five rivers of the Punjab. When Bentinck changed this to the Indus and to the Sutledge below Rupar, Ranjit Singh agreed. These were the two rivers that might be useful to the British, if Bentinck meant what he said: the Sutledge would connect the British North-West Frontier with the Arabian Sea, the Indus would provide a route to central Asia. British trade on the other three rivers of the Punjab was to be forbidden.[3] From the start Ranjit saw the British plan in political terms. Trade and the Englishmen who might follow it, even if they did not cause disturbance and stir up opposition amongst the Sikhs, would need protection: the stable balance of power sought by Bentinck must rest upon order. It was as obvious to Ranjit as to Metcalfe, Clare, and the amirs of Sind, that asking oriental monarchs to govern as well as rule would lead to collisions.[4]

In June 1832 Bentinck ratified Pottinger's treaties with the amirs of Sind; in September Wade was sent back to the Punjab, to negotiate similar treaties with Ranjit Singh and the nawab of

[1] Prinsep to Wade, 19 Dec. 1831, I.O. Bengal/SPC/365, 13 Jan. 1832, no. 5.
[2] Wade to Prinsep, 13 Feb. 1832, I.O. Bengal/SPC/365, 19 Mar. 1832, no. 10; Jacquemont to Tracy, 29 Mar. 1832, *Jacquemont*, ii. 266.
[3] Prinsep to Wade, 25 Feb. 1832, I.O. Bengal/SPC/365, 19 Mar. 1832, no. 11.
[4] Wade to Bentinck, private, 8 Feb. 1832, Portland MSS. PwJf/2165.

Bahawalpur, and to survey the river Sutledge.[1] Ranjit was sceptical, although he agreed in December to sign,[2] and would not help the amirs of Sind to oppose the British, by persuading the nawab of Bahawalpur to refuse. Ranjit's scepticism increased when the government of India produced a complicated *ad valorem* customs rate of 12 per cent on cloth and metals and 5 per cent on other goods. The revenue was to be divided between Ranjit, Bahawalpur, and Sind, but no limit was set to the additional revenue which might be raised by transit charges within each state. This invited the amirs of Sind to ruin the trade by excessive charges. If it were to flourish, the tariff would have to be renegotiated.

How Bentinck meant to apply the principles agreed with Ranjit Singh at Rupar was shown most clearly during Wade's negotiations with the nawab of Bahawalpur. Like the amirs of Sind, the nawab said that a defensive alliance, turning the British into the paramount power, would be the best way to stabilize the North-West Frontier. Wade replied that this was not necessary, because the Anglo-Sikh treaty of 1809 already obliged the British to protect the states on the left bank of the Sutledge.[3] The government of India were quick to correct this interpretation. The treaty, they told Wade, 'authorises us to protect them . . . but does not . . . impose any obligation on us . . . This distinction it is necessary to observe and maintain for a contrary supposition might at times prove very embarrassing.'[4] If the British were to extend so far southwards the territory on the left bank of the Sutledge covered by the treaty of 1809, they could not object to Ranjit's doing the same on the right bank, which would give him a better claim to Shikarpur. Bentinck would not promise to defend Bahawalpur or Sind. The frontiers of both states had been settled at Rupar: they were to be preserved, and order within them was to be increased, by the expansion of British trade.

Although the nawab failed to persuade Bentinck to promise to defend Bahawalpur, he could behave as if Bentinck had, by granting the concession the amirs of Sind had steadfastly refused. After the commercial treaty was signed in February 1833,[5]

---

[1] McNaghten to Wade, 19 Sept. 1832, I.O. Bengal/SPC/368, 1 Oct. 1832, no. 19.

[2] Aitchison, *Treaties*, ii. 240.

[3] Wade to Prinsep, 25 Feb. 1833 I.O. Bengal/SPC/378, 23 Apr. 1833, no. 21.

[4] Prinsep to Wade, 23 Apr. 1833, ibid., no. 26.

[5] Aitchison, *Treaties*, ii. 357.

Lieutenant Mackeson, who had gone with Wade on his voyage down river as a surveyor, was left behind as British resident at Mithankot, to watch over shipping and the payment of the tariff. By April, when Mackeson had completed the survey of the Sutledge, and Wade had returned overland to Ludhiana, however handicapped were the British, the Great Game in Asia, as Bentinck meant to play it, might begin. The first stage of the road to Bokhara was open.

Underlying the debate in the board of control and the government of India in 1830 and 1831, about the use to be made of trade for purposes of defence, was an awareness that British India, as a continental state, in which a foreign administration ruled over a discontented population, needed a strong military frontier to guard against the remote danger of invasion, and a stable political frontier between the European and Indian political systems, to guard against the dangers of rebellion and crippling expense likely to follow the unchecked expansion of Russia. In 1831 the British had neither. Ellenborough had planned to move the military frontier forward to the Indus, the line which everyone had agreed since 1798 an invading army must not be permitted to cross, but whereas others, Metcalfe, Wade, and the Ludhiana School of Indian defence, were content to use the Sikhs as Britain's necessary ally, both to defend British India against invasion and to provide a stable and peaceful North-West Frontier beyond the Sutledge, Ellenborough, like Malcolm, Wade, and the Bombay School, wanted to turn Sind, and when the right moment came, the Punjab, into protectorates, in order in emergencies to set up forward military posts beyond the Khyber Pass and the Bolan Pass, and to defend British India in alliance with a united Afghanistan. To the west of Afghanistan the political frontier was to be constructed, in a chain of buffer states separating the European and Indian political systems, stretching from Bokhara through Khiva and Teheran to Erzerum, in which the British, with paramount influence at Baghdad as well as at Kabul, could use the expansion of trade to forestall the spread of Russian influence.

Both Ellenborough and utilitarian and evangelical Utopians like Trevelyan and Grant meant to rely on trade and settled frontiers to win the Great Game in Asia, but not in the same way. Ellenborough was forced to rely on trade in areas either too politically sensitive or too geographically remote to make possible the immediate exercise of power; as someone who preferred to rely on power, he doubted whether trade could do what must be asked of it. Trevelyan and Grant, expecting trade, by reforming upon a liberal and English model the social and economic structure of all the states between the Sutledge and the Caspian, to create both a satisfactory military frontier and a barrier between the European and Indian political systems, had no such doubts. The notion that changes in habits, the organization of labour, and the distribution of wealth, need not be accompanied by unrest or violence was peculiarly British; politically peculiarly liberal, and intellectually peculiarly whig.

Lord William Bentinck, as always, appeared more cautious, and was more perceptive. If the reforms to follow the expansion of trade should destroy Sind and the Punjab as states, the security of British India against invasion would be bought at the cost of unrest along the North-West Frontier, possibly compelling the government of India, as Metcalfe had predicted, to pursue forward policies, acceptable to Ellenborough, but which Bentinck as well as Grant had hoped to avoid. By 1833, whereas Trevelyan and Grant hoped to rely on trade, by turning feudal nomads into settled farmers, to create a stable balance of power in the near east, Bentinck saw, that although trade might forestall the expansion of Russia in Turkestan, which could also be checked by pressure at St. Petersburg, trade could not create a stable North-West Frontier; it could work only if one already existed. In 1833 and 1834, therefore, Bentinck tried to apply in Afghanistan, and assumed the board of control would apply in Persia, the principle he had explained to Ranjit Singh at Rupar.

Because the British admitted that they meant to benefit the inhabitants of the near-eastern states more than their rulers, the hostility of Asiatic princes towards British proposals for the expansion of trade is easily understood. Sind and the Punjab would serve British purposes merely by existing as territorial states with agreed frontiers. Within them the British aimed at social revolution, and asked the amirs and Ranjit Singh to protect the instrument of their own destruction. Ellenborough had feared that the upheaval caused by Russian intervention would have dangerous repercussions in India: Grant and Trevelyan feared no similar danger from British intervention. Nobody would want to turn himself into a Russian, but Afghans, Turcomans, and Sikhs, were waiting, eager, and must be given the chance, to become Englishmen. One must sympathize also with the British. However bigoted, they were consistent; they were as busily denouncing their own government for pernicious interference with the laws of nature. 'The general rule', observed Bentinck's mentor, Jeremy Bentham, 'is that *nothing* ought to be done or attempted by Government . . . The request which agriculture, manufactures and commerce present to government is as modest and reasonable as that which Diogenes made to Alexander, "*Stand out* of my Sunshine"!'[1]

[1] 'Manual of Political Economy', *Bentham*, iii. 33.

V

The Road to Bokhara 1833-1834

A man cannot be too careful
in the choice of his enemies.

LORD HENRY WOTTON,
The Picture of Dorian Gray,
Chapter I

THE BRITISH HAVE always had a healthy respect for ignorance;
ruling India as if it were uninhabited, partitioning Africa along
rivers or lines of longitude, and playing the Great Game in Asia
without maps. As late as the congress of Berlin Disraeli's were
hopelessly inaccurate. Few Englishmen thought this mattered,
and equally few Russians: Gorchakoff was as ignorant as Disraeli.
Lord Grenville, as foreign secretary, was one who apparently
objected. When Henry Dundas in 1798 wanted to hire Russian
troops to defend British India from Bonaparte in Egypt, Grenville
could not see what Russia was 'to do, whom she is to attack, nor
where her army is to march', and demanded of his colleague 'a
calculation of distances, a reference to history, and a consideration
of the present state of the intervening countries'.[1] One is not to be
deceived by this. Despite his hobby collecting maps, Grenville
knew nothing about the near east, and did not want to learn. The
greatest diplomatic historian writing today—let us flatter the man
whose name will occur to Englishmen—in an epigram by which
everyone will identify him, once said that the greatest masters of
statecraft are men who do not know what they are doing. By this
exacting standard Ellenborough succeeded, but Lord William
Bentinck was to fail.

The master's epigram is, as always, amusing, and, as sometimes,
shrewd. Ellenborough and Sir John Malcolm as romantic imperialists, and Charles Grant and Charles Trevelyan as Utopian

[1] Grenville to Dundas, 20 Sept. 1798, Historical Manuscripts Commission:
The Manuscripts of J. B. Fortescue, Esq., Preserved at Dropmore (London,
1892–1929), iv. 319.

utilitarians, had been equally confident they could solve British India's defence and frontier problems without having to choose between them, because they were certain the available information confirmed their assumptions. 'So little evidence goes such a long way', said Lord Morley, 'when once your mind is made up, and circumstances call for decision and Act.'[1] From opposite premisses both movements agreed that after 1829 decisive action must be taken: the utilitarians redefined the Great Game, they were just as eager to play. Lord William Bentinck, forced to listen to the plangent chorus of Sir Charles Metcalfe, became more and more hesitant. His willingness in 1834 to open Sind and the Punjab to British trade on terms offensive to the utilitarians, showed that the government of India knew they might have carefully to choose between defence and frontier policy, depending on who was the enemy and where was the greater threat.

II

The Great Game in Asia exposed the young men who played to irresistible temptation. Ambassadors at St. Petersburg or members of council, at the pinnacle of their careers, might scoff at the suggestion that Britain might have to resist Russia in Asia, but youngsters in the Indian Army, longing for action and promotion, were bound to confirm and not inquire, to suggest what should be done not whether it was necessary. A forward policy might lead, as it led for Alexander Burnes, to an invitation to Fort William or to an introduction to the governor-general, the surest way to promotion despite regulations stipulating that it depended on seniority. If nothing were to be done, one went back up country and was soon forgotten. How unhappy John Malcolm had been in 1801, when he returned from parading around Persia to his post as assistant to the resident at Mysore.

While Henry Pottinger in Sind and Claude Wade in the Punjab had been opening the Indus route to central Asia, and trying to create a stable balance of power along the British North-West Frontier, to suit Grant's and Trevelyan's utilitarian ideas about the role of buffer states, Lord William Bentinck had also been making more detailed inquiries about the chance of increasing the sales of

---

[1] Morley to Minto, private, 9 Nov. 1906, Lord Morley, *Recollections* (London, 1917), ii. 190.

British goods.[1] The inquiry was the famous journey of Alexander Burnes to Bokhara, so famous that it sometimes seems nobody else had begun to play the Great Game. Burnes left Ludhiana on 2 January 1832, and travelling by way of Lahore and Peshawar reached Kabul in May. From Kabul he went north through Balkh and on 27 June he reached Bokhara. By the middle of September he was at Meshed, later in the autumn at Teheran, and early in December sailed from Bushire. Having narrowly missed instructions from the board of control to go straight to London, on 18 January 1833 he came back to India at Bombay. His story of 'anthropophogi and of men whose heads do grow beneath their shoulders', as Lord Clare described it,[2] has always and deservedly been popular; its rivals are *Kim* and *The Lotus and the Wind*.

On his travels two things impressed Burnes, the river Oxus and the amir of Kabul, Dost Mahomet Khan: the first might be an opportunity or a danger, the second British India's best defence. Since the previous year Burnes had changed his mind about the likely invasion routes from Turkestan. Because, except for the last fifty miles of marshy delta, the Oxus was navigable from Kunduz to the Aral Sea, the Russians might turn the Hindu Kush, not at Herat as Conolly had predicted, but by marching farther eastwards towards Chitral, and be at Peshawar in two campaigns. The best defence would be to advance the army on the North-West Frontier to the Indus, and instead of setting up the forward posts of which Lacy Evans and Ellenborough had talked, to ally with Dost Mahomet. Swift's rule would be obeyed, and European diplomatic practice, as the British practised diplomacy, exported to Asia, by this reliance on Afghanistan as the ally chosen to defend British India.

Conolly, who saw Herat as the strategically vital point, had recommended an alliance with the Sadozai Kamran Khan. Burnes had met two previous Sadozai amirs, Zeman Shah and Shah Shuja, at Ludhiana, who had not impressed him. He preferred to support their opponents, the Barakzai. Because his own hardships in the desert had convinced Burnes that the Russians would not try to march to Herat from the Oxus or Bokhara, whether they marched through Persia by way of Herat to Kandahar, or up the

---

[1] Ggic to sc, 19 Nov. 1831, I.O. L/PS/5/42. Metcalfe, naturally, was opposed to this. Memorandum by Metcalfe, 2 June 1833, Kaye, *Metcalfe Papers*, p. 218.

[2] Clare to Bentinck, private, 9 Mar. 1833, Portland MSS. PwJf/709.

Oxus towards Chitral, Dost Mahomet at Kabul was poised to attack them in the flank. Burnes understood the obstacle to an alliance with Dost Mahomet, his bitter quarrel with Ranjit Singh. If the British wanted to increase their exports in Turkestan, this would have to be surmounted. Both Dost Mahomet and Ranjit Singh controlled vital stretches of the road to Bokhara. If, when Ranjit died, the Dost should capture Peshawar from his brother, who ruled it as a protectorate of the Sikhs, he might control the whole road beyond Sind;[1] his alliance would be indispensable. While Ranjit lived, as Ellenborough and Malcolm had feared, peace along the North-West Frontier and security from invasion seemed to depend upon contradictory policies.

In May 1833 Burnes did not repeat his mistake two years earlier of planning a defensive instead of an offensive strategy; he had learned the difference between Malcolm and Trevelyan, between Ellenborough and Grant. If the Russians could use the Oxus as the last in a chain of rivers, likely to enable them always to ship heavy goods to Turkestan more easily than the British could move them across the Hindu Kush, the British had an equivalent advantage: their products were superior, particularly their cloth.

A more extended exportation of British goods into these countries [said Burnes in May 1833], in particular of white cloths, muslins, and woollens . . . would have the immediate effect of driving the Russians from that branch of commerce . . . The transport of merchandise by the route of Caboul costs little; and, if Russia navigates the Volga, the greatest of the European rivers, Britain can command like facilities, by two more grand and equally navigable streams, the Ganges and the Indus.[2]

Britain's superior manufactures were symbols of her greater virtue, and cotton was the zenith of her achievement; her booming exports of cotton in the 1830s could surely be relied upon to bring her victory in the Great Game in Asia.

This vision was sufficiently Utopian to suit the utilitarians. Burnes added two suggestions for bringing it about. The British should start an annual fair on their North-West Frontier, to

---

[1] 'A Military Memoir [by Alexander Burnes] on the Countries between Russia and India', [5] May 1833, I.O. Bengal/SPC/374, 6 June 1833, no. 4. See also 'Memorandum [by Capt. A. Gerard] upon Some of the Countries North of the River Sutledge', Portland MSS. PwJf/2682.

[2] Burnes, *Travels to Bokhara*, ii. 443.

challenge the fairs at Leipzig and Nishi-Novgorod, and an Englishman should be stationed as a commercial resident at Kabul. Both were meant to draw trade south eastwards towards the Indus and Ganges basins. Unfortunately, to travel openly in Afghanistan and Turkestan was risky for an Englishman. James Baillie Fraser, who was as perceptive as Burnes, travelling in Khorassan ten years earlier, had quickly realized that his

> situation, placed among savage tribes, who cared nothing for Europeans, . . . differed widely from what it had been . . . at Teheran, where the name of Englishman is known and respected; and that it would not answer here to stickle for the same punctilious attention, which it is proper to demand there for the sake of national dignity.[1]

The resident at Kabul might find himself in a quandary, as in need of protection as able to provide it. This salutary warning was ignored by Bentinck, who was willing in the summer of 1833 to appoint a resident at Kabul. Unless Turcomans and Afghans were eager for everything British, the Great Game in Asia could not be played.

The resident's duties were to be few. Bentinck wanted to avoid an alliance with the Afghan states, because the Persian Connection had proved that alliances led straight to subsidies, to demands for help not offers of it. Alliances were also unnecessary: the British only needed the chance to sell their manufactures. Sometimes Bentinck could be as vague as Ellenborough. Whereas alliances would not strengthen British India against invasion, the appearance of one with Kabul might help to preserve peace along the North-West Frontier, by overawing the stubborn amirs of Sind.[2] Bentinck, under the influence of Trevelyan, wanted to open all three states beyond the North-West Frontier to British traders; he was equally determined that they should respect each other's frontiers, and so create a stable balance of power.

Utilitarians believed in free trade, because they believed in equal opportunity; they attacked barriers to trade abroad as they attacked privilege at home. If others did not wish to trade, the benefits must be explained to them: if they did not understand— but Grant and Trevelyan were certain they would. In commenting upon Burnes's proposals in June 1833, Charles Metcalfe, of course,

---

[1] Fraser, *Journey into Khorasan*, p. 475.
[2] Minute of Bentinck, 1 June 1833, I.O. L/PS/5/125, 6 June 1833, no. 13.

did not agree. Any attempt at persuasion might lead to threats; as long as the purpose of trading was political influence, separating commercial from political functions could not be done. Dost Mahomet had already asked for British help against his rivals in Afghanistan;[1] if the British seemed to be responding, they would alarm not only the amirs of Sind but also Ranjit Singh. Instead of preserving peace along the North-West Frontier, by creating a stable balance of power amongst the Afghan and Indus states, the probable outcome would be war. Past experience had shown that as long as the British had to choose between the Afghans and Sikhs, they must choose the Sikhs: as long as Ranjit lived they would have to choose. His death, said Metcalfe, would be the proper moment to negotiate with Dost Mahomet, when he and the British might both move forward their frontiers to the Indus.[2]

Bentinck knew that the board of control had decided the previous year, that 'our course is to meet Russian agents, Russian commerce, and Russian influence, on all routes approaching India'.[3] Such a course could be charted only at London. The government of India could not act in Afghanistan, nor in Persia and Baghdad, even if ostensibly on behalf of trade, in any way likely to complicate Anglo-Russian relations. India's most important interest was to preserve peace along her North-West Frontier. To prevent an anti-Russian policy from disturbing the peace, Bentinck wanted it carried out in more accessible areas, where the British might more easily send for reinforcements. When in June 1833 he let Metcalfe persuade him to ask the board of control whether he should set up a residency at Kabul,[4] Bentinck meant that the Great Game in Asia should partly be shifted westwards back to Persia, where the board of control must safeguard British India from the probable effects of the expansion

[1] Wade to McNaghten, 17 Jan. 1833, I.O. Bengal/SPC/372, 19 Mar. 1833, no. 40; Mohan Lal, *Life of the Amir Dost Mahomet Khan* (London, 1846), i. 149–50.
[2] Minute of Metcalfe, 2 June 1833, I.O. L/PS/5/125, 6 June 1833, no. 15.
[3] Memorandum by Henry Ellis, 14 June 1832, I.O. Persia/48.
[4] Ggic to sc, 6 June 1833, I.O. L/PS/5/8. The board, where Ellenborough was briefly back in office, refused to decide, lest it restrict the government of India's initiative, an initiative of which Bentinck wished to be rid. Sc to ggic, 7 Mar. 1835, I.O. L/PS/5/545. Perhaps this was because the project was opposed by the chairman of the East India Company, the first vigorous chairman in years, who supported Metcalfe. Sir J. W. Kaye, *Life and Correspondence of Henry St. George Tucker* (London, 1854), pp. 495–6.

of Russian influence, by preventing the capture by Persia of Herat. The board, where Henry Ellis was imposing on Charles Grant views remarkably similar to Bentinck's, was trying to do so, and was also trying, by explaining the reasons why British India might be endangered by the ambitions of Mahomet Ali, either because he occupied Baghdad, or because he drove the sultan into dependence upon Russia, to persuade the foreign office to help.

A bitter feud between Sadozai and Barakzai had divided Afghanistan for thirty years. During the Napoleonic Wars this had suited the British. A group of trivial and warring principalities were the best available defence against French invasion: if one joined Napoleon, the others would attack him.[1] As a barrier to Russian expansion, and to provide a larger and more stable outlet for their manufactures, the British would have preferred Afghanistan united. Conolly would have united it under Kamran Khan at Herat, Burnes under Dost Mahomet at Kabul: Bentinck chose the third candidate, the exiled Sadozai, Shah Shuja. The British, who had always been anxious not to meddle in Afghanistan, were attracted to Shah Shuja by his offer to work on their behalf. Bentinck's support of the shah in 1833 was one of the oddest incidents in the Great Game in Asia; because he failed to regain his throne, it appears to have been a mistake. Had he succeeded, it would have opened the second stretch of the road to Bokhara, and might have created the stable balance of power beyond the British North-West Frontier Bentinck, Grant, and Ellenborough, had all been seeking.

For years, Shah Shuja, a pensioner of the British since 1809, had been asking them to help him recover his throne. They had as regularly refused. As long as Metcalfe was at Delhi, he refused to give the shah arms and subsidies, but made no attempt to dissuade him: civil war in Afghanistan was no concern of the British.[2] In May 1832 Shuja asked again. Remembering their alarm at General Gardane's mission to Persia, and Mountstuart Elphinstone's costly embassy to Peshawar in 1808, he expected the British to be equally frightened by the rumours of a Russo-Persian expedition against

[1] For the political history of Afghanistan and the effects of the dynastic struggles upon the British see B. Varma, *English East India Company and the Afghans, 1757–1800* (Calcutta, 1968); Sir W. K. Fraser-Tytler, *Afghanistan: A Study*, (London, 1950), chs. 2–3; and Bilgrami, *Afghanistan and British India*, chs. 2–3.

[2] Cd to ggic, 10 Nov. 1830, I.O. L/PS/6/244; ggic to cd, 9 Oct. 1830, I.O. L/PS/6/42.

Herat. He was mistaken. Bentinck replied that the British government

> religiously abstains from intermeddling with the affairs of its neighbours, when this can be avoided.
>
> Your Majesty [he said] is, of course, master of his own actions, but to afford you assistance for the purpose which you have in contemplation, would not consist with that neutrality which on such occasions is the rule of guidance adopted by the British government.[1]

This policy, commented the East India Company in February 1833 was 'highly proper'.[2] Their commendation was badly timed. In December 1832 Bentinck seemed to change his mind. Shuja had once in 1818 been given an advance on his pension; Bentinck now gave him a second, 16,000 rupees which was a third of his annual income, and also allowed him to buy arms duty free at Delhi.[3] Shuja reacted by immediately trying to negotiate an alliance with Ranjit Singh, then by invading Sind in preparation for marching to Kandahar.

Shah Shuja had been supported by Captain Wade, who, like many meeting the exiled prince at Ludhiana, but unlike Burnes, overestimated the strength of his character. According to Wade, the amirs of Sind would help the expedition and the Afghans welcome it. 'A quick succession of revolutions', he had said in May, 'has exhausted the wealth of the country; the people are tired of the wars and factions which have distracted it, and generally look to the re-establishment of their former government as the only chance which presents itself of ensuring tranquillity.'[4] One wonders whether this argument had been meant to tap Bentinck's utilitarianism: apparently supporting Shah Shuja might both unify Afghanistan, and create the order necessary for expanding British trade and for stabilizing the balance of power beyond the North-West Frontier. Arthur Conolly, preoccupied with the defence of India against Russia, had worried about who ruled at Herat; Bentinck, preoccupied with preserving peace along the frontier, worried more about who ruled at Kandahar and

---

[1] Wade to McNaghten, 11 May 1832, McNaghten to Wade, 16 May 1832, with encl., I.O. L/PS/5/122, 2 July 1832, nos. 69–70.

[2] Cd to ggic, 6 Feb. 1833, I.O. L/PS/6/245.

[3] McNaghten to Wade, 13 Dec. 1832, I.O. Bengal/SPC/371, 21 Jan. 1833, no. 2.

[4] Wade to McNaghten, 11 May 1832, I.O. L/PS/5/122, 2 July 1832, no. 69.

Kabul. Shuja had a second advantage over his nephew Kamran Khan. Anglo-Indian foreign policy was supposed to be cheap: Shuja asked for no subsidy, only for the money he was owed.

Lord William Bentinck was neither excitable nor a fool. The court of directors later criticized his policy as a breach of neu-trality,[1] but Bentinck thought that this was one occasion on which the government of India ought to take steps beyond the frontier, because the gain might be enormous. The British, hoping to cross from Peshawar to Kunduz more easily than the Russians could cross from the Caspian Sea to Khiva, dreamt of steamers laden with ironmongery and cotton goods, travelling up the Indus from Tatta to Peshawar, and of sail boats travelling down the Oxus from Kunduz to the Aral Sea. Between them stood the Khyber Pass and the Hindu Kush. To sustain this dream, unity and calm were needed in Afghanistan; more important to Bentinck, they were also needed to create a stable balance of power beyond the North-West Frontier. Should Shah Shuja recover his throne, the British would have an ally, strong enough to encourage their trade and open the road to Bokhara, but not strong enough to disturb the peace by attacks on Sind and the Punjab.

That this was the British aim was made clear to Ranjit Singh, when he tried to grab Shikarpur as a reward for permitting Shah Shuja to advance.

The British government [said Bentinck in March 1833] apprehended no injury either to its own interests or to those of his Highness (which are considered identical) from any movement which may be made by Shah Shuja. Should his Highness, however, be of different opinion he is of course at liberty to adopt any measure which he may deem necessary for his own security, though . . . to advance upon Shikarpur, the country of a friendly power, merely on the ground of the Shah having proceeded thither would hardly seem to be reconcilable with those principles by which the conduct of nations is ordinarily governed.[2]

Here stated clearly were three rules of the Great Game in Asia. British allies should realize that common interests and the pursuit of their own interests both meant following British advice; their diplomatic practice should apply European principles; and they

---

[1] Cd to ggic, 18 Mar. 1835, I.O. L/PS/6/248.

[2] McNaghten to Fraser 5 Mar. 1833, I.O. Bengal/SPC/372, 5 Mar. 1833, no. 18.

should aim to maintain a balance of power, by giving up wars of conquest beyond the British North-West Frontier.

One change was to be permitted, indeed welcomed. Ranjit Singh refused Shikarpur, asked for Peshawar, to which, by the terms of their alliance ratified during the summer of 1833, Shah Shuja agreed.[1] As soon as the frontier between the two states was settled, the British would be freed from their dilemma of having to choose between the Afghans and the Sikhs. Instead the amirs of Sind would be forced to choose. Either they would pay homage to Shah Shuja, or they would become more friendly towards the British.[2] The latter was so much the more sensible, that to the British the choice was obvious; but either choice would lead to better terms for trading up the Indus. With the friendship of Shah Shuja at Kabul, Ranjit Singh at Lahore, and the amirs at Hyderabad, all three could be treated as the territorial states, with agreed frontiers, on which a stable balance of power depended, and could be expected similarly to treat one another. Their inhabitants might then be turned by the purchase of cotton goods into the copies of Englishmen Trevelyan and Grant were confident they were anxious to become.

The government of India, following the tenets of the Ludhiana School of Indian defence, having thus created, by the introduction of steamers on the Ganges, the Sutledge, and the Indus, a satisfactory military frontier, at which in an emergency to defeat an invading army, might also maintain peace along the frontier by means of the balance of power between Afghanistan, Sind, the Sikh Confederation, and British India, to be stabilized partly by trade, and partly by the efforts being made by the board of control and the foreign office to maintain a similar balance of power between Britain and Russia, in an attempt, by turning Turkey and Persia into buffer states whose frontiers had been equally clearly delineated, to create a barrier between the European and Indian political systems.

---

[1] The treaty was drawn up in March 1833 and ratified in August. There is an account of the negotiations in Wade to McNaghten, 17 June 1834, I.O. India/SP/1, 19 Aug. 1834, no. 1.

[2] For this reason, Pottinger was told to suspend his negotiations with the amirs until the result of their quarrel with Shah Shuja was known. McNaghten to Pottinger, 5 Mar. 1834, I.O. Bengal/SPC/380, 10 Apr. 1834, no. 24.

III

The scenario was magnificent; unfortunately the actors rehearsed the wrong script. In his perceptive study of the Malagasies, O. Mannoni argued that colonizers are arrested in childhood; unable to deal with other people, they live in a world full of fantasies. Mannoni illustrated his argument from *Robinson Crusoe*; Crusoe being the colonizer, the others on his island the colonized, whose characteristics showed how a colonizer needs to be able to control their behaviour.[1] A distinguished colleague of mine, John Franklin Hutchinson, scoffs at this comparison. Crusoe's island, he says, was a house of correction, Crusoe's life an illustration of the belief that poverty could be eliminated, not by reforming society, but by correcting the failings of the poor. Because colonizers and houses of correction both have to deal with vagrancy, there need be no contradiction here. Eighteenth-century society was threatened with social and colonizers with psychological collapse, unless the behaviour of everyone was adjusted to their view of the world. The Great Game in Asia was a magnificent daydream. Like any other, it was often interrupted.

Shah Shuja spent most of 1833 at Shikarpur collecting troops and raising money in Sind, where his demands on the amirs so angered them, that they tried to drive him out. In January 1834 he defeated them at the battle of Rohri, and later claimed as a result to have made them pay homage. Emboldened by his victory, he then crossed the Bolan Pass to attack Dost Mahomet's brothers, who ruled at Kandahar. Although this city had traditionally been a Sadozai stronghold, in July Shuja was narrowly defeated by Dost Mahomet, who came down from Kabul to help his brothers, and fled again to India.[2] 'It has always been the bane of the shah', said one well-informed observer, 'to be deficient in the actual crisis of his battles, and to be more expert in providing for his personal safety than for victory.'[3] The two men to benefit from the escapade were Dost Mahomet and Ranjit Singh. The Dost had made himself more powerful in Afghanistan, but his family had lost Pesh-

---

[1] O. Mannoni, *Prospero and Caliban: The Psychology of Colonization* (New York, 1956), part ii, ch. 2.

[2] Wade to McNaghten, 1 Feb. 1834, I.O. Bengal/SPC/380, 10 Apr. 1834, no. 17; same to same, 25 July 1834, I.O. India/SP/1, 9 Sept. 1834, no. 11; Mohan Lal, *Dost Mahomet*, i. 160–7.

[3] C. Masson, *Narrative of Various Journeys* (London, 1842–3), iii. 260.

awar; Ranjit had used Shah Shuja as the British used their allies in Europe, to fight at the decisive point of battle while he won easy prizes on the periphery.

Because Shah Shuja had boasted of British support, every precedent proved that the British should have suffered by his defeat. In tribute to Bentinck's acumen, good luck, or high rank, while he was playing the Great Game what appeared set-backs were virtually successes. All Bentinck had offered Shah Shuja was money; which had been permitted by Ellenborough, and not forbidden by Grant. Bentinck had been just as careful to avoid political entanglement: should Shah Shuja prove too feeble to set up a stable government in Afghanistan, a connection with him would have no value. Many of Dost Mahomet's friends had tried to find out how close was the connection between the shah and the government of India, hinting that if Bentinck asked them they would change sides. 'In order to avoid committing the Government to any opinion,' said Wade in May, 'I have thought the most prudent course for me to adopt was to be silent.'[1] At Bombay Lord Clare spoke out, telling Dost Mahomet's agent that the rumours of Bentinck's plans to conquer Afghanistan were false.[2] This may have hurt Shah Shuja, but made certain his failure would not hurt the British. Dost Mahomet's quarrel with them began later.

Bentinck's achievement was to shift the danger point on the North-West Frontier from Shikarpur north to Peshawar. Ranjit Singh would have to station a large army there to hold off Dost Mahomet's counter-attacks; to threaten Sind as well might be beyond him. Sind and the Punjab might now become the territorial states Bentinck hoped they would, and might yet be followed by Afghanistan. In the north, Ranjit Singh had no plans for farther expansion. If Dost Mahomet should withdraw beyond the Khyber Pass, and turn his ambitions, as the British hoped, towards Herat, British India would have created a stable balance of power along their North-West Frontier: if he refused, it would be less unsettled than previously, because of its greater depth. The British had always had to choose between the Afghans and the Sikhs; they had always chosen the Sikhs. They still had reason to: Shah Shuja had fought for Ranjit Singh, and Ranjit Singh for them.

[1] Wade to McNaghten, 17 May 1834, I.O. India/SP/1, 24 June 1834, no. 26.
[2] Clare to Bentinck, private, 16 Feb. 1834, Portland MSS. PwJf/760.

Bentinck knew, as Ellenborough had, that every defence policy should carry with it a frontier policy: if the two were not co-ordinated, the British would have to choose between them. Ellenborough had put defence before the frontier; as a conservative he assumed that British India would always be slightly unsettled, because always ruled by force. Bentinck, who wanted an interval of tranquillity, to give Indians a chance to copy Englishmen, put the maintenance of peace along the frontier before the creation of a barrier to Russian expansion. He showed this by his attitude to the civil wars in Afghanistan.

As far as this government is concerned [Wade was told] it is matter of indifference whether the Barakzai or Sadozai families hold paramount sway in Afghanistan, but under any circumstances it is of real import-ance to us that our national character should stand well with the peoples of the countries beyond the Indus, and that we should maintain such a cordial and friendly intercourse with the leading men as will pre-dispose them to espouse our interests in case of the future occurrence of a state of affairs which may demand a more decided course of policy.[1]

Here Bentinck pointed to the choice that had bedevilled Anglo-Indian diplomacy since Minto had sent Mountstuart Elphinstone to negotiate an alliance with Shah Shuja in 1808. As long as Afghanistan remained turbulent and divided, it was no certain barrier to invasion, nor to the expansion of Russian influence. Similarly, as long as the British would not take part in Afghan politics, they could not expect in moments of crisis to choose one of the Afghan princes, and expect him to fight for them, unless they were willing to fight for him against his rivals. If they did, they entangled themselves in local squabbles in which they had no interest, and endangered the peace of their North-West Frontier: to maintain an influence in Afghanistan would mean either com-pensating the Sikhs at the expense of their Afghan ally, or turning Sind into a protectorate to provide a safe route to Afghanistan from Bombay.[2] The alternative to this forward policy was to fight at the Indus, when the Sikhs might prove as demanding as the

[1] McNaghten to Wade, 19 Mar. 1833, I.O. Bengal/SPC/372, 19 Mar. 1833, no. 1.
[2] See S. R. Bakshi, *British Diplomacy and Administration in India, 1807–13* (New Delhi, 1970), pp. 36–52; and E. Ingram, 'The Defence of British India—II: A Further Examination of the Mission of Mountstuart Elphinstone to Kabul', *Journal of Indian History*, xlix (1971), 57–78.

Afghans, or to shift the campaign to Europe and the foreign office, in an attempt to forestall the danger. Bentinck planned to; he also hoped that given enough time to create a stable balance of power along the North-West Frontier, according to the principle set out at Rupar in 1831, British India would never have to fight.

The contradiction between defence and frontier policy became more obvious, when Bentinck tried in the autumn of 1833 to take advantage of the amirs' quarrel with Shah Shuja, by renegotiating the commercial treaty with Sind. The tariff on the Indus and Sutledge had proved too high; the trade unprofitable; Indian merchants less eager to use the route than had been expected. Wade had been sure the trade southwards from the Punjab would be immediately diverted to the Sutledge from the traditional caravan route through Malwa, from which the states of Rajputana not Bahawalpur and Sind earned revenue, and that Indians would rush to boats from camels.[1] In 1833, on his voyage to Bahawalpur, he had persuaded merchants at Ludhiana to ship a trial cargo. They found the Sutledge easily navigable, and in the markets at Bahawalpur and Mithankot, under the eye of a British agent behind whom stood the eager nawab, they sold at a good price. As soon as they entered the stretch of the Indus belonging to the amirs of Sind, in order to try the market at Shikarpur, 'the merchants were received with the utmost distrust'. Although the amirs of Sind had agreed to the trade, everyone knew they would do all they could to thwart it.[2]

The following year Wade persuaded the merchants at Ludhiana to try again, issuing passports all the way to Bombay to test the policy of the amirs.

We cannot now recede without loss of reputation . . . [Wade warned Bentinck in December]. The native merchants, by whom the navigation is likely in the first instance to be opened, scarcely think that we are in earnest, and Ranjit Singh and Bahawal Khan begin to suppose that our plans are to be defeated by the obstinacy of the Sindians.[3]

The government of India had already decided that if, as Pottinger

[1] Wade to McNaghten, 27 Feb. 1832, I.O. Bengal/SPC/366, 9 Apr. 1832, no. 71.
[2] Mackeson to Wade, 4 Oct. 1833, I.O. Bengal/SPC/379, 29 Jan. 1834, no. 5; Wade to McNaghten, 27 Mar. 1833, ibid. 373, 28 Apr. 1833, no. 28.
[3] Wade to McNaghten, 13 Dec. 1833, I.O. Bengal/SPC/379, 29 Jan. 1834, no. 4.

had suggested in July, the tariff were changed to a toll, to be levied on each vessel and not on the value of its contents, the Sikhs, who traded heavily in shawls from Kashmir, would find the new route more profitable, while the amirs of Sind would have fewer opportunities to interrupt it.[1]

According to Sir Charles Metcalfe, the new trade-route was leading to the quarrel with the amirs he had predicted. Bentinck has asked the board of control to decide whether he should try to place a commercial resident at Kabul; he was certain one would be needed at Hyderabad, to see that the toll was levied fairly. Metcalfe in June alone opposed the appointment, with his usual arguments, illustrated by Pottinger's troubles with the amirs. Because the British did not control the Indus, they could not protect the trade. The amirs would not protect it, the British might demand greater control: both would lead to war, and the commercial treaties would turn into a protectorate.[2] Bentinck hoped to prevent this by separating defence from frontier policy; by drawing a line between foreign and local trade. The amirs might co-operate, were they convinced that the treaty would regulate only the toll to be levied on vessels travelling through Sind to Afghanistan and the Punjab. 'The moment goods are landed at Tatta, Hyderabad, or anywhere else in their dominions', said Bentinck in October, 'they will become subject to the local duties levied by the amirs.'[3]

Throughout 1833 the amirs were busy with Shah Shuja and a family crisis. In October the last of the older generation died. The amirs, all cousins when they had once all been brothers, who had previously thought unity would be the best defence against the British, now decided that as none of them was to be looked up to as the leader, the British should negotiate with them individually. Pottinger refused: in return they refused to negotiate.[4]

The anarchy and want of authority which prevailed during the lifetime of the late Murad Ali Khan has increased one hundredfold since his death [said Pottinger in December] . . . They are very much inclined if we will permit them to drop all intercourse with us . . . I think the

[1] 'Remarks on the Indus Tariff by H[enry] Pottinger', 4 July 1833, I.O. Bengal/SPC/377, 10 Oct. 1833, no. 13.

[2] Minute of Metcalfe, 2 June 1833, I.O. L/PS/5/125, 6 June 1833, no. 15.

[3] McNaghten to Pottinger, 10 Oct. 1833, I.O. Bengal/SPC/377, 10 Oct. 1833, no. 14.

[4] Pottinger to McNaghten, 30 June 1834, I.O. India/SP/1, 18 July 1834, no. 2.

sooner this neutral state of warfare . . . in which we may be said to be engaged with Sind, [is] brought to a close the better.[1]

When the amirs proved Pottinger's point by holding up vessels from Mandavi, he suggested in February 1834, that Bentinck should place an embargo against Sindian vessels at Indian ports, and threaten force: 'The only method that now remains of bringing them to a proper sense of their relative station, and of turning the late treaty to account, is to *dictate* on that and all other topics, and not to attempt to *persuade*, for . . . our forbearance is invariably ascribed . . . to dread of their power.'[2] The only alternative Pottinger could think of was to try to divide the amirs into quarrelling factions, some of whom would then agree to co-operate.

Bentinck turned down both suggestions as too provocative: they would lead, as Metcalfe had predicted, straight to a protectorate. Security against invasion and the expansion of Russian influence could not be purchased at the cost of frontier wars, whereas if peace along the North-West Frontier depended upon preserving the balance of power between Sind, the Punjab, and ideally Afghanistan, sovereignty in Sind must be located. In the autumn of 1834 Bentinck grew impatient. The amirs were to be offered a time limit. Then, if they still refused to renegotiate the commercial treaty, they should be threatened.[3] This proved unnecessary: on 2 July 1834 they had agreed to introduce the toll.[4]

The negotiations with Sind were followed by similar revisions, in August with the nawab of Bahawalpur, and in November with Ranjit Singh.[5] Wade postponed the negotiations with Ranjit until the amirs and the nawab had signed, because he sensed that the Sikhs distrusted the scheme as acutely as the Sindians. Ranjit consented for the reason he had before: as he grew older and more frail, friendly relations with the British were an essential prop to his power. The same might be said of them. Bentinck had realized, that if he aimed to maintain peace along the North-West Frontier, by treating Britain's neighbours as independent states with agreed

[1] Pottinger to Clare, private, 9 Dec. 1833, F.O. 705/23.
[2] Pottinger to Bentinck, confidential, 8 Feb. 1834, Portland MSS. PwJf/1885; Huttenback, *British Relations with Sind*, pp. 26-9.
[3] McNaghten to Pottinger, 5 Sept. 1834, I.O. India/SP/1, 24 Sept. 1834, no. 2.
[4] Aitchison, *Treaties*, vi. 41.
[5] Ibid. ii. 361, 244; B. K. Hasrat, *Anglo-Sikh Relations, 1799-1849* (Hoshiapur, 1968), pp. 128-32.

frontiers, they must be treated differently: whereas stability in Sind would depend upon permitting the amirs to continue ruling in relative disorder, stability in the Punjab depended upon buttressing Ranjit Singh.

To operate the new system proved complicated. The toll was fixed at 570 rupees a vessel from Rupar to the Arabian Gulf, of which 240 were to be paid to the amirs, 106 to the nawab, and 224 to Ranjit Singh. The toll was to be levied at three places: Harike where the Sutledge joins the Beas, Mithankot where the Sutledge joins the Indus, and Tatta at the head of the Indus delta. Vessels travelling upstream paid 240 rupees at Tatta to the amirs, the remainder due the nawab and Ranjit Singh at Mithankot; those travelling downstream paid their dues to the nawab and Ranjit at Harike and to the amirs of Sind at Tatta. The system was supervised by Lieutenant Mackeson at Mithankot, who worked under Wade, as did an Indian agent stationed at Harike, and by two Indian agents stationed at Hyderabad and Tatta, who worked under Pottinger.

The British were not satisfied with these arrangements. Although Ranjit Singh had reminded them in September to station an Englishman at Mithankot, because at the border of the three states 'frequent collisions [would arise] which would be prevented if an agent were stationed somewhere in that direction to arbitrate disputes',[1] the amirs of Sind would not allow Bentinck to station a second Englishman at Hyderabad. Pottinger had suggested as a compromise, that a British agent should visit Sind whenever disputes arose, and assumed he might stay there as long as Bentinck wished.[2] This turned out to be a mistake, because there was never enough trade to cause disputes. One must understand what angered the amirs of Sind. The British asked Ranjit Singh, who was always bragging about his friendship with them, only to allow trade along his frontiers, and they did not ask to station a British resident at Lahore. The amirs, echoing their spokesman, Sir Charles Metcalfe, feared to suffer for their strategic situation: to utilitarians Sind was more important than the Punjab. Because the amirs controlled the Indus and the Bolan Pass, unless Pottinger were held firmly in check, British policy in Sind would be drawn beyond Grant's instructions to act on Ellenborough's, and the

---

[1] Wade to McNaghten, 5 Sept. 1834, I.O. India/SP/1, 2 Dec. 1834, no. 6.
[2] Pottinger to McNaghten, 30 June 1834, I.O. India/SP/1, 18 July 1834, no. 2.

Ludhiana School would return the initiative in the Great Game in Asia to the Bombay School of Indian defence.

IV

The right have the advantage over the left of seeing the world as it is. Perhaps this is unfortunate, perhaps the world should be changed into Utopia, but, until it is, they will remain untroubled by the disappointments befalling the likes of Trevelyan and Grant. Instead, like Ellenborough and before him Henry Dundas, they suffer from nightmares. The terms of the commercial treaties showed that Metcalfe had been right, Grant and Trevelyan wrong: the natives had turned down British offers of enlightenment and progress. The British might trade through Sind and the Punjab to Afghanistan, and the first stage of the road to Bokhara was open, but, unless the Turcomans should prove as malleable as Conolly and Burnes had said, trade would do less than diplomacy in Europe and Turkey to defend British India from the effects of Russian expansion. Trade had already proved unable without help to create a stable balance of power along the North-West Frontier. The amirs of Sind and Ranjit Singh, who had allowed the British to trade through their territories but not with them, had agreed only under pressure; any further concessions would have to be extracted by force. As Metcalfe said, the danger of free trade as a doctrine was its rapid degeneration into demands for freedom to trade. This, he repeated to Bentinck's successor in 1836, led to a 'plunge into a labyrinth of interference from which I fear we may never be able to extricate ourselves'.[1]

As long as Bentinck and Metcalfe were in India, this temptation was resisted. Renegotiating the commercial treaties, and changing the tariff to a toll, did nothing. The route was unsafe, because between Harike and Mithankot it was jungle; anyone who slept ashore might be attacked by bandits, who had only to cross the river to be safe in foreign territory. In 1833 Wade had persuaded the Sikhs and Bahawalpur to make arrangements jointly to police the Sutledge,[2] but nothing could be done to improve conditions in Sind. By 1836 the scheme was admitted to have failed.[3]

---

[1] Metcalfe to Auckland, 15 Oct. 1836, Add. MSS. 37689, fo. 39.
[2] Wade to McNaghten, 5 Feb. 1833, I.O. Bengal/SPC/373, 23 Apr. 1833. no. 17.
[3] Minute of Auckland, 29 Aug. 1836, I.O. India/SP/5, 5 Sept. 1836, no. 11.

Bentinck, during the negotiations, had been prepared for failure. He had chosen to surrender defence to frontier policy, to make the choice Grant and Trevelyan had thought would not be necessary, and Ellenborough would not have made, preferring the other choice, because he soon sensed that Trevelyan had been mistaken. In playing the Great Game in Asia Bentinck showed himself although eager for adventure, perhaps because of his earlier disappointments at Madras and Sicily, more and more cautious by temperament. His defence policy was as hesitant as his steps towards the reforms for which he is famous, and for the same reason: reforms were not worth trouble, particularly in the army, which might endanger the government of India.[1]

Although Bentinck knew that the amirs had negotiated under duress, and wondered in February 1834, whether the 'inevitable consequence [would be] the employment of military force and eventually perhaps the occupation of the country to establish the free and uninterrupted navigation of the Indus', he was careful not to tell this to Pottinger. Bentinck would demand the right to trade up the Indus, because 'the use of this river is the natural right of all the states bordering upon the river itself and of its tributary streams';[2] he was equally careful to avoid victories in principle likely in practice to jeopardize British interests.

By 1834 Bentinck had learned that a choice had to be made beyond the North-West Frontier between demanding order or stability; and that the amirs, as they had always said, did not govern Sind and therefore could not protect British trade. Because Bentinck did not believe Wellesley's and Malcolm's dictum, as echoed by Wade, that the British must push forward or risk defeat, he drew back in Sind; he turned down Pottinger's suggestion that the British might be able to control the amirs of Sind, were Shah Shuja treated as their overlord. In supporting the shah

---

[1] For Bentinck's attitude to the burning of widows see N. G. Cassels, 'Bentinck: Humanitarian and Imperialist—the Abolition of Suttee', *Journal of British Studies*, v (1965–6), 77–87. This contrasts strongly with the influence of Trevelyan over Bentinck's education policy, which was less likely to cause discontent amongst the troops. See K. A. Ballhatchet, 'The Home Government and Bentinck's Educational Policy', *Historical Journal*, x (1952), 225–9. Ballhatchet criticized the assumption that the impetus came from England made in P. Spear, 'Bentinck and Education', *Cambridge Historical Journal*, v (1938), 78–101.

[2] Bentinck to Pottinger, private, 5 Feb. 1834, [not sent], Portland MSS. PwJf/1887.

Bentinck had hoped to create a stable balance of power between three independent states beyond the North-West Frontier which might preserve peace. Encouraging Afghanistan to bring forward defunct claims to paramountcy over Sind would have caused as much trouble as Ranjit Singh's behaviour before the conference at Rupar, and might have led to collisions between the two.

Histories of the First Afghan War treat Sir Charles Metcalfe as a prophet crying in the wilderness, like Vansittart in the 1930s boring everyone with his cries against the Nazis. This is not true. Bentinck's policy owed as much to Metcalfe as to Trevelyan; his most difficult job was trying to reconcile the two. Because Metcalfe stoutly resisted both Ellenborough's and Grant's instructions, Bentinck had drawn a line between a commercial defence policy, the expansion of trade with Afghanistan and Bokhara in an attempt to forestall the expansion of Russia, and a political frontier policy, delineating the borders of the Punjab, Sind, and ideally Afghanistan. The defence policy based on trade needed order; the frontier policy based on territorial restraint needed stability. When Bentinck realized that the two did not necessarily go hand in hand, he worked for stability in preference to order. Trade was supposed to be able to manage without help, and should be left to prove its worth.

Bentinck had tried to reconcile Trevelyan's faith in the ability of trade to impose order by causing social revolution, turning Baluchis, Sikhs, and Pathans, into Englishmen, with his own policy of preserving a balance of power between the frontier states in the interests of maintaining peace. This caused an argument as it would in Turkey about the meaning of reform; whether the British hoped to cause social change to increase order, or to buttress existing social and political structures to maintain stability. Metcalfe thought the argument academic, because neither disorder nor instability beyond the frontier need worry the British. Bentinck agreed that this was true in Sind, weak and isolated beyond the Great Indian Desert. It was not true in the Punjab: the Sikhs who were neighbours and strong, were a valuable connection as long as Ranjit Singh could maintain order, and so peace along the frontier. Metcalfe assumed he would. If he conquered Sind, he would strengthen the North-West Frontier and provide greater opportunities and security than the amirs of Sind for British trade; when he died, the British, if they wished, could prevent future disturbance by annexing the Punjab, and moving forward their North-West Frontier to the Indus.[1]

Bentinck had steered carefully between Bombay's eagerness to annex Sind, which Malcolm, Pottinger, and Clare, had all demanded, and Metcalfe's demand that the amirs, as they asked, should be left alone. Bentinck would not ignore what was happening in Sind, because he believed it unsafe to ignore events in the Punjab; he agreed under pressure from Metcalfe to ignore Afghanistan, which would have proved easier had Dost Mahomet, as Shah Shuja had agreed to do, given up Peshawar. Unless the borders of Sind and the Punjab were settled, the restlessness of the Sikhs would cause trouble on the North-West Frontier. The commercial treaties showed that the British, as Bentinck had warned Ranjit Singh at Rupar, would treat Sind and the Punjab as independent and territorial states with agreed frontiers, and expected them to behave the same way to one another; that trade was permitted through and not within their territory meant that the policy would buttress the existing structures not cause social change. There was one qualification: neither the Sikhs nor the amirs were to be permitted policies of expansion. Instead of causing change, the policy forbade it; and would succeed only if the situation remained static, or by limited intervention meant to keep it so.

This was Bentinck's compromise between Trevelyan and Metcalfe. Trade might be given its chance well beyond the frontier, where it might or might not create unrest without endangering British India; on the North-West Frontier, where keeping the peace was more important, Bentinck wanted to preserve a temporary situation which he and Metcalfe both thought suited British interests. According to Bentinck, unless the British had done something to preserve it, the Sikhs would have destroyed it by invading Sind, and would have created a state beyond the frontier too powerful and aggressive for comfort.

Bentinck's anxiety to create a stable balance of power along the North-West Frontier was the result of his attitude to the Indian Army. As well as being evangelical, Bentinck was a soldier, and like so many generals of his time despised both Indian Army officers and their native troops. The wars in Nepal and Burma had convinced him that the sepoys, lacking moral fibre as much as physical strength, could not be relied upon to stand up to Euro-

[1] Metcalfe to Auckland, 15 Oct. 1836, Add. MSS. 37689, fo. 39.

peans or Afghans and Sikhs. Increasing the number of British officers was not a solution: 'Any number of European officers you could allot them could not make the sepoys equal to European troops.'[1] Expanding the irregular cavalry, although these were the troops best suited to the defence of the North-West Frontier, was only partly one. The solution, so Bentinck said, was steamers.[2] The British showed most clearly at Baghdad what they expected of steamers, but Bentinck hoped a flotilla on the Ganges might defend the North-West Frontier by quickly moving reinforcements forward from Allahabad. A similar flotilla on the Indus might operate from Bombay.

This explains what most irritated Bentinck with the amirs of Sind. The stipulation of the treaty he most disliked, and which he thought might one day lead to a quarrel and the threat of force, was not their refusal to admit a British resident, nor their refusal to allow British traders to live in Sind, but their insistence that British vessels should not be armed. If Sind were to remain an independent state, the British must be given the right to send through their troops. Otherwise they could not preserve the existing and satisfactory relations between their neighbours, by defending India on the Indus, should it ever prove necessary, from the threat of foreign invasion.

Bentinck chose to work for a stable balance of power along the frontier, because he believed that the defence of British India against Russia was better left to others, the board of control and the foreign office at London. Annexing Sind and if necessary the Punjab might, by moving forward to the Indus, have solved the problem of finding a satisfactory and stable military frontier; it had been Ellenborough's solution. It would not help to hold back Russia in central Asia. The British could not as easily control Afghanistan and Bokhara, and beyond the Indus there was no natural frontier nearer than the Paropmisus between Bamian and Herat, only a choice between forward military posts. If demanding

---

[1] Bentinck to Salmond, 16 July 1832, Portland MSS. PwJf/2040.

[2] Minute of Bentinck, 13 Mar. 1835, I.O. India/MP/35/12, 13 Mar. 1835, no. 11. Parts of this minute are printed in Boulger, *Bentinck*, pp. 193-9. 'Our principal securities,' Bentinck had said before sailing to India, '. . . are, first, our European force, and secondly, the establishment of European officers with the native army.' Memorandum by Bentinck, [1827], Portland MSS. PwJf/2584. For this reason Bentinck, like Wellesley, believed that units of the British army should always number one-third of the troops in India.

freedom to trade caused trouble, or nobody would buy, the British would have to choose between a military offensive in Asia, and defending British India by manipulating the balance of power in Europe; if the Afghans and Turcomans would not defend British India, the Turks and Austrians might, and the board of control and the foreign office should be left to persuade them. For this reason Bentinck had persistently refused to set out British policy in Persia and Baghdad.

By 1834 it was becoming clear how far Wellesley and Ellenborough had been right in assuming, that Britain and British India could not be separated, and treated as Castlereagh and Canning, echoed by Webster and Temperley, had tried to treat them, as two states carrying out when necessary two foreign policies, but only as one state, in two places, made up of halves radically different in geographical and strategic location, as well as political and constitutional type. The best evidence was the determination of evangelicals and utilitarians to avoid the problems likely to follow from admitting this, by turning India, and ideally the near-eastern states, into a copy of the new Britain of which they dreamt. The government of India could create a satisfactory military frontier at the Indus, and could try to maintain a stable balance of power amongst the states immediately beyond their North-West Frontier, but, because they could not construct a barrier between the European and Indian political systems, unless the utilitarians and evangelicals could succeed in transforming India into a copy of Britain, they could not prevent Russia from using her expansion in the near east as a lever against Britain in Europe. Upon the security of British India depended the security of Great Britain.

In 1831 and 1832 the board of control worked in Persia and at Baghdad, and in 1833 and 1834 the foreign office worked at Cairo, Constantinople, and on the Euphrates, to create, by restraining Daud Pasha at Baghdad, Abbas Mirza in Persia, and Mahomet Ali in Syria, conditions in the near east able to compensate British India for lacking the defensive strength Britain drew from the navy and the Channel, and to give her, although a continental state, the advantages of a peripheral one, secure against others if having difficulty in threatening them. As a result the British looked in the near east for the prerequisite of their power in Europe, firstly for an ally with an army in a good strategic position, who could be expected in any issue affecting their interest to be equally interested and on the same side; secondly for a way to maintain a stable balance of power, based as they understood the Vienna Settlement upon a fair division of territory, by the creation of an Asiatic Burgundian Circle, buttressed by an Asiatic Holy Alliance. If a crescent of buffer states with agreed frontiers could be created between Bokhara and Constantinople, as a barrier between the European and Indian political systems, the British could preserve peace amongst the states immediately behind it, and immediately beyond their North-West Frontier, while at the same time strengthening their regimes, by forbidding all changes likely to lead to war, and, as far as it proved possible, forestall unrest and demands for change by expanding their trade. Bentinck treated Ranjit Singh as Metternich treated the king of Naples, which leaves one wondering what the British had meant by their support of Spanish and Italian nationalism during the Napoleonic Wars.

Whereas Ellenborough would have created a stable North-West Frontier by turning the Punjab, Sind, and ideally Afghanistan, into protectorates, Bentinck, like Henry Ellis working simultaneously at the board of control, hoped to obtain the same degree of control by drawing lines on maps. Between 1832 and 1834, as the board of control and the foreign office set out to persuade Russia to treat Turkey and Persia as territories with agreed frontiers drawn on maps in 1828 and 1829 after the treaties of Turkmanchay and Adrianople, they were trying to apply throughout the near east the principle accepted by Ranjit Singh at Rupar. If the south-east frontier of Russia were fixed, the North-West Frontier of British India were fixed, and the British could delineate the frontiers of all the states between them, they might create a stable balance of power in the near east, and help to keep it stable by the limited expansion of a limited trade, however commercially hazardous and unrewarding. This could not be done, unless Sind were freed of claims to sovereignty from the Afghans and threats from Ranjit Singh; Afghanistan could be united; the eastern frontier of Persia could be drawn to the west of Herat; Turkey, whatever should be happening inside it, were treated as one state, ruled by the sultan, with whom alone the European powers should deal; and, most controversially, a ring should be drawn around Turkestan, within which the sale of ironmongery and cotton goods might forestall Russian intervention, by ending the slave trade and so contributing, as utilitarians and evangelicals dreamt, to the abandonment of nomadic for settled habits.

The beginning of the Great Game in Asia coincided with the end of an era in the history of British India. For forty years since Cornwallis had introduced his great reforms, two movements had struggled for supremacy in India, and had won alternate victories.[1] Malcolm and sometimes Metcalfe stood for the romantic imperialist view that India, bizarre, turbulent, and irreligious, as it might appear to Englishmen, should be cherished for its antiquity and infinite variety. This view was challenged in India, as in England, by the Utopianism of utilitarians, whose stern morality and love for justice were shown in their energetic search for converts; everyone should be similar, and ideally similar to Englishmen. To bring this about sometimes led to foreign and defence policies more aggressive than those of the men who thought of the Raj as a military conquest. Perhaps this is not surprising. Disciplined Victorians depended upon fantasies to prevent stress. One was the Great Game in Asia.

[1] The best account is in Bearce, *British Attitudes to India*.

VI

The Great Concession at Baghdad
1828-1832

Still eyes look coldly upon me,
Cold voices whisper and say—
'He is crazed with the spell of far Arabia,
They have stolen his wits away'.

WALTER DE LA MARE,
Arabia

ON HIS MARCH eastwards from the conquest of Egypt, early in
the autumn of 331 B.C. Alexander the Great, having reached the
banks of the Euphrates at Thapsacus, and been permitted by the
Persian army to cross unopposed, went on to victory at Arbela over
Darius Codomanus. Darius, who is reported to have mobilized
an army of more than a million men, had awaited Alexander on a
plain near the ruins of Nineveh, because he was relying for victory
upon his cavalry. Two thousand years later, classically educated
Englishmen, remembering his defeat, compared it to the defeat of
Crassus by the Parthians at Carrhae. They were puzzled that
Darius had not used his cavalry earlier, to harass Alexander on the
march, and to stop him from crossing the Euphrates. 'If the
passage of the Euphrates had been properly guarded,' the resident
at Baghdad told the British government in 1802, 'Darius might
have been saved.'[1] Over the history of British India these two
battles cast long shadows. Bonaparte and Nicholas I were not to be
allowed to copy Alexander.

As famous as any outpost of the British empire was the residency at Baghdad in the middle of the nineteenth century, when
Sir Henry Rawlinson entertained with pomp and splendour a
procession of his countrymen, who took their leisured and sight-
seeing way overland from India. Baghdad may also claim the
symbolic use of gunboats. Despite the failure of the Euphrates

---

[1] Jones to Inglis, 29 Nov. 1802, Kentchurch Court MSS. 8380.

Expedition, the British flotilla of tiny steamers, stationed up river during the Second Mahomet Ali Crisis, were expected to overawe the Arabs as effectively as the Mediterranean fleet would Mahomet Ali. The president of the board of control had no doubt of their success: 'Navigation of the Tigris and Euphrates', he said, '. . . may silently obtain that influence with the Arabs which will more than half ensure our permanent predominance.'[1] At the beginning of the Great Game in Asia, steamers were the only rival to cotton goods.

However decayed since the splendours of the Abbasid Caliphate, Baghdad remained with Constantinople and Herat one of the three strategically most important places in the near east. Certainly the British thought so. Baghdad stood at the junction of their favourite routes to India; they sent their post through and their enemies. The East India Company had sent letters to India overland across Turkey since the middle of the seventeenth century. For eighty years, until after the opening of a British factory at Basra in 1723, they arrived no more quickly than by sea around the Cape of Good Hope. During the eighteenth century attempts were made to speed up the service; an alternative route through Egypt failed because it tended to draw the British into near-eastern politics.[2] By the end of the century, and before Bonaparte invaded Egypt, it had been set down as the guiding principle of British policy in the near east, to discourage all European interest, if necessary at the sacrifice of British trade, and to treat the area as empty and uncomfortable desert.

The overland post became more important during the French Revolutionary and Napoleonic Wars; in 1798 the British started a monthly service through Baghdad, to be met at Basra by a monthly pacquet from Bombay. The service regularly caused arguments because it was so expensive. If dispatches alone were sent, the East India Company complained of the cost; when private letters were added, the government of Bombay made a profit from the

---

[1] Hobhouse to Lynch, 26 Dec. 1838, I.O. H/839, p. 63.

[2] H. Furber, 'The Overland Route to India in the Seventeenth and Eighteenth Centuries', *Journal of Indian History*, xxix (1951), 105–21; Amin, *Persian Gulf*, pp. 57–67; D. Kimche, 'The Opening of the Red Sea to European Ships in the Late Eighteenth Century', *Middle Eastern Studies*, viii (1972), 63–71. Hoskins, *British Routes to India*, pp. 4, 21, misled many historians by his claim that the Baghdad route was introduced as an alternative to the Egyptian. The opposite is true.

fees, but the bigger packets had to be sent express, which raised the cost to the company.

Trials of steam navigation in the 1820s held out little hope of a reduction. Bombay wanted to send their post through Egypt, and only in emergencies through Baghdad: the annual emergency was the south-west monsoon, when the Persian Gulf was difficult and the Red Sea impossible to reach. Remembering Alexander's way back from India, in 1832 the governor of Bombay suggested, that during the south-west monsoon the post might be sent overland alongside the Persian Gulf. Instead, in the late 1830s, while the technical problems of steam navigation in the Red Sea were being overcome, a camel post through Syria, set up by the British consul-general, temporarily revived the importance of the direct route.[1]

The British sent their letters after Alexander, and expected their enemies to follow him. Napoleon had been expected to march overland from Egypt, later from Constantinople; the resident at Baghdad had offered, and had been expected, to bar his way. When the British turned their attention from the French to the Russians, although they knew of the Russian interest in Khiva, they were as frightened that the Russians, too, might prefer to march south to Baghdad and then turn east along the coast. During their wars with Persia and Turkey, Russian troops had been reported at Sulemanieh and near Mosul, where the Tigris became navigable to the Persian Gulf. Nobody could have stopped them, had they moved troops and stores overland from the Black Sea and floated them down on rafts. So claimed Thomas Love Peacock in 1829 in his first and most famous paper on steam. 'If the Russians choose to take it,' he said, 'the whole country from the Black Sea to the Persian Gulf is theirs (as, if we choose to occupy it, it is ours).'[2] The British believed that fortunately they had the chance to occupy it, and to establish a paramount influence in those areas away from the Russian frontier, because the Russian invasion of Persia had frightened the governor of Baghdad. British India, unlike Achaemenid Persia, should be defended on the

---

[1] The route through Egypt and the Red Sea was called the 'overland' route, and the route through Baghdad and the Persian Gulf the 'direct' route.

[2] 'Memorandum [by T. L. Peacock] Respecting the Application of Steam Navigation to the Internal and External Communications of India', 10 Nov. 1829, *Wellington*, vi. 330.

Tigris and Euphrates. At Baghdad the Great Game in Asia began, ahead even of Ellenborough's and Grant's attempt to advance up the Indus towards Afghanistan and Bokhara, in a magnificent if momentary dream of assimilating the Arabs.

II

In January 1828 the British resident at Basra, Major Robert Taylor, asked the government of Bombay whether he might move to Baghdad, to take over training the governor's army. The governor had been inviting Taylor for two years, but as long as Mountstuart Elphinstone was governor of Bombay, who thought the residency at Basra a waste of public money,[1] Taylor knew that he would not be allowed to go. He hoped that his reasons for wishing to go, backed by the Russian victories over Persia, would persuade Elphinstone's successor in 1828, Sir John Malcolm. The governor had employed Europeans to train his army for some time. This was dangerous for Britain, equally so for the governor. His troops were bad: frontier clashes in Kurdistan were always won by the Persians, and his power in the province rested upon playing the Arab tribes one against another.[2] If the government of India sent British officers to train the governor's troops, they might put an end to the unrest and increase their influence in the province. Taylor argued that the probability of a Russian advance into Kurdistan 'rendered the necessity of our aid, to them a matter of first importance, if not equally one of policy and expediency to us'. Given the weakness of Turkey, the governor had to be protected; and were Russia not to, Britain must. 'No time is to be lost in acceding to the entreaties of the pasha,' said Taylor. 'He may yet be strengthened and saved; but delay is ruin to his power.'[3]

Discussions of British policy in the near east in the early nineteenth century were always charmingly idiotic, because the world they took for granted did not exist; both the utilitarians and their rivals, the romantic imperialists, sensed that in planning to safeguard British India, by reform or by strategy, the fewer concessions made to local conditions the better. Because nobody tried harder to obey this rule than Sir John Malcolm, who hoped not

---

[1] Cd to gicB, 13 Jan. 1828, I.O. L/PS/6/474.
[2] J. B. Fraser, *Travels in Koordistan, Mesopotamia, etc.* (London, 1830), i. 268 ff.
[3] Taylor to gicB, 13 Jan. 1828, I.O. Bombay/SP/67, 9 Apr. 1828, no. 1.

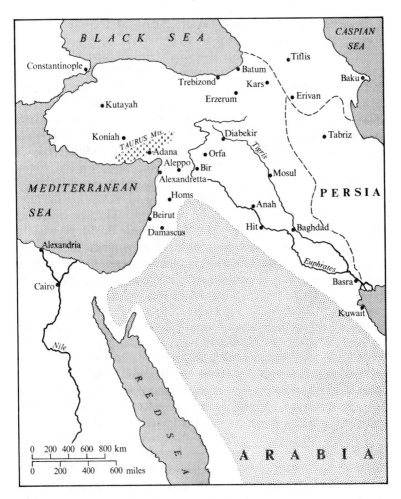

Syria and Baghdad

to change but to ignore local conditions, Taylor's request caused an argument in the government of Bombay in the spring of 1828, between them and the government of India, and between successive governments in England. Although so small a matter, the reasons for and against it illustrate many of the myths of the Great Game in Asia; and, as in Persia a year earlier, the decisions taken in 1831 turned into a policy for holding back both Nicholas I and Mahomet Ali.

Because Malcolm shared Taylor's alarm at the expansion of Russia, he had been shrewd to wait for Malcolm to take over from Elphinstone. Malcolm also shared Ellenborough's assumption that the British might be able to hold back Russia by pacifying Persia and Baghdad. When young he had believed the opposite; that turbulence was the best barrier to invasion. He had not changed his mind about this. Just as the Russians could invade Azerbaijan and Kurdistan from the Caucasus, the British could defend Fars and Baghdad from the Persian Gulf, and theoretically attack the Russians in the flank. Malcolm, however, like Ellenborough at the board of control and the British resident, Sir John Macdonald, at Tabriz, was learning that invasion was not the most serious threat: Russian expansion was. It would cause unending alarm in India, unending expense, and destroy British prestige.

Malcolm believed the impression of superiority to be vital. Unless the British lived up to their role, and set out to prove their superiority in the near east, they would find it more difficult to keep up in India. For too long the British had neglected Baghdad and Persia. Both were willing to be friendly, because natives preferred Englishmen of all Europeans, and, unlike in Turkestan, British capital already regulated the local trade. All Britain needed to increase her influence was a little of Malcolm's two favourites, energy and show. The governor of Baghdad, said Malcolm in March, should be given 'every encouragement and every means of resistance that it is in our power to afford without violating those relations in which we stand to other governments'.[1]

Taylor's suggestion aggravated a quarrel in the government of Bombay similar to the government of India's quarrel about North-West Frontier policy. Elphinstone and Malcolm had both been made governor after a career up country; their opponents, led firstly by Frances Warden and after he went home in 1828 by William Newnham, who had always worked in the secretariat, preferred to apply abstract utilitarian principle rather than base decisions upon detailed knowledge of local situations. The two groups quarrelled about whether they should try to change Indian habits. The symbolic issues, as elsewhere in India, were education and the burning of widows; trying to persuade Indians to stop burning widows, instead of compelling them as Warden wished, was one of Malcolm's attempts to conciliate the Indian aristocracy,

[1] Minute of Malcolm, 23 Mar. 1828, I.O. Bombay/SP/67, 9 Apr. 1828, no. 4.

whom he was anxious to preserve. This policy was more and more criticized from England for interfering with equality before the law; its justification was that attacks on privilege might provoke unrest.[1] Conservatives in India had always argued that the best way to conciliate Indians was not to meddle with them.

To utilitarians privilege was anathema. Education in English would give every Indian the chance to better himself, by adopting English habits. While Warden wished to end education in local languages, Elphinstone and Malcolm wished to keep it up in another attempt to conciliate the Brahmin castes. It was justified as Malcolm justified helping the governor of Baghdad: 'If it tends to the popularity and good name of Government, it is politic to support it.'[2] Warden and Newnham, who believed that popularity and respect would follow assimilation, demanded, what Sir Charles Metcalfe demanded in Bengal, thorough reform within India, while ignoring everything that happened beyond the frontier, where the British had no control.

According to Warden and Newnham, Malcolm's and Taylor's arguments were unsound. As a result of the battle of Navarino, the sultan might misunderstand the policy underlying a closer connection with Baghdad, and expect a protectorate to lead to a partition; as long as the government of Baghdad were so weak a connection could have no value. Bombay's traditional interest in the near east was trade; they had traditionally protected it in co-operation with the sultan of Muscat, and after he became too weak, by policing the Persian Gulf themselves. This was all they had tried, all they had thought necessary, and neither Persia nor Baghdad could do it for them. 'The history of our connection with Turkish Arabia from the earliest period', they reminded Malcolm in March, 'exhibited a series of insults and reconciliations without redeeming advantages, political or commercial, and the less we extend that connection the better.'[3] Taylor should be forbidden to move to Baghdad, and the governor-general should be asked whether a military mission should be sent to train the governor's troops.

---

[1] Ballhatchet, *Western India*, pp. 278, 289, 295, 301–11.
[2] Quoted in ibid., p. 295. For Elphinstone's views see also R. D. Choksey, *Mountstuart Elphinstone: The Indian Years, 1796–1827* (Bombay, 1971), pp. 381–96.
[3] Minute of Warden, 23 Mar. 1828, I.O. Bombay/SP/67, 9 Apr. 1828, no. 5. For details see Kelly, *Persian Gulf*, chs. 3, 6.

This outburst needs to be turned around. It meant that the residents at Baghdad and Basra had persistently gone beyond their instructions, and quarrelled with the governors of Baghdad and each other. Between 1798 and 1805 the first resident, Sir Harford Jones, had quarrelled with one governor after another, who had finally persuaded the Porte to have him recalled. His contemporary at Basra, Samuel Manesty, spent a year trying to ruin Jones at London, later swapped posts with the resident at Bushire, visiting Teheran as a self-styled ambassador, and finally went mad. Jones's successor, James Rich, at first did better, as was usual, but then quarrelled so seriously, even threatening to shell the governor's palace from the terrace of the residency, that the residency at Baghdad was closed in 1821, after Rich had died during a visit to Persia, and Basra was placed under the resident at Bushire.[1]

This rearrangement itself showed that Bombay believed residents were sent only to protect trade in the gulf. Taylor had been assistant to Rich since 1818, but, until he was made resident at Basra in 1822, had spent much of his time, firstly at Mohammarah then at Kuwait, to which the resident usually withdrew in times of trouble. He did not return until 1824. From a distance these quarrels seemed unnecessary. Apart from forwarding the post, a little trade or archaeology, and writing letters, the residents had nothing to do. Bored, they fidgeted. Malcolm's colleagues feared that given a chance, Taylor, like Jones and Manesty, would meddle 'in matters which it would have been better for the public interest they had taken no concern'.[2]

Malcolm was less afraid. He had when young regularly gone beyond his instructions, and was willing to risk Taylor's doing so, he told his colleagues, because, even if better relations with Baghdad would do no good, bad ones would be dangerous:[3] the governor might then ask for Russian help.[4] As a compromise, Taylor was told in March that he might visit Baghdad, but not live there; that he might show the governor how to make his army more efficient; and, that if the governor wanted them, Bombay would

---

[1] For an account of Rich see C. M. Alexander, *Baghdad in Bygone Days* (London, 1928); also Wolff, *Travels*, p. 202.

[2] Edmonstone to Warden, 21 Jan. 1806, I.O. Bombay/SPP/382/18, p. 4236.

[3] Second Minute of Malcolm, 23 Mar. 1828, I.O. Bombay/SP/67, 9 Apr. 1828, no. 6.

[4] As usual, Sir John Macdonald agreed with him. Macdonald to Malcolm, 17 June 1829, E.U.L. MSS. Dk/2/37, fo. 39.

allow him to buy steamers and weapons in India. The most important decision, whether to send British officers, was left to the governor-general.[1] Malcolm, no Utopian, doubted whether these other measures would either strengthen the government or cause unrest at Baghdad; they certainly need not frighten the sultan and the shah of Persia, nor complicate Britain's foreign relations, but they should convince the governor of Britain's friendliness.

Earl Amherst had already left Calcutta to return to England; his successor, Lord William Bentinck, had not arrived. When Malcolm's decision was sent to Bengal, the acting governor-general was the senior member of council, William Butterworth Bayley. Malcolm had reacted to Taylor's request as Wellesley or Hastings would have; Bayley reacted as Cornwallis or Sir John Shore would have, and he was backed up on the Bengal council by Sir Charles Metcalfe, who clashed with Malcolm about Baghdad for the reason they clashed about Sind. Metcalfe believed that the British should defend India in India: good government rather than prestige abroad would offset the effects of Russian expansion by making rebellion less likely. If the Russians should try to invade, the British would have to fight for themselves, if necessary in Europe; they should not expect the near-eastern states to fight for them, nor to defeat the Russians if they did. Nothing, in the opinion of Metcalfe and Bayley, could be gained by 'wasteful ineffective expenditure' in the near east.[2]

The government of India agreed with Malcolm's opponents at Bombay, that Britain's only interest in the near east was enough influence in the Persian Gulf to protect her trade. Because the governor of Baghdad, who would immediately assume that the British could be persuaded to support him whatever happened, would ignore all their advice, trying to use him to hem in Russia would prove ruinously expensive and cause trouble with the sultan and the shah. In India the British had learned this lesson early. Nobody pretended that their protectorates in India were independent, but it was impossible to remove the governor or to annex Baghdad. Although the government of India agreed in May to allow Taylor to visit Baghdad, and the governor to buy weapons at Bombay, if Bombay were certain he could pay for them, they

---

[1] Newnham to Taylor, 23 Mar. 1828, I.O. Bombay/SP/67, 9 Apr. 1828, no. 7.
[2] Acting ggic to gicB, 2 May 1828, I.O. Bombay/SP/68, 11 June 1828, no. 1.

refused to send British officers to train his army. By misleading the governor about the extent of Britain's interests at Baghdad, this would merely have increased not lessened the danger against which it was supposed to guard.

Malcolm protested that he had been misunderstood. He had meant the governor of Baghdad to pay for both the weapons and officers supplied, and would not allow his agent to buy on credit. Subsidies Malcolm claimed he had always criticized as a sign of weakness. This was true, although the government of India must have been amused to remember his extravagance on his two missions to Persia. In replying, Malcolm again argued that if the governor asked again, and promised to pay, it would be wise to agree, 'to keep him in good humour, and to aid those impressions we desire to make on his mind and that of his subjects of the sincerity of our friendship'.[1] This was exactly what the government of India feared. The only impression of friendship likely to mean anything to the governor would entangle the British in near-eastern politics, and the Persian Connection during the Napoleonic Wars had shown how costly this would be. To end the argument, in June the board of control were asked to decide what should be done.[2]

The timing suited Malcolm as well as Taylor. Malcolm's dispatches reached London in time to be answered by Ellenborough in October, one month after he became president of the board of control. Wellington was already a good friend of Malcolm; Ellenborough soon became one. His near-eastern policy was partly the result of corresponding with Malcolm, and he reorganized the British mission at Teheran to suit two of Malcolm's relatives who were members of it. Ellenborough proved as willing as Malcolm to help the governor. Taylor might move permanently to Baghdad, and, if he should, Bombay were to send someone to replace him at Basra; the governor might buy weapons at Bombay; and, if he would promise to pay them, British officers might be sent to train his army.[3] That the governor should pay was certain. Ellenborough, who hoped to persuade the East India Company to pay

[1] Minute of Malcolm, 11 June 1828, ibid., no. 2; gicB to acting ggic, 11 June 1828, ibid., no. 3.
[2] GicB to sc, 3 Apr. 1828, I.O. L/PS/5/325; acting ggic to sc, 6 June 1828, I.O. L/PS/5/5.
[3] Sc to gicB, 7 Nov. 1828, I.O. L/PS/5/573.

if necessary for the British officers being sent to Persia, knew they would never agree to pay for others at Baghdad. If the governor promised to pay, then failed, the officers would have to come home.

Before these instructions were sent, they were cancelled, because the board of control, who had afterwards heard from Bengal, knew they had missed their chance. It was not to be missed again: 'Pray jump at any offer of the pasha of Baghdad', Ellenborough told Malcolm the following year, 'if he comes at us again.' To Bayley's and Metcalfe's arguments Ellenborough paid no attention. Instead he explained in greater detail his four aims. Firstly, British officers would keep out others. Secondly, whether or not they would strengthen the governor, which was doubtful, the officers might supply useful information. Ellenborough had been shocked on taking office to find that nobody at London knew anything about the near east. 'What we ought to have is *Information*', he told Malcolm. 'The first, the second, and third thing a government ought always to have is *Information*.'[1]

As far as British officers could strengthen the government of Baghdad, by training the army, as the officers in Persia were to train the shah's, to act as a police force, they would strengthen Turkey. The government of India, therefore, were thirdly to adopt the new British policy towards Turkey: the battle of Navarino was to be treated as an unfortunate mistake. 'It is our interest both as an European and Asiatic state', they were told in December, 'that the Ottoman Porte should preserve all its present power . . . You will make the maintenance of the integrity of the Turkish dominions the unvaried object of your policy.' Finally, the more closely the British were known to be watching Baghdad, the less likely was Russia to work up frontier clashes similar to the ones she had used to justify her war with Persia. Even if the tsar's policies were what he claimed, said Ellenborough, 'it would be unreasonable to expect that generals commanding on a frontier so distant from the seat of government should not seek opportunities of gratifying their ambition'.[2] Ellenborough never trusted Paskievitch, the Russian commander in Georgia, but, as Taylor's activities at Baghdad were again to show, Englishmen were just as likely as Russians to disobey their orders.

[1] Ellenborough to Malcolm, private, 27 Oct. 1829, P.R.O. 30/9/4 pt. 5/2.
[2] Sc to ggic, 2 Dec. 1828, I.O. L/PS/5/543.

III

In May 1829 Major Taylor finally moved to Baghdad. The rest of the year, and all the following, he spent trying to strengthen the government. He was helped by his son, Lieutenant Robert Taylor of the Indian Army, who was at Baghdad on leave, and by an expatriate Englishman named Littlejohn. Between them they trained a regiment of 500 guards, for duty at the governor's palace, citadel, and treasury, and afterwards a brigade of cavalry and horse artillery, of whom the governor put Taylor in command. To expand the programme, instead of the officers the government of India had refused to send, the governor agreed to hire in England sixteen sergeants, who were to be paid British army pay, with quarters and rations, and eleven artificers, to be paid £150 a year and equivalent allowances.[1] Taylor, in turn, formed cadres that could be filled out to 5,000 infantry and a cavalry corps of 2,500 Georgians and Kurds.[2] To help him control these growing forces, and to raise his personal standing with the governor, Taylor asked Bombay to allow his son to stay with him, as his assistant and commander of his bodyguard. At the same time, to spread a complementary truth, an English missionary, the Revd. A. N. Groves, opened at Baghdad a school.

These administrative reforms at once brought political gains. As Ellenborough had hoped, the governor of Baghdad dismissed his foreign officers, and promised, as soon as the sergeants arrived, to have all his regular troops trained by Englishmen. 'Every improvement in contemplation, or progress,' said Taylor in July 1830, 'will be entrusted to the control of British talents and energies.'[3] 'There seems a strong impression in the mind of [Major Taylor]', added Groves, 'that things will not remain as they are now here; but that England will exert a much more decided influence than she has done in the government of these countries, as a counterpoise against Russia.'[4]

Their growing influence at Baghdad seemed to have given the

[1] Taylor to Auber, 14 July 1830, with encls. nos. 6–7, I.O. Persia/45. Taylor sent copies of his dispatches to the secretary to the government of Bombay to the secretary to the East India Company.

[2] 'Notes [by F. R. Chesney] on the Pashalic of Baghdad', as revised 28 Apr. 1832, Broadlands MSS. GL/CH/70.

[3] Taylor to Norris, 14 July 1830, I.O. Bombay/PP/387/6, 1 Dec. 1830, no. 11.

[4] A. N. Groves, *Journal . . . during a Journey from London to Baghdad . . . also . . . of some Months Residence at Baghdad* (London, 1831), p. 135.

British a chance to stop the spread of Russian influence. British agents in the near east could never resist the temptations of diplomacy; and Taylor believed he had an opportunity and ought to try to settle the Turco-Persian quarrel over Kurdistan. As soon as the defence of British India became less a military problem of defence against invasion, than the political problem of holding back Russia, the enmity between Turkey and Persia, once useful in stopping their both joining Britain's enemy, became equally annoying. In the Caucasus both had been more easily defeated, because less wary of Russia than of each other. Similarly, co-operation between them might be a good way to hold back Russia in future, and, even if they would not co-operate, quarrels in the buffer zone had to be prevented, lest they gave the Russians an opportunity to intervene.

Finding ways to hold back the Russians, and to prevent them from increasing their influence in Kurdistan, had become increasingly urgent during 1829, because, as Sir John Macdonald, who supported Taylor's arguments, said in July, owing to the weakness of the Turkish armies, the British must get ready for the capture by Russia of Erzerum. This fortress was the key to Asiatic Turkey: unless its capture were followed at once by peace negotiations, Turkey would fall apart. The capture of Erzerum, Macdonald told Malcolm,[1] 'will shake to the foundation the authority of the Grand Signior . . . [leave] all the countries east of the Euphrates open to the insults of the Russians, [and] lift them at once into the centre of Asia'. Although the governors of the eastern provinces of Turkey were asking for help from Persia, they would undoubtedly prefer the help of Britain.

The Kurdish chiefs of Sulemanieh had often tried to make themselves more independent by switching their allegiance between Baghdad and Persia. In 1821, during the Turco-Persian war, only the death of a Persian general stopped an army of Kurds and Persians from capturing Baghdad. The governor had tried to build up a rival party in Kurdistan, but failed, and had also offered Abbas Mirza, who refused it, an annual payment, if he would give up the connection. In 1830 a tribal feud in Kurdistan gave the governor a better chance. Two years earlier, Mahmud, the chief of Sulemanieh, had hired from Abbas Mirza, a patron of

[1] Macdonald to Malcolm, 16 and 27 July 1829, E.U.L. MSS. Dk/2/37, fos. 55, 61.

Kurds as well as a client of Europeans, a force of cavalry and two European officers to train a similar force of infantry. Mahmud's rapacity, and local dislike of European ideas, gave his brother Suleiman the chance to overthrow him: both brothers then asked Abbas Mirza for help. Abbas chose Suleiman, who agreed to pay 10,000 tomauns due in tribute; when Suleiman then failed to pay, Abbas changed back to Mahmud, and sent Persian troops to reinforce him. Although Suleiman fell back to Kirkuk, it was clear that Mahmud would be in trouble as soon as his Persian auxiliaries went home.[1] This gave the governor of Baghdad his chance.

Taylor suggested that because Mahmud, as the elder brother, would never defer to a Turk, instead of siding with him, as the governor had planned, he should side with Suleiman, if he would break all ties with Abbas Mirza. The reason for thus checking Persia, said Taylor, in the first statement of what soon became a commonplace, was 'the probability of all Persian conquests being used for the attainment of Russian ends'.[2] In case there should be similar opportunities to check Russia, Taylor asked Bombay in July for instructions with 'the amplest latitude and means for conciliating' all the inhabitants of Baghdad.[3]

This administrative and diplomatic empire building was overshadowed by the British enthusiasm for a technical novelty, steam navigation. As a way to spread British influence and check Russian influence in the near east, officers gave way to steamers, cavalry to gunboats. Seagoing steamers were still not proved, but river steamers were in use on major rivers and lakes throughout Europe; on the Indus and the Tigris–Euphrates they might back up or stand in for military missions. Everyone admired steamers. Utilitarians valued their help in changing native habits. Charles Trevelyan said they were the natural herald of railways in the war against superstition: the bishop of Calcutta said they were 'the universal agent and recipient; the highway cast through the wilderness of waters; the entrance and forerunner of all missions, education, commerce, agriculture, science, literature, policy, legislation, everything'.[4] Conservatives, as anxious not to meddle with natives,

---

[1] Draft by McNeill of Campbell to Swinton, 30 Sept. 1830, *McNeill*, p. 145.
[2] Taylor to Norris, 23 Dec. 1830, I.O. Bombay/PP/387/10, 21 Mar. 1831, no. 718.
[3] Taylor to Norris, 14 July 1830, I.O. Bombay/PP/387/6, 1 Dec. 1830, no. 11.
[4] 10 June 1833, *Bishop Wilson's Journal Letters*, ed. D. Wilson (London. 1863), p. 8.

were equally enthusiastic. Steamers would help to defend India by strengthening allied rulers of near-eastern states.

Steamers seemed to have three advantages over military missions. They would be freer from the embarrassments of working alongside natives. They would be more effective. The British knew the strength of near-eastern armies, or such strength as they had, to be their levies of irregular horse. These might harass an invader, as the Parthian mounted archers had harassed Crassus, but in peacetime they were a liability not an asset; the governor of Baghdad's difficulty in controlling the Kurds was later matched by the shah of Persia's with the Bakhtiari. The British might train a force of regular infantry strong enough to police the capital, as Taylor had, and to prevent civil war when their ally died: steamers might strengthen the government and spread British influence throughout Baghdad. Finally, if they carried letters, passengers, or goods, instead of being costly, steamers might earn money. They might combine a nineteenth-century middle-class Englishman's two loves, parsimony and profit.

The British, sensibly enough, were always looking for a way to defend British India from the sea. This had usually meant plans for an island fortress in the Persian Gulf, suggested by Malcolm for thirty years, but never built, partly because the shah of Persia would not have it, partly because none of the islands was suitable. In 1829, Ellenborough, frightened that the Russians might invade Baghdad, had wondered whether to occupy Kharrack in an attempt to blockade the Tigris.[1] However useful a defence against invasion, a fortress on Kharrack could not have checked the spread of Russian influence, unless the British could have turned the island into the central bazaar of Persia and Arabia. Malcolm had always planned to. He complained in 1829 that trade with Persia was still suffering from the unrest in Fars; moving the British residency from Bushire to Kharrack would protect English merchants from the 'weakness, or wickedness of the local government'.[2] Imperialists, unlike utilitarians, knew that trade needed protection.

Steamers apparently offered a way for a naval power to take the offensive, and, while retaining strategic mobility to operate far inland. The governor of Baghdad, who wanted to match Mahomet Ali's steamers on the Nile, had asked to buy some when in 1828

[1] 3 Sept. 1829, Ellenborough's *Diary*, ii. 92.
[2] Malcolm to Macdonald, 4 Feb. 1829, E.U.L. MSS. Dk/2/37, fo. 24.

he had asked for British officers. This request caused some confusion, because the board of control thought he wanted a navy in the Persian Gulf, which they had always frowned upon:[1] gulf rivalries were complicated enough. Malcolm, however, who had admirals for brothers, and who was a great supporter of steam, seized his chance in 1830 to send a former officer of the Bombay Marine named Bowater, to find out whether the Euphrates and Tigris could be sailed.

Bowater, echoed by Sir John Macdonald at Teheran,[2] decided that the Persian Gulf would be better than the Red Sea for a steamer service to England, because calms were its worst hazard, whereas the Red Sea was known for strong winds, uncharted reefs, and poor harbours. Furthermore, should the Euphrates prove navigable above Baghdad, the current would flow the right way, by speeding up news from England.[3] In July 1830, Bowater, with Major Taylor's brother and some friends, a party of six high-spirited Englishmen, as might often be found passing by when there was a chance of adventure in the near east, set out to discover whether steamers of two feet draught could sail down the Tigris from Mosul and the Euphrates from Bir. With great self-confidence the resident did not wait for their report. Like a miniature de Reuter, he had persuaded the governor to grant his brother a great concession for the reform of Baghdad.

It happened that the resident's brother James had been one of the two promoters of steam communication with England by way of the Red Sea. He had first tried to raise money for a voyage around the Cape; when he failed he turned to the Red Sea, and came up against his better-known and more successful rival, Thomas Waghorn. In the autumn of 1829 both left London hoping to reach India through Egypt in record time. Unfortunately, they met in the Red Sea, and had to travel to Bombay together. Taylor proposed with four steamers between London and Alexandria, and six between India and Suez, to introduce a monthly service. This would have to be subsidized from private subscriptions for two years, when it would start to make a profit.[4] Sir

---

[1] Sc to ggic, 2 Dec. 1828, I.O. L/PS/5/543.

[2] Macdonald to Ellenborough, 10 Mar. 1830, E.U.L. MSS. Dk/2/37, fo. 116.

[3] 'Remarks [by John Bowater] on the Persian Gulf and the Red Sea as Applicable to Steam Navigation', 17 June 1830, I.O. Persia/46.

[4] A. N. Groves, *Journal of a Residence at Baghdad during the Years 1830 and 1831* (London, 1832), pp. 9–11; Hoskins, *Routes to India*, pp. 116–21.

John Malcolm was not impressed, and refused to help Taylor. Many Anglo-Indian officials thought little of private enterprise; Malcolm wanted the steamer service to England to be run by the government, and even Bentinck, who hoped it might eventually be run privately, thought it could not start unless the government backed its capital or made use of it for the post.[1] Undaunted by these failures, Taylor set out for Baghdad in 1830 to try the third possible route, the Tigris and Euphrates.

Taylor's plans for reforming Baghdad were as ambitious as his plans for the Red Sea. By the terms of the concession, before Christmas 1831 he was to be running fortnightly sailings between Bir and Basra, paying the governor of Baghdad a toll of a guinea a passenger. In return the governor gave Taylor a monopoly for the first two years of the service, and promised to protect it. The resident warned his brother to arm his steamers, nevertheless, and suggested buying the co-operation of the most powerful Arab chiefs along the route. The governor was also persuaded that he would be strengthened, if more of the Arab tribes gave up their nomadic habits, so promised Taylor large areas of land, at a nominal rent, and to levy only a 3-per-cent duty on any exports, provided he started indigo and sugar plantations.[2]

Major Taylor's vision of Baghdad resembled Trevelyan's and Conolly's of Sind and Afghanistan: the 'moral plague of this vile government', as he described it,[3] was to be wiped out. Whether the Arabs would value the features of English life they were to be offered was a question not worth asking. Visionaries, knowing the answers, rarely trouble themselves with questions; nor do they have to choose. There was to be no conflict between strengthening the governor by reforming his army, and causing a social revolution by reforming trade and farming. Conflict between social change and political stability was prohibited by an Englishman's ingrained respect for property: wealth spread, it did not have to be spread by government. Nor would there be any conflict between local and imperial interests. The plan depended upon reopening a disused canal between the Tigris and Euphrates, and the resident was counting upon Bombay to help. Steam communication, he promised them in July, would prove 'in connection with the introduction

---

[1] For Bentinck and steam see Rosselli, *Bentinck*, pp. 285-92.
[2] Encls. nos. 7-8 in Taylor to Auber, 14 July 1830, I.O. Persia/45.
[3] Taylor to Norris, 7 Aug. 1830, I.O. Bombay/PP/387/6, 1 Dec. 1830, no. 15.

of British colonies and arts, a political lever of inestimable power and consequence, in repressing or meeting any hostile advance through the pashalic'.[1]

Here was to be a classic example of British power and skill helping one another. The resident would use Britain's growing influence over the governor of Baghdad, to keep out foreigners, and to hold him to his agreement; as farming and trade flourished they would increase order in Baghdad, the governor's dependence upon the British, and as a result the security of British India. Sadly, the surveying party went up the Tigris to Mosul, but before James Taylor could go on to England to raise capital and form his company, or Bowater come down the Euphrates, they were ambushed, and three of them, one of whom was James Taylor, were killed. Baghdad was too like Sind. As Metcalfe would have assumed, any attempt to increase British influence and hold back Russia by expanding trade and investment was bound at best to fail, at worst to lead to collisions and the increased political control for which it had been meant to substitute. The governor of Baghdad, like the amirs of Sind, could not provide protection, consequently the glorious vision of British-trained troops and British steamers taming Arabs, and bringing security to farmers and artisans, vanished.

Unable to force their hand by private initiative, Major Taylor would have to go on trying to interest the government of Bombay in Baghdad, by proving that the direct route would be the best for steam communication with England. In the spring of 1831 he sent out a second surveying party commanded by Lieutenant Henry Ormsby of the Bombay Marine, who had been told by Sir John Malcolm to survey the harbours in Syria, and suggest which would best suit mail pacquets from Malta. Crossing the desert from Hit to Damascus, the 'short but unusual route'[2] the British consul-general in Syria wanted to use for a camel post, they reached Beirut in June, mapped the harbours in Syria, and came back down the Euphrates from Bir. Here they found that they had been beaten by the man who made the direct route famous, Francis Rawdon Chesney.

Chesney's visit to Baghdad was the result of a second line of inquiry, begun in 1829 by one of the chief assistant examiners at

[1] Taylor to Auber, 14 July 1830, I.O. Persia/45.
[2] Encl. in Villiers to Auber, 28 Sept. 1831, I.O. E/2/37.

East India House, Thomas Love Peacock. Peacock, who read nothing but classical literature,[1] had as a result more certain opinions about the geography of the near east than most of his contemporaries, and stressed the importance of Baghdad. The prospect of Russian influence there alarmed Peacock more than Ellenborough. Some years later, he asked Chesney 'rather quaintly whether . . . he thought Persia was a Russian province, and how soon there will be a Russian dockyard at Basra with timber floated down from Armenia'.[2] There would be, Peacock was certain, if the British did not act first, and he could think of no geographical nor political obstacles to stop them. The Russians would not strike back against British steamers on the Euphrates by moving towards the Tigris, because the Oxus was their best route to the east. Russians on the Oxus might be compared to Americans in the Mississippi basin; so might Englishmen on the Euphrates. 'The protecting arm of a civilized government', said Peacock in November, 'is all that is required to do as much for the now thinly peopled and devastated regions that border the great rivers of Asia.'[3] As visionaries Major Taylor and Charles Trevelyan had a rival.

This was the first time anyone at London had suggested putting steamers on the Euphrates. Because Ellenborough shared Peacock's assumption that the Russians would move up the Oxus, or into Persia, and should be checked from the Indus or the Black Sea, he was less enthusiastic, given his suspicions of Russian influence in the near east, than might have been expected. His greatest interest in steamers was in increasing his control over the government of India. This attracted him to the Red Sea route: Mahomet Ali's Egypt, unlike Baghdad, was already safe. Ellenborough nevertheless told the government of India in March 1830 to survey both routes,[4] and Aberdeen promised to ask the British consul-general at Alexandria what he thought.

John Barker, the consul-general, was a famous figure in the near east, who had represented Britain for thirty years, most of the time

[1] H. Mills, *Peacock: His Circle and his Age* (Cambridge, 1969), pp. 19–30.

[2] Chesney's journal, 12 Sept. 1833, *Life of General F. R. Chesney, by his wife and daughter*, ed. S. Lane-Poole (London, 1885), p. 265.

[3] 'Memorandum [by T. L. Peacock] Respecting . . . Steam Navigation', 10 Nov. 1829, *Wellington*, vi. 330.

[4] Sc to ggic, 14 Mar. 1830, I.O. L/PS/5/543. For details see Philips, *East India Company*, pp. 264–8.

as agent of the East India Company at Aleppo. Although he preferred the Euphrates to the Red Sea route, unlike Peacock he
admitted that it might be dangerous: in the dry season the water
might be too shallow for steamers, sailing ships could not go up
river against the wind. The only way to find out how to overcome
these difficulties would be a trial run.[1]

With perfect timing, Chesney, an engineer officer on leave, who
had persuaded Sir Robert Gordon to send him to report on conditions in the Asiatic provinces of Turkey, arrived at Alexandria in
the summer of 1830, and volunteered to carry out a preliminary
survey. Here began his career as the Mesopotamian Burnes. He
went down the Euphrates from Anah opposite Damascus in the
spring of 1831, then, travelling overland through Persia and Asia
Minor, came back to England in September the following year.
He was just in time to join in the debate about British policy in the
near east, begun at the board of control then taken up at the foreign
office.

Chesney came back convinced, as Taylor was, and probably
convinced by Taylor, that the greater technical difficulties of
sailing on the Euphrates would be offset by the greater political
benefits. This route would be the cheaper to run, which would
please the East India Company, who were about to lose their
monopoly of trade with China, and, because it went by Persia,
British agents throughout the near east would be better able to
co-operate. The squadron of the Bombay Marine policing the
Persian Gulf already had a rendezvous at Basidu; letters for the
resident at Teheran could be dropped at Kharrack. Finally, the
effects in Baghdad of steam navigation would be cumulative, and
worthy of a free trading imperialist's dream;

the prospect of gradually civilizing Arabs, of increasing facilities to our
commerce, and also strengthening the hands of the sultan in the pashalic,
by inducing the people and the pasha to attend to the defence of Euphrates and Tigris; which as they now are offer an easy and irresistible inlet
to a northern enemy.[2]

---

[1] Barker to Aberdeen, no. 19, 2 May 1830, F.O. 78/192. Barker's career is
recounted in *Syria and Egypt under the Last Five Sultans of Turkey: Being
Experiences during Fifty Years of Mr. Consul-General Barker*, ed. E. B. B.
Barker (London, 1876).
[2] 'Reports on the Navigation of the Euphrates by F. R. Chesney, 1831–1833',
I.O. L/MAR/C/565.

The British being seen there would promote order, order trade, trade civilization, and all of them would conveniently keep out the Russians. Reform and security might advance hand in hand.

This report merely echoed the arguments Taylor at Baghdad and James Farren, the consul-general in Syria, had been repeating for four years. Nevertheless, as the leading apostle of the direct route, Chesney pushed aside both of them. Taylor and Farren had seemed to be supporting one another, they told each other so,[1] but were in fact at odds. Taylor wanted steamers and reform, and cared about the post only so far as it might need one and encourage the other: the post alone mattered to Farren. He had little influence in England. His colleagues at Constantinople resented his appointment; Palmerston, when he read them, found his dispatches infuriating; and, although Farren had argued since 1831 that the post should be sent overland by camel through Damascus, as the crossroads of the principal caravan routes in Asiatic Turkey,[2] he could not have arranged for this, because until 1834 he was not allowed to move inland and had to hover on the coast.

Taylor wanted the post sent from Latakhia or Alexandretta to Bir, and then down the Euphrates by boat. Despite a change in 1831 in the government of Baghdad, the new governor was as eager as the old for steamers, and Taylor wanted to encourage him for the same reason as the old: steamers would be the best way to obtain 'a commanding influence over the soil, resources, and waters of the pashalic'.[3] The post had other charms than news: properly set up it would help reform Baghdad.

Chesney robbed not only Taylor but the government of Bombay of the leadership in steam communication, because he pressed for action when they agreed to a pause. In June 1831 the whig president of the board of control, Charles Grant, repeated Ellenborough's instructions to the government of India to look into both overland routes.[4] As in Sind, Grant's enthusiasm for steamers on the Euphrates stemmed from his hope of reforming the Arabs from a distance, without being entangled in their politics. The

[1] Farren to Taylor, 11 Mar. 1832, Taylor to Farren, 10 Apr. 1832, I.O. Persia/47.

[2] Farren to Grant, 28 Jan. 1831, I.O. L/PS/3/117.

[3] Taylor to Norris, 11 Jan. 1832, I.O. Bombay/PP/387/22, 4 Apr. 1832, no. 1011.

[4] Sc to gicB, 18 June 1831, I.O. L/PS/5/544. Ormsby had not sent to London a copy of his report on the harbours in Syria.

government of Bombay had also changed; Malcolm had resigned in 1831 shortly after Ellenborough. His successor, the earl of Clare, who never grew used to the hyperbole of Anglo-India, or not in others, complained that everyone who spoke up for either route exaggerated the ease and the benefits to be expected.[1] Clare himself preferred the Egyptian route, and suggested that dispatches should be sent through Baghdad only when the monsoon closed the Red Sea. The East India Company, who feared the cost of sending steamers to the Red Sea, told the government of India in March 1832 not to spend any more of their money.[2] Because the governor of Baghdad seemed willing to spend his own, and on river steamers he would have to spend less, three months later the board of control agreed, if he would pay for them, to supply them, and also to send him an engineer to cut the canal between the Tigris and Euphrates at Baghdad.[3]

This decision was the result of a long dispute between Taylor and the government about the likely effects of his work at Baghdad upon Britain's foreign relations. Unfortunately, by the time Taylor had calmed everyone, Mahomet Ali had invaded Syria. In September 1832, just when Chesney was parroting his arguments to Grant, Taylor told the government of Bombay, that he could not finish surveying the rivers, and that as a result they should neither send engineers to cut the canal, nor permit the governor to buy steamers, until the war between the sultan and Mahomet Ali was over.[4] Long before this, the myth of the help to be expected from steamers on the Euphrates in reforming Baghdad, either by strengthening the governor or by persuading his Arab subjects to exchange nomadic for settled habits, had been exploded.

IV

The governor had invited Taylor to Baghdad at a time when he feared a Russian invasion. When Taylor dreamt his dreams, he was expecting Turkey to fall apart; and assumed, as Sir John Malcolm had once suggested, when the sultan had joined Napoleon against the Third Coalition, that if this happened, Britain should turn

---

[1] Clare to Bentinck, private, 5 Jan. 1832, Portland MSS. PwJf/624.
[2] Cd to gicB, 14 Mar. 1832, 25 Sept. 1833, I.O. L/PS/6/474.
[3] Sc to ggic, 1 June 1832, I.O. L/PS/5/544.
[4] Taylor to Norris, 15 Sept. 1832, I.O. Bombay/PP/387/34, 12 Dec. 1832, no. 4185.

Baghdad into a protectorate. Taylor's lineage was impeccable. Every agent sent to the near east since 1798, spellbound by the corruption and unrest in the near-eastern states, and the rabble their troops appeared to Europeans, was both more frightened than his superiors of the threats to British India, and more certain a bold advance was needed to parry them. Each was just as certain he should be put in command: disorder was a challenge awaiting an Englishman, as it awaited St. John Rivers, a test of the virtues of decision, activity, and sobriety, his nineteenth-century countrymen so heartily admired. Each ignored all states but his own, forgetting that the vast distances they covered, and their quarrels with one another, might have been enough to defend British India.

The geography of the near east might have been sufficient against invasion, but not against Russian or even Egyptian expansion; yet if the British were to challenge Russian influence, they had carefully to avoid making contradictory offers: to create a buffer zone they needed a connection with all the near-eastern states, not to have to choose between them. Baghdad was unique in being a province of the only state, although not European a component of the European balance of power, to be dealt with by the government of India. They had predicted, when they told Malcolm in 1828 not to allow Taylor to move from Basra, that he might forget to harmonize British policy at Baghdad with their policy at Constantinople and Teheran. The sequel was more dramatic. Eighteen months after he reached Baghdad, Taylor looked as if he were encouraging the governor to rebel against the sultan.

Throughout the reign of Sultan Mahmud II, onlookers had difficulty remembering that Baghdad was part of Turkey. The governors had time and again refused tribute; and had been regularly replaced by nominees of the sultan, who had been just as regularly tyrannized by the Mamelukes, their only support against the Arabs. The sultan did not control the governor: the governor did not control Baghdad. Mahmud, who had failed to reassert the imperial authority in Europe, was determined to obtain control. Taylor's governor, Daud Pasha, 'cunning, deceitful, bloody, [and] penurious',[1] had ruled at Baghdad since 1817, when Mahmud had sent him to turn out his predecessor. In October

---

[1] 'Notes [by F. R. Chesney] on the Pashalic of Baghdad', as revised in April 1832, Broadlands MSS. GL/CH/70.

1830, when Mahmud sent an envoy to Baghdad to ask for tribute, Daud knew what was meant. As a result he arranged for the envoy's 'secret and sudden disappearance', as Taylor called it,[1] but paid the tribute. Taylor, who feared that the governors of Mosul and Diabekir were waiting to invade, hoped that, if Daud had paid enough, Mahmud would accept the explanation that his envoy had died of cholera. If he refused, he might ruin Taylor's plans for turning Baghdad into a barrier to Russian influence.

In Turkey Daud's action was not necessarily rebellion, certainly not a declaration of independence. The governors of outlying provinces well knew, as their behaviour in the Napoleonic Wars had proved, the advantages of autonomy within Turkey. Despite this, if Mahmud proved stubborn, Daud might. Taylor argued that the British should then support Daud, who had proved a good ally, and in February 1831 asked Sir Robert Gordon to work for his reinstatement.[2] Gordon disagreed. He did remind the Turks of their need of tranquillity in Asia, but warned Taylor not to meddle in their internal affairs. If Mahmud chose to depose him, Daud was merely a rebel.[3] Unfortunately Taylor had already offered in December to help Daud, telling him of his 'willingness to render him every service in my power'; whereupon the governor had replied that he 'counted upon . . . [Taylor] as his most effective friend in necessity'.[4] Here in Taylor's opinion, was the chance to obtain a decisive influence in a vital strategic area, by turning the province of Baghdad into a British protectorate.

The likely result of Taylor's behaviour was clear enough to the Revd. A. N. Groves. Although he was always being told that the inhabitants of Baghdad would prefer British rule to Turkish, he doubted whether they were attracted by British ideas. 'The effects' of Taylor's plans, he said,' . . . none can tell, but that they must be very great everyone may see.'[5] If they succeeded they would cause a social revolution: 'If the Turks will not adopt European principles of government, they cannot resist the pressure from without,

[1] Taylor to Norris, 23 Dec. 1830, I.O. Bombay/PP/387/10, 21 Mar. 1831, no. 718.
[2] Taylor to Gordon, no. 4, 11 Feb. 1831, in Gordon to Palmerston, no. 30, 15 Apr. 1831, F.O. 78/198.
[3] Gordon to Palmerston, no. 31, 26 Apr. 1831, with encl. to Taylor, F.O. 78/199.
[4] Taylor to Norris, 23 Dec. 1830, I.O. Bombay/PP/387/10, 21 Mar. 1831, no. 718.
[5] Groves, *Journal at Baghdad*, p. 11.

and if they do, they will fall from within as Mahometan powers.'[1] Whereas Taylor's plans, whether or not they succeeded, might provoke the crisis in Turkey they were meant to prevent, the British had begun to realize that their most vital interest was to devise a method by which the Turks might escape from one of Groves's alternatives without succumbing to the other.

At this point, wearily, the government of Bombay called a halt. Taylor, as Metcalfe and Malcolm's colleagues had said he would be, had been carried away. They were not surprised at this, because it had happened before. In 1808 the governor of Bombay noticed that a new governor had been sent to Baghdad, and that the resident at Basra 'seems determined to resist his taking possession'.[2] This had previously meant that the resident feared his profitable private trading arrangements might be ended. Taylor's plans, however ambitious, were for the public good: he had turned to private enterprise out of necessity. The government of India could not decide how to prevent this happening again. In October 1831, Bombay praised Taylor for his success in training the governor's troops, and in surveying the Tigris and Euphrates, but told him not to start cutting the canal between them, and to return temporarily to Basra.

If Taylor's behaviour had been foolish, the government of India's was worse. Bombay complained that if he thought they had meant to do anything more than encourage the governor in order to keep him happy, Taylor had misunderstood their purpose. If this meant anything, it meant that the British were trying to suit only themselves. They habitually did this, and in the near east, where their interests were negative, holding back others, with good reason, but as so often they misled and disappointed their friends.

The government of Bombay knew that Baghdad was part of Turkey; but, as long as the sultan's rule was titular, they had not seen how to accommodate to the fact. They preferred either to ignore Baghdad, or to fit it onto the Persian Connection. The new governor-general, Lord William Bentinck, who was determined not to be drawn into near-eastern politics, argued that training the governor's army might alarm the shah of Persia. To prevent this, the resident at Basra should be placed under the orders of the resident at Teheran. Bombay replied that this was not a solution,

---

[1] Ibid., p. 9; Groves, *Journal of a Journey*, p. 135.
[2] Duncan to Minto, private, 11 Jan. 1808, Minto MSS. M/337.

because, when the shah learnt of it, he would embarrass the resident at Teheran by inventing claims to Baghdad. Instead, Bombay told Taylor to be guided by both the foreign office through their ambassador at Constantinople, and by the resident at Teheran, who worked under the governor-general.[1] This too was not a solution: being adrift between two governments had been the cause of successive residents' successive indiscretions. Bentinck, however, was being consistent. In 1830, when the resident at Teheran died, Bentinck had refused to name his successor. Because Persia could not be separated from the balance of power in Europe, he would not take over the Persian mission; as long as the foreign office would also not, the board of control must. The same was true of Baghdad: Taylor had proved it.

In the summer of 1831 the board of control also called a halt. Their decision was the origin of a policy invariably associated with Palmerston, later derided by Salisbury, who kept it up, as backing the 'wrong horse'. Palmerston's ideas were not all inherited from Canning, as we are usually told,[2] some of the most significant came through Charles Grant from Henry Ellis. Ellis was the bastard of the earl of Buckinghamshire, president of the board of control at the start of Liverpool's ministry, and an Addingtonian. Is it not fun to believe that this important British policy was handed down not by Pitt the Younger, the fount of all wisdom, but by Sidmouth riding on his crocodile? The method by which Palmerston by 1834 was trying to protect the integrity and independence of Turkey and Persia had been devised in 1831 by Henry Ellis, who had solved the problem he had been set in 1814, of how weak states could be turned into a strong barrier.

By the time Charles Grant, who had been first secretary for Ireland and president of the board of trade, reached the board of control in 1830, he had disappointed everyone who had predicted, after hearing him speak at Cambridge, a brilliant political career. His health had been ruined in India; he was too fussy to be efficient; the board of control required high administrative not oratorical ability: as a result the East India Company accused him of being lazy and unbusinesslike.[3] He tended, as a result, to rely

---

[1] GicB to sc, 17 Oct. 1831, I.O. L/PS/5/326.

[2] See e.g. H. W. V. Temperley, *England and the Near East: The Crimea* (London, 1936), pp. 59–61.

[3] Auber to Bentinck, 24 Nov. 1831, Portland MSS. PwJf/261; Ravenshaw to

heavily upon his colleagues, even when he disagreed with them. In December 1832 he appointed his friend Thomas Macaulay, whom 'he seemed really to think . . . a conjuror' because he worked so quickly,[1] secretary to the board of control. 'He told me yesterday, with tears in his eyes,' said Macaulay a year later, 'that he did not know what the board would do without me . . . Grant's is a mind that cannot stand alone . . . It turns, like ivy, to some support.'[2] The results were most noticeable in foreign policy.

As a Canningite who had resigned from Wellington's government along with Palmerston and Melbourne, Grant tried in India to reverse the policies of Ellenborough and the assistant secretary at the board of control, Benjamin Jones, who had assumed that the habit of not meddling in the internal affairs of allied states would in time compel the British to annex them, and that forward policies were needed in central Asia, both to ensure tranquillity in India by hemming in Russia, and to create stable political conditions along the British North-West Frontier. Jones's success at browbeating Grant was shown in 1834 by his policy in Oudh; he resisted so long because he preferred to meddle. Indians like Sindians and Turcomans would surely seize their chance to copy Englishmen, as soon as they were given security for the just rewards of labour. Unfortunately, Grant's way of giving them security was to force allied rulers to satisfy the exorbitant and unwarranted claims made by British creditors.[3] *Laissez-faire* depended upon everyone's paying his debts.

Grant's policy towards the near-eastern states was equally erratic: he disliked threats, would not offer help, but eagerly awaited signs of improvement. His mainstay here was Henry Ellis. Grant disliked Ellis, and they disagreed as much as Grant and Jones: when the board of control were reconstructed after the renewal of the East India Company's charter in 1833, Grant tried to remove Ellis without finding him another post. Earl Grey accused Grant of ingratitude,[4] well aware that Ellis, although

same, 19 Nov. 1831, ibid., no. 1923/1. Philips, *East India Company*, p. 276, denies the charge of laziness, but not of inefficiency.

[1] Macaulay to his sisters, 29 June 1832, *Letters of Thomas Babington Macaulay*, ed. T. Pinney (Cambridge, 1974), ii. 143.

[2] Macaulay to his sisters, 5 Dec. 1833, Trevelyan, *Macaulay*, p. 251.

[3] Philips, *Easy India Company*, pp. 278-85.

[4] Grant to Grey, 29 June 1832, Grey of Howick MSS. This despite the support Ellis gave Grant in getting Macaulay appointed to the governor-general's council. Macaulay to his sister, 22 Nov. 1833, *Macaulay*, ii. 338.

opposed by Grant, had thought of the method being used to sustain Turkey after the treaty of Unkiar Skelessi. Although Grant opposed Ellis, he could not resist him; on one occasion despatches were sent to him in France, where he was on holiday. By the time the ministry resigned, British policy at Teheran and Baghdad, as well as at Constantinople, was based on Ellis's assumptions.

Ellis had warned Castlereagh in 1814, that one day a way must be found to hold back Russia in the near east without trying to turn Turkey and Persia into protectorates, and so complicating Anglo-Russian relations in Europe. Ellis's mentor, Sir John Malcolm, had thought that turbulence in the near east was the best defence of India; but although it might prevent invasion, it would tempt, not hold back Russia. Ellis preferred to answer the oft repeated request of the shah of Persia, and turn Persia and Turkey into buffer states; that is to settle their frontiers, actually to persuade everyone including Russia to agree to the frontiers settled at Turkmanchay and Adrianople, and sufficiently strengthen the government to ensure the stability of the regime. Ellis sided firmly with the imperialists not the utilitarians: reform was to buttress the existing political and social structure, not to aim at social revolution.

This meant that Ellis had to change Ellenborough's priorities: it became essential to avoid a quarrel with Russia. Whereas Ellenborough had assumed that as long as British policy, in deference to Wellington and Aberdeen, was cautious at Teheran and Constantinople, it might be bold in Baghdad as well as Sind, Ellis separated the two. Sind, Afghanistan, and Bokhara, all the responsibility of the government of India, might be persuaded to give up nomadic for settled habits, and might be turned into protectorates, by buying British goods; Baghdad was to be treated henceforth solely as a province of Turkey. Britain's policy at Baghdad must not hamper her policy in more sensitive and important areas; it must help to turn Persia and Turkey into buffer states. This explains the board of control's reaction to Taylor's dealings with Daud Pasha.

The board were more critical than the government of India of all Taylor's efforts.[1] In July 1831 they firstly told him not to meddle again in the affairs of Kurdistan. Their reason was curious. Not

---

[1] Owing to the death of Taylor's brother, who was to deliver them, his despatches describing his work on the rivers and with the governor's troops

the ambassador at Constantinople but the resident at Teheran was to protect British interests in Kurdistan; Taylor was to follow his instructions in all disputes between Turkey and Persia. As Kurdistan was usually treated as part of Turkey, not Persia, the board meant that they would not allow their connection with Baghdad to complicate Anglo-Persian relations. They were still hoping to keep up their Persian Connection by encouraging trade, in an attempt to strengthen the shah as head of the dynasty, and to create a stable political situation in Azerbaijan.

The board went on to criticize Taylor's efforts to train the governor's army, because they understood Taylor 'to assume it as a principle', that Britain should help the governor to raise a regular army 'in order to maintain his independence'.[1] Their criticisms may seem curious.

Without recurring to the obvious inadmissibility of this principle, as trenching on the rights of the sultan, and on our obligations to that prince, we must on the narrowest grounds of selfish policy, question the expediency of so identifying ourselves with the interests of the reigning pasha. Not only are we precluded from acknowledging his independence *de jure*, but it appears to us that he is far from such independence *de facto*, as would warrant an undoubted reliance on the security of his power. Nor is this security, whatever be its amount, enhanced by the prospect of hereditary succession. The heir-apparent is only six years of age.

The board of control seemed unable to decide, whether to forbid what Taylor was doing, because it ought not to be tried, or because it would not succeed. In fact, appearances deceived.

The board were trying to decide how far the governors of outlying provinces 'can from the laxity and decay of the Turkish government be deemed, for purposes of international intercourse, independent rulers'.[2] The decision they came to was that in future not at all. Baghdad was not to become Egypt, nor Moldavia and Wallachia: the disintegration of Turkey, as far as international practice might stop it, must cease. The governor was to be treated 'only as the dependent and subject of the sultan'. Similarly, nothing

eventually reached London at the same time as his account of the murder of the sultan's envoy and his offer to support Daud Pasha.

[1] Sc to ggic, 1 July 1831, I.O. L/PS/5/544.

[2] 'Note [by Henry Ellis] on the Despatches from Baghdad', May 1831, I.O. Persia/45. This note was the basis for the secret committee's despatch.

was to be done at Baghdad without the sultan's permission; nothing 'which could in any degree excite in the mind of the Grand Signior any apprehension of our countenancing any scheme which should weaken his authority'.[1] This was a revealing qualification. If Mahmud should succeed in imposing his authority at Baghdad, either because Daud gave way, or because he was turned out, then a British mission training at Baghdad an army capable of holding back Persia and maintaining order might be welcomed; and, being an equivalent to the privileges already possessed by Russia in European Turkey, should not provoke the tsar. The board, on the advice of Henry Ellis, were beginning the policy, not only of defending British India by challenging Russian influence throughout the near east, but of challenging it by reforming Turkey. They were also rejecting the utilitarian and evangelical meaning of reform. The Turkish Empire was to be preserved by the cultivation of its appearance from without as a single state; nothing was to be done to upset its appearance, ideally nothing was to be done at all, except in answer to an invitation from the sultan, likely to show him as equally susceptible, but not more susceptible, to British interests as to Russian.

These instructions controlled Taylor's relations with a new government at Baghdad. Mahmud had proved stubborn: Ali Rida, the governor of Aleppo, was told to turn out Daud by force. At first he failed. In June 1831 he laid siege to Baghdad, when Daud, his army weakened by the plague, nevertheless stood up to him for three months. Taylor hoped that this would persuade Mahmud to pardon him. Instead, in September, traitors opened the gates at Baghdad to Ali Rida, who slaughtered Daud's Mamelukes, but spared him.[2] He had a distinguished career elsewhere in the empire.

In Taylor's opinion this change of government changed nothing; rather the need for British aid at Baghdad became more urgent. Taylor had left Baghdad for Basra at the end of May to escape the plague: in the autumn he was asking whether he might go back. His reasons were those he had previously given, except that this time he was certain the sultan would not be offended, because he had sent positive orders to the new governor to train a regular

[1] Sc to ggic, 1 July 1831, I.O. L/PS/5/544.
[2] Taylor to sc, 29 Oct. 1831, with encls. nos. 1, 6–7, 10, I.O. Persia/46.

army and start a steamer service. The Turks would prefer British officers and machinery, but what Britain would not supply they would look for elsewhere. If Taylor were not allowed to help, they would hire foreigners: if he were, as he had previously claimed, Britain would obtain paramount influence at Baghdad. There was a further attraction. Ali Rida was to govern not only Baghdad, but Mosul, Diabekir, and Aleppo. For 'the complete and final subjugation of the Arabs, the pacification of Syria and Mesopotamia, for the prosecution of commerce, and the ultimate civilization of the people on European principles', Ali Rida and the governor of Syria were to divide the Levant between them.[1] Here, if they would seize it, was the opportunity for which the board of control in Ellenborough's day claimed to have been waiting.

The governor, as Ellenborough had hoped, had given the British a second chance. This time they jumped at it: by influence in Baghdad they might strengthen Turkey. J. B. Kelly makes a mistake in saying that Taylor, because of his russophobia, had disgraced himself and lost all influence.[2] His arguments were backed up in September by the resident at Teheran, who thought that Taylor had exaggerated the extent of Russian influence, but not the danger from it. In Persia the situation was similar. Trade could not re-establish for Britain influence equivalent to Russia's without a gesture of support for the regime. The obvious gesture was a military mission: unless the British undertook to train their allies' armies, they might seek Russian help.[3]

Because of a spasm of energy in Charles Grant, in the spring of 1832, the board of control, who were about to reappraise their policy in Persia, apparently changed their policy at Baghdad. They had been convinced by Taylor's explanation of his dealings with Daud Pasha; and although they had just told him not to meddle in Turkish politics, they now told him he might move permanently to Baghdad, as the best way of 'establishing such an influence in the pasha's councils as will be requisite for the discharge of the duties properly belonging to his office'. These were the two things Taylor had always wanted to do: to look after the British military mission, which the board now agreed to send to Baghdad, if the

[1] Encl. no. 2 in Taylor to sc, 16 Nov. 1832, I.O. Persia/46; Groves, *Journal at Baghdad*, p. 263.
[2] Kelly, *Persian Gulf*, pp. 269–70.
[3] Campbell to sc, 15 Sept. 1831, I.O. Persia/46.

governor would pay them, and to oversee cutting the canal between the Tigris and Euphrates, which would be needed for the steamers the board were now willing to allow the governor to buy at Bombay. The board's aims, in a lurch towards utilitarian Utopianism, were as grandiose as any of Taylor's or Ellenborough's, and as grandiose as their aims in Sind, 'to promote the cause of civilization and the establishment of beneficial rule'.[1] The rule would benefit, naturally, not only the Arabs but Britain: to the utilitarians, the security and prosperity of Britain and India was the cause of civilization, and they thought the Russians uncivilized for standing in the way.

In July, when, during the discussions about Persia, Henry Ellis reasserted himself and Grant relapsed, the board reminded Taylor that his duties were strictly limited. The military mission were to be used only as instructors; without the consent of the governorgeneral, and at the express wish of the sultan, sent in writing through the ambassador at Constantinople, they were not to take the field. As far as possible the attempt to settle the unrest in Baghdad should be left to trade. The East India Company had long ceased to make a profit on trading to the Persian Gulf, but the private and country traders at Bombay had flourished; in Baghdad the end of the company's monopoly had not ended the possibilities of British trade, nor of encouraging trade for political reasons. By 1832 these political had formally taken over from commercial considerations. The board were worried by Mahomet Ali's success in Syria; they wished to be certain, that, if the sultan should be defeated, Ali Rida could not make use of the British military mission to support a claim to independence. 'The pasha,' the board reminded Taylor, 'is not to be regarded as an independent sovereign, but as the temporary governor of a Turkish province.'[2]

Although the government of Bombay had not yet sent the military mission, the board had reason to worry. Their chance to begin the new policy, of trying to strengthen the sultan's control of the empire with as little intervention as possible in his affairs, had been denied them by Mahomet Ali. Taylor understood this. In September he told the government of Bombay, that, until the war was over, they should not send the engineers to cut the canal between the Tigris and Euphrates, nor the military mission and

---

[1] Sc to ggic, 28 Apr. 1832, I.O. L/PS/5/544.
[2] Sc to ggic, 5 July 1832, ibid.

the steamers, because the governor could not afford them.[1] The governor had applied to the sultan, who also could not afford them: nor could he defend Baghdad from Mahomet Ali. 'Troops we have none to spare,' replied the Porte to the governor's entreaty, 'ammunition we have not the means of sending. The sultan has sent a small supply [of funds] out of his private coffers, but scarcely enough to meet the wants of the pasha for his domestic expenses.'[2]

While the war, or, as the board of control were determined, as long as they were able, to think of it, the rebellion, had curtailed Taylor's opportunities, it confirmed his political role. Throughout this period, the British had hoped to make political gains while economizing: the future of the residency at Basra was continuously in doubt. Malcolm, who had wanted to join it to the residency at Bushire, moving both to Kharrack, had been held back by the Russo-Turkish war. He remembered, that by bringing home all their residents in the near east during the war of the Third Coalition, the East India Company had driven the shah of Persia into an alliance with France. In 1832 Clare took up the idea, arguing that whenever there was peace in the near east Taylor had nothing to do, but Bentinck preferred to allow the board to decide.[3] If they were to carry out British policy in the near east, they must choose where to place and how much to spend on agents: in 1829 the residencies at Basra and Bushire had cost the East India Company £14,000.[4] No decision was taken until February 1834, when the board persuaded the company, despite the cost, not to bring home the resident at Baghdad until the rebellion in Turkey had been suppressed.[5]

This decision stirred up the old argument between Bombay and Fort William, echoing their argument six years earlier, when Taylor had first asked whether he might move to Baghdad. The Bombay council always said that British residents in the near east were sent to protect British trade in the Persian Gulf. This justified the residency at Bushire, but in September the councillors 'were at a loss to point out one specific advantage which has occurred from

---

[1] Taylor to Norris, 15 Sept. 1832, I.O. Bombay/PP/387/34, 12 Dec. 1832, no. 4185.

[2] Canning to Palmerston, no. 60, 10 Aug. 1832, F.O. 78/211.

[3] GicB to sc, 17 Oct. 1832, I.O. L/PS/5/326.

[4] Accountant-general at Bombay to Norris, 18 Nov. 1830, I.O. Bombay/PP/387/7, 8 Dec. 1830, no. 50.

[5] Cd to gicB, 26 Feb. 1834, I.O. L/PS/6/474.

our establishment at Basra and Baghdad since the downfall of the Great Napoleon in 1814, nor . . . any that are to be derived in future, except it be watching the acts of Russian agents in that quarter'.[1] Trade at Basra needed only a native agent, without an escort, who were attacked by Arabs whenever they travelled up river; a political connection with Baghdad would offend the sultan. As Taylor's plans for training the governor's troops and starting a steamer service had been postponed, he should be brought home to Bombay.

Now that fighting had broken out again, Clare again echoed Sir John Malcolm. He agreed that if Britain's only interest were her trade, the resident at Bushire should be able to protect it. At a time, however, when British policy in the near east was being debated at London between the foreign office and the board of control, and when the government of India must be careful not to contradict them without meaning to, the resident at Baghdad carried out useful, even if limited, political duties.[2] These were the ones he had been given during the Napoleonic Wars; to improve the overland post to India, provide the board of control with a quicker and more reliable source of news, and stop the French expanding eastwards from Egypt. Bonaparte had merely been swapped for Mahomet Ali.

At Fort William Lord William Bentinck in October supported Clare.[3] Taylor had already been severely checked; he might spend money to obtain information, and in the autumn of 1834 he was given more to spend, but he might not travel about Baghdad, and he was not to take sides. This did not mean that Britain's interest in Baghdad was lessening, exactly the opposite; Baghdad was a peculiarly sensitive area, because, owing to the danger from both the Russians and Mahomet Ali, Britain's behaviour there must be an example of the behaviour she was trying to make them copy. This mattered more at a time when the British thought they had found a way to stabilize the political situation in Syria and Baghdad, regardless of who happened to be ruling there. In August 1834 parliament had agreed to the Euphrates Expedition. As the per-

---

[1] Minute of Newnham, 6 Sept. 1834, I.O. Bombay/SP/82, 24 Sept. 1834, no. 89.

[2] Minute of Clare, 18 Sept. 1834, ibid., no. 90.

[3] McNaghten to Wathen, 10 Oct. 1834, I.O. Bombay/SP/82, 29 Oct. 1834, no. 118.

sonification of Britain at Baghdad, Taylor was to be superseded by Chesney.[1]

After 1832 Taylor lost his chance at Baghdad, because his plans for a steamer service, for ending the unrest in Baghdad and Syria, and for cutting the cost of influence, all waited for peace between Mahmud II and Mahomet Ali. In times of crisis the government of India might not act as an independent state; as long as Lord William Bentinck was at Fort William, in the near east they were more and more unwilling to try. Nor might the board of control carry out British policy in Turkey separately from the foreign office. Owing to the activities of Mahomet Ali, then the Russians, the Great Game in Asia shifted westwards, when Palmerston in 1833 reacted to the treaty of Unkiar Skelessi as Ellenborough had to the treaties of Turkmanchay and Adrianople, and dealt with the results as Henry Ellis suggested.

The best-known result of Ellenborough's equally well-known attempt to increase British influence in the near east was the journey of Alexander Burnes to Bokhara; in comparison Taylor's work at Baghdad may seem unimportant. The comparison is misleading. The First Afghan War was a disaster: Palmerston's defeat of Mahomet Ali is usually considered a success. Taylor upset his superiors because he began the Great Game in Asia so quickly. Whereas the government of India had time to persuade the board of control to alter their instructions about Sind, Taylor began while Ellenborough and Aberdeen were alarmed by the treaties of Turkmanchay and Adrianople. If Turkey should have been partitioned, or begin to act as a protectorate of Russia, British influence at Baghdad might have served the same purpose in Asia Minor as Greece in the eastern Mediterranean. The attraction of Baghdad and Greece as successor states was equally brief. Taylor soon had to obey a new rule for British agents in the near east; that Britain would try to preserve Turkey as drawn on a map in 1829. The constant upheavals in the near east, of which the government of Bombay complained, were partly the result of changes in British policy.

Taylor, Chesney, and when permitted Charles Grant, all dreamt dreams of the future of Baghdad similar to Trevelyan's of Afghanistan. Because, by undermining the authority of the sultan, they might have led to the partition Taylor had expected rather than to

[1] For the situation at Baghdad in 1834 see Ch. IX, pp. 282–4.

strengthening Turkey, firstly Ellenborough, then Henry Ellis, changed the goals at which the British might effectively aim. The social revolution implied in persuading the inhabitants of Baghdad to give up nomadic for settled habits mattered less to Ellenborough than increasing the governor's control over the province and British control over him; and Ellenborough relied less on commercial treaties and concessions, more on steamers and military missions. In areas well away from the Russian frontier, and as strategically important to the British as Moldavia and Wallachia were to Russia, Ellenborough hoped that Wellington would not think such attempts provocative, and would resist Russia's attempts to pretend they were: Ellis thought them so. Any demand for privileged status in a particular province of Turkey tended to destroy the political cohesion of the empire, and the possibility of the sultan's reasserting his control; conversely, the best way to reach Aberdeen's goal of increasing the stability of Turkey as a state was to keep out. If the British wished to hold back Russia in the near east, as in the eighteenth century they had tried to hold back France, they had carefully to hold back themselves. Baghdad must not be controlled by another strong state, as in the eighteenth century the British had been determined Egypt should not be, but they need not control it themselves.

If Turkey were to have been partitioned, Baghdad would have become a protectorate of the government of India; if it were to remain a province of Turkey, British activities there would have to be taken over by the foreign office, and must wait for Palmerston to realize it. Mahomet Ali's rebellion made this more urgent, but also less dangerous. The point the British wished the Russians to understand, that Turkey was to be treated, like Austria or Prussia, as a territorial state with fixed frontiers, could be more easily explained in dealing with Mahomet. In theory this was easier, in practice not so, because in 1832 the British missed their chance. While they waited for another, they tried to make sure that their position at Baghdad would help them to make use of it. As a result, and against their wishes, the British took one step forward: the Euphrates Expedition were sent to restrain both Mahomet Ali and the sultan, in an attempt to destroy the treaty of Unkiar Skelessi.

VII

The End of the Persian Connection
1828-1832

> This story has no moral. If it
> points out an evil, at any rate
> it suggests no remedy.
>
> SAKI,
> *The Unbearable Bassington*

AT THE END of the nineteenth century, Lord Curzon knew more about the near east than anyone in politics. His contemporaries did not mind this, they did mind being told of it: the length of his speeches offended them more. The house of commons never respected Curzon because he stood for knowledge before judgement. What Curzon said about the near east was true, but, because nobody listened, he continued as viceroy of India a habit the British had begun a century earlier of wandering in the near east in a circle. Either they paid too great attention or too little:[1] each extravagance was followed by another supposed to remedy it. The selection was limited. Although civil servants stayed longer and longer in India, diplomatic capers in the near east never lost their attraction for newcomers, nor failed to imprint them for their careers. A good example was Persia at the beginning of the Great Game in Asia. Henry Ellis, who thought out British policy there, had been thinking for twenty years.

From reading Webster and Temperley one might not know that Britain had a connection with Persia. One might also not know of the existence of an Indian empire,[2] nor of the influence over the foreign office of the board of control.[3] They wrote as if Britain

---

[1] G. N. Curzon, *Persia and the Persian Question* (London, 1892), ii. 605.

[2] Persia is mentioned four times by Webster in his *The Foreign Policy of Castlereagh* (London, 1925–31) and twice by Temperley in his *Foreign Policy of Canning*. Temperley thought it hardly necessary to mention Persia in a book called *England and the Near East*.

[3] The omission may partly have resulted from Webster's peculiar view of British India was a separate state, and of the president of the board of control

were merely a peripheral European state, able for reasons never explained to balance the other states of Europe. Englishmen may have thought this, and some of them certainly thought it about the near east, where their view of Persia was typically odd and often unrealistic. Persians, because more closely connected and for longer with Englishmen, were expected by utilitarians and whigs to appreciate more than Afghans, Arabs, and Baluchis, their superiority and the higher virtues they stood for. Tories and imperialists, who had been more closely connected and for longer with Persians, expected nothing of them but a calculation of national interest. Both assumptions led to the same conclusion; that Persians would prefer Englishmen to Russians.

It should be assumed as a fundamental principle of diplomatic conduct in Persia [said Ellis], that every shah of Persia is disposed to prefer a British connection and British advice to Russian, and that all his subjects not positively bought by Russian gold have a natural dislike to the Russian name and people.[1]

Poor relief, trade unions, and connections with Russia, were against both utilitarian laws of nature and imperialist common sense.

Henry Ellis, obeying the rules laid down by the foreign office in the twenty years following the fall of Wellesley in 1812, knew that the government of India, or when they refused to look the board of control, must find a way to prevent the expansion of Russia, without affecting Anglo-Russian relations in Europe. Because, as long as Castlereagh and Canning could ignore the near east, the concert of Europe might successfully maintain the European balance of power, the concert was to take precedence over the security of British India. Unfortunately, while disentangling Britain from her alliance with Persia, through fear of the effects in Europe of Russo-Persian enmity, Castlereagh and Canning failed to foresee the equally dangerous effects in India of their friendship. How to counteract these was the problem puzzling firstly Lord Ellenborough, then Charles Grant and

as 'only an intermediary between an almost all powerful governor-general and an East India Company tenacious of its rights and eager for dividends'. *Castlereagh*, i. 13. This is neither a convincing description of an office created and long filled by Henry Dundas, nor a convincing explanation of Castlereagh's failure there.

[1] Memorandum by Ellis, 20 May 1835, F.O. 60/37.

Henry Ellis. The Great Game in Asia was their answer, to be played in Persia as it was being played in Sind and at Baghdad.

Turbulence in the near east might have defended British India against invasion, as long as Persia and Turkey were enemies of Russia; if they became her protectorates, their weakness would make the problem more serious. The British would be unable to prevent the gradual but persistent expansion of Russia's influence, who could offer Persia compensation in areas where exchanges of territory would threaten British interests. For this reason, as soon as the defence of India was turned from a military into a political problem, the board of control became as anxious to create stable frontiers in Persia as the government of India were to create them between the Punjab and Sind.

Because Persia shared a frontier with Russia, not British India, more was needed than stability; in Persia, unlike Sind, stability after the treaty of Turkmanchay depended upon order. Persia, like Turkey, need not be strong, although given time she might grow stronger. Correct diplomatic practice and a military mission sent to train the Persian army might sufficiently strengthen the imperial government, while increased trade might help to end the unrest in the frontier provinces. The Indus and the Euphrates were not the only waterways to catch the eye of a sea power on the map. There was a third, not the Persian Gulf, because the British, who had no wish to encourage Indian manufactures, preferred to export their own through the Black Sea. In recognition of the strategic importance of Anatolia to the security of British India, the Great Game in Asia was to be played at Trebizond.

II

When the duke of Wellington became prime minister in 1828, Charles Arbuthnot was hurt at not being offered a place in the cabinet. He was one of Wellington's closest friends; or, if he were not, his wife was. Arbuthnot, like most good tories, was incapable of coherent speech.[1] Canning and Peel both owed their position in the party to their ability to make better speeches than their colleagues in the house of commons. Ellenborough could speak, but in the lords it mattered less. This had its effect on the Great Game. When Ellenborough demanded an office of business,

---

[1] E. Longford, *Wellington: Pillar of State* (London, 1972), p. 153.

Wellington made the mistake of thinking that at the board of control he would be held in check by the other members.[1] Instead Ellenborough pressed constantly for forward policies throughout the near east. In Sind he had his way, but in Persia British policy had to conform to the limits set by Wellington.

Canning's successor at the foreign office, obeying his rule that the possibility of a quarrel with Russia over Persia should not be allowed to strain Anglo-Russian co-operation in Greece, had seized the chance in 1828 to purchase by one payment of the subsidy the abrogation of the subsidiary articles of the treaty of Teheran. Ellenborough's belief in the importance of India to Britain, and his ambition, both forbade him Canning's lack of interest in the near east. Arguing that unless held back the Russians might have to move south-eastwards, as the British in India had moved north-westwards, in an unending search for a stable frontier,[2] in October 1829 Ellenborough asked his colleagues to warn Russia that this would threaten Britain's interests as an Asiatic state. Wellington promptly refused. Ellenborough was not disheartened, because he knew there was no immediate danger to India from Russian policy in Persia; nor need there ever be, if Britain worked to prevent it. What the Kajars needed, as Sir John Malcolm had recommended at Baghdad, was a little encouragement from Britain. 'Our influence in Persia', said Ellenborough, 'has been much weakened by our vacillating conduct. I must endeavour to retrieve our affairs there.'[3]

What most worried Ellenborough was the political situation in Persia. Wellington vetoed a forward policy, because he knew Britain could no longer turn Persia either into an ally against Russia, or into the protectorate his brother Wellesley had planned. Ellenborough had to settle for a less ambitious plan, to prop up the dynasty and prevent revolution. Throughout 1829 the British resident at Teheran, Sir John Macdonald, bombarded the board of control with details of the anarchy in Persia. A rebellion in Kerman had been so serious, it had forced the shah to divert troops from the Russian front. 'Had the war . . . continued a

[1] Wellington to Peel, 16 Aug. 1828, *Wellington*, iv. 615.
[2] 25 Sept. 1828, Ellenborough's *Diary*, i. 224. For an explanation of this phenomenon see John S. Galbraith, 'The "Turbulent Frontier" as a Factor in British Expansion', *Comparative Studies in Society and History*, ii (1959–60), 150–68.
[3] 1 Oct. 1828, Ellenborough's *Diary*, i. 231.

month longer,' said Macdonald in March, 'the whole of Persia from Khorassan to Tabriz would most probably have presented a frightful scene of confusion, anarchy, and bloodshed.' Unless the British supported the Kajar dynasty in this crisis, and promised the throne to Abbas Mirza, they would ask for Russian support, and Abbas, if not the shah, would pay whatever price was asked, 'which would render him entirely dependent on the Emperor'.[1] After the treaty of Turkmanchay, the British in Persia had to solve a new and dangerous problem; how to stop Persia from becoming a protectorate of Russia.

Wellington's method in 1828 of propping up the Kajars was to help them reform their army and finances. The army's duties were to be paramilitary, to crush rebellion and make certain that Abbas Mirza obtained the throne; they were not to defend Persia or British India against Russia. To make this clear any officers the British sent out were to be paid by the shah. If Persia could best serve Britain's interests by acting as a buffer state between the British and Russian empires in Asia, she must remain at peace with Russia; but, in Ellenborough's opinion, this was 'not inconsistent with her entire independence of, and freedom from Russian control and even counsel'.[2] Ellenborough, of course, meant to cheat, as Nicholas I meant to cheat when he called Turkey after the treaty of Unkiar Skelessi a buffer state: each expected only his advice to be followed. The shah, frightened by Canning's modification of the treaty, was not to feel that it would 'change the relative position of the two powers towards each other, or effect an alteration in their real interests'.[3] The Persians were not to forget that they should prefer Englishmen to Russians.

In 1829 the situation in the near east became more threatening to Britain after the treaty of Turkmanchay had been followed by the treaty of Adrianople: Canning's attempt to separate the balance of power in Europe from the defence of British India had undermined both. The British had feared that as soon as Russia was fighting Turkey, the shah might invade Georgia.

[1] Macdonald to Amherst, 28 Mar. 1828, same to sc, 5 Oct. 1828, I.O. Persia/43. 'That the court of St. Petersburg is bent on establishing a secret influence here,' argued Macdonald two years later, 'is . . . quite evident.' Same to Ellenborough, 10 Mar. 1830, E.U.L. MSS. Dk/2/37, fo. 116.

[2] Sc to ggic, 7 Nov. 1838, I.O. L/PS/5/543; Wellington to Ellenborough, 9 Oct. 1828, *Wellington*, v. 117.

[3] Sc to ggic, 13 Dec. 1828, I.O. L/PS/5/543.

You will perceive [Macdonald warned the East India Company in May] . . . the difficulty I experience in preventing our Persian allies from rushing headlong into another war with Russia, for which they feel all the inclination in the world under the idea that the time is now arrived, when they are destined to recover all their lost provinces on this side of the Caucasus.[1]

Alternatively, the British feared that the Russians, following their traditional policy of exploiting victory over one near-eastern state against the other, might follow their victory over Turkey by invading Azerbaijan. This seemed to become more likely during the summer, after a mob at Teheran had murdered a Russian envoy.[2] It is also what happened, except that the Russians had changed their policy. The famous turnabout in Russian policy towards Turkey that followed the treaty of Adrianople can also be seen in their reaction to the murder of Griboedoff.

Continuing the new Russian policy of turning Turkey and Persia into protectorates, the tsar seized his chance to dominate Abbas Mirza. By the terms of the treaty of Turkmanchay Persia had agreed to pay Russia an indemnity of ten crores of tomauns. Helped by Canning, they had paid eight in exchange for the evacuation of Azerbaijan. When a Persian embassy arrived at St. Petersburg to apologize for the death of Griboedoff, the tsar gave up one of the two crores outstanding, and in September offered the Persians five years to pay the other.[3] This trapped Abbas Mirza. The shah refused to pay. He did not have to; everybody knew that in five years he would be dead, and, were he not, he had no war for the succession awaiting him. Abbas Mirza was unable to pay; yet his accession might depend upon Russian help. The British, watching closely, knew where this was leading. 'They mean,' noted Ellenborough a month later,' . . . to rule Persia *by influence.*'[4]

Macdonald claimed that the biggest barrier to matching Russian influence was the character of the Kajars. A government

---

[1] Macdonald to R. Campbell, 24 May 1829, E.U.L. MSS. Dk/2/37, fo. 14; Heytesbury to Aberdeen, no. 93, 13 Aug. 1829, with encl., F.O. 65/180. The Russians, too, were expecting this, or so they said. Encl. by Nesselrode in Lieven to Aberdeen, 28 June 1829, F.O. 65/183.

[2] Ellenborough to Macdonald, private, 25 Oct. 1829, P.R.O. 30/9/4 pt. 1/5; Heytesbury to Aberdeen, no. 26, 27 Mar. 1829, F.O. 65/179.

[3] Heytesbury to Aberdeen, no. 122, 26 Sept. 1829, F.O. 65/181.

[4] 19 Oct. 1829, Ellenborough's *Diary*, ii. 116.

of 'idiots', their foreign policy was carried on by 'a weak and perfidious prince that would without scruple betray any one'. Their lack of faith mattered less than their lack of sense.

The Persians are so perverse, so perfidious, and so wanting in wisdom [said Macdonald], that it is difficult to calculate on their procedure. In matters of foreign policy, they frequently act more like children than men, being alternately swayed by their fears, their petty dissensions, and their individual interests, to which everything is sacrificed without a scruple. The more Russia conciliates the more they will presume.[1]

Fortunately in breaking down this barrier the British had, or so Macdonald believed, an equally great asset, his own strength of character.

Reports from British agents in the near east were usually untrustworthy, because designed to prove how a loyal Englishman, lonely, far from home amidst strangers and barbarians, had averted grave peril. As soon as he learnt that the government wanted to prop up the Kajar dynasty, Macdonald's gloom turned to confidence. 'If government are inclined to grant their aid and support,' he told the government of Bombay, commenting upon the difference between the policies of the board of control and the government of India, 'I should not yet despair of being able to put Abbas Mirza on the throne without the intervention of Russia.' Macdonald said that Britain should send weapons as well as a military mission to Persia, and stressed that the success of the policy would depend upon his continuing influence over Abbas Mirza: 'It rests with him to be an independent prince or an empty pageant. If he sinks into the latter, the influence of those who place him on the throne will soon reach the Indian Ocean and the mountains of Kabul.'[2] To be independent meant following British advice.

The greatest danger from Russian influence over Persia would have been Russian officers training the Persian army. The Persians had dreamed for many years of reconquering Herat, Bahrein, and sometimes Baghdad. Ellenborough assumed, that because the Russians could most effectively have threatened British India by

---

[1] Macdonald to Malcolm, 25 May 1829, same to Ellenborough, 18 June 1829, E.U.L. MSS. Dk/2/37, fos. 26, 43.
[2] Macdonald to Newnham, private, 2 Sept. 1829, same to R. Campbell, 28 Nov. 1829, ibid., fos. 79, 100.

using Persians as henchmen, they would encourage what the British must forbid.

If we allow the Persians to think we have ceased to trouble ourselves about them [said Ellenborough in October] . . . fear of Russia will secure the compliance of the Persian government with any demand, and our only security will be in the chance of the dissolution of the government, and of the irregular and uncombined action of the several tribes.[1]

Persian imperialism might threaten British India; its failure would be equally calamitous. Turbulence in Persia might or might not defend India against Russia, but was certain to unsettle the British North-West Frontier. The obvious defence, as Macdonald had said, was to outbid the Russians for influence over Abbas Mirza, by helping to make certain he would obtain the throne.

For these reasons, during 1829 Wellington had gradually been persuaded to give way a little to Ellenborough. The Persians were to be sent as many British officers as they could be persuaded to employ; they were to be encouraged to pay for them, but the officers were not to be brought home should they refuse. They were also to be sent the weapons Macdonald had suggested, and Ellenborough, who raised the number, asked in December for payment only by instalments.[2] These measures were supposed to appear administrative. The political counterpart was avoided. Abbas Mirza was not to assume that the British would guarantee his accession; they were trying to prevent his buying a guarantee from Russia. In a civil war for the succession, Macdonald, as directed by the government of India, who were technically responsible for Anglo-Persian relations, although both they and Ellenborough wanted the board of control to take over again, was to maintain an 'inviolable neutrality'.[3] Persia was an independent state, and Canning had told everyone for years how much he disliked people who meddled in the internal affairs of others. As always this meant only that the British wished to hold back Prince Metternich and the tsar, or that they were unable to intervene effectively themselves.

---

[1] Ellenborough to Wellington, 18 Oct. 1829, *Wellington*, vi. 238; 17 Nov. 1829, Ellenborough's *Diary*, ii. 136.
[2] Sc to ggic, 24 Aug., 27 Oct., 7 Dec. 1829, I.O. L/PS/5/543.
[3] Swinton to Macdonald, 26 Dec. 1829, F.O. 248/61.

The British had not offered enough. In March 1830 the Persians asked them to replace the abrogated subsidiary articles of the treaty of Teheran by one article offering general protection, which might 'add strength to the existing government in the eyes of the people [and] . . . serve to avert, on the part of the Imperial [Russian] cabinet, the assumption of so high and haughty a language'.[1] Abbas Mirza's chief minister explained why the Kajars needed this. He feared, he said,[2]

not the prospect of another war . . . but the necessity Persia would feel of submitting to every demand of the Russian government, however injurious and oppressive it might be, unless she could be assured that she was not left quite alone to struggle against the overweening power of that government.

If the British saw Persia as a buffer between British India and the Russian empire in Asia, and if they hoped that stability in Persia would help stabilize the balance of power amongst the states beyond their North-West Frontier, they must match the interest in Persia of the Russians. Buffer states can exist only during a balance of tension between two unfriendly, equally powerful, and equally interested neighbours.

The Russians not only threatened the Persians, as expected they tempted them. They were trying to persuade Abbas Mirza to send a joint expedition against Khiva, and offering to go without the final crore of the indemnity as a reward. This did not particularly alarm the British, although they were determined to prevent it. Macdonald thought that he had enough influence over the shah so to do.[3] Because Turkestan could most effectively be kept as a buffer by negotiation between London and St. Petersburg, should Macdonald fail, Wellington seemed 'disposed [in March] to make it a European question'.[4] All the cabinet would allow Ellenborough to offer the Persians in July was a vague statement that Britain would not permit the subjugation of Persia to go unnoticed.[5] None of this was as detached as it appeared: Ellenborough believed

---

[1] Macdonald to sc, secret and confidential, 10 Mar. 1830, I.O. Persia/45; same to Ellenborough, private, 7 Mar. 1830, ibid.

[2] Campbell to Swinton, 23 June 1830, in same to sc, 23 June 1830, I.O. Persia/45.

[3] Macdonald to Ellenborough, private, 10 Mar. 1830, E.U.L. MSS. Dk/2/37, fo. 116.

[4] 6 Mar. 1830, Ellenborough's *Diary*, ii. 206.

[5] Ellenborough to Abbas Mirza, 14 July 1830, F.O. 60/32.

that from the Indus he could beat the Russians to Turkestan. Expanding Britain's trade might also challenge Russia in Persia, while both avoiding the expense and embarrassment of renewing the treaty of Teheran, and demonstrating the interest in Persia for which the Persians had been pleading.

When Sir John Macdonald died in June 1830, the Persians again asked the British to put into the treaty of Teheran an article providing general protection. In October they were again refused. The British thought that Abbas Mirza was trying to take advantage of Macdonald's acting successor as resident, Captain Campbell; that he wanted to be bought off with a subsidy.[1] Because the Persian Connection had proved so expensive, Wellington hoped to stop Russia from gaining enough influence 'to dispose of the resources of Persia', while Britain stayed 'unbound by specific stipulations'.[2] Despite the Persian warnings, the British could not believe that they might have to choose between these objectives. Persia was bound to resist Russia: Abbas Mirza had himself stated that 'nothing short of coldness and neglect on our part will ever induce them to throw themselves into the arms of a power from whose known ambition and haughty temper they have everything to dread and nothing to expect'.[3] 'The steady opposition of Persia to any Russian designs formidable to us,' concluded one official paper, 'is ensured without any endeavour on our part.'[4]

Conservatives often rely on leadership rather than ideology. The British lost influence in Persia, which puzzled them, partly because between 1828 and 1832 two families fought a long and venomous battle to take over the residency at Teheran. Sir John Macdonald was Sir John Malcolm's brother-in-law; Macdonald's second assistant and eventual successor, Captain John Campbell, was Malcolm's second cousin. The first assistant was Sir Henry Willock, who had been British chargé d'affaires at Teheran for ten years before Macdonald arrived, and had been persuaded to stay on as first assistant to support Canning's claim, that the size and splendour of the mission would be increased when the government of India took back control of it. Macdonald disliked and

[1] Campbell to sc, 23 June 1830, I.O. Persia/45; same to Ellenborough, confidential, 23 Nov. 1830, I.O. L/PS/5/120, 5 Aug. 1831, no. 32.

[2] sc to ggic, 4 Oct. 1830, I.O. L/PS/5/543.

[3] Macdonald to Ellenborough, private, 29 Nov. 1829, E.U.L. MSS. Dk/2/37, fo. 101.

[4] 'Memorandum Relative to the Persia Mission', 1830, I.O. L/PS/3/1, p. 180.

resented Willock, and tried to have him sent home, so that Camp-bell could be promoted.[1] With the help of Malcolm, who libelled Willcock to Ellenborough, Macdonald eventually succeeded. Ironically, at the moment Willock's recall reached Teheran, Macdonald died. The struggle immediately became more bitter: Willock and Campbell both wanted to be resident. 'In no part of the world', commented Bentinck wryly, 'has party work and clan work run higher than in Persia.'[2]

Macdonald and Campbell had friends at Bombay and the board of control; Willock's friends were at Fort William. Lord William Bentinck, under pressure from his secretariat, criticized Macdonald for never explaining why Willock should be brought home. However, because he refused to devise British policy in Persia, 'from the greater importance of its connection with the politics of Europe with respect to Russia',[3] in August Bentinck asked Ellenborough to choose Macdonald's successor. Ellenborough had already decided to: he was as eager to seize control of British policy as Bentinck was to lose it, and had decided that someone eminent and famous was needed to recover Britain's influence at Teheran, and to win a diplomatic victory sufficiently striking to propel Ellenborough towards the foreign office. Unfortunately, nobody eminent in England would go. After months of searching Bentinck was told to look. Because the allowances were to be cut down, nobody in India would go. This left a choice between Campbell and Willcock, who had been waiting in Persia for eighteen months to learn which, if either of them, had been chosen.

Ellenborough argued that the shah would interpret the re-appointment of Willock to mean that Britain was going back to Castlereagh's and Canning's policy. Willock's friends at Fort William also proved powerless in 1831 against Campbell's father, who happened to be chairman of the East India Company. 'What a glorious job his appointment is,' said the earl of Clare at Bombay. 'It brings one back to the good old days when Pagoda trees grew in India.'[4] The appointment was also foolish. For ten years in

---

[1] For extracts from Macdonald's correspondence see E. J. Harden, 'Griboedev and the Willock Affair', *Slavic Review*, xxx (1971), 74–91. One must remember that Mrs. Harden writes as if Willock were intriguing against Macdonald. The letters she chose to publish were Macdonald's intrigues against Willock.

[2] Bentinck to Ellenborough, private, 16 Jan. 1831, I.O.L. MSS. Eur. D/556/1.

[3] Bentinck to Ellenborough, private, 26 Aug. 1830, P.R.O. 30/9/4 pt. 1/4.

[4] Clare to Bentinck, private, 28 Dec. 1831, Portland MSS. PwJf/624.

Persia Willock had replied to embarrassing questions and to abuse with discretion and tact. Campbell, who was vain, bombastic, bad tempered, and a liar, had in less than three years driven his assistant to London to work for his recall.

The British had been squandering their influence, at a time when a civil war in Persia was becoming more and more likely. Abbas Mirza's defeat by Russia had caused a new struggle for the succession, and whatever happened Britain seemed likely to suffer. To the shah and the Russians, the Russo-Persian war had been fought over the only strategically satisfactory frontier between Georgia and Persia, which controlled the passes from the Caucasus into Azerbaijan. By the treaty of Turkmanchay the shah lost and the Russians won it. This affected the internal politics of Persia as greatly as the security of British India.

Abbas Mirza, defeated in a war he had risked for his own interests, and fearing he might lose his pre-eminence, became more and more anxious to keep up his foreign connections. When his minister warned Campbell in June 1830, that 'a conviction of the impossibility of preserving the independence of Persia had become prevalent amongst all ranks',[1] he meant that if Britain did not help Abbas Mirza, he would seek help from Russia. The help he wanted was British officers to lead as well as train his troops. Ellenborough, held back by Wellington, had no choice but to hope that training would be enough; that Abbas Mirza would then be strong enough to hold down all his brothers. Abbas need not pay for these instructors, in case he should be offered Russian officers paid for by their government, but they were not to take the field. Firstly the government of India, then in October the board of control, reminded the resident at Teheran, that should war break out between the brothers, Britain would remain neutral.[2]

British leadership, as Indian Army officers knew, was more important than training in reforming native armies and propping up Indian allies; without it, the military mission in Persia would do no more good than they had in the Napoleonic Wars. To strengthen Abbas Mirza, and his reliance on Britain, the detachment would have to join him against his greatest rival for the throne, his half-brother the governor of Kerman. Campbell knew

[1] Encl. in Campbell to sc, 23 June 1830, I.O. Persia/45.
[2] Sc to ggic, 4 Oct. 1830, I.O. L/PS/5/543.

that 'non-intervention . . . now seems to form the basis of European policy', but he could not 'see the justice or propriety of applying such a system in the present state of Persia'.[1]

Most Anglo-Indians assumed the priorities of an insular state, protected by its navy and certain the majority of its population were loyal, to be no guide to successful British policies in Asia. To argue, that by helping Abbas Mirza against the governor of Kerman the British detachment would be meddling in the internal affairs of Persia, was only theoretically true, and, were it true, helping him was unavoidable, because in the spring of 1831 his half-brother was trying to force the shah to name him the heir apparent. This would compel the British to support one side or the other. The prince of Kerman was a brother of the governor of Fars, who had been trying unsuccessfully to persuade the government of Bombay to send a military mission to Shiraz to train his troops. Unless the British helped Abbas Mirza, he would expect them to help his half-brothers, in the hope of turning southern Persia into a protectorate, and would himself seek help from Russia.[2] Partitioning Persia into spheres of influence might have been a defence against a military threat to India from France. As soon as Britain's interests in the near east had been redefined in political terms, partition, by leading on not holding back Russia, and by tempting her to expand eastwards towards Khorassan and Herat, would have been tantamount to a defeat.

This was the situation in Persia when Charles Grant and Henry Ellis took over from Ellenborough at the board of control at the end of 1830. Because they looked at it as they looked at the situation at Baghdad the following year, and in Syria in 1832, they had to decide how to react to civil war in the near-eastern states, and how to hold them together, and ideally stable, with as little interference as possible. Their explanation of the relationship between the governor of Baghdad and Mahomet Ali of Egypt and the sultan resembled their earlier explanation of the relationship between Abbas Mirza and the shah.

Their reasoning on both occasions seemed curious. Campbell was reminded in May 1831 that the treaty of Teheran prohibited British intervention in the internal affairs of Persia. Apparently the prohibition was not absolute; the British detachment might

---

[1] Encl. no. 3 in Campbell to sc, 27 Feb. 1831, I.O. Persia/46.
[2] Encl. in Campbell to sc, 27 Nov. 1830, I.O. Persia/45.

fight for Abbas Mirza against the governor of Kerman, just as a British military mission might train the governor of Baghdad's troops at the invitation of the sultan, because Abbas was acting as deputy for the shah. Ellenborough had treated Abbas Mirza as heir apparent, but Ellis and Grant thought this 'tended to involve us too deeply in the internal concerns of Persia'.[1] Because the Russo-Persian frontier was the most sensitive spot for which the board of control were responsible, Ellis believed that Ellenborough, in trying to match Russian influence over Abbas Mirza, had pursued the wrong policy. The British should not seek and should not recognize particular claims, and, by dealing as far as possible with the shah, should attempt to impose equal restraint on Russia: Persia was not to be treated as Europeans had hitherto treated Turkey. In future Campbell was to treat Abbas Mirza merely as the shah's deputy in 'the management of wars, and of negotiations of an important character'. As the sultan might recall the governor of Baghdad, the shah might transfer Abbas Mirza's powers to one of his brothers; he was to be treated 'not as the Prince Royal nor as the ruler of powerful provinces, but as the person appointed by the king to act in his name and on behalf of His Majesty'.

This was a method of trying to hold together the near-eastern states, as Castlereagh and Canning had tried to hold together the Vienna Settlement in Europe, by behaving as if changes in government did not matter to the British, as long as they did not lead to changes in foreign policy. Metternich thought his Holy Alliance a better method, because if small states were permitted to change their governments, changes in foreign policy could be expected. The appearance of British policy was actually an illusion. Persia and Turkey might do as they wished, provided they were no more attentive to any other state than to Britain. Grant and Ellis warned Persia, in the words Palmerston would later use to the sultan, not to flirt too closely with Russia: 'If His Majesty the shah should be disposed to weaken or dissolve his connection with this country, the effect might be to place us under the necessity of turning our attention to other means of guarding ourselves from the consequences of conduct so unjust and so unreasonable.'[2] The British, having no wish by 1831 to turn Persia into a protectorate,

---

[1] Grant to Grey, 14 May 1831, Grey of Howick MSS.
[2] Encl. to ggic in sc to Campbell, 21 May 1831, F.O. 248/65.

did not seek paramount influence there, but would not surrender it to Russia, because they hoped, in Anatolia and Azerbaijan as later at Baghdad, that if diplomacy could create a stable balance of power between the two states in the form of a buffer, trade would afterwards maintain it.

III

Because British India resembled the Hapsburg Monarchy, the British treated their manufactures as an alternative and more effective Holy Alliance, by which they might defend themselves cheaply and far away. British manufactures were to stabilize the political situation in Persia as well as in Baghdad, by developing the trade-route to Tabriz through Trebizond and Erzerum. The board of trade had suggested in 1826, when the Levant Company gave up their monopoly, and the foreign office under Canning, anxious to avoid entanglements, took control of British consuls, that the time had come to try to expand Britain's trade in the near east.[1] Nothing was done, and in 1829 British merchants who traded to the Black Sea were still complaining, that if they were to expand their trade with the Caucasus and compete with the expanding Russian trade with Persia, they needed the help of a British consul in the Black Sea. Sir Robert Gordon argued in December that all barriers to British trade in the Black Sea had been removed,[2] but the foreign office, where Lord Aberdeen was as interested in the near east as Canning had been bored by it, agreed that the appointment of a consul 'appears most desirable . . . Why', asked Aberdeen in January 1830, 'has it been so long delayed?'[3] Less than two months later, in March 1830, James Brant was appointed vice-consul at Trebizond, with a salary of £200 a year and permission to trade for himself.

According to C. W. Crawley, the needs of trade had a considerable influence on British policy in the near east during the 1830s. To imply, however, that the British wanted to stabilize the Russo-Persian frontier because by the treaties of Turkmanchay, Adrianople, and St. Petersburg, the Russians came far enough south to menace the road from Trebizond to Tabriz, and so to

[1] Lack to Douglas, 20 Aug. 1830, B.T. 3/22, p. 44.
[2] Gordon to Aberdeen, no. 79, 15 Dec. 1829, F.O. 78/181.
[3] Minute of Aberdeen on Turkey merchants to Aberdeen, 29 Jan. 1830, F.O. 78/195.

endanger an important British trade route, is to reverse Britain's order of priorities.[1] The trade was to stabilize the frontier: the British interest was the stability, not the profit. What had frightened them was the fall in 1829 of Erzerum, which Sir John Macdonald explained in July,[2] 'will shake to the foundation the authority of the Grand Signior, leave all the countries east of the Euphrates open to the insults of the Russians, lift them at once into the centre of Asia, and enable them to make a direct communication with the Black Sea by the capture of Trebizond.' Although Erzerum was evacuated by Russia under the terms of the treaty of Adrianople, the British hoped that similar dangers could be forestalled by ending the unrest and increasing the prosperity of eastern Anatolia and Azerbaijan, so helping to create stable frontiers between the two provinces and Russia, and equally important between one another.

The British consul-general at Constantinople agreed that the appointment of Brant might expand British trade with eastern Anatolia. If it were to have any effect in Azerbaijan, the co-operation of Captain Campbell and the East India Company would be needed. Because the Russians, who might resent political initiatives, could not object to British merchants, in July 1830, Ellenborough, eager as always to check Russia, asked the East India Company to help.[3] About to lose their monopoly of trade with China, they did not expect to make up for it by expanding trade with Persia and the gulf. Because the decline of the company's trade made the residency at Basra redundant, they were pressing the government of India to amalgamate it with the residency at Bushire.

Brant reached Trebizond in August 1830. By the end of the year it was obvious that the hopes he had held out to Aberdeen were false. 'A direct trade between Europe and this port does not exist,' he admitted, and little trade was done with the Caucasus.[4] Even that would be stopped in 1832, when the prohibitive Russian

---

[1] C. W. Crawley, 'Anglo-Russian Relations, 1815-40', *Cambridge Historical Journal*, iii (1929), 66-7.

[2] Macdonald to Malcolm, private, 16 July 1829, same to Ellenborough, private, 27 July 1829, E.U.L. MSS. Dk/2/37, fos. 55, 61.

[3] Cartwright to Bidwell, no. 5, 26 May 1830, F.O. 78/195; Jones to Auber, 10 July 1830, I.O. E/2/37.

[4] 'Report [by J. Brant] on the Trade of Trebizond', 25 Mar. 1831, in Brant to Palmerston, no. 2, 25 Mar. 1831, F.O. 78/205.

tariffs would be extended to Georgia. This left the trade with Persia, and Trebizond in the wrong place for the consulate. British merchants might need help at Trebizond, because their goods would arrive by sea: Persian and Turkish merchants, whose goods travelled overland from Tabriz to Constantinople, would prefer to settle their European business as Erzerum. Ideally British agents should be posted at both cities. Brant offered in January 1831 to take a lower salary were he named British consul at Erzerum, provided his partner succeeded him at Trebizond. There would be no conflict between their official and private interests, he told Aberdeen, because, so sparse was British trade, the government's success was indistinguishable from theirs.

Erzerum, unlike Trebizond, lay astride the caravan routes between Tabriz to the east, Angora and Constantinople to the west, Kars to the north, and Baghdad and Damascus to the south. 'Nothing seems wanting to make the place a great commercial mart', said Brant, 'but merchants to supply their wants and receive their produce.'[1] This conclusion was belied by his own analysis. After the treaty of Adrianople, the Russians, anxious to increase the ratio of Christians to Mahometans in their frontier provinces, had moved 50,000 Armenian families from Erzerum behind the Russian frontier. The Turks had promptly confiscated their property. Brant was certain, that if the Turks could be persuaded to restore it, the Armenians would find ways to return, but the Turks must hurry, or the Russians would build the Armenians new towns. Instead of political stability being the result of trade, as a substitute for political intervention, intervention was apparently needed to expand the trade.

The trade would also depend upon more precise definition of the terms of trade between Britain and Persia. The Persians were levying higher charges on British goods entering Persia from Erzerum than on those being shipped from Bombay through Bushire. At Bushire the Persians levied duties from the purchaser at 3 per cent and on certain articles at only 1 per cent; at the border between Persia and Turkey the duty paid by the vendor was 5 per cent, which came on top of the 3 per cent levied by the Turks, whether or not the goods were only in transit. Campbell had persuaded the Persians to lower their charges in individual

---

[1] 'Note [by J. Brant] on the Commercial Prospects of Erzerum', 20 Jan. 1831, in Brant to Aberdeen, no. 1, 20 Jan. 1831, F.O. 78/205.

cases, but, because he could not speak for the British government, only for the government of India, he could not try to negotiate a new tariff.[1] Canning's policy of separating Persia politically from Europe was making it impossible to rejoin them by means of trade. In the summer of 1831 Campbell warned the board of control, and Brant the foreign office, that until the British negotiated a new commercial treaty, and gave the resident at Teheran the power to enforce it, they would not be able to expand British trade through Erzerum. Brant urged on Palmerston in the same language he had used to Aberdeen. 'One motive which I imagine may be considered a strong one,' he repeated, 'is the increase of British influence which would probably follow a more active commercial intercourse.'[2] In Persia as in Sind, and as so often throughout the east, the British were being asked to calculate, whether a little political pressure might not produce a great commercial gain. Expanding trade was politically as well as economically desirable, but free trade did not always lead to freedom to trade.

The foreign office, who always found trade distasteful, in the spring of 1831 asked the board of trade and the board of control to decide what should be done. Free trade and *laissez-faire* were the watchwords of nineteenth-century liberal England: they were enshrined at the board of trade as deities. Nobody worshipped them at Bombay. The British Indian economy was the exception to the rules of British economic policy throughout the nineteenth century: in the near east it also tried to change them. British merchants at Bombay, and Indian merchants financed by British capital, interpreted equal opportunity to mean privilege, ideally monopoly.[3] In Persia they were used to and would want to go on paying lower duties than the Russians. The frontier between Turkey and Persia, the boundary between the European and Indian political systems, also divided two economic systems. This offended the board of trade. They reacted sharply in

---

[1] Brant to Campbell, 2 Apr. 1831, F.O. 248/65; encl. in Campbell to sc, 23 Sept. 1831, I.O. Persia/46. The Persians caused endless disputes by levying duties on goods evaluated by the customs master, whereas the Turks levied them upon the invoice price. In individual cases the Persian duty had been lowered to 2 per cent on piece goods and 4 per cent on hardware.

[2] Brant to Palmerston, no. 3, 21 May 1831, F.O. 78/205.

[3] See H. R. C. Wright, *East Indian Economic Problems in the Age of Cornwallis and Raffles* (London, 1961), and P. Nightingale, *Trade and Empire in Western India, 1784–1806* (Cambridge, 1970).

June, after the Turks prohibited the export of Turkish goods from Trebizond in European ships, because that interrupted trade, and disobeyed the capitulations: they would do little to promote trade. They thought a consulate at Erzerum a likely waste of public money, unless someone should offer to do the job unpaid in order to use the title.[1] Similarly a new treaty would be useful only if it improved the mechanics of trade, such as transport, arrangements for settling disputes, and, although the board of trade never learnt that this was a sensitive political question, the safety of merchants. Beyond this nothing should be done. The board were strongly opposed to anything 'which should have for its object, on either side, the obtaining of exclusive or distinctive privileges'.[2]

The East India Company were no more interested than the board of trade. When the board of control asked for their advice, they replied in May that the last commercial treaty between Britain and Persia had been negotiated by John Malcolm in 1800, and, although the Persians treated it as cancelled by the treaty of Teheran, British goods were allowed in at Bushire as if it were still in force. As long as excessive charges were not levied at Bushire, the company did not care what happened to goods from Erzerum: they did not see how the proposed trade 'can affect directly or indirectly either the interests of the Company or the countries subject to their governments in India . . . [nor] should they expect that much advantage would be derived from it'.[3]

This left the board of control, who had, as Ellenborough had had, a political interest in the trade, as a weapon in the Great Game in Asia, but were true to their form in 1831 and so cautious. The British, they explained in June, had become interested in Erzerum too late; the Russian gains at Turkmanchay had cut the best route between Erzerum and Tabriz through Erivan. As a result 'the intercourse by the ports of the Black Sea with the north of Persia may probably become either more complicated or more circuitous . . . [and] the port of Trebizond may not so easily, as might otherwise be expected, supersede the more circuitous channels of trade' through the Persian Gulf.[4] The board of control wanted to avoid all initiatives likely to justify similar

---

[1] Lack to Backhouse, 27 May, 17 June 1831, B.T. 3/22, pp. 346, 369.
[2] Lack to Backhouse, 18 June 1832, B.T. 3/23, p. 329.
[3] Auber to Villiers, 19 May 1831, F.O. 248/65.
[4] Villiers to Backhouse, 17 June 1831, F.O. 248/65.

concessions to Russia, or demands from Persia. If he could, Campbell was to persuade the Persians to levy on British goods arriving from Erzerum the same duty paid on goods arriving at Bushire; but he was not to do it by persuading the Persians to agree that Malcolm's commercial treaty was still in force. This was a trap Henry Ellis was anxious to avoid, because, whereas the Persians would claim such a concession to be worth an offer of protection, trade was politically useful to the British, only if it could manage without help and without creating entanglements. It must, however, be encouraged, because the board were 'fully alive to the importance, political as well as commercial, of extending our trade with Persia'.[1]

Two months later the board became more aggressive: trade was one subject on which Grant had strong views. Confident in the wish of the Persians to expand their trade with Britain, for nobody turned down the chance of progress and happiness, he told Campbell to negotiate a new tariff on goods travelling through Erzerum. The duty levied should be lower than the duty paid on goods at Bushire, because it was legitimate practice to charge more on goods that were trans-shipped; goods through Erzerum would be travelling directly to and from England. The board were still assuming that this tariff might be introduced without negotiating a new commercial treaty or reviving Malcolm's.[2] They had explained their determination to treat Persia as a sovereign state: diplomatic practice, and foreign trade organized according to European practice, would hold it together and would be followed by prosperity and tranquillity. To encourage the trade, in October the board, unlike the board of trade, urged the foreign office to follow Brant's advice and post a British consul at Erzerum.[3]

As trade turned out to depend upon the support of the imperial governments, whose efficiency it was supposed to increase, in Persia in 1832 and in Turkey two years later Britain's priorities were turned about; more attention being paid to strengthening the government and less to expanding British trade. The foreign policy, as well as the domestic politics, of Persia became increasingly unsteady in 1831 and 1832, because Abbas Mirza, his military reputation damaged by defeat against the Russians, was

[1] Ibid.; sc to ggic, 17 June 1831, I.O. L/PS/5/543.
[2] Sc to ggic, 24 Aug. 1831, I.O. L/PS/5/544.
[3] Villiers to Backhouse, 29 Oct. 1831, I.O. L/PS/3/117.

looking for ways to repair it, and to make certain of the throne. Turbulence in Persia was itself threatening to the British; it became more so at a time when it might have been expected to become less. The struggle with Russia was over. The treaty of Turkmanchay had given the Russians a strategically satisfactory frontier in the Caucasus; they could prop up Persia as a protectorate on their southern frontier, and soothe Abbas Mirza by turning him towards the east. As long as Persia and Turkey were closely connected with Russia, should they recover control of their eastern provinces, they would make her southern frontier more secure. The British did not see that the policy was defensive, although it would not have mattered if they had: they only saw that if Russia gained in Persia the influence they assumed she hoped to gain in Turkey by the treaty of Unkiar Skelessi, she could not help but endanger British India.

Their defeat by Russia had had an equally marked effect on the Kajar dynasty. In 1830 the shah appointed Abbas Mirza governor of Hamadan and Kermanshah. In consequence he governed the whole of Persia west of Teheran, and became so much more powerful than any of his brothers, that in an attempt to challenge him, the governor of Kerman, Hassan Ali Mirza, seized Yezd and marched on Isfahan. Were his brother, the governor of Fars, to support him, Persia would be partitioned, with a narrow strip between Isfahan and Teheran as the frontier. Whatever happened British interests would suffer. Campbell feared, that unless asked by the shah to suppress Hassan Ali, Abbas Mirza might threaten Baghdad, in an attempt to exact tribute from the governor. Instead he marched against Kerman, where Hassan Ali, deserted by his brother, at the beginning of May gave in without a fight. This success revived Abbas Mirza's self-confidence. He had been responsible for Persia's foreign and defence policy in the west since the Napoleonic Wars; the shah now gave him responsibility for the east.[1] By the autumn he was ready for an expedition to Khorassan, rumoured to be the prelude to marching against Khiva or Herat. Abbas Mirza had to find somewhere for his troops to plunder, as he had not been paying them. 'Whatever they intend to do,' said the commander of the British detachment in August,

[1] Campbell to Swinton, 27 Feb. 1831, I.O. Bengal/SPC/361, 29 July 1831, no. 4.

'they had better be quick about it, or I fear the staff and colours will be all that will remain.'[1]

This placed Captain Campbell in the same predicament as Charles Metcalfe back in 1808, when he had been dragged from camp to camp by Ranjit Singh on his campaign against the cis-Sutledge states. Campbell was torn between staying at Tabriz, to prevent the Russian mission from gaining too great an influence over Abbas Mirza's ministers, or following the prince in the hope of dissuading him from invading Khorassan. Despite the board's instructions, to prevent Abbas Mirza from accusing the British of supporting the rebellion, Campbell had permitted the detachment to accompany him to Kerman. It did no good. Persian generals, used to levies of irregular cavalry supplied by the tribes, had always resented the British preference for infantry. Although the least advantage the British hoped to gain from fighting this local prejudice, and sharing their military as well as technological skills, was the exclusive right to train their allies' troops, the British detachment were followed to Kerman by a battalion of infantry under the command of Russians. Campbell, irritated by the intrigues and the competition, tried to find an excuse to withdraw the detachment. Some way had to be found to increase his influence, for here in the autumn of 1831 was the first sign that Persia might be moving eastwards, as Palmerston later put it, as 'the advanced guard of Russia'.[2]

Englishmen in the near east have never been backward in trying to help their government. In the autumn of 1831 Campbell's task was not made easier by the arrival in Persia of Captain Chesney, on the tour of the near east which had already taken him to Egypt and Baghdad. Chesney had a solution to all Britain's problems; to draw Abbas Mirza westwards, reverse the south-eastward expansion of Russia, and sever the connection between Russia and Persia. Persia was to take advantage of the rebellion in Poland— Chesney did not know it was already over—to plan with the sultan a joint invasion of Georgia. 'Such a measure', he told Abbas Mirza in September, 'would be most acceptable to England, on whose assistance he might rely.'[3] This indiscretion caused a flurry

[1] Encl. no. 2 in Campbell to sc, 22 Aug. 1831, I.O. Persia/46.
[2] Quoted in Kelly, *Persian Gulf*, p. 464.
[3] Campbell to sc, confidential, 10 Oct. 1831, F.O. 60/32; Chesney to Gordon, 13 May 1832, F.O. 78/218.

at London. 'Some check should be given to the unauthorized proceedings of Captain Chesney,' said one senior official at the board of control, 'who is usurping the functions of the British envoy and may, if not speedily prevented, involve us in considerable embarrassment.' 'Quite right,' agreed Grant,[1] and early in February 1832 mentioned the matter to Palmerston. Palmerston was to warn Stratford Canning at Constantinople to curb Chesney, and Heytesbury at St. Petersburg to calm the Russians: Grant would remind Abbas Mirza of the fiction that Anglo-Persian relations were dealt with by the government of India.[2]

Poland played her part in the Great Game in Asia, as in every international crisis until 1870; Polish nationalism was the pillar upholding the Holy Alliance. Chesney had echoed Lacy Evans, by implying that as Great Britain had become an Asiatic as well as a European state, a Polish lever against Russia should be used to prevent the development by Russia of an effective Indian lever against Britain. Unfortunately, and it placed the British in a dilemma, Poland was covered by the Vienna Settlement, whereas Turkey and Persia were not. 'We must stand upon our treaties,' replied Palmerston, when asked to help the Poles, 'and while, on the one hand, we should remonstrate if Russia were to depart from the treaty of Vienna, on the other hand, we could not do so ourselves by helping to make Poland entirely independent.'[3] The partition of Poland regulated the power of France; as far as it also increased the power of Russia, the British were trying at the beginning of the Great Game in Asia to forestall the potentially threatening consequences, by devising a near-eastern equivalent to the Vienna Settlement.

The most odd aspect of this incident was the surprise of the British, that with two Englishmen to proffer him advice, Abbas Mirza should have ignored both of them. Chesney could not persuade him to invade Georgia, nor Campbell dissuade him from invading Khorassan. The success or failure of this expedition would be equally calamitous. Campbell was certain that the Russians were its authors, and had planned it as the prelude to a

[1] Minutes of Cabell and Grant, 30 Jan. 1832, on Campbell to sc, 10 Oct. 1831, I.O. Persia/46.
[2] Grant to Palmerston, 1 Feb. 1832, I.O. L/PS/3/117; Palmerston to Grant, 14 Feb. 1832, F.O. 60/32.
[3] Palmerston to Granville, private, 29 Mar. 1831, P.R.O. 30/29/404; same to Holland, private, 9 Apr. 1831, Add. MSS. 51599, fo. 60.

joint attack on Khiva.[1] Should the Russians capture Khiva, they would extend their influence far to the south-east, and, as Lacy Evans had predicted, would have the opportunity, by advancing along the Oxus, to cause unrest beyond and along the North-West Frontier of India. Abbas Mirza, on the other hand, might be defeated. This would provoke civil war in Persia, and force him to offer Persia to Russia as a protectorate as the only way to ensure himself the throne. In the new year of 1832, unless these nasty circumstances in Turkestan and Persia could be forestalled as Ellenborough had planned, the British might lose their chance to create a buffer zone, a protectorate in Afghanistan, and a satisfactory frontier between the European and Indian political systems.

Campbell must have seemed a pest, because he regularly reminded Abbas Mirza how weak he was. His army had never defeated the Russians, and had no reason to risk defeat in Khorassan; they had done what the British wanted by keeping down his brothers and ensuring his accession, 'a chain of successes achieved more by the appearance than the actual power of the army'.[2] Trying to increase his power by pacifying Khorassan might defeat its object. Campbell, who had not yet found an excuse for bringing the British detachment back to Azerbaijan, feared that if he now forbade them to go with Abbas Mirza to Khorassan, Russian influence would be unchallenged, whereas if they went, they were likely to become more involved in Persian politics than the board of control would wish. As a compromise, in November Campbell said they should go, but warned them not to join an expedition against Khiva or Herat. If the British in Persia were not merely to jog behind events, they had to find a way, either by inducement or pressure, to convince Abbas Mirza that his interests would be best served by attending as closely to Britain as to Russia.

The shift in Persian foreign policy to the east was equally worrying to the government of India. The resident at Ludhiana, Captain Wade, had warned them in the spring that a connection between Persia and Sind, to follow a dynastic marriage being planned, might give the Russians the chance to prevent the British from opening up the Indus. Campbell explained in December that

[1] Campbell to sc, confidential, 10 Oct. 1831, I.O. Persia/46.
[2] Campbell to Swinton, 6 Nov. 1831, I.O. Bengal/SPC/365, 12 Mar. 1832, no. 3.

it was nonsense to see Persia as a protectorate of Russia. The shah hated the Russians; Abbas Mirza was merely trying to humour them. He hoped that in return for planning expeditions against Khiva, they might go without the last crore of the indemnity, still owing under the treaty of Turkmanchay, and again promise him the throne.[1] Campbell often warned the board and the government of India that this was one cause of their lack of influence: the state of his relations with the Russians mattered more to Abbas Mirza than the state of Persia. If they would support him when the time came, he would win the civil war. The British were always telling him to stand alone. That was risky, and, until the indemnity was paid, impossible.

The British were infuriating allies. As a welfare office they had numberless plans for improvement; arriving at intervals during the nineteenth century armed with constitutions, training manuals, ideas about civil liberty, designs for steamers, telegraphs, and railways, when all one needed were troops and a little cash. So niggardly were they, that often they cheated. Abbas Mirza claimed that when the British had first tried to buy out the subsidiary articles of the treaty of Teheran, they had offered 400,000 tomauns. As soon as he agreed, because he needed the money to pay the Russian indemnity, the sum was halved.[2] In the new year of 1832, he offered the British a bargain.

When Captain Shee, the acting commander of the British detachment, reached Meshed, 'frightened out of his wits' by what was happening,[3] he was persuaded in April to sign an agreement promising Abbas Mirza 100,000 tomauns, the amount owed by Persia to Russia, in return for giving up his expedition to Khiva and dismissing his Russian advisers. Campbell, not yet confirmed as resident, was furious, disavowed the agreement, and told Shee not to meddle in politics.[4] Nevertheless Campbell warned the board of control in May that they must do something to help Abbas Mirza, who was the best barrier to paramount Russian influence over Persia. The governor of Fars, 'a miserable debauchee of no weight in the kingdom . . . who sleeps eighteen hours out of the

[1] Campbell to Prinsep, 4 Dec. 1831, I.O. Bengal/SPC/367, 30 July 1832, no. 2; see above, Ch. IV, p 93.

[2] 'Record [by Revd. J. Wolff] of a Conversation with Abbas Mirza', 10 Jan. 1832, F.O. 60/32.

[3] Clare to Bentinck, private, 19 July 1832, Portland MSS. PwJf/667.

[4] Campbell to sc, 8 May 1832, with encls. nos. 3–8, I.O. Persia/47.

twenty-four',[1] who had been angling for Russian advisers, as he had been refused British, would be far more easily overawed. The results of Shee's blunder were to have been expected: the khan of Herat, the beg of Bokhara, and even Shah Shuja, all offered in return for subsidies to defend British India against Russia. Abbas Mirza's argument, however, was irrefutable: if the British had not deserted him, he would not have needed the help of Russia. He had taken the board of control at their word. If they wanted him to regain his independence, they must help him pay off the indemnity.

In 1832 Campbell's reports became more erratic than the situation in Persia they described. In the spring he continued his lament that the greater danger to Britain from the expedition to Khorassan was the likelihood of Abbas Mirza's being defeated. His own provinces were ravaged by plague and cholera, his revenues all spent on the campaigns in the east, and 'self-glory seems to have taken possession of his mind'.[2] The British should pay for moving his army back to Azerbaijan; otherwise, said Campbell in May, 'want and anarchy' would lead to the 'utter dissolution of his power'.[3] Abbas Mirza was advancing against Herat, in the hope that Kamran Khan and the khan of Khiva would agree to pay tribute, and Campbell feared a decisive counter-attack. Instead, by the autumn, he was hailing Abbas, who had managed to Campbell's surprise to pacify Khorassan, as a soldier 'unknown in Persia since the days of Nadir Shah'.[4]

This did not alter Britain's predicament. Abbas Mirza must still be persuaded to return, before his success became as damaging to Britain as his failure: by preventing her from turning Afghanistan into a protectorate, the fall of Herat to Persia, even more than the fall of Khiva to Russia, would endanger the security of India. To increase Britain's influence, in the autumn Campbell sent his assistant, John McNeill, to Abbas Mirza's headquarters at Torbat. McNeill, who Clare told Bentinck would prevent Campbell 'from getting you into scrapes',[5] decided that the attack on Herat was a feint. It had been planned to deceive the rebel chiefs

---

[1] Macdonald to Malcolm, 25 May 1829, E.U.L. MSS. Dk/2/37, fo. 26. The prince-governor of Fars, like the prince regent of England, had not aged well.

[2] Campbell to Malcolm, 16 June 1831, I.O.L. Film. MSS. 2408.

[3] Campbell to Grant, 9 May 1832, same to sc, 9 May 1832, I.O. Persia/47.

[4] Campbell to Swinton, 25 Sept. 1832, I.O. Bengal/SPC/371, 14 Jan. 1833, no. 13.

[5] Clare to Bentinck, private, 5 Jan. 1832, Portland MSS. PwJf/624.

of Khorassan and to frighten Campbell: Abbas Mirza had hoped, as the board of control had feared would follow from entanglement in Persia's dynastic quarrels, that the British, in fear of Russia, might buy him off. McNeill, trying to disillusion him, warned him that 'coquetting with other powers would most certainly be abortive'.[1] McNeill was mistaken. The board of control had finally decided that something must be done.

In Persia, as in Asiatic Turkey, the British could not expand their trade until they had dealt with existing political problems. Contrary to the board's instructions, in the autumn of 1831 Campbell had pressed the Persians to recognize that Malcolm's commercial treaty was still in force.[2] They refused, and Campbell doubted whether they would be willing to negotiate an alternative tariff, because Britain's trade in Persia like her political influence came second to Russia's. Persia could not permit British goods from Erzerum to pay the same duty as goods landed at Bushire, which would have been lower than the duty paid by Russian merchants on goods from Tiflis. By the terms of the treaty of Turkmanchay both Russian and Persian goods paid a single customs duty of 5 per cent *ad valorem* at the frontier. This suited the Persians, because, although trade boomed between 1828 and 1830, owing to the closure of the overland routes through Anatolia during the Russo-Turkish war, and slumped shortly afterwards, not to recover for fifty years, in both cases the balance favoured Persia.[3] This made a pleasant contrast to the unfavourable balance of trade between Persia and British India.

Campbell had hoped that the Persians would be more amenable in 1832. In July, the Russians, trying to protect their manufactures, had introduced prohibitive tariffs against the shipment of goods from Europe to Persia through Georgia. Abbas Mirza said he wanted to develop an alternative route; the balance of Russo-Persian trade favoured the Persians, partly because they could circumvent the tariff by shipping European manufactures into Georgia paying only 5 per cent in duty. Unfortunately for the British, trade came second to politics. Abbas Mirza's anxiety about the succession bound him to Russia more closely than the

[1] Encl. no. 10 in Campbell to sc, 24 Dec. 1832, I.O. Persia/47; *McNeill*, pp. 157–61.
[2] Campbell to sc, 20 Sept. 1831, I.O. Persia/46.
[3] M. L. Entner, *Russo-Persian Commercial Relations, 1828–1914* (Gainesville, 1965), pp. 7–10.

potential profits from trade drew him to Britain. There was a second reason. By the terms of the treaty of Turkmanchay Russia might post consuls 'wherever the good of commerce will demand it'.[1] The Kajars, who resisted all appointments on the ground that the trade was not big enough to warrant them, were less interested in its expansion than in strengthening their dynasty; and did not share the British assumption that one would follow the other. The British were always slow to realize that theirs was the only society where political stability depended upon the expansion of trade. By the end of 1832 the most successful importers into Persia were the members of the British mission, who could obtain luxuries more cheaply at London than at Bombay.

Brant at Trebizond had done no better; until the Persian mission should be returned to the foreign office, he could not be expected to. In October 1832, after 'fruitless endeavours to establish a commerce with Persians here', and certain that nothing could be done without a tariff, Brant decided to visit Campbell at Tabriz.[2] Brant's analysis of the potential of Anatolia remained ambivalent. Potentially it was rich. The best way to tap its wealth would be by allowing the Turks, when the tariff was renewed in 1834, to raise the duty from 3 to 5 per cent, in return for the removal of all restrictions on what might be imported and exported. Expanding British trade was becoming urgent, as the best means of 'counteracting Russian influence, which is increasing every day, and which seems to be less offensive to the population than it was'. Here was the catch. 'Nothing is wanting but the proper protection,' Brant had claimed of the transit trade to Persia, 'to cause it to become of importance.'[3] Unfortunately, he reported in September, in Anatolia 'everyone is as discontented as possible' with the Turks.[4] In addition to revising the tariff, the British would have to find a way to make the Turkish government more efficient, by increasing the sultan's control over his eastern provinces. Nowhere was this more urgent than in Syria. Erzerum had not recovered its previous commercial eminence, said Brant, because Mahomet Ali's rebellion had interrupted all trade.

The invasion of Syria also interrupted a discussion at the board

[1] Hurewitz, *Near and Middle East*, i. 96–102.
[2] Brant to Backhouse, separate, 2 Oct. 1832, F.O. 78/215.
[3] 'Report [by J. Brant] on the Trade of Trebizond', 31 Dec. 1831, in Brant to Palmerston, no. 10, 31 Dec. 1831, F.O. 78/205.
[4] Brant to Bidwell, 8 Sept. 1832, F.O. 78/215.

of control about how the British could re-establish their influence in Persia. Grant had been mortified to learn that British trade was not being given the chance to improve Persia it deserved. In May 1832 he reminded Abbas Mirza, that he was relying upon him to protect British merchants from 'vexations impediments' and 'unauthorised exactions'.[1] Persia's commercial as well as diplomatic habits ought to take Britain's as their model. Until the end of the year the board pressed Persia to reduce the duties being charged on goods entering through Erzerum; they also wanted Alexander Burnes, on his return from Bokhara, to travel directly from Persia to London, to report on the prospects of trade in Turkestan. 'We continue of the opinion', said the board, 'that an improvement in our commercial relations with Persia . . . is a desirable object, the pursuit of which should steadily be kept in view.'[2] They had realized, however, that they would have to risk negotiations for a new tariff, and that the chances of success would depend upon first re-establishing their influence.

IV

King William IV had been a sailor. This may account for his preferences in foreign affairs: the admiralty had never been particularly interested in the European balance of power, and William saw that the defence of British India was as important. 'I am decidedly of the opinion', he said in July 1832, 'that our intercourse with Persia ought to be encouraged, and a friendly intercourse built up in order to strengthen our influence and diminish the attempts of Russia to hold Persia under subjugation.'[3] When he mentioned this to Palmerston, the foreign secretary replied that it was Grant's affair, but the king was not so easily discouraged. He had been reading Brant's reports, and was anxious the foreign office should not miss the opportunity provided by the new Russian tariff to develop the alternative routes to Persia through the Black Sea or down the Euphrates.[4] British policy in Persia and Baghdad owed much to William IV.

---

[1] Encl. to ggic in sc to Campbell, 1 May 1832, I.O. L/PS/5/544.
[2] Sc to ggic, 12 Dec. 1832, ibid.
[3] Memorandum by William IV, 16 July 1832, I.O. Persia/48. One can never be certain what William IV thought, because his letters were written by his secretary, Sir Herbert Taylor. He said that he wrote only what the king thought.
[4] Palmerston to Grant, 17 July 1832, Taylor to Palmerston, 26 July 1832, F.O. 60/32.

The board of control, who had at first been confident that any-thing British must win the day, were soon surprised. Henry Ellis had tended to discount the reports of a joint Russo-Persian expedition against Khiva, because he had expected Abbas Mirza to realize that his most vital interest was to husband his military strength in order to overawe his brothers. When it became clear that Campbell was being ignored, the board were disappointed. 'We can attribute to nothing short of infatuation', they remarked, 'the conduct he has adopted in respect to his troops.'[1] Was Abbas Mirza showing a preference for Russian advice? In October 1831 Grant asked to be told what was meant '*by Russians*, for although by reports we have heard of a Russian force being with Abbas Mirza, this is the first intimation in any official paper'.[2]

The campaign in Khorassan confirmed their fears. In the spring of 1832 the board had to admit, that they must work out the likely repercussions of a closer connection between Persia and Russia; what was the best defence against them; and how far and by what means they should intervene, if they decided to re-establish sufficient British influence in Persia to counteract them, and to demonstrate to Russia that Britain had the determination and the means to prevent Persia's being turned from a buffer into a protectorate. Ellis, accordingly, collected during the summer from past and present British agents in the near east a series of papers, 'in view to the adoption of some decisive proceedings in respect to the treaty with that state',[3] and which read like the papers collected by Ellenborough two years earlier.

It is a testimony to the influence of Henry Ellis, that having spent the spring and summer of 1832 thinking what ought to be done in Persia, the board of control were persuaded to do little. That something would have to be done was suggested by the names of the men from whom they sought advice. Two of the papers were written by Sir Gore Ouseley and Sir Henry Willock, the first a casualty of Castlereagh's, the second of Canning's determination to sever the Persian Connection.

---

[1] Sc to ggic, 9 Nov. 1831, I.O. L/PS/5/544.

[2] Minute of Grant, 21 Oct. 1831, on Campbell to sc, 22 Aug. 1831, I.O. Persia/46.

[3] 'Memoranda Relating to Persia, Prepared Principally by Mr. Ellis, in View of the Adoption of some Decisive Proceeding in Respect to the Treaty with that State, in Consequence of the Abrogation of the 3rd and 4th Articles of the

What most frightened Willock, as it had Colonel de Lacy Evans, was the possibility of a Russian expedition against Khiva. At Khiva the Russians could threaten to cause unrest in both Khorassan and British India, because they could expand along the Oxus virtually unnoticed. As Ellenborough had realized, this was far more dangerous than any threat of invasion.

The extending influence of Russia in the East [said Willock] gives the prospect of change to the disaffected [in India], and the ferment which the hope is calculated to produce on the public mind is more likely to undermine our authority and rule than any overt act of hostility on the part of that power.

Unfortunately, once the expansion of Russia had begun, Britain would have no means of stopping it.

The irregularities of bordering states will continue to afford Russia a plausible pretext for further interference and encroachment [added Willock], and her gradual progress may be pursued to our very frontier in India without affording the slightest tangible ground for the expression of umbrage on our part.

Willock assumed that the Russians' experience in Turkestan would resemble Britain's in India: surrounded by decaying and unruly oasis states, once their expansion had begun, they would have no choice but to continue it.

Willock, like Arthur Conolly and Charles Trevelyan, belonged to the Ludhiana and Ouseley, like Sir John Malcolm and Sir John Macdonald, to the Bombay School of Indian defence. Should the Russians expand eastwards from the Caspian, 'it at once excludes Persia from all possibility of checking [their] advance . . . towards India,' said Willock, 'and we must attach less value to our alliance with the shah and seek to raise in Afghanistan and its rulers a new barrier'.[1] Willock, who had worked under Castlereagh and Canning, hoped that, if the foreign office took back control of the Persian mission, they might be able to preserve Persia as a buffer state; Ouseley, remembering Wellesley's vision of Persia as an Indian subsidiary ally, chose the Persian Connection as the best

Treaty of Teheran of November, 1814', I.O. Persia/48. Many of the papers were also filed in F.O. 60/32.

[1] Memorandum by Willock, 6 Mar. 1832, I.O. Persia/48. For Russian interest in Turkestan see S. Gopal, 'Reaching for the Oxus: A Study of Central Asian Politics in First Half of the Nineteenth Century', *Journal of Indian History*, Golden Jubilee Volume (1973), 745–60.

defence of India. The disorder in Turkestan, said by Willock to endanger British India, Ouseley said would help defend it: the British might use the Turcomans to prevent the Russians from settling on the east coast of the Caspian.

A hint from the Prince Royal [of Persia] would suffice [said Ouseley]; their readiness to take advantage of every commotion by friend or foe, and their want to subordination to the Prince, or even their own chiefs, would sufficiently account for their desultory attacks without any suspicion being excited to the prejudice of Persia.

To use Abbas Mirza as Britain's agent in central Asia, the British would need to recover their influence in Persia. Ouseley, even more strongly than Willock, whose career had been ruined by it, argued that British influence had suffered, from transferring the Persian Mission from the foreign office to the government of India, and from abrogating the subsidiary articles of the treaty of Teheran. These should be put back, in a form vague enough to satisfy the Persians and warn the Russians, but without committing the British, and a new minister should be sent to Teheran from the foreign office. 'The experiment', said Ouseley, 'of transferring Persian politics back to Asia, and the attempt of putting an end to the relations of Persia with Europe have been tried, and have failed.'[1]

This line of argument was opposed, as was to be expected, by Captain Campbell: it threatened his career. 'The dispenser of tomauns . . . certainly not fit for his situation',[2] survived only as long as his loyal and capable assistant, John McNeill, drafted his most important dispatches. He had drafted this one. McNeill, also following Malcolm, argued that the threat to British India from Russian expansion would be most obvious, and should be met, not at Khiva but at Tabriz. The Russians would have difficulty reaching Khiva from Orenburg: any advance from the Caspian, and Astarabad in the south-east corner would make the best bridgehead, could be barred by Persia. Like Ouseley, McNeill argued that to regain her influence in Persia was Britain's most important interest in the near east. 'An inconceivable apathy has been manifested to the affairs of Persia,' complained McNeill, who missed Ellenborough; as a result Abbas Mirza, worried about

---

[1] Memorandum by Ouseley, 5 July 1832, I.O. Persia/48.
[2] Clare to Bentinck, private, 2 Sept. 1832, Portland MSS. PwJf/673.

the succession, had turned to the Russians. So worried was he, that in return for a promise of the throne he might be willing to give them Azerbaijan. If he did, the British could retaliate only by threatening a partition, encouraging the governor of Fars to declare himself independent, or by pushing into central Asia ahead of the Russians. They could not be stopped in Persia. 'If Russia [is] resolved to take possession of Persia by force,' said McNeill, 'all our power cannot prevent her doing so.'

The British could match Russian influence, and so maintain Persia as a buffer. The ambassador at St. Petersburg should regularly remind the Russians, that Britain knew what they were about, and of their obligations to treat Persia as a sovereign and independent state. At the same time, Britain should give more help to Abbas Mirza. If a larger military mission were sent out, and his infantry were armed with modern weapons, Abbas might risk fighting for the throne without foreign help, and would become less subservient to Russia, 'who will be left no legal ground for interference'. This was all that was necessary in Persia, and all Britain should attempt: to put back the subsidiary articles, in however vague a form, 'would awaken the jealousy of Russia and afford her unnecessary umbrage'.[1] For the same reason the British, who did not want to entangle themselves in Persia but to keep out the Russians, should avoid the dramatic gesture of sending an embassy from London. A little military aid, quietly supplied from India, and a little money to spend when the shah died, would prevent a war for the throne. Because it might justify Russian expansion, unrest in Persia was the most serious threat to British India, a stable government there its best defence.

Willock and the Revd. Joseph Wolff, a well-known traveller, who had recently visited Persia and Turkestan, argued that it was dangerous to ignore the shah. Britain's influence in Persia had been destroyed partly by the utilitarian passion for economy. The board of control praised the 'masterly manner' in which McNeill had persuaded the shah to waive the customary presents due when Campbell was confirmed as resident. The shah was bitterly offended. 'They do what they like now,' he said, 'they think the waters have passed over me.'[2] Because the shah had chosen to treat Abbas Mirza as his deputy, since the Napoleonic Wars the

---

[1] Campbell [actually McNeill] to sc, 4 Sept. 1832, I.O. Persia/47.
[2] McNeill to Campbell, 30 June 1832, *McNeill*, p. 153.

British resident had spent most of his time at Tabriz. To improve his personal relations with Fath Ali would be difficult. The mission was too small; to ruin Willock, Sir John Macdonald had argued in 1828 that he needed only one assistant. In the spring of 1832 Campbell was alone, because he had sent McNeill to take up his new post as resident at Bushire. Until the autumn, when McNeill came back, there was nobody to represent Britain at Teheran. To maintain any style in either capital was becoming more and more difficult, because the resident's allowances had been cut, and the government of India would spend as little as they could to keep up his houses.[1] This was a concession; in India residents had to house themselves. That British policy in Persia was carried on by one government and was paid for by a second was another reason for the decline of British influence. The presence of a Russian mission in Persia made it risky to treat the British mission as if they were at Gwalior or Hyderabad: the political situations were too dissimilar. During 1832 it became more risky. As an omen of trouble, in December the new Russian minister, General Count Simonitch, arrived at Tabriz.

Willock and Wolff also warned the board that British influence in Persia was suffering because Abbas Mirza compared the British mission unfavourably with the Russian. Young men were the glory of British India; their bounce, thrust, and self-confidence, had served Britain well. In India there had been no competition: eighteenth-century Frenchmen had been similar. In Persia the Russians cheated: they sent as envoys men with high rank and titles. During the Napoleonic Wars the Russians had resented the British habit of sending young or bad-mannered men to St. Petersburg; the Third Coalition had been injured by Sir Charles Warren's passion for gambling and Lord Granville Leveson-Gower's for making love. Whatever the failings of his ambassadors, Castlereagh had understood that high rank and style mattered more than ability: in diplomacy, contrary to the American belief in cunning, even in Metternich's cunning, there are severe limits to what mere talent can achieve.

One must sympathize with the British. Foreign governments had an easier task: their noblemen were invited to visit London. They were so pleased to accept, and stayed so long, that English-

---

[1] Cd to ggic, 20 July 1831, I.O. L/PS/6/244; Jones to Auber, 2 July 1832. I.O. E/2/38; Carter to Villiers, 23 Aug. 1832. I.O. E/2/11.

men found it difficult to remember when Vorontsoff, Esterhazy, and Princess Lieven, had not been there. The court at Vienna was stuffy (and no British ambassador since Pembroke could muster enough quarterings to be admitted beyond the fringe), at Berlin dreary, and at St. Petersburg barbaric: nobody of eminence, even Anglo-Indian eminence, would think of accepting the residency at Teheran. Sir John Malcolm, Sir Richard Jenkins, and Mountstuart Elphinstone, had all refused.

The board's discussion of the reasons for the decline of Britain's influence in Persia, and of the possible ways to revive it, was concluded in two papers written in April and June by Henry Ellis. Whereas everyone else had dealt with Abbas Mirza, Ellis concentrated upon the shah. Britain had lost her influence by abrogating the subsidiary articles, by deserting Persia in a moment of defeat. 'No proceeding could have been taken more calculated at once to degrade Great Britain in the estimation of the Persian court and to increase the conviction of the overwhelming power of Russia.'[1] Although the abrogation was a logical result of the policy set out by Ellis himself for Castlereagh in 1814, Ellis recommended, as a symbolic appeasement of vanity, the restoration of the subsidiary articles. The shah would be flattered, and, because the Russo-Persian quarrel over their frontier in the Caucasus had been settled, there would be no danger of their causing complications.

Ellis wanted British policy in Persia to be the same as his policy in Turkey: Abbas Mirza, like the governor of Baghdad, should be treated for purposes of international relations merely as an official of the imperial government. The succession crisis in Persia made this policy easier to set out than to carry out. As soon as the crisis was over, and a new shah securely on the throne, as long as he had not bought the help of Russia by concessions likely to endanger British interests, the British would be out of danger. Although the Russians might promise Abbas Mirza the throne, and tempt him with visions of conquest in the east, Ellis, like McNeill, was adamant that the British should not try to rival them; because of Russia's superior political and strategic position, she was bound to win any contest to turn Persia into a protectorate. Britain needed Persia as a buffer; which meant persuading Russia to behave with similar restraint.

Ellis claimed that the best way to manage this was to resurrect

[1] Memorandum by Ellis, 14 June 1832, I.O. Persia/48.

the shah. Whether or not Abbas Mirza succeeded Fath Ali did not matter to Britain, but, if Fath Ali could be persuaded to give Abbas the money he needed to pay his troops and to pay off the Russian indemnity, probably he would succeed, and without having to buy the throne by concessions to Russia. Should Abbas fail, the British could prepare for the likely effects of civil war, greater Russian influence and at worst partition, by annexing Kharrack. From a base on Kharrack, they could control Arabistan, Fars, and Luristan, as effectively as the Russians from Georgia could control Azerbaijan, Ghilan, and Mazenderan. Should Abbas succeed, as Ellis naturally preferred, the foreign office could then send an ambassador with high rank to congratulate him on his accession, and to show that Britain was determined Persia should be treated as an independent state.[1]

This is how Ellis had looked at the Persian Connection in 1831; nothing had happened since to change his mind. What was new were the stories of an expedition to Khiva. This did not endanger Persia, nor could a connection with Persia defend Khiva: the defence of Khiva and the Persian Connection should be kept separate, on either side of the frontier between the European and Indian political systems, and Khiva should be defended by warning the Russians at St. Petersburg and forestalling them in Turkestan. Ellis, who agreed with Willock more than Ouseley, also agreed with Grant's forward policy in central Asia. If British agents could negotiate a grand alliance stretching from Bokhara through Kabul to Lahore, British influence accompanied by their goods might create a stable balance of power in the Asiatic Burgundian Circle, by which the British planned to separate the European and Indian political systems.[2]

This policy was based upon an assumption of superiority equivalent to the superior strategic position Ellis allowed Russia in Persia. If Russia could not object to British expeditions to Turkestan, neither could Britain object to similar Russian expeditions to free Russian citizens from slavery or to expand their trade. Russian goods, however, would never compete with British, and, as soon as the civilizing influence of Britain should end the slave trade, Russia would have no grounds for intervention. These arguments appealed to a Utopian like Grant, and in central Asia he

[1] Memorandum by Ellis, 21 Apr. 1832, I.O. Persia/48.
[2] Minute of Ellis, 22 Jan. 1833, same to Grant, 22 Apr. 1834, I.O. L/PS/5/43.

and Ellis, as the board's instructions to the government of India about the Indus trade had shown, had the same aim. Ellis realized that in Khiva and Bokhara no distinction could be drawn between stability and order: because their inhabitants must be persuaded to give up nomadic for settled habits, a stable balance of power could not be established short of social revolution. Fortunately, as long as Russia's 'successes in negotiations', as McNeill said, 'are ... to be regarded as sacrifices to the impulse of fear rather than the results of natural predeliction',[1] Britain would have a second advantage: the khan of Khiva and the beg of Bokhara would realize that Britain, unlike Russia, would never threaten their independence, because the military frontier of India would remain at the Indus.

The result of this discussion was an attempt to hold back the Russians, by more clearly separating central Asia from Persia, and without becoming more entangled in Persia's internal affairs. The board still doubted whether the Russians were planning an expedition to Khiva. The Russian ambassador told Palmerston that the rumours of one were false; and the Russians were busy trying to pacify Georgia. Nevertheless in August 1832 Britain warned Russia not to forget, that as Khiva commanded a route to the frontier of India, an attack on Khiva would threaten a vital British interest.[2] This was not quite a warning that Britain would treat the conquest of Khiva as an unfriendly act—it was not as strong as Grey's declaration to France about the Sudan, nor as strong as the warning Ellenborough had wanted to give Russia over Persia—it was a statement that Britain would protect her vital interests wherever necessary, and that Khiva, like Persia, was to remain a buffer state between the Russians in the Caucasus and on the Caspian and the British in Afghanistan and the Persian Gulf. Grant and Ellis were less impatient than Ellenborough, because, confident Alexander Burnes would be welcomed at Bokhara, they were waiting for his assurance that the government of India could forestall the Russians by selling British cotton goods in Turkestan.

If Afghanistan and perhaps Bokhara were to become protectorates, Persia might remain a buffer, as long as the British

---

[1] Campbell [actually McNeill] to sc, 4 Sept. 1832, I.O. Persia/47.
[2] Durham to Palmerston, no. 11, 13 Aug. 1832, Palmerston to Durham, no. 24, 31 Aug. 1832, F.O. 65/200.

obeyed Wellington's rule, repeated by Ellis, and did nothing to give the Russians an excuse for intervention. The British military mission were to be enlarged, as Ellenborough had planned, and the modern weapons, which he had promised Abbas Mirza in 1830 but which had never been sent, were to be given him, in the hope he might feel strong enough to defeat his rivals without the help of Russia. For the same reason Campbell was told in January 1833 to subsidize Abbas Mirza, should his father die at a time when he had no money to pay his army for marching to Teheran.[1] Ellis could agree to this. He did not mind helping Abbas Mirza as the man most likely to win the struggle for the succession; but he refused to treat him as heir apparent. The British should stay within the terms of the treaty of Teheran, which gave them a right to influence in Persia equal to Russia's right by the treaty of Turkmanchay; to extend the terms might lead to a struggle for influence with Russia the British were bound to lose.

Ellis had been looking for a way to suggest that Britain thought of Abbas Mirza only as a deputy of the shah. His own suggestion, of putting back the subsidiary articles into the treaty of Teheran, might have defeated his other objective, by appearing provocative to Russia. Instead William IV gave a knighthood to Captain Campbell.[2] These steps were all small, but they showed that Ellis had solved the puzzle he had been set by Castlereagh in 1814, of finding a way to hold back Russia in the near east without endangering the balance of power in Europe. The solution Ellis set out would sever the Persian Connection, swapping Wellesley's policy of turning Persia into a protectorate, and, if the British had ever had the chance of this, they had lost it between 1814 and 1828, for the policy of keeping Persia as a buffer. Her frontiers were settled, because she had lost Erivan and was not to attack Herat, and, provided the small obstacle of the imminent succession crisis could be overcome with the help of the British military mission, the dynasty should be secure. Persia would then be stable. A little trade to bring prosperity to Azerbaijan might also help permanently to hold back Russia, by compelling her to treat Persia as an independent state.

Behind this containing policy, as Ellis knew, Charles Grant dreamt of causing social revolution. It had to be prevented in

[1] Sc to ggic, 14 Jan. 1833, I.O. L/PS/5/544.
[2] William IV to Fath Ali, 14 Jan. 1833, F.O. 60/33.

Persia, where reform was to strengthen the existing political and social structure; it was the prerequisite of turning the oases of central Asia into the territorial states with settled frontiers they must become, if the British were to forestall Russian expansion eastwards from the Caspian. As Wellington and Ellenborough had decided in 1829, the Great Game in Asia should be shifted from Persia both westwards to warnings at St. Petersburg, and eastwards to a forward policy in central Asia. The strategy was mapped at the board of control, but, as long as Lord William Bentinck and Sir Charles Metcalfe were governors-general, the government of India refused to carry it out. The pressure from London that led after 1835 to a collision with the Afghans had its origins in decisions taken at the board of control, not at the foreign office.

The Vienna Settlement was both a rearrangement of territory to create a balance of power, and an agreement to preserve a particular political and social order. To Europeans, whether its supporters or opponents, the two were indistinguishable: to Englishmen they were not. The British respected the territorial settlement; in western Europe it suited them, and they respected all property. They had no respect for European social structure, expecting everyone ideally to copy theirs. Sindians, Afghans, and Turcomans might avoid the mistakes of Austrians and Italians: they were being given the chance to copy Britain. One must not smirk at an Englishman's belief in the forces of good and evil, and at his certainty that he stood up for good and Nicholas I and Metternich evil; nor must one doubt that foreign policy was measured in these terms. In August 1832 Grant told Palmerston that a stronger stand must be taken for liberalism against despotism: the forces of despotism were doing better than they had when the arch-reactionary Wellington had been in office, and something must be done to stop them.[1] In Syria and Baghdad something was, when Henry Ellis showed the foreign office how to play the Great Game in Asia in Turkey.

[1] Grant to Palmerston, 5 Aug. 1832, Broadlands MSS. GC/GL/205.

VIII

The Eastern Crisis 1832-1833

> Experience is the name every one
> gives to their mistakes.
>
> MR. DUMBY,
> *Lady Windermere's Fan*,
> Act III

THE GREAT GAME in Asia began twice, once in 1830 and the second time three years later, after the whigs had learned from experience what they would not allow tories to teach them. There are few descriptions of the first, just as many of the second, but, because British policy has been described in the wrong terms, all are misleading. Historians writing between the wars, mistaking Lord Holland's handwriting for Palmerston's, wrongly assumed that the British debated whether to support Mahmud II or Mahomet Ali.[1] While avoiding this mistake, Mayir Vereté and Sir Charles Webster made another:[2] they failed to see why Palmerston was not allowed to help the sultan. The British did change their policy during the First Mahomet Ali Crisis; they changed what they meant by reform: likewise, the British did not back the 'wrong horse' in 1833; they had backed it in 1830. Their policy was set out by the board of control. Palmerston was taught by Henry Ellis that Britain's proper aim was to protect her interests in the near east by treating Turkey and Persia as in-

---

[1] Crawley, *Greek Independence*, p. 212; F. S. Rodkey, 'Lord Palmerston and the Rejuvenation of Turkey, 1830–1841—I', *Journal of Modern History*, i (1929). 571–2; J. E. Swain, *The Struggle for the Control of the Mediterranean Prior to 1848: A Study in Anglo-French Relations* (Philadelphia, 1933), p. 86; H. C. F. Bell, *Lord Palmerston* (London, 1936), i. 179–80; Temperley, *England and the Near East*, p. 63; and V. J. Puryear, *France and the Levant (from the Bourbon Restoration to the Peace of Kutiah)* (Berkeley/Los Angeles, 1941), pp. 174–5.

[2] M. Vereté, 'Palmerston and the Levant Crisis, 1832', *Journal of Modern History*, xxiv (1952), 143–51; Webster, *Palmerston*, i. 278–82; D. Southgate, *The Most English Minister: The Policies and Politics of Palmerston* (London, 1966), pp. 62–7; Kelly, *Persian Gulf*, pp. 270–4.

dependent states with agreed frontiers, whose internal upheavals were to be ignored.

The board of control had shown how this could be done, in Egypt in the late eighteenth century: for purposes of international relations, Egypt was to be treated as a province of Turkey. Provided the beys, and later Mahomet Ali, did not try to declare their independence, the autonomy of Egypt might be ignored. Similarly, as long as the appearance of a united state were kept up, the Egyptian occupation of Syria might be ignored. Whether Egypt included Syria did not of itself matter to the British; what did matter was limiting the influence in the near east of other European states, firstly France, then Russia, and deciding what effect their actions would have on British India. The board of control did not seek preponderant influence in Egypt or Syria, nor did they seek it in Persia or Baghdad, or at Constantinople: they wished to deny it to others. The balance of power in Europe and the stability of British India both depended upon the existence of Turkey as a buffer state. Trying to turn it into a protectorate, or trying to turn Kajar Persia into one, would bring on a struggle with Russia the board of control feared they were likely to lose.

The emphasis in the First Mahomet Ali Crisis has always been misplaced. The fall of Acre to Mahomet in May 1832 was less threatening to Britain than the possibility of the fall of Herat to Abbas Mirza. Until 1833 the war in Syria mattered less than the succession question in Persia: holding back Russia and defending British India by creating a balance of power in the near east both meant ending the war in Khorassan. What was peculiar in 1832 were the whigs, who had to learn which were Britain's most vital interests in the near east. Palmerston had to learn first; and had then to teach his colleagues, who also had to learn the second lesson that his office gave him power. Whereas they had to learn that he would set out their policy; he had to learn that it already existed. Because the board of control were the department of government best served by an expert bureaucracy, Webster's claim that Charles 'Grant was of course under . . . [Palmerston's] influence',[1] turns out to be false. The Great Game in Asia swung westwards into Turkey in 1833, when Palmerston began to play as Henry Ellis suggested.

---

[1] Webster, *Palmerston*, i. 40.

II

Since the late eighteenth century, the needs of Indian defence had been as great an influence as the balance of power in Europe upon British policy in Egypt. This was most noticeable whenever the British debated whether to swap their traditional policy of treating Turkey as a single state for the alternative of recognizing, usually in Egypt or Baghdad, the independence of a provincial governor. In 1802, having by the treaty of Amiens driven the French army of occupation from Egypt, the British, before evacuating themselves, had to find a compromise between the beys and the sultan, which would in emergencies allow the British to return to Egypt but forbid the French. Unfortunately, to detach the beys from the French, the commander-in-chief, Egypt, had promised to put them back in power. This offended the sultan, and caused a quarrel between the soldiers in Egypt supporting the beys and the ambassador at Constantinople, who supported the sultan. To the soldiers the choice might be unpleasant, but was obvious: if Britain supported the sultan, the Egyptians 'would consider *any* invading power as a fortunate and welcome means of delivery', whereas supporting the beys would provide 'an efficient barrier ... against at least the *immediate* enterprises of the French'.[1]

The army, who always doubted whether the Mediterranean fleet could protect Britain's interests in the near east, were arguing that the policy of treating Egypt as part of Turkey was likely to endanger British India. The British resident at Baghdad agreed with them. Harford Jones was one in a long line of Englishmen, who believed that Turkey could survive as a state, stable and powerful enough to suit the British, although cut down to Anatolia, Syria, and Arabia. Egypt mattered no more than the Balkans. Britain did not need to control Egypt: her only interest there, to prevent an invasion of India, could be defended either by a naval base or by patrolling the Red Sea. Egypt must not belong to a great European power; it need not belong to the sultan.

The dangerous effects of the decline of the power of the sultan were to be sought farther east, in Syria, Persia, and Baghdad. Jones, who had been sent to Baghdad in 1798 to prevent Bonaparte's marching eastwards from Aleppo, claimed that Baghdad

[1] Stuart to Hobart, 29 Apr. 1802, W.O. 1/346, p. 33. For details see S. Ghorbal, *The Beginnings of the Egyptian Question and the Rise of Mehemet Ali* (London, 1928), pp. 157–78.

was the obvious point in advance of the frontier at which to defend British India, and the resident at Baghdad the obvious man to place in command.[1] Although the government valued the analysis, they preferred the alternative defence of relying upon the navy, to Jones's idea of a protectorate over Baghdad. As long as the enemy in the near east was France, who was vulnerable to sea power, the British had no need to choose between their European and imperial interests; and, as long as both could be defended by an alliance with Russia, they were careful to avoid actions in the near east likely, by drawing away the attention of Russia from western Europe, to endanger the interests they were meant to protect.

At the beginning of the Great Game in Asia it was understood at the board of control to be a rule of British policy in the near east, that political changes in Turkey must be measured by their likely effects upon Persia and Baghdad. Nobody knew this better than Mahomet Ali. Were he to obtain his independence through a connection with the British, he had to show them, as all his approaches between 1829 and 1833 prove, that he was the necessary ally they were looking for to defend British India in the near east. His hopes were destroyed at the same moment and for the same reason as Ellenborough's, by Wellington's inability to hold on to office.

In 1829, during the Russo-Turkish war, Mahomet Ali refused to send troops to reinforce the sultan in the Balkans; instead he offered to defend the Turkish frontier in Asia.[2] This matched Wellington's opinions about Britain's priorities. Although Aberdeen thought Mahomet Ali 'a rogue . . . [who] requires watching',[3] he also thought, that because Egypt unlike Greece was a formidable military as well as naval power, Mahomet might be better than the Greeks at holding back Russia. Sir Robert Gordon, who feared that Mahomet planned to attack not defend the sultan, warned his brother to be careful. In 1830 he changed his mind: recognizing Mahomet's peculiar status within the empire might be the best way to protect all the British interests in the near east endangered by the expansion of Russia.[4]

[1] Jones to Inglis, 29 Nov. 1802, Kentchurch Court MSS. 8380.
[2] Barker to Gordon, 7 Aug. 1829, in Gordon to Aberdeen, no. 44, 10 Sept. 1829, F.O. 78/181.
[3] Aberdeen to Gordon, private, 8 May 1830, Add. MSS. 43210, fo. 242.
[4] Gordon to Aberdeen, no. 18, 7 Aug. 1829, F.O. 78/180; same to same, no. 42, 15 June 1830, F.O. 78/190.

This was the idea Mahomet Ali tried again and again to convey.

Lord Aberdeen does not know me [he told the British consul-general in March] . . . if he did, he would perceive that the only way to strengthen the sultan is to support me. By supporting me, he would soon have at his disposal a disciplined army of 125,000 men ready to form a barrier against the Russians both at Constantinople and in Persia.[1]

If Britain ever had to fight Russia to defend India, she would have to fight in Persia, and the only state who had a strong enough army to act as the necessary ally, at a time when nobody expected anything of the Persians, was Egypt. The claim was repeated in 1831 to Sir John Malcolm, who travelled through Cairo on his way home to England from Bombay. The 'vast importance' to Britain of an ally in the near east, at a time when the power of Russia was likely to destroy Turkey, should convince the British of the value of a connection with Egypt, who alone could defend Asiatic Turkey, and by implication Persia, from Russian aggression and its effects in India. 'It was very plain', said Malcolm, 'that . . . [Mahomet Ali] was feeling his way towards some assurance that England would be willing to recognize a larger independence than that which he then enjoyed.'[2]

This was the catch. Mahomet Ali was trying to sound like Ellenborough, who, he knew, preferred Egypt and the Red Sea for overland communication with India. Unfortunately, Ellenborough's willingness to risk a collision with Russia had been subordinated to Wellington's and Aberdeen's policy of holding her back by denying her grounds for further intervention. As soon as the British decided that Russia was after influence not territory, they had to beware of anything dramatic. When in 1831 Henry Ellis explained Britain's attitude to the prince royal of Persia and the governor of Baghdad, he resurrected the principle that Turkey should be treated as a single state, whose foreign relations were carried on by the sultan. In 1832 and 1833 Mahomet Ali, by invading Anatolia, eventually collided with the board of control.

Although Aberdeen had promised to reply to Mahomet Ali's proposal for an Anglo-Egyptian connection, nothing had been done before the tories resigned. Palmerston did nothing until 1832. Mahomet Ali had not waited. In November 1831 the Egyptian

---

[1] Barker to Aberdeen, no. 9, 8 Mar. 1830, F.O. 78/192.
[2] Kaye, *Malcolm*, ii. 557.

army invaded Palestine and beseiged Acre. The Porte had had plenty of warning, but had paid no attention, and until the following year thought, that were this merely a local quarrel between two provincial governors, they would be asked eventually to settle it; nobody could tell it was 'a struggle for empire with the sultan'.[1] From the beginning the British tried to keep out: whether or not the quarrel was local, the longer it could be treated as if it were the better. When the governor of Acre asked, firstly for a British squadron to play the role of Sir Sidney Smith, then for British mediation, the British chargé d'affaires at Constantinople replied, that Britain must wait for an invitation from the sultan.

In January 1832 Palmerston 'approve[d] his answer'; and also decided not to reply to Mahomet Ali.[2] This was fair. He would help no one, and told Stratford Canning, sent in November 1831 on a special mission to Constantinople to settle the frontiers of Greece, 'to say no more . . . than to assure . . . [the sultan] of our general wishes to maintain and uphold him as an ancient ally and old friend and as an important element in the balance of power in Europe'.[3] The last is the important phrase. Greece mattered more than Syria, not merely because Palmerston had always wanted Greece to be as big as possible, nor because the stability of Greece was a more vital British interest than the stability of Asiatic Turkey—it was not—but rather, that because the sultan had never within memory governed his Asiatic provinces, Englishmen who thought only about the European balance of power did not see how a rebellion in Syria, any more than a rebellion at Baghdad, could affect the sultan's ability to carry out his most important European duty of controlling the Straits. As long as the rebellion was confined to Syria, they were right: it did not.

Mayir Vereté tried hard to disprove F. S. Rodkey's claim, that 'Palmerston . . . was misled for a time . . . as to the strength of Mahomet Ali's forces'.[4] Although Vereté did prove that British

[1] Mandeville to Palmerston, no. 28, 26 Nov. 1831, no. 38, 27 Dec. 1831, F.O. 78/200.

[2] Minute of Palmerston on Mandeville to Palmerston, no. 31, 26 Nov. 1831, F.O. 78/200; Palmerston to Mandeville, no. 1, 31 Jan. 1832, F.O. 78/202; minute of Palmerston, 20 Jan. 1832, on Barker to Palmerston, separate, 8 June 1831, ibid.

[3] Palmerston to Canning, private, 20 Feb. 1832, F.O. 352/25.

[4] F. S. Rodkey, 'The Views of Palmerston and Metternich on the Eastern Question in 1834', *English Historical Review*, xlv (1930), 627.

agents in the near east accurately reported the size of the Egyptian army,[1] this hardly mattered, as long as it was impossible to tell what Mahomet Ali wanted and what was his chance of success. The vigorous defence of Acre, which held out for six months, seemed at one moment to be destroying the Egyptian army in Syria; John Barker at Alexandria believed that Mahomet over-estimated his strength, and from Constantinople both John Mandeville, the British chargé d'affaires, and Stratford Canning, when warned that Mahomet was challenging the sultan not quarrelling with the governor of Acre, reported the Turks to be confident they could defeat him. 'The prevailing opinion here', said Canning at the end of April 1832, 'is unfavourable to the success of Mahomet Ali.'[2]

Whatever British agents said, the foreign office would pay little attention to any one but Canning. Barker, who was an abler man than he appeared, held a temporary appointment and was not respected. He 'is a good sort of nobody,' said the earl of Clare, who met him on his way out to Bombay, 'an old Levantine without any idea beyond Aleppo and Alexandria. He has no influence with the pasha and Mahomet Ali frightens him out of his wits.'[3] The consul-general in Syria, J. W. P. Farren, whose appointment left the consul-general at Constantinople who knew 'something of *him* . . . incredulous',[4] offended Palmerston by his apparently unending dispatches written in sentences equally long. 'I found him *going* when I came in,' said Palmerston bitterly in 1833, 'and *he told me* he was so fit for the employment that it was impossible to doubt that he was.'[5] However accurate their reports, Stratford Canning was permitted to leave Constantinople in August, partly because Palmerston was still not convinced that the sultan was in danger.

According to Barker, the sultan not Mahomet Ali had turned a local feud into a rebellion. At the beginning of June, news of the fall of Acre reached Alexandria. Mahomet, despite his victory,

[1] Vereté, 'Levant Crisis', pp. 143-4.
[2] Canning to Palmerston, no. 29, 30 Apr. 1832, F.O. 78/210. The French ambassador shared this opinion. Puryear, *France and the Levant*, p. 155.
[3] Clare to Palmerston, private, 11 May 1831, Broadlands MSS. GC/CL/95.
[4] Cartwright to Bidwell, private, 25 Oct. 1830, F.O. 78/195.
[5] Palmerston to Ponsonby, private, 6 Dec. 1833, Broadlands MSS. GC/PO/210. 'I cannot say,' said Macaulay, 'that I admire Mr. F[arren]'s speculations as much as he appears to admire them himself. His letter is as empty a declamation as ever I read.' Minute of Macaulay, 22 Mar. 1833, I.O. Persia/49.

now offered to partition Syria, annexing Acre and Tripoli to Egypt while leaving Damascus and Aleppo to the sultan.[1] He changed his mind as soon as he learnt that the sultan had in May declared him a rebel, and had made the European ambassadors promise, that their countrymen would not run the Turkish blockade of Egypt. This embarrassed Canning: helping Mahmud against Mahomet Ali would be an expensive way to buy his goodwill about Greece. The best compromise seemed to be warning British merchants not to supply the Egyptian army, British consuls not to hold up trade with Egypt unless they had to, and Barker to stay as friendly as possible with Mahomet.[2]

Such caution became more necessary, when in July 1832 the collision between Mahomet Ali and the Mahmud II finally took place. On 13 June the Egyptian army, commanded by Mahomet's son, Ibrahim Pasha, entered Damascus; on 8 July they routed a Turkish army commanded by the new titular governor of Egypt at the battle of Homs; a week later they entered Aleppo; and on 29 July they again defeated the Turks at the battle of the Beylan Pass and entered Adana. Anatolia and the road to Constantinople lay undefended before them. Ibrahim was eager to advance on the capital; his father made the mistake of thinking it would be wiser to ask permission of the great powers. The French, who had hoped he would conquer Syria quickly before the sultan could prevent him, now hoped to obtain it for him equally quickly by negotiation.[3]

The French misled nobody; the British may have misled every one. Mahomet Ali claimed that Canning's 'comparatively friendly' behaviour should have meant that the British, even if they would not help him, would not try to stop his annexing Syria. In June 1832 he asked them to join the French in persuading the sultan to agree.[4] The sultan may have been equally misled, although it is just as likely both knew that at this time the British wanted to keep out of their quarrels. In July the Turks turned down a French offer to mediate;[5] and may have been encouraged

---

[1] Barker to Canning, no. 37, 8 June 1832, in same to Bidwell, no. 52, 8 June 1832, F.O. 78/214.
[2] Canning to Palmerston, no. 32, 17 May 1832, with encls., F.O. 78/210.
[3] Puryear, *France and the Levant*, pp. 164–5.
[4] Barker to Palmerston, no. 55, 13 June 1832, F.O. 78/211; same to same, no. 64, 24 June 1832, no. 67, 25 June 1832, F.O. 78/214.
[5] Canning to Palmerston, no. 49, 22 July 1832, F.O. 78/211.

by Stratford Canning. Early in August, as Canning, who had finished his work about Greece, was preparing to leave Constantinople, the Turks told him they would value an Anglo-Turkish alliance. The intriguing question is to guess how Canning replied.

A firm answer must await the publication of Allan Cunningham's long delayed study of Canning as ambassador to Turkey. The traditional account of his mission in 1832, offering support against Mahomet Ali in return for a large Greece, is too simple. The sultan was as anxious not to lose his Greek revenues as to hold back Mahomet Ali; whereas Canning, who should have been a missionary not a diplomatist, preferred to tie hints of support to better government of the Christians.[1] Canning at Constantinople was the twin of Charles Trevelyan at Delhi: both offered chances of improvement, both believed in instantaneous conversion, and both dreamt of social revolution. Canning disliked Mahomet Ali, because he feared that Mahmud II, even if he succeeded, would spend so much money and energy in putting down Mahomet's rebellion, that he might have too little of either left to sustain a thorough programme of reform. This should please the Russians; nevertheless, only if Mahmud showed signs of introducing liberal reforms, should Britain offer him her help.[2]

Canning, whose dragomans detested him, could never be sure that his remarks would be repeated accurately to the Turks. At his last interview with the sultan on 6 August, when he did without them, he may have been trapped, as the French suspected, into saying more than he wished. His report to Palmerston was vague and reassuring. The Turks' 'immediate object', he explained, 'is the submission of the pasha of Egypt and they would be glad to procure the moral and still more the physical aid of England for that purpose. They offer to make arrangements for giving any reasonable advantage to England in return.' Canning added that he had offered in reply only 'the general friendly disposition' of Britain, and to draw Palmerston's attention to what was happening. This he did; but not as the sultan may have expected. 'I feel the

---

[1] Professor Cunningham, who is a colleague, kindly read to the author, over the telephone, certain pertinent paragraphs from his manuscript. See also Webster, *Palmerston*, i. 279.

[2] Canning to Palmerston, private, 14 Feb. 1832, F.O. 352/25; same to same, no. 12, 7 Mar. 1832, F.O. 78/210; same to same, no. 40, 9 June 1832, F.O. 78/211; S. Lane-Poole, *The Life of the Rt. Hon. Stratford Canning, Viscount Stratford de Redcliffe* (London, 1888), ii. 78.

Turkish Empire is in a most dangerous predicament,' he said, 'and that those powers whose interests are at all involved in its fate should lose no time in adopting towards it a steady, systematic course of policy in one way or the other.'[1] Not until the end of the year did Canning argue vigorously and cogently what that policy should be: then it was the wrong policy.

Canning's statements that Mahomet Ali was not likely to destroy Mahmud II, and that Russia would not intervene, helped to persuade the British government, that they might safely continue to ignore the Syrian war. Upheaval in Turkey did not endanger Britain, as long as its stability was not endangered by the intervention of another European state. That these were still the most important considerations was clear early in September, when Palmerston and the prime minister, Earl Grey, discussed what they should do. They were being urged on, not by any of the British agents in the near east, but by the head of a British company trading with Egypt, who had long claimed and proved to have more influence with Mahomet Ali than had Barker, Samuel Briggs of Briggs & Co.[2]

III

One of the similarities between Grey's government and Wellington's was that the foreign office and the board of control co-operated, partly because Palmerston and Charles Grant, who had little in common, both owed their appointments to being members of the small but coherent Canningite party, who had joined the whigs as a group. By the spring of 1832, dispatches from the near east, and papers arguing the merits of various policies, were regularly swapped, which allowed Grant, who admitted that he knew nothing of foreign affairs,[3] to influence policy through his subordinates, who did. During the summer the board of control were busy assessing the dangers to British interests farther east; in deciding how to recover enough influence in Persia to prevent another expedition against Herat, and how to hold back

---

[1] Canning to Palmerston, separate and secret, 9 Aug. 1832, F.O. 78/211; A. Cunningham, '"Dragomania"—The Dragomans of the British Embassy in Turkey', *St. Anthony's Papers* (1961), 89–92.

[2] F. S. Rodkey, 'The Attempts of Briggs and Company to Guide British Policy in the Levant in the Interest of Mahomet Ali', *Journal of Modern History*, v (1933), 324–51.

[3] Grant to Grey, 20 Jan. 1831, Grey of Howick MSS.

the Russians from an equally threatening expedition against Khiva. The board had also seen why the British might not for long been able to ignore the Syrian war.

For the British the near east was merely a mirror reflecting more important interests elsewhere; therefore the Syrian war might be ignored as long as it could be treated as local. This suited the board of control, who had decided in the summer of 1832, 'to meet Russian agents, Russian commerce, and Russian influence, on all routes approaching India',[1] and meant to do this in Turkey by ignoring all political changes short of a declaration of independence, and by dealing only with the sultan. Ideally, no European great powers, and none of their agents including the British resident at Baghdad, should interfere in the internal affairs of Turkey, whose independence should be maintained less by reform than by diplomatic practice. The only exception was help asked for by the sultan, likely to strengthen the imperial government, and likely, if refused by Britain, to be given by someone else.

The board's part in creating British policy in the near east during the First Mahomet Ali Crisis was first shown in the language used by Palmerston in the autumn of 1832 to describe Mahomet Ali, an echo of Henry Ellis's description of the governor of Baghdad and the prince royal of Persia.

It seems to me [said Palmerston] that the sultan being our ally and the legitimate sovereign of Syria, the *Right* is all on his side; and that therefore if we act merely on principle we must take part with him . . . That next, looking at the whole transaction as a question of *Policy*, the inconvenience which might arise to Europe and to England from the dismemberment of the Turkish Empire would be greater than those which could follow from even the expulsion of Mahomet Ali from Egypt.[2]

Unfortunately for the board of control, although the foreign secretary had borrowed their language, he had not yet borrowed the policy it set out, because he had not yet realized the extent of Mahomet Ali's ambitions, nor understood the limits of Britain's power in the near east.

Samuel Briggs had first asked the foreign office to mediate between Mahomet Ali and Mahmud II in June. Grey and Palmerston refused, believing that Mahmud would prefer to put down

[1] Memorandum by Ellis, 14 June 1832, I.O. Persia/48.
[2] Palmerston to Granville, private, 18 Sept. 1832, Broadlands MSS. GC/GR/1426.

the rebellion, and would resent European mediation, because it would prove Mahomet Ali to be more than a provincial governor.[1] In September, when Briggs asked again, Palmerston again asked Grey what they should do. Mahomet Ali's victories over Mahmud in July had changed the British problem: if they offered to bring about a settlement, Mahomet would demand Syria, Mahmud would demand military and naval aid. Palmerston did find it hard to choose between them. Mahomet should be supported because he reformed, and Canningites believed in social and economic reform, but, as they disliked political and constitutional reform, the sultan should be supported because Mohamet Ali was a rebel.

It may be well to keep friends with Mahomet Ali [said Palmerston], especially if he should succeed, but the sultan is surely of the two the most important ally for us to uphold. If Mahomet is beat the sultan re-enters into possession and there is no harm done for us; but if the sultan is beat his empire may tumble to pieces and the way in which the fragments may be disposed of may essentially affect the balance of power in Europe.[2]

Earl Grey, who agreed, nevertheless drew the opposite conclusion. 'Looking upon the dissolution of the Ottoman Empire as nearly certain', he replied, '. . . I confess I feel a strong disposition to be on good terms with Mahomet Ali.'

Grey, throughout the autumn of 1832 'in a state of feverish excitement' about Belgium,[3] was worried that Mahomet Ali, denied British help, might turn to France: 'if the French influence should be established in Egypt, it might, in the event of war, added to the possession of Algiers and their own ports, prove very embarrassing to us, notwithstanding all our naval superiority'.[4] This did not worry Palmerston, because in any Anglo-French war the navy should be strong enough to force Mahomet Ali to desert France. The two men, however, shared the board of control's assumption, that Britain should prevent any other European state's becoming influential in the near east, without trying to influence events there herself. Palmerston had another reason for doing nothing: he had not yet heard whether the Greek question

---

[1] Grey to Palmerston, 19 June 1832, Broadlands MSS. GC/GR/2117.

[2] Palmerston to Grey, 6 Sept. 1832, Grey of Howick MSS.

[3] According to Sir James Graham. J. T. Ward, *Sir James Graham* (London, 1967), p. 127.

[4] Grey to Palmerston, private, 8 Sept. 1832, Broadlands MSS. GC/GR/2144.

was settled, and before he chose between Mahomet Ali and
Mahmud, should he have to, he wanted to talk to Stratford
Canning. 'Under all the circumstances,' he said finally, 'perhaps I
had better plead the dispersed state of the cabinet as a reason for
further delay.'[1]

Having held off Mahomet Ali, during September Palmerston
and Grey also held off the French and the Austrians. The French
said that Anglo-French co-operation was the only way to prevent
Russia from taking advantage of the unstable situation in Turkey
to demand more territory from the sultan: without mediation there
was danger of partition. While the French wanted to give way to
Mahomet Ali, the Austrians wanted him checked. Prince Metternich said that unless Britain helped Mahmud against Mahomet
Ali, who was a French puppet, his success would turn the eastern
Mediterranean into a French lake, recreating the situation in 1798
and 1829, when a great European power could endanger British
India, and handicap Britain in Europe, by feinting at invasion
through Persia and Afghanistan.[2]

These appeals were easily resisted as long as the whigs, thinking
in European terms, and thinking the danger point was Egypt and
Syria, saw France as Britain's enemy in the near east. Palmerston,
like Grenville in 1798, did not believe that French naval power in
the eastern Mediterranean could endanger British India or the
balance of power in Europe, nor did he believe Mahomet Ali a
French puppet. To make sure he did not become one, Palmerston
decided in October to replace Barker by someone to whom
Mahomet Ali might listen, and, as a sign of goodwill, told him to
stop describing Mahomet as the ex-viceroy.[3] He was not to be
treated as ruler of Syria, but, whatever the sultan might say, for
practical purposes he was to be treated as still ruling Egypt. To
leave him in Syria would offend the Austrians, but to turn him
out of Egypt would defeat its object, because likely to provoke the
French to intervene.

On 17 September 1832 Stratford Canning came back to England
from Constantinople. Until the end of the year, British policy in
the near east reflected his outdated conviction, partly inherited

---

[1] Palmerston to Grey, 6 Sept. 1832, Grey of Howick MSS.

[2] Granville to Palmerston, no. 261, 10 Sept. 1832, no. 264, 14 Sept. 1832,
F.O. 27/449; Lamb to Palmerston, no. 125, 10 Sept. 1832, F.O. 7/235.

[3] Palmerston to Barker, no. 11, 3 Oct. 1832, F.O. 78/214.

from his cousin, to whose opinions Palmerston also and equally unwisely deferred, that the greatest threat to British interests in the near east was the enmity between Russia and Turkey, and that the best defence against it was to turn Turkey into a protectorate by supporting Mahmud II not Mahomet Ali. In October, when Samuel Briggs, repeating Metternich's analysis, but choosing the opposite solution, argued that Mahomet Ali as ruler of Syria might help to maintain the independence of Persia, and so help to defend British India, Palmerston asked Canning to reply. Although Canning criticized Briggs's assumption, arguing both that by losing Syria to Mahomet Ali the sultan might also lose control of Baghdad, and that Mahomet was just as likely to co-operate with the Russians to partition Turkey as to defend the sultan and the shah against them, his purpose was to convince Palmerston, that Britain should support Mahmud because he would prove the better reformer.[1] Britain was to break the rule made by the board of control and to seek paramount influence in Turkey. This was Palmerston's mistake.

Palmerston, who was seduced by Canning's argument, but doubted whether Grey would be, still hoped that the sultan would prove able to defeat Mahomet Ali without help. As soon as Mahmud learnt of the defeat at the Beylan Pass, he had ordered a new army to assemble at Koniah under the command of the grand vizier. To encourage the sultan, to forestall any danger of a palace revolution at Constantinople, and to hold back Russia, Grey suggested that an ambassador should be sent to replace Mandeville.[2] Palmerston agreed, and chose Grey's brother-in-law, the ambassador at Naples, the Viscount Ponsonby. Mahomet Ali was not to rely on France, nor Mahmud II on Britain: Mahmud was then to win the victory his legitimacy and Palmerston's anxiety to reform his empire demanded.

In the hope of treating the quarrel between Mahomet Ali and the sultan as local, the British had ignored appeals from Mahomet himself, from the French on his behalf, and from the Austrians on behalf of the sultan. Early November brought an appeal directly from Mahmud, who had been sufficiently encouraged by his conversations with Stratford Canning to send to London the

[1] Memorandum by Briggs, received 10 Oct. 1832, F.O. 78/217; Canning to Backhouse, private, 14 Oct. 1832, F.O. 352/25.
[2] Grey to Palmerston, private, 20 Oct. 1832, Broadlands MSS. GC/GR/2161.

Turkish chargé d'affaires at Vienna, Jean de Maurojeni, who was to be followed by a special envoy from Constantinople, Namick Pasha. 'I think it in the general interest of all Europe except Russia to uphold the sultan', said Palmerston three days after Maurojeni's arrival, '. . . Mahomet Ali should be left in possession of Egypt, and if he wants to extend himself let him go up the Nile.' Palmerston, tutored by Canning, now approved of the sultan, because he reformed 'from principle and conviction and from political motives', whereas Mahomet Ali reformed 'merely upon mercantile speculation'.[1] This did not mean that anything should be done to help the sultan, nor that anything could be done: Palmerston's reply to Maurojeni's appeal was a Stratfordian homily upon the need for sweeping reform.

Such advice did not help Mahmud at a moment when the levies he had ordered in all the provinces of the empire had produced few recruits. Maurojeni had been sent to strengthen them, by obtaining the support of the British Mediterranean fleet, for which the sultan was willing to pay, offering in return, as he had promised Canning, to grant Britain new trading rights in Turkey.[2] This was a fair offer, because ever since Wellesley had set out to reform Persia, reformers had hoped that increased trade would demonstrate the benefits to be expected from liberal government. Reporting the offer to Grey, Palmerston explained that should Mahomet Ali evacuate Syria, the sultan would allow him to keep Egypt, whereas, if he stayed in Syria, he would cause more disturbance in Baghdad, but did not suggest how Britain should reply. In the middle of the month he agreed to meet Grey and Canning to decide.

Their meeting, and the cabinet meeting that followed, led to an argument about the meaning and value of reform. Unfortunately Lord Holland, who began in 1830 a detailed and fascinating diary, lacked the stamina to keep it up for long, and had stopped in July. Palmerston's arguments, and the reasons for their defeat, have always been deduced from the claims he made on his own behalf at later dates. Supposedly, his answer in November 1832 to anyone supporting an increase in the power of Mahomet Ali as

---

[1] Palmerston to Granville, private, 6 Nov. 1832, Broadlands MSS. GC/GR/1439.

[2] Mandeville to Palmerston, no. 29, 11 Oct. 1832, Palmerston to Mandeville, no. 8, 5 Dec. 1832, F.O. 78/212.

the best way to strengthen Turkey as a barrier to Russia, had been 'that geography and the nature of things pointed out an alliance between Russia and Mahomet Ali for the overthrow of the sultan as the inevitable consequence of any accession of power on the part of Mahomet Ali'.[1]

Tutored by Stratford Canning, Palmerston had taken the first step towards playing the Great Game in Asia: he had swapped France for Russia as Britain's greatest enemy in the east. 'These Russians', he said, 'are the most active intriguers and the most universal meddlers in the world . . . Russia expresses a decided interest in favour of the sultan, but in a manner and tone that bespeak anything but sincerity and zeal.'[2] Until 1833, Palmerston, like Canning, saw the near east as it had been before the treaties of Turkmanchay and Adrianople: he had changed the enemy, but had not re-examined the danger. Also like Canning, he could not foresee the effects of Russo-Turkish friendship: he was expecting a partition. Russian offers of help must be meant to hide demands for territory in the Caucasus.

Palmerston in 1832 and 1833 must not be mistaken for the celebrity of later years, whose idiosyncracies became a symbol of the mid-Victorian balance of interests. In 1830 he was known only as a sound administrator, who had recently started to speak on foreign affairs after twenty-five years as secretary at war, when he had apparently enjoyed the delights of the Ton more than every-day affairs of state. He had been suggested to Grey for the foreign office by Lord Holland and the marquess of Lansdowne. Their poor health would not allow them to take the job, they were so idle they did not want it; but they meant to lay down the policy. 'Nobody can understand', said Palmerston in August 1832, 'the physical impossibility under which I laboured for many months to do anything but struggle well or ill through the public business of the day.'[3] Holland was not surprised, because he had meant Palmerston to write all the letters. Whereas the whigs, who had lots of ability, lacked talent, the Canningites were very talented: all of them had held high office, and should have been used to working hard.

[1] Palmerston to Holland, 10 Feb. 1836, Add. MSS. 51599, fo. 213; same to Grey, 22 Apr. 1833, Grey of Howick MSS.

[2] Palmerston to Granville, private, 4 Dec. 1832, Broadlands MSS. GC/GR/1451.

[3] Palmerston to Holland, 7 Aug. 1832, Add. MSS. 51599, fo. 124.

Palmerston had not been an easy colleague. He had quarrelled with the whigs throughout the passage of the Great Reform Bill, which he disliked, and in the spring of 1832 had threatened to change parties. Whom, wondered Holland, had he planned to join?[1] The tories hated him more than anyone, and accused him of giving way too easily to France; the radicals said the same about Russia; both were offended by his bad speeches, usually saying little to avoid embarrassing his relations with foreign ambassadors, which hardly mattered as he was so rude to them in person; and all of them disliked his dandified manners. The young Disraeli immortalized him as 'menacing Russia with a perfumed cane'.[2]

Palmerston was over-ruled in the cabinet in November, because he argued that the reform of Turkey was Britain's most important interest in the near east. The whigs replied that the best way to reform Turkey, and to hold back France as well as Russia, would be to support Mahomet Ali not the sultan. They also doubted whether Britain could stop Mahomet Ali. This argument was turned against them by Palmerston when applied to Portugal. 'I am inclined to think we might *propose* an armistice', he said, 'and that we should not stand worse if it were rejected. But as to *imposing* it, I cannot see our right to do so, nor our means of accomplishing it.'[3] At the beginning of December, when Maurojeni pressed for a reply, Palmerston could only try 'to put a few unmeaning phrases together'.[4] Although refusing to send the fleet, the British promised to urge Mahomet Ali to evacuate Syria, and expected the sultan to treat this as an 'unequivocal proof of the lively interest which the British government takes in . . . [his] welfare . . . and its anxious solicitude for the maintenance of the integrity of his dominions'.[5] Even if this should discourage Mahomet Ali, it did nothing to help Mahmud, but Palmerston could not do more as long as the cabinet would not agree.

During December and January, the French, who wanted Syria and Adana for Mahomet Ali, continued to offer their mediation. The Russians, just as determined to defeat him, to preserve the

---

[1] Palmerston to Grey, private, 9 Oct. 1831, Grey of Howick MSS.; Holland's Journal, 5 Apr. 1832, Add. MSS. 51869, fo. 446.
[2] J. Ridley, *Lord Palmerston* (London, 1970), pp. 151–4.
[3] Palmerston to Holland, 1 Dec. 1832, Add. MSS. 51599, fo. 142.
[4] Palmerston to Grey, 2 Dec. 1832, Guy of Howick MSS.
[5] Palmerston to Mandeville, no. 8, 5 Dec. 1832, F.O. 78/212.

existing balance of power in the near east, were just as anxious for a settlement. They hesitated in November to offer the sultan reinforcements, hoping that the British would;[1] nor would he then have accepted them. He was awaiting a reply from Palmerston. In December the Russians mobilized. Turkey suited them because she was weak, but the British envoy at St. Petersburg warned Palmerston in December that they would expect to be paid for their help: the tsar would 'realize as the price of his timely succour the wish he is supposed to entertain of obtaining . . . a free passage for his ships of war through the Dardanelles'.[2] If the British chose not to act in the near east themselves, they should take care to prevent anyone else from acting instead: to keep out everyone was their most vital interest.

The British cabinet were busy at home; the first general election since the Reform Act was about to be called. More important, as soon as the act had been passed, the ministry began to quarrel. There was trouble about Ireland; Graham at the admiralty wanted to cut down the navy, Hobhouse at the war office the army: with ships needed in Ireland, to defend Belgium from Holland and Portugal from Spain, the whigs baulked at a third crisis in the near east. 'The navy could handle two European crises simultaneously without increased estimates but not three';[3] and Althorpe, the most powerful man in the government, so hated spending money, that he would have prevented Palmerston from sending ships to Belgium, had it meant increasing the naval estimates. Only public opinion might have forced his hand, and the press ignored the near east.[4] Meanwhile, towards the end of December, Namick Pasha arrived, to be welcomed by 'a ridiculous speech from the king, with abundant flourishes about the sultan and friendship for him, which is the more droll from his having been high admiral at the time of the battle of Navarino'.[5] As

---

[1] Bligh to Palmerston, no. 14, 23 Nov. 1832, F.O. 65/201; Puryear, *France and the Levant*, pp. 172–4, 181–4.

[2] Bligh to Palmerston, no. 32, 20 Dec. 1832, F.O. 65/201; Mandeville to same, no. 5, 8 Jan. 1833, F.O. 78/221.

[3] C. J. Bartlett, *Great Britain and Sea Power, 1815–1853* (Oxford, 1965), pp. 85–91.

[4] J. H. Gleason, *The Genesis of Russophobia in Great Britain: A Study in the Interaction of Policy and Opinion* (Cambridge, Mass., 1950), pp. 135–8, 149–52.

[5] *The Greville Memoirs: A Journal of the Reigns of King George IV, King William IV and Queen Victoria*, ed. H. Reeve (London, 1888), ii. 347.

Namick often remarked, had the British not sunk the sultan's fleet, he might not have needed the help of theirs.[1]

Encouraged by Stratford Canning, Palmerston tried to convince his opponents in the cabinet by setting out the arguments against Mahomet Ali. The result was two famous papers written by Canning and Henry Ellis. They are rightly seen as the beginning of a new policy in the near east, because one of them taught Palmerston how to play the Great Game in Asia, but they are usually treated as complementary. They were not: they offered Palmerston two policies not one. Because he did not immediately understand this, and because Holland was able easily to rebut Canning's arguments, partly explains Palmerston's second defeat in the cabinet in January 1833.

Canning's defence against the possibility of Russian intervention to keep Turkey weak was British intervention to make her strong. This would be more difficult were Mahomet Ali permitted to keep Syria, because the sultan would waste all his time and energy trying to drive him out. The continuous disorder would ruin Britain's trade, otherwise the cheapest and most effective means of reforming Turkey, 'upon which the best and only hope of maintaining . . . [its] independence . . . and improving the condition of its inhabitants, may be truly said to depend'.[2]

Britain had the right to intervene, said Canning, because the sultan was a legitimate ruler, who might ask for help, whereas Mahomet Ali's right to retain possession of Syria or of Egypt without the sultan's consent can only be by 'right of force'. 'What other', quipped Lord Holland, 'has the sultan?' Canning also guaranteed that the result of offering Britain's help would be paramount British influence guiding Turkey towards a liberal future: 'There is no doubt', he said, 'that the sultan would in any emergency look with preference to the counsels or assistance of Great Britain.' Utopians knew that eastern monarchs preferred Englishmen, just as imperialists knew 'a sort of moral necessity . . . [that] *says British soldiers must be the best in the world*'.[3] As Grant

---

[1] Palmerston to Grey, 29 Jan. 1833, Grey of Howick MSS.

[2] Encl. in Canning to Palmerston, 19 Dec. 1832, F.O. 78/211; printed in Crawley, *Greek Independence*, p. 237. See also Vereté, 'Levant Crisis', pp. 149–150, and Kelly, *Persian Gulf*, p. 272.

[3] Lord Broughton, *Recollections of a Long Life*, ed. Lady Dorchester (London, 1909–11), iv. 197.

and Trevelyan had assumed in Sind and Afghanistan, so little effort was needed by the superior.

By his plans for turning Turkey into a protectorate, Canning recreated the utilitarian vision of the future of central Asia, Sind, and Baghdad. To support his claim, he sent Palmerston in December a paper written by Chesney, who had followed him home from the near east in September, arguing that a steamer service on the Tigris and Euphrates would consolidate Britain's influence at Baghdad, 'by increasing facilities to our commerce, and also strengthening the hands of the sultan in the pashalic', under British supervision.[1] This concession for a steamer service would be both a suitable reward for defeating Mahomet Ali, and a way to prevent his causing trouble again, because it would give Britain a unique opportunity to make the most of the greater freedom to trade, promised by the sultan, but which the capitulations would force him to give to everyone, by ending the unrest in Syria and Baghdad. Trade would lead to order, order wealth, wealth revenue, revenue stability, and stability paramount British influence.

These arguments were supposed to win over members of the cabinet, like Holland and Lansdowne, who did not object to paying for active foreign policies, but who disagreed with Palmerston about what they should be. Holland replied later in December that Canning had everything the wrong way round.[2] If the British wanted to strengthen the Turkish Empire, it would be better and more easily governed were it smaller; if they wanted to reform it, Mahomet Ali had proved a better reformer than Mahmud; if Mahmud had tried to strengthen the imperial government at the expense of local custom, his title was no more legitimate than Mahomet's—and here Holland spoke like the good whig he was—because he had shown no more respect than Mahomet for the rights of property. Having attacked the aim, Holland attacked the method. The sultan's behaviour in 1802, after the British had driven the French from Egypt, proved how absurd it was to assume, that if they drove Mahomet Ali from Syria Mahmud would afterwards do as they told him. Canning's assumptions were

---

[1] 'Reports on the Navigation of the Euphrates by F. R. Chesney, 1831–1833', I.O. L/MAR/C/565.

[2] Minutes of Holland on encl. in Canning to Palmerston, 19 Dec. 1832, F.O. 78/211.

unrealistic; they were also rash. If Britain meddled, so would Russia and France, and in places where Britain might not be able to stop them. As sea power could not hold back Russia in the Caucasus, trying to turn Turkey into a protectorate might cause the collision with Russia it was meant to prevent.

Henry Ellis, commenting on behalf of the board of control, agreed with Holland that Canning had the wrong solution when he, too, applied to Turkey the criticism of Utopian dreams of reform, which he had already explained to Captain Campbell at Teheran and Major Taylor at Baghdad in 1831, but he agreed with Canning that Holland had ignored half the problem. To the board of control the most important test of any policy was its likely effect on the stability of British India. Since August, when he had warned the Russians off Khiva, Palmerston had learned that if Mahomet Ali's offers to defend India were spurious, he must be checked before he could do India harm. 'If England had no possessions in India and no interest in checking the further aggrandizement of Russia towards the south, then indeed non-intervention might be the best policy,' said Palmerston in December, but he had 'the greatest doubts [whether] . . . the success of Mahomet Ali would be favourable to our security in India.' Early in January 1833 Ellis explained why;[1] he also argued that Canning's notion of intervention should be rejected. Canning thought the weakness of Turkey the greatest danger to Britain in the near east and wanted to make it a protectorate but strong. Ellis, seeing danger to British India from an unstable balance of power in the near east, wanted to turn Turkey into a buffer state and to keep her independent but weak.

Mahomet Ali had always tried to obtain British support, by arguing that the creation of a powerful state in Egypt, Syria, and by implication Baghdad, would check the expansion of Russia towards Anatolia, help Persia to check it in Azerbaijan, and so solve the problem of how to defend British India, by the creation of a triple alliance between Egypt, Persia, and the government of India. Ellis objected to Mahomet Ali's visions of the future of Turkey as strongly as to Canning's: both would upset the balance of power. 'It is not the interest of the European sovereign of India',

---

[1] Ellis to Palmerston, 9 Jan. 1833, F.O. 78/233; printed in Kelly, *Persian Gulf*, p. 838. Similar ideas had been expressed by Farren the previous summer. Farren to Palmerston, 23 May 1832, I.O. Persia/47.

he stated as a principle, 'that a powerful Mahometan state should be placed at the mouth of the Euphrates.' Such a state would make the Persian Gulf more difficult to police; was as likely to partition Persia with Russia as defend her; and the revival of Islam might lead to a Mahometan league in central Asia, likely to cause unrest in northern India. These were all spectres, not necessarily dangers, but they shared one characteristic, instability, and would all make it more difficult not easier to defend British India cheaply and far away. 'The absence of such a power', said Ellis, 'is at present a complete security against any attack upon our Indian possessions from the southern parts of the Indus.' Whereas, should Mahomet Ali annex Baghdad, the British might be compelled to annex Sind, restraining him would provide an example to Russia of the determination of the British to prevent the expansion eastwards of any strong state, or of any protectorate of a strong state, lest they should have to defend themselves by the politically contentious, because costly, method of moving equally far north-westwards the military frontier of British India.

Ellis here set out the more substantial and more immediate problem that Turkey and Egypt, even more than Persia, could not be separated from the European balance of power. A strong state in Turkish Arabia, if capable of defending British India, would be equally capable of attacking her. One reason for the Great Game in Asia was to prevent Russia from using the threat of an attack on British India as a lever on British policy in Europe. 'The political and commercial interests of Great Britain', concluded Ellis,' . . . will be best consulted by having these provinces placed, as they are now, under a government to whom relations with India and Persia are matters of secondary rather than primary importance.' The boundary between the European and Indian political systems should be kept as far west as possible, and Baghdad should be treated as a province of Turkey, part of the buffer zone between the two.

At the end of the Great Eastern Crisis, Disraeli and Salisbury, planning to make Turkey strong, talked of turning the embassy at Constantinople into an Indian residency.[1] This was what Canning meant to do; but Ellis sensed that the Russians would not permit it, because they were aware of the British habit of

[1] A. P. Thornton, *The Imperial Idea and its Enemies: A Study in British Power* (London, 1959), p. 33.

treating allied Indian states as protectorates. Turkey could not be turned into a protectorate; the British must make do with a buffer, with acceptable frontiers, preferably the frontiers accepted at Adrianople, ruled by the sultan, and recognized by the powers. If the British tried to act by themselves, and tried by their reforms to change Turkish habits, they would cause uproar in Turkey and risk a European war. Ellis shared Malcolm's preference for weak states in the near east as the best defence of India, and was trying to apply Malcolm's rule to the new situation, where it was necessary to prevent the expansion and increasing influence of Russia. This meant that Britain would have to prop up not over-turn the existing political and social structure in the near east.

Ellis had explained to Palmerston the proper meaning of reform, who after 1833 never meant what Stratford Canning or utilitarians meant by the reform of Persia and Turkey. Temporarily, this proved no help. When, on 28 January 1833, Palmerston was again over-ruled in the cabinet, and the decision whether to send the fleet again postponed, he told Namick Pasha that Anglo-French mediation might be offered instead. The sultan, replied Namick, would prefer the help of Russia.[1] This was true. The British, while arguing, had been overtaken by events in the near east. On 21 December Ibrahim Pasha had decisively defeated the grand vizier at the battle of Koniah. At the beginning of February, when the Egyptian army were within striking distance of the sea of Marmora, the sultan asked for the help of the Russian fleet; on the 20th the first Russian ships reached Constantinople. This changed the nature of the crisis, but made it no less threatening to British interests. Russian influence in Turkey would be as dangerous as Mahomet Ali in Syria and Baghdad to the stability of British India, and might also destroy the European balance of power.

Britain's choice in 1833 was not whether to protect the sultan, but how and with whom, and to decide which dangers most threatened him. Palmerston was offered alternatives. Metternich, echoing Wellington, told him in February that if Austria were willing to believe the tsar, when he said that Russia wanted to prevent a partition, Britain should believe him, because the fate of Turkey mattered less to her, as she was not a neighbour, than to them. British and French ships should join the Russians in the sea of Marmora to defend Constantinople, and, should France refuse,

[1] Palmerston to Grey. 29 Jan. 1833, Grey of Howick MSS.

Britain, Austria, and Russia, should together prevent France from supporting Mahomet Ali.[1]

The danger Metternich foresaw was French hegemony in Europe: the French would try to use Mahomet Ali, as in the eighteenth century they had used the sultan, as a lever to tilt the balance of power in their favour.

Upon the wreck of that empire [said Metternich] . . . will arise an Arab empire closely related to France, extending her preponderance throughout the Mahometan world of Asia and Africa, taking Austria and Russia in reverse, and ready to act in concert with France whenever she may be engaged in hostilities with them in Europe.[2]

Perhaps he exaggerated, to others Austrians always seemed to exaggerate the dangers of revolution, as the government of India did their fears of rebellion, but Metternich saw that such a diversion might fulfil Napoleon's ambitions, by driving Britain and Russia out of Europe. If Austria were to keep down the Revolution, and Britain were both to hold back France in western Europe, and defend British India as far away as possible, Turkey must be held together.

Palmerston liked Metternich's suggestions, because they would hold back France; the French were pressing him equally hard to offer Anglo-French mediation as the best way to hold back Russia. They were less anxious to hold back Mahomet Ali, although they were willing to blockade Syria and Egypt, should he refuse reasonable terms, and said that they were not trying to turn Egypt into a protectorate.[3] Although Palmerston did not tell Metternich, he did not believe them; he was sure they would include all Syria in the reasonable terms to be imposed on Mahomet Ali.[4]

Until March, when he learnt how much help the Russians were giving the sultan, Palmerston saw Mahomet Ali as the greater

[1] Metternich to Neumann, 15 Feb. 1833, *Mémoires de Metternich*, ed. Prince Richard Metternich (Paris, 1880–4), v. 490; Lamb to Palmerston, no. 2, 8 Jan. 1833, no. 7, 17 Jan. 1833, F.O. 7/240.

[2] Lamb to Palmerston, no. 18, 14 Feb. 1833, F.O. 7/240; same to same, no. 54, 13 Apr. 1833, F.O. 7/241.

[3] Granville to Palmerston, no. 27, 21 Jan. 1833, no. 31, 25 Jan. 1833, F.O. 27/463; Palmerston to Grey, 28 Jan. 1833, Grey of Howick MSS.

[4] Palmerston to Granville, private, 4 Dec. 1832, 12 Feb. 1833, Broadlands MSS. GC/GR/1451, 1465.

danger to Britain's newly defined interests in the near east, and would have worked with Metternich, except that the cabinet would not risk a collision with France. At the beginning of February he warned Mahomet Ali, through Barker's successor as consul-general at Alexandria, Colonel Patrick Campbell, that the government's reason for postponing a decision on whether to send their fleet to help the sultan, 'was not because they viewed with indifference the events which were passing in the east'. If war in Syria might, by making Turkey unstable, threaten the European balance of power, it must be treated as rebellion; the sultan as a legitimate ruler, Mahomet Ali as 'only the governor of a Turkish province, appointed during the pleasure of the sultan, and removable at will'. Palmerston hoped Mahmud would deny Mahomet Ali both Syria and Adana, but, were he to keep Syria, the grant must be made 'with such obligations in point of tribute and military aid, as might leave the revenue and resources of the Porte undiminished, and with such limits as might least endanger adjoining provinces'.[1] If the rebellion should spread to Baghdad, it might also endanger British India.

When Campbell asked Palmerston how to reply, should Mahomet Ali again ask for British help, Palmerston decided that 'the British government could not countenance any such project'.[2] In the spring of 1833, guided by Henry Ellis, Palmerston moved closer to a proper understanding of the effects of the Syrian war upon Britain's interests in the east. Mahomet Ali's

real design is to establish an Arab kingdom [Palmerston told his brother in March] including all the countries of which Arabic is the language. There might be no harm in such a thing in itself; but as it would necessarily imply the dismemberment of Turkey, we could not agree to it.

Mahomet Ali might not himself destroy Turkey; he might give Russia the chance to do so later. The tsar would help the sultan, only to keep him 'a weak neighbour fit for preying on at a convenient season'.[3]

Ellis had convinced Palmerston that the partition of Turkey

---

[1] Palmerston to Campbell, no. 1, 4 Feb. 1833, F.O. 78/226.
[2] Minute of Palmerston on Campbell to Backhouse, 24 Jan. 1833, F.O. 78/227.
[3] Palmerston to Temple, 21 Mar. 1833, Bulwer, *Palmerston*, ii. 144; same to Ponsonby, private, 17 Feb. 1833, Broadlands MSS. GC/PC/655.

was not the only likely result of the creation of an Arab state. 'Russia would soon come to an understanding with our new sovereign,' predicted Palmerston. 'Persia would probably be nibbled at by both, and their union might produce inconvenient consequences to our eastern possessions.' Mahomet Ali's victory would make the defence of British India more difficult, and the European balance of power less stable. 'The sultan', Palmerston added, 'would be squeezed to death unless the powers of Europe made war to assist him; and there is no telling how far it might be convenient for them to do so, and how easy it might be for them to bring their assistance to bear upon the points assailed.'[1] The British had good reasons for treating the Syrian war as a local quarrel for as long as possible: as soon as it became an international question, they were caught between Metternich's prediction that a French protectorate over Mahomet Ali would lead to French hegemony in Europe, and Sir George de Lacy Evans's prediction that a Russian protectorate over Mahmud II would lead to Russian hegemony. Because the British government could not agree which of the two was more likely, Henry Ellis's proposal of turning Turkey into a buffer state seemed the best way to avoid both of them.

The British were ineffective at Constantinople in the spring of 1833, and Webster blamed Mandeville,[2] which was unfair: he had been sent no instructions for months, and assumed that Palmerston was waiting for Ponsonby, who did not arrive until May. The new French ambassador at Constantinople, who boasted in February that he could persuade Ibrahim, acting on behalf of Mahomet Ali, to settle for most of Syria without Adana, promptly failed. Ibrahim continued his advance; the sultan sent for Russian troops; the French, having failed to outbid the Russians, urged him to yield all Ibrahim's demands. This, at last, alarmed Palmerston's colleagues.[3] On 3 April, he persuaded them to reinforce the Mediterranean fleet, and to send a squadron to Alexandria to back up Campbell. The British expected the French to join them, assuming that, if Mahomet Ali still refused reason-

---

[1] Palmerston to Granville, private, 29 Jan., 5 Feb. 1833, Broadlands MSS. GC/GR/1461, 1463.

[2] Webster, *Palmerston*, i. 289.

[3] Talleyrand to Broglie, 25 Apr. 1833, *Mémoires du prince de Talleyrand*, ed. duke of Broglie (Paris, 1891–2), v. 151.

able terms, they should blockade, to prevent his reinforcing the Egyptian armies for an attack on Constantinople.[1]

Unfortunately, the British and French could not force Mahomet Ali to agree to a settlement quickly enough to prevent the sultan's needing more and more Russian help: the Russians, willing enough to protect the sultan, did nothing to hold back Mahomet Ali. By April 1833 Britain's priorities in the near east had been turned about: Russia replaced Mahomet Ali as the enemy. As long as the British talked about the reform of Turkey, they could argue a case for supporting the sultan or Mahomet Ali. As soon as reform was redefined to mean stability not change, they had to support the sultan; as soon as they thought of Turkey not as a protectorate but as a buffer, holding back Russia became more important than the defeat of Mahomet Ali.

Earl Grey feared that Britain could not have done anything sooner to accomplish this, and that it was now too late. 'It is evidently impossible to support the resurgence of the Turkish Empire', he said in April, 'without foreign force; and if this is to be afforded by Russia, it establishes at once a sort of protectorate, the result of which cannot be doubtful.'[2] Grey had not kept up with Palmerston, who no longer planned the resurgence, merely the continuation of Turkey. Nothing more was said about better government: 'We must try to help the sultan in organizing his army, navy, and finances; and if he can get these departments in good order he may still hold his ground.'[3] This would depend upon a settlement; Mahomet Ali must be appeased or the Russians would never leave Constantinople. Palmerston, sounding more and more like Aberdeen and Sir Robert Gordon three years earlier, had taken his second step towards the Great Game in Asia: he had learned that Russian influence was as dangerous as her territorial expansion to Britain's interests in the near east and to the security of British India.

To demand a settlement was easier than to devise one. Palmerston would have been happy to accept the abortive settlement suggested by the French ambassador in February, because, by denying Mahomet Ali the northern part of Syria as well as Adana,

---

[1] Palmerston to admiralty, secret, 3 Apr. 1833, F.O. 78/223; Grey to Palmerston, private, 10 Apr. 1833, Grey of Howick MSS.

[2] Grey to Palmerston, 23 Apr. 1833, Broadlands MSS. GC/GR/2223; printed in Webster, *Palmerston*, ii. 832.

[3] Palmerston to Temple, 21 Mar. 1833, Bulwer, *Palmerston*, ii. 144.

it might have brought greater stability to British India as well as Turkey, by also denying him 'the avenues of Mesopotamia'.[1] After its failure, Palmerston tried in April to revive the concert of Europe. The British, always suspicious of and impatient with Austria's hesitations, nevertheless sensed, although they would rarely admit it, that the two states had similar interests in the near east.

Metternich wanted any negotiations about a settlement to take place at Vienna. Palmerston could not agree to this, because 'the *pure* principles of absolutism which would mark the acts and language of such a conclave would not do here'.[2] Palmerston was echoing Canning's opinion about Greece: 'to do any good we must . . . [act] *alone*. Combined operation is nonsense, in a case in which the principles on which we and our allies act, are as different as the objects at which we respectively aim.'[3] Differences about Greece, Belgium, and Portugal, had left a legacy of incurable suspicion. Grey was just as suspicious of the French proposal for a self-denying ordinance, to be signed by all four powers. Palmerston could not convince him, that even if it would not affect the terms of the settlement already being negotiated directly between Mahmud and Mahomet Ali, it might ensure its success by holding back Russia in the future.[4] Such an agreement might also, as a result, have met one of the requirements of winning the Great Game in Asia set out by Henry Ellis. If Turkey were to be seen and treated by other states as an independent state with recognized frontiers, the British might by such an agreement have found allies to help in creating the buffer zone between Britain and Russia in the near east, and so defend British India on their behalf. Owing to the xenophobia of firstly Grey then Palmerston, the British, who had to stand alone against Russia in Persia and Turkestan, missed in 1833 and 1834 many chances to create a stable balance of power in Turkey, and, when they tried to manage it themselves on the Euphrates, they failed.

Palmerston had moved by April as far as Ellenborough in 1829; he had perceived that Russian influence was as dangerous to

---

[1] Ibid.

[2] Palmerston to Grey, 18 Apr. 1833, Grey of Howick MSS.; Lamb to Palmerston, no. 54, 13 Apr. 1833, no. 56, confidential, 14 Apr. 1833, F.O. 7/241.

[3] Canning to Granville, private no. 88, 8 Nov. 1825, P.R.O. 30/29/8/9, no. 396.

[4] Grey to Palmerston, 19 Apr., 23 Apr. 1833, Broadlands MSS. GC/GR/2221, 2223; Palmerston to Grey, 25 Apr., 7 and 9 May 1833, Grey of Howick MSS.

Britain as Russian annexations, but just as Ellenborough would not believe Heytesbury, Palmerston could not believe that Russia and Austria were not secretly planning a partition. The tsar, said the ambassador at Vienna, Melbourne's brother Frederick Lamb, had taken 'a solemn engagement, if the Turkish empire should fall to pieces, not to appropriate a single village'.[1] Metternich believed him, but Palmerston did not; nothing Metternich could say would persuade him. On 25 April the cabinet agreed to Palmerston's suggestion, that the powers should be invited to attend a conference at London, to negotiate joint proposals for a settlement, and then to send identical instructions to their ambassadors at Constantinople. When Metternich refused to take part, for the reason Palmerston would not take part in negotiations at Vienna, Palmerston was convinced his suspicions were justified.[2] Throughout the crisis Metternich and Palmerston were unable to co-operate, partly because neither would defer to the other. 'When I ask what has prevented him and you from perfectly understanding each other . . .', said Lamb in July, 'I can find no other reason than in his determination to treat . . . at Vienna and yours to treat . . . in London.'[3]

This squabble had no immediate effect, but in the autumn a decisive effect, upon the situation in the near east. On 9 April, after the French had failed to mediate, the Egyptians had advanced as far as Kutayah, and the first Russian troops had reached Constantinople, Mahmud agreed to appoint Mahomet Ali governor of all four provinces of Syria. Mahomet Ali, pressed at Cairo by the British, French, and Austrian consuls, agreed at the same time to the same terms. What should happen to Adana remained undecided. Mahomet Ali said he wanted it because its timber was needed by the Egyptian fleet; the sultan, who knew that its true value lay in controlling the passes through the Taurus mountains, did not mention it on 18 April, when he announced the new arrangements for Syria. One month later, on 16 May, he surrendered it to Ibrahim.

Allies were supposed to serve Britain's interests. Because both

---

[1] Lamb to Palmerston, no. 26, 8 Mar. 1833, F.O. 7/240.

[2] Lamb to Palmerston, nos. 69 and 73, 8 May 1833, F.O. 7/241; Palmerston to Lamb, private, 2 May 1833, Broadlands MSS. GC/BE/440.

[3] Lamb to Palmerston, private, 9 July 1833, Broadlands MSS. GC/BE/108; for details see Webster, *Palmerston*, i. 290–300.

the French and the Austrians had failed him, Palmerston had to fall back on the British fleet. By the beginning of May, ships had been found to carry out the cabinet's orders; in the meantime their function had been changed. They were to stay off Alexandria only until the fate of Adana had been decided, and were then to move to Besika Bay to put equal pressure on the Russians.[1] Palmerston hoped to persuade Mahomet Ali to evacuate Adana for the reason he had hoped Mahomet would evacuate Syria, because outside Egypt the unrest he caused would encourage the sultan to look for foreign support. Not until Palmerston learnt that the sultan had surrendered Adana did he tell Campbell in June not to oppose the settlement any longer.[2]

The peace of Kutayah was the equivalent of the battle of Navarino in its stunning effect on the balance of power within Turkey, and as a result on the relations between the powers. Both also left the British wondering what to do. Wellington and Aberdeen, knowing the limits of sea power, had thought it better not to fidget, not to provoke Russia by frivolous opposition, but to wait and see what steps should or could be taken to lessen the damage done to British interests by Russia's victory and the peace of Adrianople. Palmerston could not wait: he was born a fidget. If Turkey were to be turned into a buffer state, the fleet must show the flag at the Straits, to equal Russian influence at Constantinople. This was Palmerston's second mistake. The fleet could not challenge Russia; they had arrived too late. Instead they may have strengthened the determination of the Russians to turn Turkey into a protectorate by negotiating the treaty of Unkiar Skelessi.[3] What Aberdeen and Ellenborough had feared after the treaty of Adrianople had happened, and had proved Henry Ellis right: he had always said, that in battles for political influence against Russia, the British were likely to lose.

The new ambassador at Constantinople, Lord Ponsonby, knew that Palmerston had made a mistake. If Britain's most vital interest in the near east were to make sure the Russians left Constantinople, she must persuade the sultan to surrender Adana, to bring about a final settlement with Mahomet Ali. Then,

[1] Palmerston to Ponsonby, no. 2, 10 May 1833, F.O. 78/220.
[2] Palmerston to Campbell, no. 6, 10 May 1833, no. 7, 1 June 1833, F.O. 78/226; same to same, private, 10 May 1833, Add. MSS. 48451, fo. 7.
[3] Bartlett, *Great Britain and Sea Power*, p. 93.

until the Russians had gone, the British should keep silent. After a squadron of the Mediterranean fleet arrived at Tenedos on 28 June, Ponsonby warned Palmerston that 'it might be a dangerous thing to enter the Dardanelles by force . . . [because] if the Russians are about to retire, it would be prudent to avoid raising questions'.[1]

In May Holland criticized the threats against Mahomet Ali. The British should be careful not to do more than France, because 'that France will ultimately have him, if we do not, I think most probable'.[2] If Holland feared that Palmerston would turn Mahomet Ali into a French client, William IV feared that he would turn Mahmud II into a Russian one. The moment for decisive action had been missed.

It is impossible to deny [said the king], that this demonstration on the part of England and France, this threatened interposition, has been produced by the appearance of the Russian armament at Constantinople, rather than by the dangers to which the sultan was exposed by the success of Mahomet Ali.[3]

In any new crisis the sultan would demand a protectorate from Russia, who encroached gradually, rather than risk destruction by waiting for the states who claimed to be eager to hold together his empire to offer their help.

The king also reminded Palmerston that he should not forget to calculate the likely effect of his behaviour, and of any settlement between Mahomet Ali and the sultan, upon the security of British India. Naval demonstrations could add nothing, whereas the friendship of Mahomet Ali as ruler of Syria, the king had always claimed, would buttress British India by holding back the Russians in Persia.[4] William IV and his secretary, Colonel Taylor, were not the 'two fools' arrogant whigs pretended.[5] The sultan had turned to Russia partly because he feared the social revolution implicit in Palmerston's demands to Maurojeni and Namick for reform as much as he feared an Egyptian attack upon Constantinople.

---

[1] Ponsonby to Palmerston, no. 2, 2 May 1833, no. 6, 6 May 1833, F.O. 78/223; same to same, no. 25, 7 June 1833, F.O. 78/223; for details see G. H. Bolsover, 'Lord Ponsonby and the Eastern Question (1833–1839)', *Slavonic Review*, xiii (1934–5), 99–100.

[2] Holland's journal, 22 May 1833, Add. MSS. 51869, fo. 588.

[3] William IV to Palmerston, 20 May 1833, Grey of Howick. MSS.

[4] William IV to Palmerston, 1 June 1833, Grey of Howick MSS.; Holland's journal, 8 June 1833, Add. MSS. 51869, fo. 606.

[5] The phrase was Lord John Russell's. Broughton, *Recollections*, v. 38.

Palmerston had since learned that Turkey must be turned into a buffer; not until 1834 did he learn how. During the summer of 1833 he had first to learn, that if the security of British India were to be treated as one of Britain's most vital interests in the near east, the war in Persia was just as important as the war in Anatolia, the siege of Herat just as ominous as the Russian troops at Constantinople.

IV

The origins of the First Afghan War cannot be explained solely by tracing chronologically Britain's relations with the Punjab, Afghanistan, and Sind; nor can Britain's interest in the Eastern Question be explained solely by tracing the relations between Mahomet Ali and the sultan. The sequence must be arranged geographically, as the focus moves from east to west and back again. Lord William Bentinck at Fort William could subordinate defence to frontier policy, because he assumed that the board of control would think of a way to hold back Russia farther west. Similarly, British policy in Turkey had not to jeopardize the security of British India. Between the two stood Kajar Persia, always a puzzle to the British, who, because it seemed unable to help with either, would have preferred to separate it from both.

Despite the success of his campaign in Khorassan in the summer and autumn of 1832, Abbas Mirza, hard pressed for funds, was compelled to retire for the winter to Meshed, and to send back what was left of his army to Azerbaijan. This only postponed the threat to Britain's interests of which the members of the British mission in Persia had been too sceptical a year before, but about which they had since changed their minds, the capture by Persia of Herat. John McNeill now said, in January 1833, that were Abbas Mirza to bring order to Khorassan, 'nothing is likely to prevent his incorporating Herat, sooner or later, within the Persian dominions'.[1] Here was as great a danger to Britain, and to be as vigorously prevented, as the partition of Turkey. Mahomet Ali's Egypt must not become an independent Arabian kingdom; Herat must not become part of Persia. According to the Bombay School of Indian defence, to which both Sir John Campbell and McNeill belonged, Herat was the key to British India. Nobody

---

[1] McNeill to Campbell, no. 4, 20 Jan. 1833, no. 8 in Campbell to sc, 25 Feb. 1833, I.O. Persia/49.

foresaw, should it fall to Persia, Russian armies pouring across the Indus; nobody foresaw them pouring across the Channel after the partition of Turkey. Instead the stability of British India would be permanently endangered.

British India, as the Austrian Empire, was a continental state, with poor frontiers, a varied population, and alien rulers, which needed to be defended at a distance, preferably by forestalling attack. Should Herat fall to Persia, this would become more difficult, because the buffer zone between the European and Indian political systems would have been extended eastwards and closer to the British North-West Frontier; or worse, if Persia were assumed to be acting with the encouragement of Russia, it would have been destroyed. The zone had already shifted from the Mahometan Khanates to Persia, when the British after the Napoleonic Wars realized, that, because of Persia's connections with other European states, they could not turn her into a protectorate upon the Indian model. Herat must remain part of Afghanistan, part of an Asiatic states' system that, if the British did not yet, they might control. The fall of Herat to Persia, and Persian intervention in Afghan politics under pressure from Russia, would extend the European system beyond the Hindu Kush, and leave the British no alternative but to defend India, as Lord William Bentinck assumed, at the frontier or by European alliances. At the same time the North-West Frontier would have to be moved westwards: the need to control territory beyond the Indus would compel the British to annex the Punjab and Sind.

McNeill suggested that the British should forestall Persia at Herat by negotiating alliances with the Afghans. Helping the Afghans against Persia was forbidden the British by the ninth article of the treaty of Teheran, but McNeill believed that an opportunity would be given them to amend it. In January 1833 Abbas Mirza again asked the British to substitute for the abrogated subsidiary articles of the treaty an article offering general protection.[1] Both Campbell and McNeill, who had opposed the idea the previous year, when Ellis had suggested it, now agreed. As it stood the treaty was worthless, said McNeill in February, because the whole burden of it fell on Persia. British policy based on it was absurd. The British had argued that they could not help Persia,

[1] McNeill to Campbell, no. 5, 20 Jan. 1833, in Campbell to sc, 21 Feb. 1833, I.O. Persia/49.

firstly because she might provoke Russia, then because she was subservient to her. If the British feared Persian subservience, they must give the dynasty enough help to maintain their independence.[1] This was true; and it was not true. The degree of stability necessary to hold Persia together as a buffer state might have been obtained more effectively and cheaply by negotiations between London and St. Petersburg; by a change in the behaviour of foreign states rather than the dynasty.

Campbell, as usual, embroidered on McNeill. Because the British no longer financed Persia's resistance to Russia, they could not expect Persia to attack a Russian army marching eastwards towards India; consequently the end of the Persian Connection might increase the difficulty both of defending British India against invasion, and of preventing the expansion of Russia. Abbas Mirza might turn to Russia for the help the British were so reluctant to give him. 'So fast as England recedes,' said Campbell, 'Russia in the same ratio advances.' The easiest way to stop this would be the replacement of the subsidiary articles of the treaty by a statement offering Britain's protection, for which Abbas Mirza had asked, and which 'would leave no doubt in the minds of this nation of the good feelings which England entertained' for him.[2] By settling the dynastic quarrel amongst the Kajars in favour of Abbas Mirza, the British might, without unduly interfering in Persia's internal affairs, equal the influence of Russia, and, by succeeding in turning Persia into a buffer, prevent the capture by Persia of Herat.

Campbell and McNeill both assumed that Shah Shuja's expedition to Sind in 1833 was to be the start of an attempt to unify Afghanistan; Lord William Bentinck had hoped it would be. They also assumed, and this revealed their different priorities, that the united state would include Herat. Bentinck wanted to create a stable balance of power along the North-West Frontier, McNeill and Campbell to stabilize Persia as a buffer state. This could not be done until the frontier dispute between Persia and Afghanistan had been settled. Both Britain and Persia, therefore, would benefit from the revision of the treaty of Teheran. Should Britain offer to replace the subsidiary articles, Persia might agree to take out

---

[1] Memorandum by McNeill, 12 Feb. 1833, I.O. Bengal/SPC/374, 23 May 1833, no. 22.

[2] Campbell to sc, 22 Feb. 1833, I.O. Persia/49.

article nine,[1] which would also be tantamount to giving up her plans to annex Herat. As soon as the British had negotiated an alliance with Kamran Khan, the Persians would not attack Herat unless put up to it by the Russians, when the British would have to strike back equally hard.

Without such alterations to the treaty, Persia might meddle in Afghanistan, and the Russians would undoubtedly encourage them. The shah had promised to receive at the end of March the new Russian envoy, Count Simonitch, who had with him a secretary, two assistant secretaries, a physician, three aides-de-camp, and two consuls. Campbell feared that Simonitch had been sent to open a permanent Russian embassy at Teheran, until 1828 an exclusively British privilege, and one reason they still had any influence in Persia.[2] Campbell, by comparison, had only one assistant in John McNeill, and his eyesight was failing so badly that he could barely read the Persian passports, necessary to clear the way for British merchants and officials. The governor of Bombay, who thought him incompetent, suggested that Alexander Burnes should be sent out to help him.[3]

The British were lucky that the behaviour of Simonitch and his suite offended the shah, because it appeared during the spring of 1833 as if the Russians were trying to increase their influence in Persia and might succeed. The first to suffer was Captain Shee, dismissed in March from the command of Abbas Mirza's infantry, to show his goodwill to Russia, but not, Campbell hoped, to make way for Russian officers. Campbell, who in a rare example of family disloyalty—Shee was Sir Pulteney Malcolm's bastard— said that he was anyway incompetent, urged the government of India to send out someone capable of commanding Abbas Mirza's troops, because he had been waiting four years for the officers Ellenborough had promised him. Campbell told Abbas, however, that until they arrived he must make do with Shee, who was the only symbol of British influence available; if he dismissed him, Campbell would send home the British detachment.

[1] Campbell to sc, 20 Feb. 1833, with encl. by McNeill, 21 Jan. 1833, I.O. Bengal/SPC/374, 23 May 1833, nos. 17–18.

[2] Campbell to Swinton, 16 Mar. 1833, I.O. Bengal/SPC/374, 6 June 1833, no. 14. Masson, *Travels*, ii. 189–91, records the arrival at Kandahar of an envoy allegedly from Abbas Mirza; and negotiations were allegedly still continuing for the Perso-Sindian marriage.

[3] Clare to Bentinck, private, 9 Mar. 1833, Portland MSS. PwJf/709.

Abbas Mirza, meanwhile, had been waiting in Khorassan for funds and reinforcements from Azerbaijan, in order to attack Herat. When they had not come by June, he reluctantly obeyed a summons from his father to return to Teheran, because he hoped to prise money out of the imperial treasury. Although the shah remitted debts and offered a subsidy together equal to 80,000 tomauns, when Abbas Mirza left Teheran on 9 August, he had 'gained nothing in credit or influence by his visit to the capital, where he displayed little wisdom or address'.[1] Abbas, who had dropsy, was clearly weakening, which spurred those of his brothers who wanted to take his place. Hassan Ali Mirza, the brother of the governor of Fars, who had lost Kerman in 1831, now bought it back for 30,000 tomauns; Yezd was given to a son of the governor of Teheran; and Hamadan taken from Abbas Mirza and given to one of the shah's ministers.[2] His rivals sensed Abbas Mirza to be sufficiently near death, or sufficiently overtaxed in Khorassan, to risk a coalition against him.

This dynastic rivalry would endanger Britain, if it gave the Russians a chance to move forward in central Asia. They had plans, Campbell reported in August, for settlements in Ghilan or Mazenderan and on the east coast of the Caspian. Simonitch had asked permission to open a Russian consulate at Rasht, where Russians did little trade, and which would alarm the shah, because Ghilan was traditionally unsettled; a fleet of steamers were simultaneously being launched on the Caspian, which, although merchant vessels, 'are no doubt in furtherance of the future designs entertained by Russia towards the east'.[3] Despite the Russians' denial in 1832, these signs all pointed to a Russian expedition against Khiva. However potentially threatening to the British, the prospective danger could nevertheless be turned to immediate advantage, were the Persians, either suspicious of the Russians or busy intriguing one against another, to break off the campaign against Herat.

What most worried Campbell in 1833 was the likely effect of the death of Abbas Mirza. Russia had recognized the claims of his son, Mahomet Mirza, but 'the princes who have threatened to

---

[1] Campbell to McNaghten, 11 Aug. 1833, I.O. Bengal/SPC/377, 7 Nov. 1833, no. 3.

[2] Diary of 8 June 1833, in Campbell to sc, 10 Aug. 1833, I.O. Persia/49.

[3] Diary of 31 July 1833, in Campbell to sc, 1 Oct. 1833, I.O. Persia/49.

dispute the succession with an elder brother are not likely to submit without resistance to a nephew'.[1] Campbell suggested that Britain should support Mahomet Mirza, were he named heir apparent by the shah, but should otherwise not choose between the rival claimants. Whether or not Abbas died, and if he did regardless of who succeeded him, Britain must help the Kajars to settle this dynastic quarrel, or Persia would become a Russian protectorate. Having tried to remember that the board of control's policy, as Henry Ellis had explained, was to avoid a struggle for influence with Russia, Campbell shortly forgot. Abbas Mirza was still demanding compensation for the abrogation of the subsidiary articles, and in September Campbell suggested, that in return Abbas might agree not to seek help from anyone but the British, and not go to war with a European state without their permission.[2] This suggestion echoed Wellesley, whose ambitious plans had been abandoned on the advice of Henry Ellis nearly twenty years before. To control Persia's relations with Russia was to turn Persia into a protectorate, and the British could not protect Persia. Nothing came of these proposals for revising the terms of the Persian Connection, however, because Abbas Mirza, who had reached Meshed on his way back to his army, died on 21 October. His son had to break off the attack on Herat and return to Teheran to fight for the succession.

When news of the state of affairs in Persia filtered through to the foreign office, one fact stood out, that Persia might change the terms of her connection with Russia as well as with Britain. This immediately caught the attention of Palmerston. 'Is it likely', he asked Grant in October, 'that the object or result of . . . [Simonitch's] mission may be the conclusion of a treaty with Russia similar to that which Russia has concluded with the Porte?'[3] This had to be prevented, lest by turning Turkey and Persia into protectorates of Russia, it should, before the British had succeeded in turning Afghanistan into a protectorate, both destroy the buffer zone the British had been hoping to create between the European and Indian political systems, and, as a result, push back the

[1] Campbell to McNaghten, 13 Aug. 1833, I.O. Bengal/SPC/377, 7 Nov. 1833, no. 4.
[2] Campbell to sc, 4 Sept. 1833, F.O. 60/33; same to Grant, private, 1 Oct. 1833, I.O. Persia/49.
[3] Palmerston to Grant, 29 Oct. 1833, I.O. Persia/48.

political frontier of India to the Himalayas. August 1833 was the month of Palmerston's realization of the realities of international politics in the near east. This 'masterpiece of Russian intrigue and Turkish folly',[1] as Palmerston called the treaty of Unkiar Skelessi, had the same effect on him as the treaty of Adrianople on Wellington and Aberdeen. It might upset the balance of power in Europe; copied in Persia it might destroy the security of British India. In consequence the foreign office could not limit the help they gave the board of control to restraining Russia from an advance towards Khiva; they must also follow Henry Ellis's advice about how to play the Great Game in Asia in Turkey.

[1] Palmerston to Ponsonby, private, 7 Aug. 1833, Broadlands MSS. GC/PO/659.

IX

Towards the Euphrates Expedition
1833–1834

> Remember the golden rule: when the game's
> going against you, stay calm—and cheat.
>
> HARRY FLASHMAN,
> *Flashman at the Charge*,
> Chapter VIII

BETWEEN 1828 AND 1832, British policy in Persia and at
Baghdad had stayed within the limits set by Aberdeen and
Wellington, later set out as principles by Henry Ellis. The British
had offered enough help, not to commit themselves, nor to turn
Persia and Baghdad into protectorates, but to maintain them as
buffer states, by dissuading them from seeking help elsewhere.
This policy was to be severely tested by the effects of the campaigns in Syria and Khorassan. More decided intervention might
be needed to prevent both the shah, in the person of Abbas
Mirza, and the sultan from threatening British interests under the
influence of Russia: increasing Russian influence was in itself a
threat to Britain. Ellenborough had originally criticized the
policy, because he doubted whether Russia would ever do anything in the near east dramatic enough to justify retaliation in
Europe. In Persia in 1833 this proved true; the dangers to be
expected from the campaigns in Khorassan were future ones. In
Turkey it was not true; the danger was imminent. On 8 July the
sultan had signed the document which would shape the Eastern
Question for the rest of the decade, the treaty of Unkiar Skelessi.

Throughout the spring of 1833 the British, despite Palmerston's
suspicions, had never questioned the tsar's statements, that his
troops would leave Constantinople as soon as peace was made
between Mahmud II and Mahomet Ali.[1] On 10 July the Russians
left, two days after the signature of the notorious treaty. The

---

[1] Palmerston to Bligh, private, 7 and 21 May 1833, Broadlands MSS. GC/BL/
99, 101.

public treaty was merely a defensive alliance between the sultan and the tsar to last eight years. The controversy, both at the time, and amongst historians, was caused by the secret article; not that it long stayed secret. This did not change the rule, to which the British had agreed by the peace of the Dardanelles in 1809, that the Straits should be closed to all warships as long as Turkey was at peace. The treaty did not permit Russian warships to go in and out of the Black Sea in peacetime, nor, despite warnings from the British embassy at St. Petersburg of the tsar's intentions, did Palmerston believe it did. The effect of the article would be felt in wartime, because the sultan, as an ally of Russia, was pledged 'to closing the strait of the Dardanelles [but not the Bosporus], that is to say, to not allowing any foreign vessels of war to enter therein under any pretext whatsoever'.[1]

The British objected to the treaty because it turned Turkey into a protectorate of Russia.

The sultan with respect to foreign relations [said Palmerston] binds himself to adopt the quarrels of Russia as his own, and with regard to the internal concerns of his dominions is taught to look to the Russian army for the maintenance of his domestic authority. It is obvious that he thus ceases to be independent either at home or abroad.

Britain's protests against the treaty had to be 'directed against the right of interference as a matter of course',[2] because it would tilt the European balance of power dangerously against Britain, and at the same time threaten the stability of British India. The campaigns against Herat threatened to extend dangerously far eastwards the zone of buffer states the British were trying to create in the near east; the treaty of Unkiar Skelessi would destroy it. As the British found out later in the century, how, if the Black Sea were closed to them, could they hold back the Holy Alliance, or retaliate in Europe against Russian threats to India?

The British were always annoyed when their allies failed to defend themselves, and also British interests, and settled instead

---

[1] The treaty is printed in Hurewitz, *Near and Middle East*, i. 105. For the correct interpretation of the treaty see P. E. Mosely, *Russian Diplomacy and the Opening of the Eastern Question in 1838 and 1839* (Cambridge, Mass., 1934), pp. 10–12; for the incorrect one see S. M. Gorianov, *Le Bospore et les Dardanelles* (Paris, 1910), pp. 43–4.

[2] Palmerston to Bligh, no. 93, 13 Oct. 1833, F.O. 65/206; same to Grey, 6 Aug. 1833, Grey of Howick MSS.

with Russia. The sultan 'must reign like other sovereigns by his own means', Palmerston had told Ponsonby in May, 'and if he cannot be safe unless surrounded by Russian bayonets, instead of keeping the Russians in Turkey he had better go with them to Russia'. Palmerston had even thought of using Mahomet Ali to drive them out. The Russians had gone, but, if Turkey remained a protectorate, they might return, which left Palmerston in a dilemma.

As long as the sultan has the power or the will to remain independent [he told Ponsonby], every motive must lead us to support him; but if he becomes a slave to Russia he ceases to be what we want to see at Constantinople, and Mahomet Ali may then be a better support for the balance of power in the east . . .

Our best policy seems to be to pledge ourselves to do nothing for the future; to keep ourselves free to act according to circumstances; to prevent Mahomet Ali and the sultan from going to war again; to help the sultan to strengthen himself so as to be able to be independent of Russia if he chooses to be so; to keep well with both Mahomet and Mahmud; to hold the balance between France on the one hand and Russia on the other should either endeavour to encroach.[1]

Under the shock of the treaty of Unkiar Skelessi, Palmerston began to sense the wisdom of Ellis's rule, that owing to her geographical position Britain was more likely to lose than win any contest with Russia for paramount influence in Turkey, and began to work for stability in the near east, not demanding paramount influence for Britain, but determined to take it away from Russia. Turkey was to join Persia as a buffer state, and the treaty of Unkiar Skelessi was to be ignored. 'The British government', explained Palmerston in August, in protesting against the treaty to the Turks, 'will hold itself at liberty to act . . . in any manner which the circumstances of the moment may require equally as if the treaty . . . were not in existence.'[2]

The danger of instability at Constantinople, and of the sultan's asking the Russians to come back, was not ended by the settlement with Mahomet Ali, because a rebellion seemed likely. 'If it produces civil war,' Palmerston told his brother, 'the sultan, at the head of one party, may call in the Russians to put down the

---

[1] Palmerston to Ponsonby, private, 21 May, 1 July 1833, Broadlands MSS. GC/PO/656, 658.
[2] Palmerston to Ponsonby, no. 16, 7 Aug. 1833, F.O. 78/220.

other, and then comes the question, shall we let them return, or can we prevent them from doing so?'[1] Ponsonby, much more decisive as soon as the Russians had gone, said that the only way to prevent their return, and to match their influence at Constantinople, was to give him discretionary orders to call up the fleet. Grey was willing enough, because he saw that if the Russians arrived first, the fleet could not drive them away, but, because Ponsonby would have the power to create a state of virtual war with Russia, he said in September that the cabinet, down in the country for the summer, must first be consulted. Until the Mediterranean fleet had been reinforced from Portugal (not by much: Palmerston assumed six British ships could easily sink twelve Russian), there were no ships for which Ponsonby could send.[2] The autumn of 1833, when 'a schism in the ministry is approaching',[3] was not a good time for bravado, and until the end of the year Palmerston had not decided in what circumstances Ponsonby should act; whether he should prevent the sultan's being threatened by the Russians or supported by them.

The British attached 'great importance to the independent existence of a powerful state in the countries which now constitute the Ottoman Empire'.[4] They did not now mean by this a state powerful enough to fight other European states, just as they did not mean this by the independence of Persia, but one able to govern its own territories without foreign help. Nor did they mean to drive Mahomet Ali out of Syria. As long as Britain and France held him in check, and prevented his frightening the sultan into sending for the Russians, Turkey seen from outside was a single state. In October Palmerston told Campbell to remind Mahomet Ali that he would endanger its stability, as long as his naval and military preparations caused the Russians to stay on the alert in the Black Sea.

Because Britain's interest in Turkey was external, 'to maintain the independence and integrity of the Turkish Empire, as an important element in the general balance of power', Britain

---

[1] Palmerston to Temple, 6–7 Oct. 1833, Broadlands MSS. GC/TE/216; printed in Bulwer, *Palmerston*, ii. 169.

[2] Ponsonby to Palmerston, separate and secret, 27 Aug. 1833, no. 54, 7 Sept. 1833, F.O. 78/224; Grey to same, 18 and 23 Sept. 1833, Broadlands MSS. GC/GR/2251–2; Palmerston to Grey, 25 Sept. 1833, Grey of Howick MSS.

[3] Macaulay to his sister, 17 Aug. 1833, *Macaulay*, i. 323.

[4] Palmerston to Campbell, no. 16, 2 Oct. 1833, F.O. 78/226.

offered to help the sultan strengthen the imperial government, which was the meaning of better government to conservatives, by reforming his army and system of taxation. If the sultan would not reform, better Mahomet Ali at Constantinople than a Russian puppet.

The British government . . . [Palmerston told Ponsonby in December] believing that the well understood interests, both commercial and political, of the two countries, must generally be the same . . . [thought] that all these inconveniences and dangers might be avoided, by reverting to the ancient policy of the Porte; and by looking for aid to England whose interests cannot be averse to those of Turkey, instead of leaning upon a powerful and systematically encroaching neighbour. That if the alarms of the sultan are really excited by Mahomet Ali, Great Britain can effectually control the pasha, and protect the sultan from such danger; and it may be added that as long as the Ottoman Empire continue really independent, and does not become the satellite of any other power, the disposition of Britain to assist the sultan will always be equal to her power of doing so. But if the British government should be reduced to the necessity of choosing between the establishment at Constantinople of the power of Mahomet Ali, or the subjugation of that capital to the power of Russia, it would be impossible that we should not prefer the former of these two alternatives.[1]

Mahomet Ali as sultan would be less objectionable than as ruler of Baghdad: Turkey was a useful buffer, precisely because she was larger and weaker than the Arabian kingdom of which the British were convinced Mahomet Ali must dream.

Reading about the First Mohamet Ali Crisis gives one the feeling that it followed the Crimean War. As it did not, one can see why Palmerston, during the crises to follow the Holy Places dispute, was so impatient with Clarendon and Aberdeen. He had been through it all before: the issue was the same as in 1833, and, as Aberdeen should have remembered, the same as in 1829. Were Russia allowed to turn Turkey into a protectorate, having persuaded or forced Austria to agree, the balance of power in Europe would be destroyed, because Russia would then act as if she could not be checked. Even Napoleon to invade Russia had firstly to defeat, and then demand the help of Austria and Prussia. It was

---

[1] Palmerston to Ponsonby, no. 23, 6 Dec. 1833, F.O. 78/220; same to same, private, 6 Dec. 1833, Broadlands MSS. GC/PO/662; the former printed in R. L. Baker, 'Palmerston and the Treaty of Unkiar Skelessi', *English Historical Review*, xliv (1928), 83–9.

not enough, therefore, to ignore at Constantinople the existence of the treaty of Unkiar Skelessi, it must be protested at St. Petersburg and eventually replaced by an international agreement. When Grey hesitated, Palmerston explained in October that unless they protested, Russia would not realize how serious was their determination to resist her in Turkey. Policy must be seen in action, and Russia and Austria must be warned that Britain would fight to prevent their treating Turkey as a second Poland.[1] The historical allusion was doubly valid: the security of British India depended upon preventing a successor to Poniatoffski as well as the partitions.

Protesting against the treaty of Unkiar Skelessi became more important in the autumn of 1833, but it became equally difficult to decide how, after Austria and Russia signed in September the treaties of Münchengrätz. The British had been unable to decide, whether Metternich had known in advance about the treaty of Unkiar Skelessi, or had not, and had been deceived by the tsar. Having at first decided that Metternich had deceived them, they later decided that the tsar had deceived him.[2] This did not excuse him and his actions at Münchengrätz, although the British did not know for certain what he had done, annoyed them more.

Metternich claimed that at Münchengrätz he had been able to counterbalance the treaty of Unkiar Skelessi.[3] Nobody in England believed him, and, had they known the terms of the treaties, they would have seen that they showed up the most important difference between British and Russian policy in the near east. Britain wanted to preserve a piece of territory suitable to act as a buffer state. Who ruled it mattered less. Russia was willing to protect the Ottoman dynasty, because they controlled the Straits, but not to give them a guarantee of their territory. Despite this, the treaties of Münchengrätz must be seen as one of Metternich's most successful diversions. The tsar, who in the spring despite everything he said had been thinking about a partition,[4] was willing to forget the idea, not only because the sultan had agreed to a protectorate, but also because the rebellion in Poland had given

[1] Palmerston to Grey, 8 and 14 Oct. 1833, Grey of Howick, MSS.
[2] Lamb to Palmerston, no. 129, 25 July 1833, F.O. 7/242; same to same, no. 155, 1 Oct. 1833, F.O. 7/243.
[3] Metternich to Esterhazy, 7 Oct. 1833, communicated 18 Nov. 1833, F.O. 7/245.
[4] G. H. Bolsover, 'Nicholas I and the Partition of Turkey', Slavonic Review, xxvii (1948–9), 115–21.

Metternich his first chance to prove, that the Revolution threatened
Russia as much as Austria, therefore both states should return to
their policy at the end of the Napoleonic Wars, and subordinate
their interests in the near east to the maintenance of the Holy
Alliance.

Metternich agreed with Palmerston that nobody should be
allowed to change the situation in the near east, which meant
holding back both Mahmud II and Mahomet Ali, but he saw no
reason why the Anglo-French as well as the Russian forces should
not now be withdrawn. Austria was more easily reassured than
Britain, because the situation to remain unchanged, as both the
Russians and the British understood, was a Russian protectorate
over Turkey. Austria, as well as Russia, preferred a vassal sultan at
Constantinople to Mahomet Ali (whom they saw as a vassal of
France and as an agent of Revolution),[1] whereas Britain would have
preferred Mahomet Ali at Constantinople to a sultan who had been
turned into a vassal of Russia. Until the end of the year, the danger
of European war was considerable, because Palmerston, misunderstanding Metternich's priorities, remained convinced that at
Münchengrätz Austria and Russia might have planned the
partition of Turkey. 'The dismemberment of that empire', said
Palmerston, 'could not be effected without a contest between the
other states of Europe, and . . . when effected, would in all probability alter the balance of power, in a manner dangerous to the
peace and security of many of the European states.'[2]

In October, despite the opposition of Grey, whose turn it was
to fall under the spell of Princess Lieven, Palmerston persuaded
the cabinet to strengthen the Mediterranean fleet, and to make the
same protest against the treaty of Unkiar Skelessi at St. Petersburg
as had been made earlier at Constantinople. The Russians only
increased Palmerston's annoyance, by replying in November that
they had merely done what he and Stratford Canning had been
planning, and had seized the opportunity Britain had missed.
Palmerston did not like to be reminded of his mistake, nor of its
causes; and he denied the Russian claim that a Russian protectorate over Turkey, making Russia invulnerable, would endanger the

[1] Lamb to Palmerston, no. 155, 1 Oct. 1833, nos. 178 and 179, 26 Dec.
1833, F.O. 7/243.
[2] Palmerston to Temple, 6-7 Oct. 1833, Broadlands MSS. GC/TE/216:
printed in Bulwer, *Palmerston*, ii. 169.

peace of Europe, and the balance of power on which it depended, no more than a British protectorate, making Britain and British India invulnerable. To the British sea power was liberal, defensive, and less threatening to Russia than Russian expansion eastwards to British India: military power was aggressive and inherently despotic. 'We consider . . . [the Russian] answer to our protest flippant and impertinent,' said Palmerston in December, 'especially the concluding *tu quoque*.'[1]

However angry with the tsar, in the winter of 1833 Palmerston was more angry with Metternich: because Austria had agreed to the treaty of Unkiar Skelessi, Britain could not force Russia to replace it by an international agreement.[2] Whenever Britain, Austria, and France could agree, it mattered little how firm a stand Russia took; they could challenge it. The treaties of München-grätz strengthened the treaty of Unkiar Skelessi, because, in forcing Metternich to keep silent, the tsar forestalled Palmerston's attempt to create a near-eastern triplice, and, more importantly, prevented the sultan from hoping for, or counting on, its support. For Metternich, who obtained Russian backing against the Revolution, the bargain was worth while; Britain had to find another way to make certain that Russia had no choice but to act with restraint. This moved the focus of attention to the near east. What could not be arranged at Vienna and St. Petersburg might be tried at Constantinople and Baghdad.

In December 1833, the Russians explained that their policy in Turkey was defensive. The embassy at St. Petersburg, taught by Heytesbury, knew this to be true, and what it meant; that a protectorate was preferred to partition.[3] Palmerston, while planning to force the Dardanelles, and to attack the Russians in the Baltic, should they return to Constantinople in the spring, was gradually realizing, that as the treaty could not be destroyed, Britain must also attack them politically in Turkey, by preventing anything happening which might cause the sultan again to ask them for their help. 'If we can only keep Mahmud and Mahomet quiet, Turkey may yet be saved', he said, 'and while we have a good

---

[1] Bligh to Palmerston, no. 119, 6 Nov. 1833, F.O. 65/208; Palmerston to Bligh, private, 10 Dec. 1833, Broadlands MSS. GC/BL/110.

[2] Grey to Ponsonby, private, 4 Dec. 1833, Broadlands MSS. GC/PO/663.

[3] Bligh to Palmerston, no. 134, confidential, 21 Dec. 1833, F.O. 65/208; same to same, private, 21 Dec. 1833, Broadlands MSS. GC/BL/54.

fleet in the Mediterranean we can answer for Mahomet.'[1] This turned out to be not true. As a result, in 1834 Britain's answer to the treaty of Unkiar Skelessi was the Euphrates Expedition.

II

Throughout the late summer and autumn of 1833, while the foreign office had discussed the threat to Britain's interests in Turkey, and how to deal with it, the board of control had discussed the threat in Persia. The difference between them was the board's clearer perception of the issues, and what should be done, although they were less confident than Palmerston of success. Whereas he wanted to free Turkey from the shackles of the treaty of Unkiar Skelessi, Henry Ellis wanted to free Britain from the treaty of Teheran. This treaty was an advantage only so far as it stood for the right of Britain to an interest in Persia equal to Russia's interest by the treaty of Turkmanchay, and only as long as the echoes of Wellesley's hope when negotiating it, of turning Persia into a protectorate, could be ignored.

The board had to decide how to treat Sir John Campbell's warnings in February and March that the siege of Herat would shortly endanger British India. 'It is decidedly opposed to our interests that the Persians should conquer the country', said William Cabell at the board of control in June, 'and thus pave the way for the establishment of Russian influence in that quarter.' He suggested that Britain should try to remove the Afghan article from the treaty of Teheran by offering to mediate 'in [any] case of unjust aggression' against Persia. The risk involved in offering such a bargain was bringing about the situation it was meant to prevent. As Cabell admitted,[2]

we should know to what extent Russian influence had been carried, if the Persians, at their instigation, should refuse to accede to an arrangement . . . calculated to replace Persia under our protection and to secure us from injury through the instrumentality of operations among the Afghans, which, if successful, would prove seriously detrimental to our interests.

The tendency to treat all who are not with one as against one was

---

[1] Palmerston to Granville, private, 6 Dec. 1833, Broadlands MSS. GC/GR/ 1501.

[2] Memorandum by Cabell, 7 June 1833, I.O. Persia/49.

one trap Henry Ellis was anxious to avoid by the creation of a zone of buffer states.

Cabell had accurately set out Britain's dilemma. Ellis explained in August how it should be solved, and once again formulated British policy when, in December 1833, Palmerston began to play the Great Game in Asia. Ellis argued, as usual, that Britain had created her own dilemma by taking out the subsidiary articles of the treaty of Teheran, which had, if nothing else, demonstrated to Russia the extent and legitimacy of Britain's interest in Persia. She could not solve her dilemma by negotiating a new treaty meant to turn back Persia into a protectorate, because Britain could not, and had proved she could not, protect Persia from Russia; she had not protected the sultan from Mahomet Ali. To propose the removal of article nine so soon after Abbas Mirza had pacified Khorassan would merely repeat the previous blunder: Abbas was bound to see the British as thwarting him at every turn. Instead he should be held back where he threatened British interests by offers of help where he defended them; he should be offered Britain's backing against future Russian demands on Persia, and the British military mission should be made large and effective enough, to make him feel confident of succeeding to the throne without Russian help.[1]

Britain's backing was to be limited to an offer of mediation, and to a statement that Britain might take further action to defend Anglo-Persian interests, should the mediation be unsuccessful. Although the aim of this concession was limited to matching Russian influence, its success would depend upon three developments. The first was yet another reorganization of the Persian mission. If Persia like Turkey were to become a buffer state, the same policy must be carried on in both; because the frontier between the European and Indian political systems had moved eastwards from Erivan to Herat, this could be done only by the foreign office, who must take back control of the mission. The other two developments concerned the fate of Herat. Persia could not be turned into a satisfactory buffer state, until she had agreed to an eastern frontier drawn to the west of Ghorian, which controlled the approach to Herat, and until Herat had become part of a united Afghan state, and ideally a British protectorate.

---

[1] Ellis suggested one field officer and two captains of infantry; and one captain, two lieutenants, and ten sergeants of artillery.

Because these were all contentious questions, Ellis suggested in August that before the government acted, they should send to Persia someone capable of reporting accurately the state of affairs.[1]

The British could never decide whether to demand help from allied states, or to be satisfied that they continued to be independent. In commenting in September for the secret committee of the East India Company, Thomas Peacock echoed Cabell. Britain should send to Persia a large enough military mission to assuage Abbas Mirza's fears about the succession; this had been urgently needed since the treaty of Turkmanchay. In return, as Sir Gore Ouseley had said the year before, Abbas should agree to forestall any future Russian expansion from Khiva up the Oxus, by setting the Turcomans against the Russians, whenever they tried to settle on the east coast of the Caspian. Paramount influence in Persia was vital to the defence of India in central Asia, because, were the Russians to prevent such a coalition, they 'would make Kharasm an easy conquest'.[2]

This was a line of argument Ellis had been criticizing for nearly twenty years: it meant another, certainly expensive, and probably unsuccessful struggle against Russia. When Grant and Palmerston decided in November 1833 to take steps to prevent Persia from following Turkey into dependence upon Russia, they accepted Ellis's assumptions that greater influence in Turkestan must follow closer relations with the Afghans, and be arranged by the government of India; that Persia's contribution to the stability of British India was to match the newly defined relationship between Mahmud II and Mahomet Ali. All that mattered in Persia, as in Turkey, was the stability of the imperial government. Although Palmerston was not yet willing to take back control of the Persian mission, he was willing to plan a co-ordinated strategy for the near east, because he now saw, as the king put it, that without one Britain would witness 'the gradual encroachment of Russia upon Persia, the result of war and of protection with respect to Turkey'.[3] 'It really seems of great importance not to repulse . . . Persia', said

[1] 'Memorandums [by Henry Ellis] on Relations with Persia', [about 20 Aug. 1833], in Ellis to Palmerston, 21 Aug. 1833, F.O. 60/33. They were also sent to Grant.
[2] 'Memorandum [by T. L. Peacock] on the Affairs of Persia from the Commencement of Sir John Macdonald's Mission', 21 Sept. 1833, I.O. L/PS/3/1.
[3] Memorandum by William IV, 2 Nov. 1833, I.O. Persia/48.

Palmerston, 'and if we can secure her as an ally we shall greatly thwart the schemes of Russia in that quarter—why stint the Persians in British officers and men, and if we give them enough why should they take [them] from any other power?'[1] Therefore, despite muttering at the East India Company about the cost, in November the board of control told the government of India to pay whatever was necessary to persuade competent young officers to serve in Persia.[2]

The arrival of the military mission was to be preceded by revisions to the treaty of Teheran, to be negotiated under instructions from the foreign office, but to take the form of the revision of an existing treaty, not the negotiation of a new one; both to prevent the Persians from making new demands, and the Russians from pretending that the British were making them. The offer of mediation, as drafted by Ellis, was to be put in, to show that the subsidiary articles had not been taken out because Britain had lost interest in the Persian Connection, nor through fear of a misunderstanding with Russia. In return, and contrary to the advice of Ellis, who thought it unnecessary, Persia was to be persuaded to take out article nine, because the state of war between Abbas Mirza and Kamran Khan 'would make the obligation imposed on Britain . . . extremely embarrassing'.[3] The British would have liked Persia also to take out the article of the treaty giving her the right to hire the soldiers of any state not at war with Britain, but knew that such a request must be offensive, when they had repeatedly offered their own help and never given it.

If her soldiers could carry Britain through the succession crisis in Persia, her trade might replace them thereafter. Campbell, as instructed in 1831, had been trying to improve conditions of trade, in order to develop the trade-route from Trebizond to Tabriz. The Persians said that the duty could not be lowered below 5 per cent without offending Russia; they did agree that whenever the value of goods was disputed both sides should appoint an arbitrator. These, claimed Campbell in June, were the best terms to be had: they would not change much, unless British consuls were

---

[1] Palmerston to Grant, 3 Nov. 1833, I.O. Persia/48. Grey also had been consulted.
[2] Macaulay to Auber, 23 Oct. 1833, I.O. E/2/37; cd to ggic, 20 Nov. 1833, I.O. L/PS/6/245.
[3] Palmerston to Campbell, no. 1, 4 Dec. 1833, with encl., F.O. 60/33.

appointed in Persia to see to their enforcement.[1] As long as the resident at Teheran was employed by the East India Company, this could not be done, because any consul would automatically have had the higher rank. Here was another reason why Campbell needed a credential from the Crown: trade as well as the balance of power demanded that Persia should be treated as part of the European rather than the Indian political system.

Henry Ellis, whose opinions about trade matched his strategy, thought that Britain should be satisfied with the rights of a most favoured nation. British goods, like British values, did not need protection: with equal opportunity they would always sell. As Persia was willing to grant this, a new commercial treaty would not be needed, and Campbell was told in November to treat the commercial negotiations, like the political, as tidying up an existing treaty. The duty was to be fixed at 5 per cent; arbitration accepted as a method of settling disputes, which were to be settled within three days, to guard against the Persian passion for putting things off; and the local Persian authorities were to be compelled by the imperial government to make certain that debts due British merchants were paid. The appointment of consuls was not to be pressed. The resident, his assistant, and the resident at Bushire, would all be sent consular credentials.[2] To demand more would offend the shah, who had refused to allow the Russians to appoint consuls, although by the treaty of Turkmanchay they had the right to appoint them wherever their trade seemed to require it.

Finally, the government did something to end the ill effects on Anglo-Persian relations of the struggle for the Persian mission, and of the incompetence of Sir John Campbell. 'Your envoy's letters from Teheran drive me mad,' complained Clare to Bentinck the following year. 'They are wordy essays with little if any information . . . [He] eternally complains of Russian influence and intrigues, but he never tells you *what* thay have actually done and *what* is the effect produced. Dr. McNeill's reputation must be over-rated if he looks over his despatches.'[3] On the advice of Henry Ellis, at the beginning of December Palmerston and Grant

[1] Campbell to Grant, 1 June 1833, I.O. Persia/49.
[2] 'Supplementary Memorandum [by Henry Ellis] on Relations with Persia', [about 20 Aug. 1833], F.O. 60/33.
[3] Clare to Bentinck, private, 18 June, 8 July 1834, Portland MSS. PwJf/773, 777.

decided to send out to Persia, to investigate the state of affairs, and to report on the competence of Campbell and McNeill, a well-known British traveller, James Baillie Fraser, who had travelled through Persia ten years previously, and who had been Ellenborough's first choice in 1830 to escort his horses to Ranjit Singh. Fraser, who had missed the chance to begin the Great Game in 1830, was to begin it again in 1834.

Fraser was to report on the condition of Erivan and Nakitchevan, Russia's new frontier provinces on the Arras; on the extent of her influence and trade in Persia and the states between the Caspian and the Indus; and whether the Russian demand to post consuls in Ghilan and Mazenderan was justified by the volume of trade, or was meant to create unrest as the prelude to annexation. He was to gauge the power of Abbas Mirza, his ability to hold on to Khorassan and capture Herat, to rely upon his troops, to overawe his rivals, particularly the governor of Fars, and to obtain the throne, when his father should die, without foreign help. He was also to gauge the state of affairs at Baghdad, and whether, in the event of the partition of Turkey, it might successfully declare its independence. All this information was to be obtained unobtrusively: Fraser was 'sedulously to avoid all appearance of being invested with any diplomatic character or mission whatever'.[1]

The government of India were told to collect similar information. Similar information of similar places by similar methods for similar reasons: on 19 December 1833, four years but ten days since Ellenborough and Aberdeen had begun, the Great Game in Asia began again. The East India Company merely found it repetitive. They had already spent large sums, supposedly to obtain the information necessary to combat Russian influence, and saw no reason to spend any more. They knew that the government of India opposed such policies, and were determined not to carry them out; if the British government chose to begin them, they should pay. The company refused to give Fraser any money, except 'under the positive understanding that the advance is a loan; that the expense of Mr. Fraser's mission does not belong to the East India Company and shall not be charged to its account'.[2] The company were right to scoff at Fraser's disguise, and to worry

[1] Palmerston to Fraser, 4 Dec. 1833, F.O. 60/33.
[2] Mill to Jones, 7 Dec. 1833, I.O. L/PS/3/118. Fraser was to be paid his travelling expenses and £1,200 a year.

whether his advice would have expensive consequences, because Palmerston, although still uncertain exactly how to, knew that he had begun to play the Great Game in Asia. Fraser, he told Ponsonby, was being sent to Persia 'to throw up there some outworks against Russia'.[1] One month later, in January 1834, the government decided to throw up similar outworks on the Tigris and Euphrates.

III

The Great Game in Asia began for the second time in Persia, but was played with greater daring in Turkey. At the end of January 1834, the cabinet decided to ask parliament in the forthcoming session for a grant to experiment with steamers on the Euphrates, as the best way to stabilize the situation in Syria and Baghdad, and to stabilize the situation at Constantinople by sending Ponsonby the discretionary orders to call up the fleet, for which he had been asking. Ponsonby was to act only at the invitation of the sultan, and the British admiral might refuse to co-operate, should he think the operation too hazardous.[2] These instructions have often been criticized, but they were meant to be a defensive, not an offensive weapon.

The peace of Turkey [said the king in February at the opening of parliament], since the settlement that was made with Mahomet Ali, has not been interrupted; and will not, I trust, be threatened with any new danger. It will be my object to prevent any change in the relations of that empire with other powers, which might affect its future stability and independence.[3]

The fleet would hold back Mahomet Ali, and there seemed less chance of a rebellion at Constantinople: the sultan, therefore, would not need the help of Russia, and Ponsonby was not empowered to stop the Russians, should they return to Constantinople by invitation. He was empowered to act only if the Russians, despite all they had promised and Metternich had promised for them, should try to impose their will on the sultan by force, or threaten a partition.

[1] Palmerston to Ponsonby, private, 6 Dec. 1833, Broadlands MSS. GC/PO/662.
[2] Palmerston to Ponsonby, secret and separate, 10 Mar. 1834, F.O. 78/234.
[3] The speech from the throne, 14 Feb. 1834, *Parliamentary Debates*, 3rd series, xxi. 3.

Upon the affairs of the Levant [said Palmerston in August] our system remains the same. We are determined to resist Russia, if Russia should attempt encroachment, but we do not mean to break with her by taking the offensive ourselves. We wait till she becomes the aggressor, knowing the advantage of having to repel an aggression instead of being the party to make one.[1]

If Turkey were to be held together as a buffer state, the British needed to be able to exert as much pressure as might be necessary, but only so much, to hold back the Russians without having to replace them.

At Constantinople, Lord Ponsonby was trying to make certain he would never need to use his discretion, by convincing the sultan that Britain and France would not tolerate, and even without the help of Austria were strong enough to prevent, Russia's treating Turkey as a protectorate. Ponsonby doubted whether the sultan ever would be convinced, unless Britain should offer a substitute for the treaty of Unkiar Skelessi, and during the summer talked in private of the need for a war to prove that Russia could be defeated. This was not literally meant. 'I have never (though you seem to have misunderstood me)', he told Palmerston in October, 'intended to throw upon you the moral disadvantage of beginning a war. My measures . . . have always had for their end the avoidance of that evil, and I think I have sufficiently shown how it can be avoided.'[2]

This was true, nevertheless since 1833 the two men had changed stations; Ponsonby having become more eager than Palmerston for decisive action to restore Britain's influence in the near east. According to Webster, Ponsonby 'alone of Palmerston's subordinates and colleagues foresaw what British policy could achieve in the Eastern Question'.[3] This may have been the case at the foreign office: the statement betrays Webster's habitual disregard of the board of control, and peculiar definition of the subject. Ponsonby stands out because under the influence of Robert Urquhart he wanted, like Stratford Canning, if for less apparently Utopian reasons and with less missionary zeal, to turn Turkey into a protectorate of Britain. To destroy the value to Mahmud II of

[1] Palmerston to Ponsonby, private, 22 Aug. 1834, Broadlands MSS. GC/PO/ 667.
[2] Ponsonby to Palmerston, separate and secret, 19 Dec. 1833, F.O. 78/225; same to same, no. 166, 22 Oct. 1834, F.O. 78/239; same to same, private, 3, 12, and 17 Feb. 1834, Broadlands MSS. GC/PO/181, 183, 185.
[3] Webster, *Palmerston*, i. 302.

the treaty of Unkiar Skelessi, Mahomet Ali must be forced to evacuate Adana and Syria; the fleet should stay in the eastern Mediterranean to hold back the Russians; and the British should then make use of the opportunity they would have created to reform the sultan's army and finances, as much to strengthen their influence over him as his government.

Ponsonby was a dangerous man to employ at Constantinople, because he did not understand the relationship between the British government and British trade. The most serious threat to Britain during the Russian occupation of Constantinople in 1833, was not that the Russians would not leave, which would have meant a European war (for which they were not ready, although Ponsonby told Palmerston to be ready), but rather that they would give the defence of Mahmud II against Ibrahim as a reason for occupying Trebizond, Erzerum, and Sivas. Britain could hardly have asked France, and certainly not Austria, to fight to evict them; were they to stay, they would destroy the trade-route to Persia, and might plan at any time 'from thence an attempt to attack the British possessions in India'.[1]

This danger reappeared in March 1834, when the Russians and Turks signed the convention of St. Petersburg. In return for going without part of the indemnity still owed by the terms of the treaty of Adrianople, as a pledge for the payment of the rest Russia was allowed to occupy Silistria, which controlled the routes into European Turkey, and to move her Asiatic frontier nearer to Kars and the trade-route from Anatolia to Persia. The Russians said that this showed their disinterest: Palmerston and Ponsonby saw only their ambition. Whereas the board of control had hoped that in Turkestan, and even Persia, trade might end the unrest and so prevent crises, Ponsonby believed that in Turkey, where the crisis had taken place, the damage could be undone only by the exercise of power. Then trade, which would always need protection, might benefit. 'Protection given to our political interests', he said in November, 'will throw open sources of commercial prosperity perhaps hardly to be hoped from our intercourse with any other country upon earth.'[2] At the beginning of the Great Game in Asia, the British were nothing if not en-

---

[1] Ponsonby to Palmerston, no. 1, 22 May 1833, F.O. 78/223.
[2] Ponsonby to Palmerston, no. 187, 25 Nov. 1834, F.O. 78/240; Bolsover, 'Ponsonby and the Eastern Question', pp. 101–5.

thusiastic. Utilitarians forgot that European trade might need protection; Ponsonby, unlike Ellenborough, forgot that, as the Turks had little to sell, they might have difficulty in paying for everything they were to buy.

Between 1829 and 1845 the value of Britain's trade with Turkey more than quadrupled. Because the balance was so favourable, indeed too favourable, to Britain, while the British enlarged their capital available for reinvestment, the Turks had to devalue the piastre to pay their bills. Ponsonby, trying to end the sultan's reliance upon Russia, and seeing that trade and influence did not necessarily march hand in hand, supported in 1834 a Turkish proposal to raise the duties they were entitled to levy from 3 to 5 per cent, bringing them into line with Persia, and argued that as British merchants would pay in devalued Turkish piastres they would be paying no more.

This upset the board of trade. Turkish trade, they replied, was regulated by the capitulations not the sultan, and the board, who sought no privileges, would grant none: they would not tolerate the creation in Turkey of monopolies as a way to avoid European competition.[1] Nor did they accept the Turkish argument for raising the duties; only if this concession would bring sufficient political gains might the foreign office agree to it for political reasons.[2] Palmerston, perhaps surprised that Stratford Canning's paragon should prove such a half-hearted reformer, repeatedly told Ponsonby to explain that freedom of trade and the prohibition of monopolies was the only way to increase the sultan's revenue, which could alone strengthen his government and end his need of foreign support.[3]

Ponsonby's anti-Russian extravagance in 1834 was encouraged by Robert Urquhart, the 'most prolific, most single-minded, and extreme of . . . all' the young men who toured the near east at the beginning of the Great Game in Asia, and who came home to tell what they had seen;[4] his only rivals were Chesney and Burnes. Urquhart had gone out to Greece a Philhellene; had stayed to change his mind; had been employed by Stratford Canning at Constantinople in 1832 as a confidential agent; and had returned

[1] Lack to Backhouse, 27 Nov. 1833, B.T. 3/24, p. 330.
[2] Lack to Bidwell, 6 Dec. 1834, B.T. 3/25, p. 365.
[3] Palmerston to Ponsonby, no. 22, 6 Dec. 1833, F.O. 78/220; same to same, no. 24, 1 June 1834, F.O. 78/234.
[4] Crawley, 'Anglo-Russian Relations', p. 62.

to England in September full of the opportunities for Britain in Turkey. His book *Turkey and its Resources* was such a success with William IV, that he sent a copy to each of his ministers, and foisted Urquhart upon Palmerston as someone who should be sent to tour the near east from Turkey to Afghanistan and Bokhara, and report upon political and economic conditions.

Until Urquhart reached Constantinople at Christmastime 1833, his mission had no political purpose; it was not supposed to be complementary to Fraser's. It was Ponsonby who guessed how useful Urquhart might be in supporting his arguments for a bold policy, kept him at Constantinople throughout the spring, and in July 1834 sent him on a tour of the northern coast of the Black Sea. This led to the first of Urquhart's collisions with Palmerston. Urquhart, like Ponsonby, argued that to hold back Russia, Britain must offer the sultan an alliance; he added that its immediate result would be to divert the Russians from the Straits, by encouraging the Circassians to keep on fighting them in the Caucasus. Without a British alliance to replace the treaty of Unkiar Skelessi, the sultan would never break away from the Russians. Palmerston, who thought such arguments hastened the war he wished to prevent, in September and October told Ponsonby that Urquhart was merely wasting public money and should be sent home to London.[1]

This proposal for intervention in Circassia illustrated both how far the importance of Britain's interests was being measured throughout the near east in the same terms, and how far Palmerston was reflecting the assumptions of the board of control. 'Will England', asked Ponsonby in September, 'leave the Caucasus to the fate of Poland, or will England remember that in condemning those natives to Russian serfage, the balance of power in Europe is changed, the commerce of Britain limited, and Turkey, Persia, and India endangered?'[2] If British India were to be defended as cheaply and as far away as possible by curtailing the expansion of Russia, Circassia was the place to do it. Palmerston knew that it could not be done. Intervention in the Caucasus from the Black Sea would be at least as offensive to Russia as the British had

---

[1] G. H. Bolsover, 'David Urquhart and the Eastern Question, 1833–37', *Journal of Modern History*, viii (1936), pp. 445–53; Sir C. Webster, 'Urquhart, Ponsonby, and Palmerston', *English Historical Review*, lxii (1947), 329–36.

[2] Ponsonby to Palmerston, no. 144, 16 Sept. 1834, F.O. 97/344.

declared Russian intervention from the Caspian in Turkestan, and to be effective would require the military action it was Britain's most vital interest to avoid.

If Great Britain were at war with Russia [replied Palmerston in November], and if we had the means of affording the Circassians such effectual succour as would not only enable them to make a temporary stand against the Russians, but would place them in a condition to secure themselves permanently against the vengeance of the Russian government, it would be allowable and it might be expedient to assist these people.[1]

This was not the case. Because Britain could not protect Circassia any more effectively than Persia, intervention there should be avoided, as one of the policies meant to strengthen Turkey which Ellis had argued should be given up, in return for the creation of a zone of buffer states, of which Anatolia and Azerbaijan, but not Circassia, must be part.

Because Ponsonby defended Urqhart, in December 1834 Palmerston was proposing to make him consul at Constantinople; perhaps his ideas about Turkish politics made up for his Russophobia. Urquhart argued that Turkey was an underdeveloped market for British manufactures, and a source of raw materials hitherto found only in Russia. Despite this echo of the Ochakoff Affair, Vernon Puryear, by attributing to Urquhart the commercial rivalry between Britain and Russia which became the economic origin of the Crimean War, exaggerated the importance of his mission to Constantinople.[2] As important to Urquhart as the Turkish trade was the Turkish system of government. Turkey would be more easily held together than Englishmen often feared, for the reason it had always held together in times of stress, and had puzzled many European observers including Napoleon by so doing, because its institutions were designed to create stable local self-government. Turkey was an empire, and the British should avoid the mistake of trying to turn it into a centralized European state. This was not incompatible with a flourishing trade. If the British matched their opposition to monopolies by lowering their prices, they might unloose 'those administrative chains, those commercial prohibitions that lock its resources from the light', and

---

[1] Palmerston to Ponsonby, no. 67, 16 Nov. 1834, F.O. 97/344.
[2] V. J. Puryear, *International Economics and Diplomacy in the Near East: A Study of British Commercial Policy in the Levant, 1834–1853* (Palo Alto, 1935), pp. 23–7.

make Turkey 'the largest mart in the world for English manu-factures'.[1]

The appeal of such ideas to Palmerston is obvious. From a different premiss they reached the same conclusion as Henry Ellis; that as bold steps against Russia were impossible, they must be made unnecessary. The treaty of Unkiar Skelessi, which bound Russia to support Mahmud II, and the treaty of Turkmanchay, which bound her to support Abbas Mirza, must both be destroyed by making certain that the circumstances in which they would operate never arose. Turkey like Persia was to be treated for purposes of international relations and international trade as one state; how it was organized did not matter, and how power was divided inside it did not matter, as long as the division was stable. In 1834, in both states, this was a big qualification.

As the British often tried in the nineteenth century, in the summer of 1834 Palmerston was trying to find a way to create a stable balance of power in the near east without British inter-vention. Unfortunately, although the fleet temporarily held back Russia, they did not strengthen the sultan, who would never feel strong enough to govern his empire without the backing of the treaty of Unkiar Skelessi, until he had forgiven or overthrown Mahomet Ali. Metternich and the French repeatedly proposed a four-power treaty of guarantee (the one missing from the Final Act at Vienna), but Palmerston doubted whether the Russians would now be bound by it. Because the only way Russia could control her own economic development was 'the actual possession of the Straits . . . I shall never believe [he said] that anything but the consciousness of insuperable difficulty prevents her from attempting the possession'.[2] Palmerston in July and August was beset by a British statesman's habitual dilemma; where to find the continental ally with a powerful army capable of defending British interests. As long as the enemy was Russia, in the near east that ally must be Austria, or, in the late nineteenth century, preferably Germany. Tiresomely neither would do as Britain asked. Had Germany been willing to, and Austria able, not only

[1] Report by Urquhart, 10 Oct. 1834, in Ponsonby to Palmerston, no. 159, 11 Oct. 1834, F.O. 78/239; see also 'Memorandum Compiled from Mr. Urquhart's Notes . . . respecting the Affairs of Turkey', 12 Jan. 1833, in H. Taylor to Backhouse, private, 12 Feb. 1833, F.O. 78/223.

[2] Palmerston to Ponsonby, private, 22 Aug. 1834, Broadlands MSS. GC/PO/ 667.

the Eastern Question, but the problem of how to defend India, would have been solved, and the British would not have needed to play the Great Game in Asia.

Prince Metternich claimed that by the treaties of Münchengrätz he had already done as Britain asked, that is preserved Turkey by diverting the tsar's attention to Poland and the Revolution. Palmerston, who did not believe in the Revolution or when he did supported it, and did not want to defend Turkey at its expense, knew why Austria could not openly oppose Russia, but this made him more impatient not less, because he hated the choice offered, the choice Castlereagh would have made, that to hold Turkey together meant co-operating with the Holy Alliance.

The policy of Austria [he said] . . . is timid, tricky, and insincere. Fear seems Metternich's guiding principle; craft his established course of action. He fears Russian encroachment on Turkey, but on the whole he fears still more the political encroachment of those parties to the west-ward [the Revolution], to resist whom he thinks he shall want the cordial assistance of Russia. He therefore lets Russia go to a certain way in encroachment in order not to lose her goodwill if the other party should move on his other side . . . He has latterly invited England and France to open their mind to him on these affairs, but he has not explained to us his own views, or any other source of security except his own alleged conviction that the emperor is sincere in his abjuration of any views of aggrandizement at the expense of the sultan. All this leaves the matter just about where it stood. The emperor is not ready as yet to make a second move; the time for doing so is not yet come, and he will not act prematurely. For the year 1834 we may all feel full confidence in the moderation of Nicholas: but who is to answer for him in 1835, 6, 7, or 8? . . . What are we to do for future security, and how are we to obtain any permanent guarantee against Russian encroachment on the Turkish Empire?[1]

This question, asked by the government of India and the board of control, had led to the Great Game in Asia. Palmerston, who could not guess that Metternich's diversion would be kept up until 1849, was anxious to make use of the time he had provided. If the British were not to co-operate with Mahomet Ali, the Great Game was the only alternative bastion against Russia, and source of future security.

The first requirement of stability was the maintenance of peace

[1] Ibid.

between Mahmud II and Mahomet Ali. A rebellion in Syria during the summer had encouraged the sultan to plan an attack on his vassal. Ponsonby in July and August warned him not to; telling him he would be beaten, and that Britain would neither help him nor allow Russia to.[1] Palmerston approved of Ponsonby's firmness; he was himself equally firm with Mahomet Ali. The governor chose this moment to try again to prove his usefulness to the British, by reminding them that he alone was strong enough to compel the Russians to respect the independence of Turkey and Persia. His insistence upon ruling all of Syria was partly the chance it would give him to raise 150,000 troops, the army needed by Britain to defend her interests in the east.

So far as regards the resistance of Russian encroachments . . . on the side of Asia [said Colonel Campbell, who agreed], perhaps the establishment of an Asiatic caliphate under Mahomet Ali would be a better barrier and more likely to afford effectual opposition to Russia than the Porte could now be expected to offer, and in case of need Mahomet Ali could give great assistance to Persia (supposing him to rule over Baghdad) in any struggle of Persia against Russia.[2]

By standing in for Austria, Mahomet Ali might help Britain to win the Great Game in Asia.

Palmerston had been convinced by Henry Ellis that such hopes were false. Mahomet Ali might be acceptable as sultan; an independent Arab kingdom could not be set up without risking war with Russia and the partition of Turkey, the crisis the suggestion was meant to prevent. The strength and wealth of Egypt helped to stabilize Turkey by checking the French in the eastern Mediterranean; in Syria Mahomet Ali threatened her stability, and by his control of the overland routes might aggravate not solve Britain's problem of how to defend British India. 'Mahomet independent', replied Palmerston in September, 'would soon come to an understanding with the powers; Baghdad and something else would be offered him, as the price of his co-operation with Russia in her attempt to appropriate to herself European Turkey

---

[1] Ponsonby to Palmerston, no. 99, 25 July 1834, no. 115, 16 Aug. 1834, F.O. 78/237.

[2] Campbell to Ponsonby, private, 21 Aug. 1834, in same to Palmerston, no. 42, 25 Aug. 1834, F.O. 78/246; encl. in same to same, secret and confidential, 4 Sept. 1834, ibid.

and the whole of the Black Sea.'[1] It all sounded too like the situation in Persia.

Palmerston was willing to help Mahomet Ali rule Egypt, by sending him a British military mission, the traditional method of surveillance, who would keep out the French, but should he attack the sultan he would be driven from Egypt as well as Syria. As usual the British were trying to maintain peace without committing themselves, by telling both sides in a dispute that they would be beaten, and neither that they could expect British help. The man who was given the chance to arrange this was Chesney, because in August 1834 parliament voted the funds for the Euphrates Expedition.

IV

Captain Chesney, like Urquhart, had returned to England from his tour of the near east in the autumn of 1832, and in December his opinions had been used by Stratford Canning to support the argument, that Britain should try to turn Turkey into a protectorate by assimilation. Baghdad would be easily assimilated, they supposed, because British trade could be protected by steamers on the Tigris and Euphrates. The board of trade doubted it: 'I fear', said the president, 'that this is a little visionary.'[2] As soon as the sultan had taken fright, and turned instead to Russia, this is exactly what the proposal turned out to have been. Because of the cost, the East India Company had forbidden further trials of steam in the Red Sea; the resident at Baghdad had explained that similar trials on the Euphrates must await a settlement between the sultan and Mahomet Ali. Instead the steamer service, and the trade expected to follow it, were to bring about the settlement.

Throughout 1833, as Palmerston groped towards an understanding of Britain's true interest in the near east, Chesney could convince nobody in the government of the need for action at Baghdad. To the foreign office the province was less important than the Straits and Syria, to the board of control less important than Turkestan and Persia, to the government of India less important than Afghanistan and Sind. That Baghdad should have become a focus of attention in 1834 shows how obvious it had

---

[1] Palmerston to Campbell, private, 29 Sept. 1834, Broadlands MSS. GC/CA/61.

[2] Auckland to Palmerston, private, 14 Aug. 1832, F.O. 60/32.

become, that Britain's interests throughout the near east were similar, and that the Eastern Question and the Great Game in Asia must be treated as one. Baghdad was where they met.

Many of the directors of the East India Company, remembering Ellenborough's thoroughness between 1828 and 1830, feared that dramatically improving communications would result in an attempt to govern India too closely.

Ah! but that is the very thing we do not want [Chesney was told]. What is to become of us if you give us a monthly mail to India? No, No! Now we write our letters, and get our answers every six months, and have peace and leisure between whiles; life will not be worth having if you get your way.[1]

Chesney's supporters, the under-secretary, John Backhouse, at the foreign office, Peacock at East India House, who persuaded Chesney to publish a full report of his travels, and John Sullivan (a relative of Henry Ellis) at the board of control, who tried to interest Palmerston, all failed. Nothing more was heard of a cabinet committee Lansdowne had talked about; and Palmerston, remembering what a nuisance Chesney had been in Persia, refused to recommend his promotion to the brevet rank of lieutenant-colonel.[2]

Chesney's connections did him no good. His argument, echoing Peacock's ideas in 1829, that if Britain did not seize control of the Euphrates route Russia would use it in future wars, appealed to the king, with whom Sullivan arranged Chesney an interview in April. According to Chesney, the king immediately spotted the navigational advantage of the Euphrates route, that the winds blew ahead on the Red Sea but abeam on the Euphrates. 'I am a sailor,' said the king, 'and these points are, in my opinion, quite conclusive.'[3] He also saw the political advantages of the route as a defence against Russia and as a way to strengthen Persia. His promise to urge the government to consider Chesney's proposals was likely to prove a handicap, however, because the king had already foisted Urquhart on Palmerston, and had used similar

[1] Lane-Poole, *Chesney*, p. 254.

[2] Chesney to Backhouse, private, 11 Apr. 1833, F.O. 60/33; minutes of Backhouse and Palmerston, 24 Aug. 1833, on Canning to Palmerston, 15 Aug. 1833, ibid.

[3] F. R. Chesney, *Narrative of the Euphrates Expedition . . . during the Years 1835, 1836, and 1837* (London, 1868), pp. 144–6.

arguments in support of Mahomet Ali. According to Palmerston, they led to the partition of Turkey not to a balance of power in the near east.

The board of control thought so too. Every proposal considered between 1828 and 1834 turned on the question of the difference between a protectorate and a buffer state. Britain did not need to reform Mesopotamia, she only needed certain access to the area. William Cabell, the board's equivalent to Urquhart and Ponsonby in his preference for decisive and provocative intervention, argued in August 1833 that the best policy would be to occupy the territory between Alexandretta and Latakhia on the coast, and Bir and Beles on the Euphrates. Britain would then stand between the Russians and the French, and between the sultan and Mahomet Ali, whom Cabell did not expect to oppose the idea. 'Whether the Porte as superior of the country might under Russian influence object to such a measure is for consideration,' he admitted, 'and the light in which it might be viewed by the European powers might doubtless seriously affect its practicability.'[1] Doubtless it would have: like the British occupation of Cyprus at the congress of Berlin, the idea was unthinkable unless Russia had first been defeated in war, or admitted that she would not continue to fight. Otherwise it would have led straight to a partition.

Chesney's proposals had to wait for a hearing until a moment when they could be interpreted as likely to stabilize the balance of power in the near east, not strengthen Turkey. This happened in January 1834. The Mediterranean fleet controlled by the discretionary orders might hold back the Russians; steamers on the Euphrates might hold back Mahomet Ali. At a cabinet committee on 30 January, 'the political bearings of Persia and the Euphrates, the march of Russia, etc., were gone into'.[2] Ministers, knowing the history of the East India Company's steam trials, were worried about the cost. Although Chesney and Peacock promised them, that a trial run made by two small steamers on the Euphrates alone would cost no more than £13,000, even this seemed excessive. The whigs were obsessed with economy. They knew the East India Company would not pay, although Chesney in March thought they might, therefore they stalled until June, when the disorder in

---

[1] 'Memorandum [by William Cabell] on the Settlement in the Bay of Scanderoon', [August] 1833, I.O. Persia/48.

[2] Lane-Poole, *Chesney*, p. 269.

Baghdad convinced everyone, that unless Britain acted the sultan would again ask for help from Russia.

This was the vexed question in 1834: how long 'the weak and inefficient pageant' that was the Turkish government of Baghdad could be allowed to fall into a 'state of almost utter abandonment and ruin'.[1] If Britain did not prevent it, others would. The 'Russians are trying to gain an influence in this country and in Persia', reported Major Taylor from Baghdad in February and March. Should they succeed, 'its central position and navigable streams' would offer facilities for 'intrigues more fatal than war'. The governor, plagued by Arab revolt, might even welcome the Russians because the alternative seemed to be Mahomet Ali.

The people here are prepared for anything on the part of the pasha of Egypt [said Taylor], and there is nothing to resist any attempt he may think fit to make on the pashalic . . . In reality the pashalic may at this moment be contemplated as scarcely belonging to the Turkish Empire and . . . should Ali [Rida] Pasha side with Russia the province is lost to the Porte beyond all chance of recovery.[2]

Only a bold stroke by Britain could avert the partition of Asiatic Turkey.

The disorder at Baghdad was aggravated by the disorder in Kurdistan. Rashid Pasha, the Turkish commander defeated at the battle of Koniah, had since been made governor of Sivas and Diabekir, and told with the help of Ali Rida to force the Kurds to stop fighting one another, and enlist in the Turkish army in time to fight Mahomet Ali. The British worried that Rashid would attack the Egyptians instead of the Kurds; in fact the Kurds kept him busy at Diabekir and Erzerum, and prevented him from moving south to Mosul, while the Arabs pinned down Ali Rida at Baghdad.

Here was the gravest danger, that the situation at Baghdad might persuade the sultan to invoke the treaty of Unkiar Skelessi. 'I fear that the weakness of the pasha [of Baghdad] to preserve his territory', said Sir John Campbell at Teheran, 'will oblige the sultan to solicit the interference of his perfidious Russian ally.'[3]

---

[1] Fraser to Palmerston, 12 Nov. 1834, F.O. 60/34.

[2] Taylor to Ponsonby, private, 20 Feb. 1834, in Ponsonby to Palmerston, no. 58, 18 May 1834, F.O. 78/236; same to sc, with encl., 14 Mar. 1834, I.O. Persia/50.

[3] Campbell to Taylor, 29 Jan., 2 Feb. 1834, I.O. Persia/50, pp. 214, 217.

How should the danger be countered? Brant at Erzerum, Campbell at Teheran, and Taylor at Baghdad, all recommended a British protectorate. The government of Bombay, Taylor's nominal superiors, who saw nothing unusual in disorder at Baghdad, forbade Taylor to move around to watch the Egyptians and the Russians; later in the year they were to debate whether to shut down the residency. The government of India expected Turkey to fall apart, and preferred Mahomet Ali to keep Russia out of Baghdad rather than step in themselves.[1] Although the board of control rejected the suggestion that they should order the government of India to send and pay for a military mission at Baghdad to match the one being sent to Persia, they understood that the disorder and the likelihood of an Egyptian invasion, the reasons why Bombay and Fort William wanted to stay out of Baghdad, were the reasons why the foreign office would have to step in.

This meant that the residency at Baghdad could not be shut down, equally that all British activity must be made to stabilize not unsettle Turkey, by being planned, as Henry Ellis had advised, in co-operation with the Porte. Because 'there is certainly something peculiar in the atmosphere of Baghdad and Basra', said Ellis, 'that diplomatizes the heads of all the company's residents there',[2] Taylor must be strongly warned against again being entrapped by the governor. In April, in instructions approved by Palmerston, Taylor was told, that should the Arab tribes drive out the governor, he might recognize any temporary ruler or go away to Basra.

If Mahomet Ali should mix himself in the quarrel or take advantage of it to attempt any fresh acquisition of territory, or again, should the Persians under cover of these commotions commit acts of aggression on the pashalic . . . [he] should abstain from interference unless directed or empowered by higher authority.[3]

Taylor need not solve Britain's problem, because with the permission and help of the sultan, so the British hoped, Chesney would.

Turkey, as Ellis had argued for three years, was to be treated as a

---

[1] GicB to sc, 7 Jan. 1834, I.O. L/PS/5/326; McNaghten to Norris, 14 May 1834, I.O. Bombay/PP/387/5, 11 June 1834, no. 22; see above, pp. 175–7.

[2] Ellis to Grant, 3 Sept. 1833, I.O. Persia/48.

[3] Sc to ggic, 18 Apr. 1834, I.O. L/PS/5/544; minute of Palmerston on Grant to Palmerston, private, 16 Apr. 1834, F.O. 60/35.

buffer state. The tsar must be made to realize that Britain would not tolerate Russian influence at Baghdad equal to her influence in Persia and at Constantinople; as far as being a neighbouring state was the justification for Russian policy, Britain, as the only sea power in the Persian Gulf, claimed a similar interest at Baghdad.[1] Ellis had also argued decisively in 1833, that although Mahomet Ali's occupation of Syria need not provoke the partition of Turkey and destroy the balance of power in Europe, his occupation of Baghdad would endanger British India. In the summer of 1834 these arguments suited Palmerston, who was determined to prevent the Russians from expanding their territory or their influence, while they pretended to help the sultan and the shah.

What lies they have told us [and in July Palmerston catalogued them] ... what a humbug is their evacuation of the Principalities! Then their great slice of Asiatic Turkey upon the principle of the most undoubted disinterestedness and moderation. Then their intended aggression against Persia; add to this their intrigues at Constantinople to set the sultan and Mahomet [Ali] by the ears again.

In fact the Russians were being most co-operative about arranging the Persian succession, but this only made Palmerston more certain, that although every sign of goodwill hid an intrigue, 'the Russian government *now* understand that we are both able and resolved to resist them. *Last year* they deceived themselves.'[2] It was necessary to act; it was also safe.

For these reasons the government finally overcame their hatred of spending money. On 2 June Grant moved in the house of commons the appointment of a select committee to inquire into the best route for a steamer service to India. Naturally he ignored the political considerations: the house of commons was not the place to discuss openly the Great Game in Asia. The committee struck under Grant's chairmanship was distinguished and well informed, including George de Lacy Evans, J. S. Buckingham, a well-known traveller in the near east, and Sir Robert Gordon, formerly ambassador at Constantinople. Between 9 June and 10

---

[1] 'Memorandum [by Henry Ellis] on the Affairs of Persia' in Grant to Palmerston, 14 May 1834, F.O. 60/35; 'Memorandum [by Henry Ellis] on Recent Despatches from Persia', 5 June 1834, ibid.
[2] Palmerston to Bligh, private, 15 July 1834, Broadlands MSS. GC/BL/112; same to Ponsonby, private, 24 June 1834, ibid., GC/PO/666.

July the committee met fourteen times, when they were interrupted by the resignation of Grey and the reconstruction of the
government.

The evidence heard by the select committee brought before
parliament some of the problems connected with the defence
of British India, which had puzzled the government of India, the
government of Bombay, the board of control, and off and on the
foreign office, for thirty-five years. The technical discussions
about the virtues and faults of the various routes need not be
repeated here: the Cape, the Red Sea, and the Euphrates all had
their supporters. Whether the Euphrates would be better suited
than the Red Sea for a steamer service was soon settled; even
Peacock and Chesney, who now forgot his previous awareness of
the difficulties involved, and argued that the river would be easy to
navigate in the eight months of flood water, and possible during
the four months of low water, did not claim it to be as easy as the
Red Sea. Their most determined opponent was Sir Pulteney
Malcolm, John Malcolm's brother, and recently in command of
the Mediterranean fleet, who said that the greatest attraction of
the Red Sea route was the prosperity and order in Egypt. The
Euphrates should be used only as a replacement during the four
months of the south-west monsoon, when strong headwinds had
so far prevented steamers from reaching Suez.[1]

Paradoxically, the turbulence in Baghdad was the reason why
the Euphrates route had suddenly become attractive. The debate
before the select committee was the third in five years about the
security of British India, and each time the subject under discussion, whether Russian influence, the expansion of trade, or the
practicability of steamers, turned into a discussion of the dangers
of invasion. In 1830, Ellenborough's questions about the extent
of Russian influence in central Asia, and how it should be matched,
had been answered by an analysis of the Oxus and Herat as
alternative routes to India. In 1832, Grant's similar questions
about Persia had had similar replies. In 1834 the third route was
to be considered; if a steamer service on the Tigris and Euphrates
would end the local unrest, it might also keep the Russians out of

[1] *Parliamentary Papers: Reports of Committees* (1834), xiv. 478, 'Minutes of
Evidence before the Select Committee of the House of Commons on Steam
Navigation to India', questions nos. 1-146, 150-388, 689-92, 1078-79, 1473,
1726-30 (Peacock and Chesney), 1769-1903, 2080-109 (Malcolm).

Baghdad and the Persian Gulf. If, according to Ellis's principles, Turkey and Persia were to be treated by the great powers as independent states, local quarrels between provincial governors, or between one of them and the sultan or the shah, were as far as possible to be ignored. Unfortunately, this could be done only as long as the imperial government were strong enough to prevent the rebellion's spreading to strategically vital areas, for example Baghdad and Khorassan, or to areas along the Russian frontier, where it might justify, as it had in the 1820s, Russian claims to intervene, in an attempt to re-establish, or, as the British would always perceive it, to destroy the near-eastern balance of power.

Thomas Love Peacock, watching the gradual but persistent expansion of Russia towards Kars and Erzerum, and ignoring both the Bombay and Ludhiana Schools of Indian defence, had begun to see the Tigris and the Persian Gulf as the most likely invasion route to India. When asked by the committee whether Britain's sea power would not force the Russians to expand from Khiva up the Oxus, he replied that 'pre-eminence at sea is not a talisman; it is to be kept up by constant watchfulness and the exertion of adequate force. I know there is danger by the Oxus, but there is also danger by the Euphrates, and I would stop both doors if I could.'[1] Steamers on the Indus might close one and steamers on the Euphrates the other, by extending the range and effectiveness of sea power far inland.

This idea was dismissed as preposterous by the first resident at Baghdad, who had later negotiated the preliminary terms of the treaty of Teheran, Sir Harford Jones Brydges. He had once scoffed at the idea of Bonaparte's marching from Egypt through Baghdad to the Persian Gulf, and thought it would be equally foolish of the Russians.

I should very willingly give them Basra [he added] and even then what could they do as to getting to India, unless they have a superior fleet . . . in the gulf of Persia; how are they to get down that gulf? If Russia could send a stronger fleet than yours around the Cape of Good Hope, why then she may get to India by the Euphrates.[2]

The Persian Gulf could be blocked by a squadron based at Bombay. As a follower of the Bombay School, Jones argued that the most likely invasion route, and the most threatening to

---

[1] Ibid., no. 65.   [2] Ibid., no. 1519.

Britain, because it could not be blocked by sea power but only by greater influence than Russia in Persia, ran from Astarabad to Herat.

As contentious as the claim that it might still be possible to defend British India in alliance with Persia was the discussion about the benefits to be expected from starting a steamer service on the Euphrates. Jones said one was not needed for the post; the overland service he had started during the Napoleonic Wars was fast and frequent enough, and a similar but alternative service was being suggested by James Farren, to run straight across the desert from Damascus to Hit. Whether there were any trade to be done at Baghdad was a guess. Robert Taylor, the resident's son, who had helped his father in 1830 to train the governor's troops, said that the Arabs, who were anxious for a steamer service, would be easily kept quiet by small gifts, and that the governor, just as eager, would do all he could to help. Two previous assistant residents at Baghdad, Jonathan Hine and Gordon Colquhoun, said exactly the opposite: the governor, who had no control over the Arab tribes, could give no help; it was doubtful whether trade could be expanded; and if it were tried trouble could be expected, because steamers would destroy the existing Arab caravan trade.[1] Where steamers would be welcomed, they were probably not needed; where they were needed they would cause trouble, and, as the British were learning on the Indus, might also need the protection they were supposed to provide.

On 4 August 1834 Grant recommended parliament to vote £20,000 to pay for an expedition to the Euphrates, to carry out the recommendations of the select committee. They had decided that, as the Red Sea was navigable except between June and September, and the Euphrates except between November and February (and it might prove to be navigable then), if both routes were used the British would be certain of uninterrupted service. The committee had not ignored the technical difficulties of the Euphrates route, the Arabs, fords, sharp bends, marshes, and rapid current, which meant that a sailing ship might take only a week between Baghdad and Basra but six weeks between Basra and Baghdad, but thought it worth trying to find out whether steamers could improve on this, because the route 'presents so many other advantages,

---

[1] Ibid., nos. 1200–78 (Taylor), 910–1071, 1588–1725 (Hine and Colquhoun).

physical, commercial and political'.[1] Parliament were to pay for the experiment, but, should a service be started, the cost was to be shared by the British and Indian governments. The organization of the expedition was also to be shared; the East India Company were to supply two steamers, one for high the other for low water; the board of control were to choose and train the officers and men; and the foreign office were to make the necessary diplomatic preparations. All of them quickly ran into trouble.

The first problem was the cost. 'I am very glad of it.' said Lord William Bentinck in September, when he heard of the expedition. 'Either by land or sea there ought to be a bi-monthly communication to and from India, and well-managed the cost would not be large.'[2] The likely cost seemed too large for Grant. Originally planned as a trial of the Euphrates, Grant soon asked Chesney to survey the Tigris and Karun as well, and to provide as much scientific information as possible. This was an absurd request given the sum advanced by parliament, but Grant, particularly after Chesney changed his mind again and said that the Euphrates would be easily navigable for only four months of the year, expected him to overspend, and wanted to have good reasons for asking for more money. The expedition eventually cost £43,000 and for doing far less than Grant had asked. 'That Captain Chesney will succeed in spending the £20,000 voted by parliament I have very little doubt,' said James Baillie Fraser, who had reached Baghdad on his tour of the near east, 'and of his establishing a permanent steam communication on the Euphrates, I have just as little doubt that he will not.'[3]

One way to lower the costs was to try during the autumn to persuade the East India Company to buy the steamers when the expedition had finished with them. They refused, unless they should prove suitable for use in India; they also refused to pay for them in advance.[4] Although in the new year they gave way, they were clearly worried, that should the service be started, the government of India would be made to pay the whole cost. 'A public mail we *must have* in some shape or other', said the chairman

[1] Encl. in Carter to Taylor, secret, 1 Sept. 1834, I.O. L/PS/5/544.
[2] Bentinck to Ellenborough, private, 27 Sept. 1834, P.R.O. 30/9/4 pt. 5/1.
[3] Extract of a letter from [Fraser], 22 Nov. 1834, P.R.O. 30/12/29 pt. 2/7.
[4] Ellenborough to chairmen of E.I.C., 23 Feb. 1835, I.O. E/2/38, p. 210; chairmen to Gordon, 8 and 27 Apr. 1835, I.O. E/2/13, pp. 350, 389.

early the following year. '. . . *Time* is a great object, I admit; but, as other things, may be purchased at too high a price.'[1]

Chesney himself proved difficult; Grant had to ask him three times before he would agree to lead the expedition. He finally accepted on 20 August, but was clearly piqued at not being promoted. Although Palmerston supported Grant's recommendation, the ordnance office refused to promote Chesney because he was too junior. Not until Wellington returned to office was the problem solved by giving Chesney the local rank of lieutenant-colonel.[2] No sooner had Chesney begun to organize the expedition than it was attacked from three sides. The first was the king. William IV was sometimes as fidgety as Palmerston. Having pestered the government not to ignore the Euphrates, in September he pestered them not to forget the Red Sea. To Grant's assurance that 'the Red Sea project has not escaped attention', because the government hoped to extend the Malta pacquet service to Alexandria, to connect with the East India Company's service to Suez, the king replied that he was delighted, seeing 'no reason why both lines should not be effectively prosecuted *at the same time*'.[3]

In November, when Lord Ellenborough returned to the board of control, he criticized Chesney and Grant for planning to start the expedition at the wrong end, at Bir instead of Basra. Chesney argued that by going down river from Bir the experiment could be made more quickly; Ellenborough replied that too much time had already been lost to justify this argument, and that it was technically more sensible to go up river in rising water, when the current would help refloat the steamers should they run aground.

I confess the more I reflect upon the matter [said Ellenborough] the more reluctant I feel to take upon myself the responsibility of exposing the steam vessels to loss, the officers to extreme risk, and the expedition to failure, by adopting the unwise determination of my predecessor to make the attempt from Bir.[4]

When Wellington, for once proving more adventurous than

---

[1] Tucker to Ellenborough, 7 Feb. 1835, P.R.O. 30/12/29, pt. 2/8.
[2] Couper to Somerset, 29 Oct. 1834, I.O. L/PS/3/118; Wellington to Hill, 21 Nov. 1834, F.O. 78/250.
[3] H. Taylor to Grant, 28 Sept. 1834, Grant to H. Taylor, 29 Oct. 1834, H. Taylor to Grant, 2 Nov. 1834, I.O. L/PS/3/118.
[4] Ellenborough to Wellington, 3 Jan. 1835, P.R.O. 30/12/29 pt. 1/4.

Ellenborough, in January 1835 over-ruled him, the trial was made as Grant and Chesney had planned, and was the fiasco Ellenborough had predicted.

The third attack on Chesney came from the consul-general in Syria, James Farren. Farren, who had been appointed because the board of trade hoped the abolition of the Levant Company would give them the chance to expand Britain's trade with the near east, had been in Syria since 1831.[1] He had supported the resident at Baghdad's arguments about the advantages of the Euphrates as a route to India, but the two men were thinking of different routes: Farren wanted to send the post through Damascus, 'the shortest and most desirable channel of communication between this country and India', and justified his choice as the best way to obtain information about, increase British influence in, and expand British trade with, the parts of Persia and Turkey of most interest to the East India Company.[2] Here was the usual panacea. Tiresomely, the Turks would not allow Farren to travel inland, nor to visit Damascus, whose inhabitants violently disliked foreigners.

This was not solely a case of religious fanaticism. 'Of all the cities of the East [said an English observer in 1836], Damascus is probably the most oriental—the city which has undergone fewest changes.'[3] It was one of the most conservative cities in Turkey, partly because its trade with Europeans had always been indirect. It had also been left alone by the Turks. By the nineteenth century their rule at Damascus, like their rule at Baghdad, was titular; payment of tribute was the sole and a sufficient sign of allegiance. Farren's appointment was seen as one of Mahmud II's centralizing reforms, threatening the traditional political and commercial structure, and offending the Damascenes for the same reason they offended Urquhart and Lord Holland. Until February 1834

---

[1] Lack to Douglas, 20 Aug. 1830, B.T. 3/22, p. 44. Farren, who was grasping, had demanded at least £1,000 in salary. Farren to Backhouse, 14 July 1830, B.T. 1/270. The board of trade said £800 was enough, and would not allow him a pension upon retirement.

[2] Farren to Grant, 26 and 28 Jan. 1831, in sc to Farren, 14 Mar. 1831, I.O. L/PS/5/543; R. Tresse, 'L'installation du premier consul d'Angleterre a Damas, 1830–1834', *Revue d'histoire des colonies françaises*, xxiv (1936), 359–80.

[3] 'Report [by John Bowring] on the Commercial Statistics of Syria', 1839, p. 306, F.O. 78/380. See also N. A. Ziadeh, *Damascus under the Mamluks* (Norman, 1964), and Edward Hogg, *Visit to Alexandria, Damascus, and Jerusalem, during the Successful Campaign of Ibrahim Pasha* (London, 1835).

Farren had to divide his time between Beirut and Sidon; he finally went inland thanks to Mahomet Ali, to limit whose power was the object of all the British schemes.[1]

In October, as soon as Farren heard of the Euphrates Expedition, he reminded the board of control of his alternative. If they wanted only to speed up the post to India, they need not go to the trouble and expense of a steamer service on the Euphrates: the fastest route to India was by steamer to Beirut, overland through Damascus to Basra, and thence by steamer to Bombay. Even if a steamer service were to be started on the Euphrates, it should terminate not at Bir but Hit; and the post should then travel overland by camel to Damascus and Beirut. Beirut was nearer than Alexandretta to Malta; Hit was half way down river between Bir and Basra; and Hit was also situated below most of the navigational hazards on the Euphrates.[2]

'Mr. Farren's proposal', said the board of control, '. . . and his general views were worthy of attention by the Home authorities.'[3] Farren implied, of course, that Chesney knew all this, but that if the steamer service were to stop at Hit his experiment would appear less sensational, and would also have to be made from Basra. As far as this was true, it reveals the true purpose of the expedition. For the post, a steamer service between Bir and Basra was unnecessary; Jones's service through Baghdad to Constantinople, or Farren's through Hit and Damascus to Beirut, would have been enough. Ellenborough was equally correct to say that the expedition should have started from Basra. The arguments were irrelevant, because in the summer of 1834 the board of control and the foreign office were not thinking about the post, nor about the routes to the east: the northern stretches of the Euphrates were the one place where a flotilla of British steamers might separate Mahmud II and Mahomet Ali. The immediate object of the Euphrates expedition was political, and it failed not because of the technical fiasco it temporarily proved, but owing to the opposition it encountered for equally political reasons. The expedition, which was supposed by sleight of hand to help the British destroy the treaty of Unkiar Skelessi, and to safeguard British India by

[1] C. Issawi, 'British Trade and the Rise of Beirut, 1830–1860', *International Journal of Middle East Studies*, viii (1977), 92.
[2] Farren to sc, 16 Oct. 1834, I.O. Persia/51.
[3] Farren to sc, 1 Aug. 1834, with minute of Grant, I.O. Persia/50.

turning Turkey like Persia into a buffer state, was instead destroyed by the treaty.

V

The Euphrates Expedition, like the Baghdad Railway, caused controversy as soon as it was seen to be a political not an economic device. The British wanted an efficient and reliable overland post to India; they wanted it to pay for itself; they wanted it, if combined with trade, ideally to make a profit; but their anxiety to control the routes to the east was not the cause of the Euphrates Expedition. Nor did they prefer the Euphrates to the Red Sea route, because it was directly under the control of the sultan.[1] Except for political reasons they did not prefer it, nor did the sultan control it.

Ibrahim Pasha controlled the area between Bir and the Mediterranean, and the right bank of the Euphrates between Bir and Hit. Although the left bank was supposedly controlled by Rashid Pasha, the governor of Sivas and Diabekir, his authority was nominal, because the Kurds were keeping him busy farther north and Egyptian troops were east of the Euphrates at Orfa; nor had the sultan any authority in the area. Chesney, who claimed that a passport from the sultan would carry great weight, knew that Mahmud's authority was as nominal as Rashid's. Of the three officials, Ibrahim, Rashid, and Ali Rida of Baghdad, upon whom the success of the expedition depended, two could give no help, and the third, who could, would not, as long as the British insisted that Turkey's foreign relations were to be carried on only by the sultan. Although 'Russia cannot be expected to remain indifferent', Chesney warned Grant, 'to this beginning of a change in the political and commercial influence of England in Turkish Arabia',[2] in the autumn of 1834 the British were in fact assuming that France, lurking behind Mahomet Ali, and Russia, lurking behind Mahmud II, would do nothing to counter Britain's attempt to destroy their influence.

On 1 September the board of control asked the foreign office to obtain a passport for the expedition from the sultan. They expected

---

[1] As Hoskins, *Routes to India*, p. 155, Bailey, *Turkish Reform Movement*, p. 66, and H. H. Dodwell, *The Founder of Modern Egypt* (Cambridge, 1931), p. 134, all suggested.

[2] Chesney to Grant, 23 Sept. 1834, I.O. L/PS/3/118.

no difficulty, because, when talking about a steamer service with Stratford Canning and Mandeville two years earlier, Mahmud II had been enthusiastic; he had also told Ali Rida to co-operate with Taylor. The Turks had no objection to a European post: they did object to the Euphrates Expedition. They had wanted British help, but as they knew how the British hated to spend public money, they became suspicious when the British planned to start a steamer service themselves, and at their own expense. 'Had it been possible to have made its material character and range of objects less imposing,' said Farren two years later, 'and, laying the groundwork without starting prejudices, to have gone on completing the plan in a progressive and unobtrusive manner', then it would have created fewer difficulties with the Turks.[1] Instead the Turks were worried that what had previously been planned as a Turkish was now to be a British steamer service.

Farren's explanation, although true, was irrelevant, because the British were not sending the Euphrates Expedition as a geographical survey but as a political symbol. Palmerston had hoped that the sultan would treat the expedition as one of Britain's attempts to create a stable balance of power in the near east, by reasserting the authority of the imperial government. He was constantly warning the Turks to concentrate upon administrative and military reorganization as the prerequisite of power; tax farming must be abolished to raise a sufficient revenue to pay the army, and Palmerston offered both modern weapons to arm and a military mission to train them. This the Turks refused.[2]

By the time Palmerston left office in November nothing had been done, and Ellenborough realized that nothing could be done without a passport, because the expedition must not appear to be an invasion, however lightly armed, able to justify Russian retaliation under the treaty of Unkiar Skelessi. To prevent this was the object of sending Chesney.[3] On 17 December Ponsonby reported that he had finally obtained a passport; in January the board told Chesney to start immediately; and on 16 February

---

[1] Farren to sc, n.d., I.O. Bombay/SP/90, 31 May 1837, no. 346.

[2] Palmerston to Ponsonby, no. 24, 1 June 1834, F.O. 78/234; Ponsonby to Palmerston, no. 115, 16 Aug. 1834, F.O. 78/237; F. S. Rodkey, 'Lord Palmerston and the Rejuvenation of Turkey, 1830–41', *Journal of Modern History*, i (1929), 575–6.

[3] Ellenborough's letters discussing whether or not the expedition should take place are in P.R.O. 30/12/29 pt. 1/4.

1835 he sailed. The passport, however, was not an order to Ibrahim Pasha, who would obey orders only from Mahomet Ali; it was merely an expression of goodwill.[1] The Euphrates Expedition had been hampered, because during the autumn it became entangled in another round of the quarrel between Mahomet Ali and the sultan.

In the autumn of 1834, the British would not permit Mahmud II to attack Mahomet Ali. Anxious for Anglo-French support, he had again sent Namick Pasha to London. Palmerston treated him as the board of control had prescribed. He echoed Ponsonby in warning Namick early in November, that Britain would not help the sultan, who would be beaten were he to fight by himself, nor allow him to ask for help from Russia. Palmerston now differed from Ponsonby, however, in refusing to send the Anglo-French fleet to Constantinople, as the preliminary to an alliance meant to replace the treaty of Unkiar Skelessi.[2] The aim of British policy was to destroy the treaty not to replace it by a British guarantee; to evict the Russians not to stand in for them. Namick Pasha's mission was itself a sign that the sultan was behaving more confidently. If he were patient, one day Mahomet Ali would die: 'What remains to him of life is nothing when set against the duration of an empire.'[3] Patience would lead to stability, all that Britain asked of Turkey. What angered Mahmud II was the thought that he might die first; nevertheless, 'peace', said Ponsonby, '. . . will not be broken by the sultan. He is too poor a wretch to act, however he may talk. We must take him by the beard when we want him, and he will thank us for the violence we may use.'[4]

Mahomet Ali was more determined, and the British had to be as firm with him as with the sultan. Since the peace of Kutayah the Egyptians had been occupying Orfa, which was supposed to have been returned to the sultan. Because its retention by Mahomet Ali gave him access to Baghdad and would give Mahmud II an excuse for war, in the summer Palmerston had insisted upon its return, one reason why in September Mahomet Ali announced his intention to declare his independence. Palmerston promptly

[1] Ponsonby to Palmerston, no. 211, 17 Dec. 1834, with encls., F.O. 78/240.
[2] Ponsonby to Palmerston, no. 166, 22 Oct. 1834, F.O. 78/239.
[3] Palmerston to Ponsonby, private, 16 Nov. 1834, Broadlands MSS. GC/PO/670.
[4] Ponsonby to McNeill, private, 29 Oct. 1834, McNeill, p. 177.

warned him in October, that Britain could not tolerate such a 'most flagrant violation of honour and good faith'.[1] Palmerston, who suspected as always a Russian plot, because the independence of Egypt would weaken Turkey, left the fleet in the eastern Mediterranean, to hold back both the sultan and Mahomet Ali, and hastened the preparations for the Euphrates Expedition.

These actions were directed through Mahmud II and Mahomet Ali against the Russians, who raised no objection to the continued presence of the British fleet in the eastern Mediterranean, and approved of the firm line taken with Mahomet Ali.

I always felt [said Palmerston] that the insolence of tone and menacing attitude of Russia were founded on a belief that England was powerless and incapable of effort: and that, as this illusion was gradually dispelled, the language and conduct of the Russian government would become more civil and pacific . . . Everything tends to show the gigantic scale upon which her projects of aggrandizement are formed and how necessary it is for other nations, who do not mean to be encroached upon, to keep vigilant watch and have their horses always saddled.[2]

Palmerston did not realize that he was doing the Russians' work. They were willing enough to let him hold back Mahomet Ali; they would do all they could to prevent his strengthening the sultan. Equally they did his work: as long as Mahomet Ali could be held back, there was no need to strengthen the sultan. Unfortunately Palmerston's methods, however temporarily effective, provided no permanent solution, either by the rearrangement of power inside the Turkish Empire, or, which Henry Ellis had repeatedly stipulated to be the primary aim of British policy, by general agreement amongst the European powers about how it should be treated. The Euphrates Expedition was the first to suffer.

The British did no better at Cairo. Colonel Campbell warned Chesney in October that orders from Mahmud would offend Mahomet Ali, who was determined not to be treated merely as a provincial governor. Chesney should rely for help upon Ibrahim Pasha, and 'should endeavour to keep entirely in the background anything like a reference to the Porte'.[3] At first Mahomet Ali was

[1] Palmerston to Campbell, no. 11, 1 Oct. 1834, no. 14, 26 Oct. 1834, F.O. 78/244.
[2] Palmerston to Bligh, private, 5 Sept. 1834, Broadlands MSS. GC/BL/114.
[3] Campbell to Chesney, 30 Oct. 1834, I.O. L/PS/3/119.

not unfriendly to the expedition; but he knew nothing about it, and was waiting to learn what Palmerston would say about Orfa and his proposed declaration of independence. No obstacles were placed in Chesney's way by Mahomet or by Ibrahim, until Palmerston rejected Mahomet's proposals;[1] then he changed his mind about the Euphrates Expedition. Instead of refusing to be treated as a provincial governor, he turned about and argued that the expedition was not his business. 'He could not *now*', he said in December, 'give any aid to the enterprise without the sanction of the Porte, and . . . he was sure that His Majesty's government would appreciate his conduct in this respect; but the sanction of the Porte once obtained, he would not then be backward in his aid.'[2] As a loyal vassal, he would evacuate Orfa and wait for the sultan to issue a passport; then he did all he could to persuade him not to issue one.

The British had hoped, that if the governor of Baghdad argued at Constantinople in favour of the expedition, he might counter-balance Mahomet Ali's arguments against it. Both Ali Rida and his predecessor Daud Pasha had wanted a steamer service on the Tigris and Euphrates, in the hope of increasing their control over the Arabs. Major Taylor was sure Ali Rida would do all he could to help the expedition when it reached his territory; but he did not control the area in which difficulties were likely to occur.[3] Rashid Pasha, who was supposed to control part of it, was busy elsewhere. Even before the Russians and Egyptians had started to urge the sultan not to issue a passport, he had warned Ponsonby in October that he could grant one, only if he were not held respon-sible for anything that happened, because he could not protect the expedition from the Arabs. Ponsonby hoped this would not matter; the steamers should be able to defend themselves.[4] Below Hit this might have been true, but for their portage from the Mediter-ranean and their protection, should they run aground between Bir and Hit, the British would need the help of Ibrahim. He would not give it: when Chesney arrived in the spring of 1835 nothing had been done to improve the roads across Syria. Unfortunately

[1] Campbell to Backhouse, private, 31 Oct. 1834, F.O. 78/247; Farren to sc, 23 Nov. 1834, I.O. Persia/51.
[2] Campbell to Palmerston, no. 63, 8 Dec. 1834, F.O. 78/247.
[3] Carter to Taylor, secret, 1 Sept. 1834, I.O. L/PS/5/544; Taylor to sc, 23 Dec. 1834, I.O. Persia/51.
[4] Ponsonby to Palmerston, no. 161, 12 Oct. 1834, F.O. 78/239.

for the British, their steamer service on the Euphrates, like their service on the Indus, needed the active help of the men who were supposed to be destroyed by it.

By the time William IV dismissed the whigs in November 1834, Palmerston had learned how to play the Great Game in Asia; he was not yet very good at it. The solution to the problem of how to hold Turkey together as a buffer state was constant exertion to preserve its stability. Palmerston expressed this clearly when he returned to office the following year.

I quite agree with you [he told Lord Holland] that Russia has no *immediate* intentions of attacking Turkey, and she will postpone any such attempt as long as she sees other powers prepared and determined to support Turkey, and thus we preserve peace by protecting the sultan.

I also entirely concur with you in the expediency of preventing if possible a rupture between Mahomet Ali and the sultan, and I hope we may be able to. But the sultan *is* the sovereign, and Mahomet *is* the subject; and it is impossible to deny the *right* of the sultan to appoint another man to govern his province of Syria, and his province of Egypt, if he chooses to. What one may dispute is the prudence of attempting to exercise a right without the full means of being able, as we say here, to 'vindicate the law'.[1]

In 1834 Britain could send the fleet to hold back the would-be combatants in the near east, and could try to use the Euphrates Expedition to forestall Mahomet Ali's dreams of expansion into Arabia, but Palmerston had failed to negotiate a European agreement to control the behaviour of the great powers in another crisis.

Britain paid a high price for Palmerston's suspicions of Metternich. In the summer of 1834 Metternich had tried to turn the treaties of Münchengrätz into a four-power agreement with Britain and France by suggesting an informal conference at Vienna. Palmerston, as always, would not hear of it: this time Metternich replied that he would have nothing further to do with Palmerston. At the end of September the Austrian chargé d'affaires explained to the new prime minister, Lord Melbourne, the disastrous effect on Britain's foreign relations of the tone of Palmerston's dispatches, making 'the cabinet realize that Palmerston was managing the foreign office with more daring than skill'.[2]

---

[1] Palmerston to Holland, 11 Feb. 1836, Add. MSS. 51599, fo. 221.
[2] G. H. Bolsover, 'Palmerston, Metternich and the Eastern Question in 1834',

The Austrian, Russian, and French ambassadors had all gone home; the tsar had refused to allow Stratford Canning to succeed Heytesbury at St. Petersburg; and Britain appeared uncomfortably isolated, lacking the connection with one of the continental powers necessary in the nineteenth century, were Britain to have any effect on the European balance of power. In October the cabinet forced Palmerston to make a conciliatory gesture; Britain, he told Lamb, would always be interested in Metternich's proposals for a settlement.[1] This did no good. The powers remained deadlocked, and nothing was done until 1838 to show that Russia had given up her claim to a protectorate over Turkey.

Although, according to the traditions of the board of control, the British were to keep out of the near east, where they had no local interests other than the overland post, exerting only as much pressure as was necessary to keep out others, they could not afford, as in Europe, merely to react to changing circumstances. The Euphrates Expedition had shown, both that circumstances likely to hold back others might sometimes have to be created, and that sea power, however apparently flexible a strategic weapon, often proved as politically ineffective an offensive weapon in the near east as in Europe. The best way to have turned Turkey into a buffer state, having the advantage of restraining the French in Egypt as well as the Russians at Constantinople, would have been a guarantee amongst the four great powers, and this could not be attempted as long as Palmerston remained as suspicious of Metternich as of the tsar.

Despite Palmerston's claim, that states have no permanent friends only permanent interests, Britain's security as an Asiatic state was jeopardized by his inability to admit to needing the help of Austria, were Britain to extend to even part of the near east the reliance on sea power and the efforts of others characteristic of her peripheral position in Europe. Austria, unlike Germany later and Persia earlier, would not have had to defend British India, only Turkey, which Metternich, by the wrong method, claimed already to have done. If the habit of treating the near-eastern states as the European states treated one another could be developed in Turkey, the board of control hoped that it might in time govern international politics in central

---

English Historical Review, li (1936), 247. The pertinent dispatches were printed by Bolsover and by Rodkey, 'The Eastern Question in 1834', pp. 630-40.

[1] Palmerston to Lamb, nos. 41 and 46, 9 and 16 Oct. 1834, F.O. 7/246.

Asia; helping them to create an equivalent to the Burgundian Circle, stretching from Constantinople through Teheran to Khiva and Bokhara, and behind which, by the creation of a protectorate over Afghanistan equivalent to the Russian protectorate over Georgia and the Mahometan Khanates, the government of India could also create a stable balance of power along their North-West Frontier, ensuring the tranquillity of British India.

During 1833 and 1834 Henry Ellis had recruited the foreign office to help with carrying out these plans for the defence of British India, by persuading Palmerston to reject the advice of Stratford Canning, beware the advice of Ponsonby, and pursue however ineffectively the correct aim of turning Turkey into a buffer state not a protectorate, by avoiding, what he suspected of Russia, 'systematic interference to preserve internal tranquillity in Turkey'.[1] Because of Palmerston's lack of success, the security of British India would still depend upon success farther east, in Persia and Afghanistan. Palmerston's confidence in his ability to hold back Russia, and to maintain Turkey as a buffer state, had been increased by Russia's willingness in 1834 to co-operate with Britain during the succession crisis in Persia. Unfortunately the end of the crisis did not end Britain's difficulty in deciding how, by altering the Persian Connection, to set up a satisfactory boundary between the European and Indian political systems.

[1] Comment by Palmerston on Metternich to Hummelhauer, 11 Sept. 1834, communicated 24 Sept. 1834, F.O. 7/251.

X

The Succession Crisis in Persia 1833–1834

> Alice could never quite make out, in
> thinking it over afterwards, how it was
> that they began; all she remembers is
> that they were running . . .
>   The most curious part of the thing
> was that the trees and other things round
> them never changed places at all; however
> fast they went they never seemed to pass
> anything.
>
> LEWIS CARROLL,
> Through the Looking Glass,
> Chapter II

THAT THE Great Game in Asia had begun again became more obvious during 1834, when British policy throughout the near east was increasingly co-ordinated. This did not make it more successful; in Persia, where the British had for years been telling the Persians, that because Britain could never threaten them, the two states had identical interests, and found in 1834 that the Persians had taken them at their word, the British gave up hope of success. Two signs of the co-ordination were the more important part played by Palmerston in supervising Anglo-Persian relations, and the attempt to make policy in Persia match policy in Turkey. 'If the Russians succeed in Persia,' said Ponsonby in May, 'their success will give them also a certainty of success here. Everybody will then be convinced that no reliance ought to be placed on England.'[1] The previous year Ponsonby had been determined to show the Russians that Britain 'will not permit them to govern the Turkish government at their pleasure so as to destroy the balance of power in Europe'.[2] In 1834 the British had

---

[1] Ponsonby to Palmerston, private, 14 May 1834, Broadlands MSS. GC/PO/195.

[2] Ponsonby to Lamb, private, 19 July 1833, Broadlands MSS. GC/PO/154/9.

to demonstrate that they would also not allow Russia to govern the Persian government so as to endanger the security of British India. Although Palmerston now understood this, as in Turkey he was slow to follow one of Henry Ellis's most sensible suggestions; that constant effort to maintain stability in the near east must partly take the form of an agreement amongst the powers to maintain the existing situation.

II

In the winter of 1833–4 the British temporarily escaped one dilemma, what to do about the siege of Herat, to face another, what to do about imminent civil war in Persia. Their solution to these related problems, the instructions to Sir John Campbell to negotiate revisions to the treaty of Teheran being taken out to Persia by James Fraser, had already become unacceptable: 'The expectations of Persia', commented Cabell, 'go much beyond the concessions authorized.'[1] Abbas Mirza did not want to revise the treaty of Teheran, but to restore it; he was planning in September and October to send an ambassador to London to demand the additional 200,000 tomauns promised in 1828 by Sir John Macdonald, but never paid, and the reinstatement of the subsidiary articles. In return, Persia offered not to go to war against any European state without the permission of Britain. This apparent willingness to turn Persia into a British protectorate, to return to Wellesley's definition of the Persian Connection, was belied by Abbas Mirza's refusal to give up his plans to annex Herat. Were Persia to become a British protectorate, supposedly this would not matter, because the boundary between the European and Indian political systems would be moved westwards from Khorassan to the Arras, and Herat would not need to become part of united Afghanistan.

As usual such proposals meant only that Abbas Mirza had the British resident on the run; and the British knew how impractical they were. Sir Charles Metcalfe was often the odd man out, but about Persia he had spoken in 1828 for everybody: 'Were we *even* [rightly ever] to expect any martial aid from Persia, in the time of our own need, we should most assuredly find ourselves

---

[1] Campbell to Grant, 1 Oct. 1833, F.O. 60/33; memorandums by Cabell on Campbell to sc, 1 Oct., 10 and 11 Nov. 1833, I.O. Persia/49.

most miserably deceived and disappointed.'[1] Britain could not
protect Persia: Persia could not protect India. Fortunately the
Persian embassy to London was postponed by the death of Abbas
Mirza on 22 October, followed by a serious illness of the shah,
who 'though a weak and inefficient ruler, formed then the only
bond that held the discordant parts of the kingdom together'.[2]
Civil war in Persia, likely for twenty years, now became a certainty.
The British had still not decided what to do about it.

The death of Abbas Mirza left four contenders for the throne of
Persia. Two of these were the brothers who ruled most of southern
Persia, Hassan Ali Mirza and Hussein Ali Mirza. That the base of
their power lay in Kerman and Fars injured their chances, by
making Anglo-Russian co-operation in support of them impossible;
nor was either likely to give way to the other. The two serious
contenders were Abbas Mirza's son, Mahomet Mirza, and another
of Abbas's brothers, the governor of Teheran, the Zil es-Sultan.
Silly Zilly, as he was irreverently called by the British, had
nothing to recommend him except fluency of speech, but he did
control the citadel at Teheran, and with it the imperial treasury:
Fath Ali had hoarded all his life, and nobody knew how much he
had hidden away. Mahomet Mirza, about whom the British were
equally rude, 'a gross, unwieldy person . . . [with] an unmeaning
countenance, and a general bearing . . . clownish and commonplace'.[3] was immediately given command of his father's armies
and control of his provinces, but was not named heir apparent.
His greatest asset was his chief minister, 'venal, avaricious, and
vindictive,' but equally able;

he is all powerful [said Fraser] . . . Mahomet Mirza is nothing . . .
Aware that were either Great Britain or Russia predominant in Persia
his own power and importance must fall . . . [he] plays the one off
against the other, exciting their respective fears and jealousies as he
finds convenient, yet always stopping short of the quarrelling point.[4]

---

[1] Memorandum by Metcalfe, 2 June 1828, Kaye, *Metcalfe*, ii, 197.

[2] Fraser to Grant, 16 Mar. 1834, quoted in memorandum by Cabell for
Wellington, 18 Dec. 1834, F.O. 65/35.

[3] Willock to Palmerston, 15 May 1834, F.O. 65/35; G. Rawlinson, *A Memoir
of Major-General Sir Henry Creswicke Rawlinson* (London, 1898), p. 48.

[4] Fraser to Grant, 31 July 1834, quoted in memorandum by Cabell, 18 Dec.
1834, F.O. 60/35. For the duties of such ministers see C. Meredith, 'Early
Qajar Administration: An Analysis of its Development and Functions', *Iranian
Studies*, iv (1971), 59–84.

Given the board of control's priorities in the near east, here was a good reason for trying to arrange a settlement in favour of Mahomet.

Knowing what had happened when the British failed to help Mahmud II against Mahomet Ali explains why Campbell, McNeill, and Fraser, in Persia, and Taylor at Baghdad, were so worried during the winter of 1833-4 about the uproar in Persia and Turkish Arabia. Campbell feared in November, that were the shah to die, his death might be 'the signal for general insurrection in which Russia . . . would mingle before the event could be known in England', by helping Mahomet Mirza in return for his allowing Russian troops into Teheran and Meshed, and pledging that Persia would not oppose Russian settlement on the east coast of the Caspian. The best way to forestall the effects on the stability of British India of this nightmare vision of a Persian version of the treaty of Unkiar Skelessi, was for the British, too, to support Mahomet Mirza, by promising him the help they should have given his father, a small subsidy and officers to command his troops. This would probably persuade the shah to name Mahomet Mirza heir apparent, and convince him that he need not look to Russia for help.[1]

John McNeill thought differently. Because the succession of Mahomet Mirza, whether or not he were named heir apparent, would cause civil war, the military mission which had finally arrived at Bushire would cause embarrassment: they could hardly avoid entanglement in the dynastic squabbles of the Kajars. McNeill, who in November was 'against the policy of interposing so decidedly in the affairs of Persia which is so strongly advocated by the envoy', thought the best way to ensure the succession of Mahomet Mirza might be 'an arrangement with Russia precluding all interference by military force in any disputes that may arise in Persia'.[2] This was the logical conclusion to Ellis's explanation in 1831 of Britain's relationship to Abbas Mirza. It did not matter who succeeded Fath Ali, just as it did not matter whether Mahomet Ali occupied Syria: civil war in Turkey and Persia would not

---

[1] Campbell to Grant, 18 Nov. 1833, I.O. Persia/49.
[2] Extract of McNeill to Wilson, 11 Nov. 1833, and memorandum by Cabell, 28 Jan. 1834, on Campbell to sc, nos. 117 and 118, 18 Nov. 1833, I.O. Persia/49.

necessarily endanger Britain, as long as Russia kept out, and agreed not to sell her support.

The foreign office and the board of control refused in the new year to be panicked by Campbell. 'Do nothing about this', said Palmerston, still trying to guess the meaning of the treaties of Münchengrätz, 'until we have further information.'[1] The British did not know whether the Russians had recognized Mahomet Mirza as heir apparent in place of his father; if they had, the shah had not yet copied them. If no heir had been named, nobody was certain to win the civil war, as Abbas Mirza had been; therefore there was nobody whom Campbell might quietly help with a little money. Consequently the board, with Palmerston's approval, told Campbell in February to remain aloof. If the shah should name an heir, and Russia recognized him, so would Britain, and would pay him the money promised Abbas Mirza. If no successor were named, and the shah's death were followed by civil war, Campbell was to keep the money and not interfere. If the shah and the Russians supported different candidates, again the British would not interfere. The military mission might work for Mahomet Mirza as successor to Abbas Mirza until an heir was named, who was recognized by everyone; but in the event of civil war they were not to take sides.[2]

One reason for this restraint was a report in January 1834 from the British envoy at St. Petersburg, the Hon. John Duncan Bligh, that the shah had asked Russia to agree to his naming Mahomet Mirza heir apparent. Bligh did not know how the Russians had answered, but thought, as they had mentioned it, that they must want to co-operate with Britain.[3] Grant, who could not see why in that case they could not have said so, nevertheless saw what Ellis and McNeill had been looking for, an 'opportunity for an attempt to place the whole question of the international relations of Russia and Great Britain . . . (as they are affected by Persia and India) in a more satisfactory position'. Grant hoped for a statement that both Britain and Russia would 'abjure any pretensions to indemnity, territorial or pecuniary, in consequence

---

[1] Minute of Palmerston, 23 Feb. 1834, on Campbell to Grant, 18 Nov. 1833, F.O. 60/35.

[2] Sc to ggic, 8 Feb. 1834, I.O. L/PS/5/544. The foreign office copy has a minute of Palmerston dated 6 Feb.

[3] Bligh to Palmerston, no. 14, 28 Jan. 1834, F.O. 65/213.

of a successful issue of their proceeding', because such a 'disclaimer . . . would be a fresh safeguard to Persia and an additional barrier against the possible designs of Russia'.[1] It would show Persia to be an independent buffer state, to be treated like any of the states of Europe.

Bligh explained that the tsar was hesitant because he 'mourns the conclusion [of the treaty of Unkiar Skelessi] in sackcloth and ashes', on account of the conflict with Britain it had caused.[2] The Russians, in succeeding in turning Turkey into a protectorate, had made the mistake Palmerston had made in 1832, or would have had he not been prevented. In 1829, when they changed their priorities from the partition of Turkey to its maintenance as a protectorate, they did not see that this could best be done by avoiding dramatic victories. Palmerston was particularly sceptical throughout the spring and summer of 1834 of any Russian offers of apparent self-restraint, because of his interpretation of the convention of St. Petersburg, by which, in return for going without part of the indemnity still owed by Turkey under the terms of the treaty of Adrianople, Russia had obtained more territory in the Caucasus than the treaty had given her in 1829. 'We should be much disposed to agree with Russia in supporting Abbas Mirza's son,' Palmerston told Bligh in February, but as they could not do so until the shah had named him heir apparent, Bligh was to say he had no instructions. Palmerston, who was sounding more and more like Wellington and Ellenborough, was frightened of falling into the trap into which Canning had fallen over Greece: Russia's policy was unlikely to be as restrained as it appeared, because, 'the military organization of her political fabric renders encroachment upon her neighbours almost a necessary condition of her existence'.[3]

In 1834 the confusion caused by the administration of the Persian mission reached one of its bizarre climaxes. Throughout 1833 the government of India had left London to set out policy in Persia; in November they merely explained, that should Abbas Mirza die, Campbell ought to cultivate the same relationship with Mahomet Mirza, if the shah named him his heir. In the spring

---

[1] Grant to Palmerston, 18 Feb. 1834, I.O. L/PS/3/118.
[2] Bligh to Palmerston, private, 28 Jan. 1834, Broadlands MSS. GC/BL/55.
[3] Palmerston to Bligh, private, 28 Feb. 1834, Broadlands MSS. GC/BL/111

of 1834 they repeated themselves: the board would provide instructions but Campbell should try meanwhile to remove the shah's scruples about naming an heir.[1] Lord William Bentinck, who shared Metcalfe's opinion of the value of the Persian Connection, had always been determined to avoid responsibility for it. More and more he thought it a waste of public money, one of the many extravagances to be cut out of the Indian budget. 'I quite agree with you,' said Lord Clare in July, 'I would not give, as we say in Ireland, a brass halfpenny to Persia.'[2] In 1832 they had sent to Persia only 3,000 of the 14,000 rifles authorized by the board of control, and the following year Bombay lost the board's instructions telling them to hasten the departure of the military mission.[3] Colonel Passmore, who had been chosen to command the mission in December 1832, did not arrive at Bombay until the middle of the following October, left for Persia on 21 November just before the news arrived of the death of Abbas Mirza, for whom he was to work, and arrived at Bushire a month later to be faced with the likelihood of civil war.

Shortly afterwards he faced the probability of a collision of authorities. The British, who had a passion for symbolic appointments, regularly sent solitary Englishmen to the near east, to defend British India or to re-establish the European balance of power. The man chosen in February 1832 to restore the shah's trust in the British, and to prevent the Russians, whatever they might say at St. Petersburg, from meddling with the Persian succession, was Sir Henry Lindsay Bethune, who had been a member of the British military mission during the Napoleonic Wars, and had commanded the Persian troops in their only victory over the Russians. Bethune offered to serve as chief of staff to the Persian army. He was to be paid £1,400 a year by the foreign office out of the secret service funds, to be given the local rank of lieutenant-colonel, but of a later date than Passmore's to make him the senior, was under no circumstances to take command of the British military mission, and was to take out with him more

[1] Swinton to Campbell, 7 Nov. 1833, I.O. Bengal/SPC/377, 7 Nov. 1833, no. 6; McNaghten to same, 10 Apr. 1834, ibid. 380, 10 Apr. 1834, no. 5.

[2] Clare to Bentinck, private, 8 July 1834, Portland MSS. PwJf/777.

[3] Swinton to Campbell, 4 Sept. 1832, I.O. Bengal/SPC/368, 8 Oct. 1832, no. 8; memorandum by Norris, 16 Nov. 1833, I.O. Bombay/SP/80, 27 Nov. 1833, no. 325.

of the weapons the British had promised Persia and the government of India had refused to send.[1]

The foreign office, having decided to make this gesture, with
true whig passion for economy then destroyed its value by halving
the number of weapons to be sent, and the treasury, the ordnance
office, and the admiralty, spent the next nine months arguing
about how the weapons should be packed and shipped. They
arrived long after the crisis they were to help avert. The ordnance
office were particularly worried that Bethune was to take the
Persians shrapnel shells, which had never before been supplied
to a foreign power and were regarded with 'great jealousy'; the
East India Company merely predicted confusion. Remembering
the feud between Harford Jones and John Malcolm in 1809, they
argued that if Campbell and Passmore were employed by them and
Bethune by the Crown, they were bound to collide. However hard
Bethune tried to prevent his appointment from misleading the
Persians, they would over-value their friendship and the price
Britain should pay for it. 'We confess', said the chairman in
March, 'our inability to perceive the advantages you appear to
expect from the appointment of Sir H[enry] Bethune in Persia.'[2]

The more detailed information of the likely consequences of
the death of Abbas Mirza upon the stability of Persia, for which
Palmerston had been waiting, was not long in coming. In 1834
payment of the remainder of the Russian indemnity under the
treaty of Turkmanchay fell due. Count Simonitch, whose language,
said Campbell, 'seems to be conclusive of the determination of his
government to bring Persia to what concessions they please by
menace and compulsion', had threatened in January that, were the
indemnity not paid, the tsar would occupy Ghilan as a security.[3]
The shah had hoped to negotiate a postponement, to find out
whether Russia and Britain would prefer him to name Mahomet
Mirza or the Zil es-Sultan his heir, and what they would offer in
return, by sending on a mission to St. Petersburg and London his
so-called minister for foreign relations, Abul Hassan Khan, who

[1] Grant to Palmerston, 3 Mar. 1834, with encl., Palmerston to Grant, 5 Mar.
1834, F.O. 60/35; Grant to Bentinck, private and confidential, 14 Mar. 1834,
Portland MSS. PwJf/1064.

[2] Couper to Backhouse, private, 13 Mar. 1834, F.O. 60/35; Loch and Tucker
to Grant, 11 Mar. 1834, I.O. L/PS/3/118. The correspondence about the
weapons is in F.O. 60/35.

[3] Campbell to Grant, private, 29 Jan. 1834, I.O. Persia/50.

had accompanied James Morier to London in 1809 with the preliminary draft of the treaty of Teheran, and was the original Haji Baba.

Simonitch was adamantly opposed to the mission; claiming that the tsar would not postpone the repayment of the indemnity and wanted Mahomet Mirza named heir apparent. McNeill told the shah in January he would be wiser to send Abul Hassan to London first, because, if he went first to St. Petersburg, the Russians might make embarrassing offers in return for going without the rest of the indemnity, whereas, if he went first to England, it was up to the British to suggest how Persia should maintain her independence. In McNeill's opinion, the best way to avoid a crisis would be to spend the money, which would have been spent helping Abbas Mirza to the throne, on subsidizing two battalions of infantry to garrison the citadel at Teheran: then Britain 'would in fact hold the power to dispose of the crown of Persia'.[1]

McNeill, now arguing for intervention, whereas in 1833 he had argued against it, was supported by James Fraser, who had the bad luck to miss his second chance properly to play the Great Game in Asia. After a most uncomfortable and dangerous journey across Anatolia in the depths of winter, Fraser arrived at Tabriz on 24 February to find, as Passmore found when he arrived about the same time at Bushire, a state of affairs entirely different from the one supposed by his instructions. 'Matters were truly in a singularly unsettled state . . . throughout Persia,' he recorded, where '. . . all that is good and worthy . . . is fast going to decay.'[2] To decide whom to support would be difficult, because the dynasty was loathed by the whole population; only the British connection might save them. Fraser said in March that McNeill's suggestion for a subsidiary force at Teheran would be 'hailed by the inhabitants with universal satisfaction'. Because the Kajars by their tyranny had forfeited their authority, if Britain acted decisively, we 'shall have with us the good will of the whole body of the people . . . [and] of that most influential part of it, the priesthood'.[3]

[1] Extract of McNeill to Wilson, 24 Jan. 1834, in Grant to Palmerston, private, 2 May 1834, F.O. 60/35; Campbell to Grant, private, 2 Mar. 1834, I.O.L. MSS. Eur. D/556/1.

[2] J. B. Fraser, A Winter's Journey from Constantinople to Teheran, with Travels through various parts of Persia (London, 1838), i. 379, 399.

[3] Fraser to sc, 16 Mar. 1834, quoted in memorandum by Cabell, 18 Dec. 1834, F.O. 60/35; Fraser, Winter's Journey, i. 401.

Fortunately, when Campbell's full powers to negotiate alterations to the treaty of Teheran reached him in March, Fath Ali
changed his mind about sending an ambassador to St. Petersburg
and London, because even Campbell realized that Abul Hassan
would have been told to ask, for the restoration of the subsidiary
articles, and for the arrears of subsidy the Persians claimed had
been due since 1828. The advice of McNeill and Fraser, 'important
and interesting' though Grant thought it,[1] also became redundant
when Mahomet Mirza, in order to obtain the nomination as heir
apparent, offered at the end of March to pay the remainder of the
indemnity owed to Russia. This according to Campbell would lead
to disaster. The campaigns in Khorassan had caused havoc and
destitution everywhere between Tabriz and Meshed, and left
Mahomet Mirza with the remains of an army, which had not been
regularly paid for four years. The prince had no money to pay
Russia; instead he would bargain, offering whatever was necessary
to escape payment and buy Russian help against his uncles. 'A
friendship thus embraced', argued Campbell, 'cannot fail to prove
fatal to the independence of the kingdom.'[2]

In 1834 every Englishman in the near east knew where such
actions were bound to lead. The lesser danger was a Persian
version of the convention of St. Petersburg, with Russia's giving
up or postponing payment of the indemnity in return for moving
forward her frontier. This was less likely in Persia than Turkey,
because the Arras was a good frontier. The greater danger would
be a Russian demand to replace the British military mission, the
symbol of Britain's legitimate claim to influence in Persia, by a
Russian one, and to impose on Mahomet Mirza a Persian version
of the treaty of Unkiar Skelessi. Russia, said Campbell in May, was
carrying out the same policy she had successfully carried out in
Turkey, and would 'under a mutual guarantee of protection
insidiously establish a pretext for interference'.[3] Then, unless the
British could dominate Afghanistan, and move the military
frontier of British India forward to meet the political frontier at
the Hindu Kush, the buffer zone between the European and Indian
political systems would have disappeared, and the tranquillity of
British India would be permanently menaced.

[1] Grant to Palmerston, private, 2 May 1834, F.O. 60/35.
[2] Campbell to sc, 5 Apr. 1834, I.O. Persia/50.
[3] Campbell to Grant, 24 May 1834, I.O. Persia/50.

Persia, however weak and decayed, argued Campbell, true to his training in the Bombay School, remained the best place at which to defend British India: 'If England loses this distant barrier . . . she will not only have to bewail what she cannot remedy, but will find herself involved in the necessitous measures of prevention elsewhere . . . for the erection and strengthening of a new and less efficient barrier.'[1] The way to prevent this was to forestall a Russian repetition of the treaty of Unkiar Skelessi, by negotiating a British equivalent. If the British lent Persia £250,000 to pay the indemnity owed to Russia, they would replace the Russian lever over the Kajars, particularly over Mahomet Mirza, by a British lever, and might demand in return, both that Persia keep up a small but efficient body of infantry, capable of preventing civil war, certainly of winning it, and that she agree to the revisions of the treaty of Teheran proposed in 1833, particularly to the removal of article nine.

James Baillie Fraser, even more upset by the decay of Persia since his last visit, was even more bold. Britain he reported in April should send a second military mission, to train a force of infantry to keep order in Khorassan as well as Azerbaijan, and they should be followed by envoys from the Crown, sent to negotiate new treaties of alliance with both Fath Ali and Shah Shuja.[2] Until the news of Shuja's defeat at Kandahar reached Teheran in September, the British seemed to have an opportunity to solve the problem of how to defend British India, by turning both Persia and Afghanistan into British protectorates. By keeping order in both of them by the expansion of British trade, the British might also win the Great Game in Asia.

III

Persia was not Turkey, and Sir John Campbell was not Stratford Canning: his advice carried no weight at London or Calcutta. During the winter Cabell had complained, that from Campbell's despatches it was impossible to tell what he thought the board of control should do; when his advice became comprehensible, it

---

[1] Campbell to McNaghten, 23 Mar. 1834, I.O. India/SP/1, 24 June 1834, no. 2.

[2] Campbell to Palmerston, no. 1, 9 Apr. 1834, F.O. 60/34; same to Grant, private, 8 Apr. 1834, I.O. Persia/50; Fraser to sc, 10 Apr. 1834, quoted in memorandum by Cabell, 18 Dec. 1834, F.O. 60/35.

was thought unsound. The earl of Clare, who read and criticized Campbell's dispatches on their way to Fort William, had never approved of his appointment; by 1834 even Bentinck, who tried for as long as possible to leave the Persian mission to the board of control, decided that something must be done. 'I have to inform you in perfect confidence,' he told Grant in September, 'of my deep conviction of the excessive unfitness of Sir John Campbell . . . besides his want of capacity and talent, his temper is most ungovernable.' His assistant, John McNeill, found it more and more difficult to work with him: 'too devoid of discretion to be entrusted with a secret', he complained, 'and too devoid of truth to be implicitly believed'.[1] Because Campbell's eyes had been troubling him, in May the secret committee told him to take six months' leave of absence at St. Petersburg, and to leave McNeill in charge in Persia. To the embarrassment of everyone Campbell, certain he was needed in Persia to defend the national interest, immediately recovered.[2]

The resident was discredited; likewise the policy he recommended. Palmerston had learned in 1832 the dangers of competing for influence with Russia; in case he should have forgotten, Henry Ellis, in a long and 'very important' paper, in May reminded him. Ellis warned Grant and Palmerston not to trust the shah. He could easily afford to pay the Russian indemnity but did not want to, hoping that if he named as heir apparent the prince chosen by the Russians or the British, either the former would go without the indemnity or the latter would pay it. If the Russians demanded Ghilan instead of payment, Britain could not object: 'the right of Russia in this matter is perfect'.[3] Britain would not lend Persia the money to pay the indemnity, and she lacked the power to bar the occupation of Ghilan, just as she had been unable to bar Russian steamers from the Caspian. Her only ground for opposition was the general one, that she could not permit the dismemberment of Persia. This had not yet been set out as Britain's policy.

Ellis recommended that the decision should now be taken,

[1] Bentinck to Grant, private, 3 Sept. 1834, Portland MSS. PwJf/1069; *McNeill*, p. 169.
[2] Sc to Campbell, 26 May 1834, I.O. L/PS/5/544; Campbell to sc, [1835], Kentchurch Court MSS. 9776.
[3] Grant to Palmerston, 14 May 1834, enclosing 'Memorandum [by Henry Ellis] on the Affairs of Persia', F.O. 60/35.

which would mean that Persia like Turkey would be held together as much by pressure at St. Petersburg as at Teheran. For this reason, Ellis was most anxious to prevent the shah from sending an ambassador to London, who would either argue, that if Britain did not pay off the indemnity Persia would have to surrender territory around the Caspian to Russia, which would endanger the security of British India, or, that as he had come to London before St. Petersburg at the suggestion of the British envoy, if no subsidy were offered Persia had again been misled. Unless Britain were prepared to guarantee the integrity of Persia, which was tantamount to declaring her a protectorate, the arrival of a Persian ambassador could cause only embarrassment.

Ellis was equally certain that Britain should not send troops to garrison Teheran, which would involve the British in the Persian civil war and lead to a collision with Russia. If the shah then nominated the Zil, Russia might declare for Mahomet Mirza and garrison Tabriz. Control of Teheran would not bring the rest of Persia under the control of the British nominee, and because it 'would throw . . . [Mahomet Mirza] at once into the arms of Russia . . . [is] rather calculated to precipitate, than prevent Russian interference'. The best way to make certain of stability in Persia would be to send out an able minister from the Crown, who could help the heir apparent were he undisputed, and help to keep out Russia were he not; to encourage the shah to name his heir, adding that Britain would approve of Mahomet Mirza; and to negotiate with Russia an agreement that both states would recognize whoever was named by the shah. Were this done, the Russians, if persuaded that the indemnity would soon be paid, might give up their demand for Ghilan, and British influence at Teheran would be restored. Ellis had no more doubts than any other Englishmen 'that the shah of Persia, whoever he may be, will always prefer English to Russian protection';[1] he merely gave a different meaning to the word.

In June 1834, Palmerston, seeing that just as Mahomet Ali must be held back in order to safeguard British India, unrest must be prevented in Persia and Baghdad to help preserve the Eurpoean balance of power, was ready to act in Persia as well as in Baghdad. Because he still expected the tsar to meddle, and whenever pos-

[1] 'Memorandum [by Henry Ellis] on Recent Despatches from Persia', 5 June 1834, F.O. 60/35.

sible to annex more territory beyond the Caucasus, he had to oppose Russia, as Ellis recommended, on the general ground that Britain was determined to prevent the dismemberment of Persia. Campbell was told to say the same to the shah.[1] Britain would not herself meddle in Persia, nor seek to turn Persia into a British protectorate—no more was heard of ambitious plans for sweeping reform—but she would not permit the tsar to dismember Persia, nor to make use of his financial lever to turn Persia into a protectorate of Russia.

On 16 June Palmerston explained to the Russian minister, why Britain opposed the tsar's demand for the payment of the outstanding sum due under the terms of the treaty of Turkmanchay.

The British government certainly never can admit [he said] the equity of the principle upon which the exaction of such payments is made to rest. That when a powerful state gets into war with a weaker one and is as it must be victorious, it seems unjust that the beaten party should in addition to its own losses in the war be crushed by the overwhelming weight of a pecuniary burden from which it has no adequate means of relieving itself. That such a mode of dealing with a discomfited power would be almost as fatal to its independence as territorial cessions would be, because the resources of a state may be crippled and its freedom of action taken away by the want of pecuniary means, as well as by the curtailment of territorial extent.[2]

Palmerston, naturally, did not follow this argument when demanding an indemnity from China in 1843. The explanation is not solely that Palmerston was a humbug, as Florence Nightingale and his biographer Jasper Ridley believed.[3] There was some truth in the British claim that as they were a naval not a military power, their pecuniary demands were less likely to lead either to a partition or to a protectorate.

Although Bligh at St. Petersburg was 'in the dark as to their intentions upon Persia', the Russians claimed in July, both that they had no designs upon Ghilan, and that they would prefer to arrange for the accession of Mahomet Mirza in co-operation with Great Britain.[4] Far from threatening Persia, were the indemnity

---

[1] Palmerston to Ponsonby, private, 24 June 1834, Broadlands MSS. GC/PO/ 666; sc to ggic, 23 July 1834, I.O. L/PS/5/544.

[2] Palmerston to Bligh, no. 26, 16 June 1834, F.O. 65/216.

[3] Ridley, *Palmerston*, p. 259.

[4] Bligh to Palmerston, private, 12 July 1834, Broadlands MSS. GC/BL/62; same to same, no. 70, 2 July 1834, F.O. 65/214.

not paid, they had offered to postpone the date for repayment until January 1836.[1] This put the British in a dilemma: they did not want the Russians to threaten Persia, but they did want the Persians to repay. Palmerston and Grant told the Persians that they thought Mahomet Mirza should be named heir apparent, but that Britain and Russia would recognize any prince named by the shah. They added that the shah must also pay the indemnity himself, not leaving the succession to depend on the 'forbearance and control of a foreign power . . . Britain [said Palmerston in August] can have no wish to obtain any undue influence over the internal affairs of Persia', and was confident that Persia would prove able to maintain her independence, 'provided the shah and his ministers do not delay the settlement of questions which ought to be placed beyond the reach of accident and foreign interference'.[2] Persia was to realize that the British would neither pay the indemnity, nor permit her to bargain with Russia. They would not step in, they would not permit Russia to step in; they did not want to turn Persia into a protectorate, nor would they permit Russia to.

Before these instructions were sent, the British had learned that on 24 June 1834 the shah had finally named Mahomet Mirza heir apparent. This did not make civil war less likely; his uncles were bound to challenge him, but, although they would all make the same claim, that he was a vassal of Russia, 'I suspect there is not the smallest confidence or concert between them,' reported Fraser; 'everyone is for himself, and hopes to retain something, at least, of what he may seize in the scramble.'[3] In this situation it was the Russians who again took the next step towards co-operation. In August they said they were 'extremely anxious' for Campbell and Simonitch to 'communicate freely and confidentially . . . upon matters of common interest', in order to work for a peaceful succession.[4] Because the British thought this would be the best way to hold back Russia, Campbell was told to co-operate, and,

[1] Palmerston to Grant, 5 Aug. 1834, I.O. L/PS/3/118.

[2] Encls. 2 and 3 in sc to ggic, 22 Aug. 1834, I.O. L/PS/5/544. Bragging as always, the British claimed that they had persuaded the Russians to postpone the date for the payment of the indemnity.

[3] Fraser, *Winter's Journey*, ii. 117–18.

[4] Medem to Palmerston, 22 Aug. 1834, F.O. 65/214; Palmerston to Grant, 23 Aug. 1834, I.O. L/PS/3/118.

in case Simonitch should hesitate to treat him as the representative of Britain, and not only of the East India Company, Palmerston wrote him a dispatch to prove it. The board of control had first asked for a credential letter. Palmerston, not knowing what this meant, agreed; his under-secretary had to explain that a credential letter would accredit Campbell to Persia on a diplomatic mission, and transfer the Persian mission from the East India Company to the Crown.[1]

Palmerston worked with the Russians in Persia, because Britain and Russia both wanted Mahomet Mirza to mount the throne as quickly and peacefully as possible, but this would not prevent collisions afterwards. Russian diplomacy, Palmerston warned Bligh in September, 'consists of intrigue within intrigue'.[2] The Russians could offer to co-operate, because if Mahomet succeeded easily or even without a fight, they would still hold over him the demand for payment of the indemnity, and the offer to help him against Herat: the British would not pay one, and must forbid the other. This was a prospective danger. Britain's immediate danger, the likelihood of civil war, was increased by the behaviour of her own officials. During 1834 both British missions in Persia became less and less effective.

Sir John Campbell had quarrelled with all the important Persian officials; as the result, he was 'seldom visited, never sent for and consulted in the business of the country, while . . . not a thing is done without the advice of' Count Simonitch.[3] It was 'comfortable and pleasant for the English to have so gentlemanly and courteous a rival as the Count': it was also dangerous, and embarrassed Campbell's capable assistant, John McNeill. Having made a successful transfer from the medical to the diplomatic service, McNeill had been brought back to Teheran from the residency at Bushire to assist Campbell, and feared he would be ruined, were Campbell called home in disgrace. 'It appears to me', McNeill told Fraser, 'that I must decide on becoming an accuser, which I cannot persuade myself to be, or I must keep quiet and

---

[1] Mackenzie to Palmerston, 26 Aug. 1834, with minute of Palmerston, 26 Aug. 1834, F.O. 60/35; memorandum by Backhouse, 27–28 Aug. 1834, with minute of Palmerston, 29 Aug. 1834, ibid.

[2] Palmerston to Bligh, private, 5 Sept. 1834, Broadlands MSS. GC/BL/114.

[3] Fraser to Grant, 31 July 1834, quoted in memorandum by Cabell, 18 Dec. 1834, F.O. 60/35.

allow the interests entrusted to the mission to be sacrificed, or I must retire, so as to induce enquiry.'[1]

Fraser and McNeill eventually thought of a fourth possibility, and persuaded Campbell, unhappy with the British government for ignoring his advice, to send McNeill to London in September to explain the gravity of the situation in Persia. This eventually ruined Campbell and made McNeill. The Persians simultaneously abandoned their plan to send an envoy to London to negotiate the revisions of the treaty of Teheran; instead they demanded the recall of Campbell and lavished praise on McNeill.[2] The following year he made a trio with Fraser and Urquhart, whom Palmerston 'set to work to *write up* the Eastern Question',[3] in the hope of causing a public outcry loud enough, to persuade his colleagues to allow him to take a more spirited line in the near east, and to back it up when necessary with public money.

The British military mission were equally ineffective. Colonel Passmore had reached Teheran at the end of March. He was followed in June by Sir Henry Bethune, whose appointment by the Persians as chief of staff to Mahomet Mirza, claimed Passmore, made him virtually Passmore's commanding officer. When Passmore protested, Bethune, in July, resigned; but Passmore, who would not serve under Bethune, would also not allow Bethune to serve under him.[4] Sir Henry, of whose influence and renown in Persia so much had been expected, was temporarily left in charge only of the Persian arsenal and artillery. This satisfied Passmore, but offended his second in command, Captain Sheil, because whereas Passmore, who was senior to Bethune, was now in command of Mahomet Mirza's troops, were he for any reason to be removed, Bethune not Sheil would replace him, leaving Sheil in command only of the British detachment. Sheil argued that this arrangement ended all his chances of promotion, and asked for compensation. Grant replied that he doubted whether the East India Company would pay any.[5]

---

[1] Fraser, *Travels in Koordistan*, ii. 244; *McNeill*, p. 175.

[2] Abul Hassan Khan to Palmerston, received 21 Nov. 1834, F.O. 60/34. The sc sent a copy to Campbell so 'that you may offer thereupon such explanations as you may think fit'. Sc to Campbell, 22 Dec. 1834, I.O. L/PS/5/544.

[3] Rawlinson, *England and Russia in the East*, pp. 52–3.

[4] Campbell to Bentinck, private and confidential, 10 Aug. 1834, Portland MSS. PwJf/572.

[5] Sheil to Grant, 1 Aug. 1834, Grant to Sheil, 13 Nov. 1834, I.O. L/PS/3/118.

The British in Persia seemed to be singing an intricate but tuneless roundelay: Campbell had offended the Persians; they, by appointing Bethune, had offended Passmore and Sheil; who had, in turn, given 'so much offence to Sir John as to induce him to refuse all further personal communication', mostly because he resented Passmore's right to report independently to the government of India on military matters. As Passmore's quarrel with Campbell was shortly followed by a quarrel with the Persian ministers, it seemed that all communication between the British missions and the Persian government would come to an end, and that Bethune would follow McNeill home to England. 'Our public agents are often too proud,' said Sir Harford Jones, when he heard what was happening, 'too lazy, and too puffed up with themselves.'[1]

This mattered more at a time when the crisis of the Kajars was imminent; nobody expected the shah to live long, and by September Mahomet Mirza's resources appeared to be in a state of 'utter destitution'. If the weapons the foreign office had promised did not reach Tabriz befor the shah died, said Bethune, 'we shall be in a sad dilemma'.[2] Mahomet had not a single organized battalion and no money to pay one, which must drive him straight into the arms of Russia. According to Campbell the choice was clear. Money when the time came, and officers to train Mahomet's troops beforehand, were not enough: 'Either England or Russia must . . . assume the management of Persia.'[3] 'The moral influence of the one will avail . . . [Mahomet Mirza] little,' added Campbell. '. . . he must rest his hopes upon the physical force of the other . . . it does not appear to me that they can act on any terms of equality with regard to Persia.' Campbell thought that Russia was only lengthening Persia's time for the repayment of the indemnity, so that 'she will have a just pretext for interference in its affairs'. As soon as Russia had helped Mahomet Mirza to the throne, he 'would become her pageant', and, because Russian soldiers would be needed to keep him there, Persia would become a Russian protectorate.[4]

[1] Fraser to Grant, 31 July, 1 Oct. 1834, quoted in memorandum by Cabell, 18 Dec. 1834, F.O. 60/35; Jones to Benjamin Jones, 24 Oct. 1834, Kentchurch Court MSS. 9770.
[2] Bethune to Backhouse, private, 26 Sept. 1834, F.O. 60/34.
[3] Campbell to Grant, confidential, 25 Sept. 1834, I.O. Persia/51.
[4] Campbell to sc, secret, 24 Sept. 1834, I.O. Persia/51; same to Bentinck, confidential, 17 Sept. 1834, Portland MSS. PwJf/574.

Campbell, like so many British agents in the near east, was mesmerized by the approaching doom. Persia, he told Palmerston towards the end of September, 'must shortly fall into the hands of Russia or England'. The way to make certain Britain controlled Persia was a subsidy. During the years of the previous subsidy, Abbas Mirza had kept up an army, although not capable of defeating Russia, capable of overawing his brothers. The Persians were claiming arrears of subsidy equal to £150,000. Campbell thought they would abandon this claim, if they were offered £30,000 annually, and, were this paid until the crisis was over, it would solve all Mahomet Mirza's problems. 'If we want Persia, my Lord,' concluded Campbell, 'we must pay the price of her alliance.'[1]

Fortunately for the British, the succession crisis in Persia happened sooner rather than later. Long before these dispatches reached London, on 20 October 1834 Fath Ali Shah finally died at Isfahan. When the news reached Tabriz early in November, Campbell and Simonitch 'conjointly and separately' hailed Mahomet Mirza as shah. The Zil es-Sultan proclaimed himself in Teheran, then gave up without a fight; in the south Hassan Ali Mirza and Hussein Ali Mirza were easily defeated by a Persian force led by Sir Henry Bethune, who by this victory justified the quixotic decision to send him. Hussein Ali was killed, Hassan Ali captured and blinded, and the Zil fled firstly to Russia, then to Turkey. More important, despite Campbell's fears, Simonitch co-operated, and made no effort to call up Russian troops from Georgia, or to offer Mahomet Mirza terms equivalent to the treaty of Unkiar Skelessi. The campaign was short, but not cheap. Campbell calculated that £30,000, or one year's payment of the subsidy he had suggested, would be needed to pay for moving Mahomet Mirza's army from Azerbaijan to Teheran.[2] Given the whigs' hesitancy in asking parliament for £20,000 for the Euphrates Expedition, this was a large sum. Fortunately it did not matter: parliament would not have to pay it.

---

[1] Campbell to Palmerston, private and confidential, 23 Sept. 1834, F.O. 60/34.
[2] Campbell to sc, 22 Nov. 1834, I.O. Persia/51. See also Hasan-E Fasai, *History of Persia under Qajar Rule; from the Persian of Farsnama-ye Naseri*, trans. H. Busse (New York, 1972), pp. 229–41. Because of the fighting in southern Persia, Campbell could not issue bills on India but had to issue them on Constantinople. This made the sum larger than it would otherwise have been because the exchange rate was so bad.

Palmerston and Grant had ignored Campbell's prophecies, and also the opinions of a former minister at Teheran, Sir Harford Jones, who had been asked by Grant in September for his advice about the revisions of the treaty of Teheran being negotiated by Campbell, and replied that something more comprehensive was needed.[1]

Persia [he predicted] will [soon] find herself in respect to Russia pretty much in the same state as the cat did to the monkey, when the latter took the chestnuts out of the fire by means of her paw, and when this happens Persia will also like her predecessor Puss . . . find that tho' her paw is miserably burnt not one of the chestnuts is to become her property.

Whereas Jones, talking after the fashion of Wellesley and Ellenborough, demanded strong steps to prevent Russia's using Persia as a lever against British India, Ellis had convinced Grant and Palmerston that the greater the unrest in Persia, and the weaker the imperial government, the more important it became not to seek to increase British influence, but to follow a policy of mutual restraint in co-operation with Russia. In October they reminded the Persian government, that although delighted by the nomination of Mahomet Mirza, they would be better pleased when the indemnity was paid, which was just as 'essential to the present and future independence of Persia'.[2] By the time news of the shah's death reached London, as usual through St. Petersburg, Grant and Palmerston were out of office and Wellington and Ellenborough were back.

Palmerston could leave the foreign office happily, because 'as to Russia I know . . . [Wellington] hates her with deep and long-standing bitterness, and is quite as little disposed to yield to her as we could be'.[3] This was true, but Wellington was a more sensible man than Palmerston, and did not allow personal grievances to influence national policy. He and Peel named Lord Heytesbury to succeed Lord William Bentinck in India, itself a symbol of Britain's determination to reach if possible an accommodation with Russia in the near east, and, on 20 December, two days after the news of

---

[1] 'Memoir [by Sir H. Jones] on Persia', 22 Sept. 1834, Kentchurch Court MSS. 9764; see also Jones's letters to Benjamin Jones at the board of control, ibid. 9766–73.

[2] Encls. 2–3 in sc to ggic, 23 Oct. 1834, I.O. L/PS/5/544.

[3] Palmerston to Holland, 21 Jan. 1835, Add. MSS. 51599, fo. 205.

the death of the shah was known at London, decided that Britain had at last been given the chance to alter the Persian Connection to suit the needs of India's defence. Because of his 'great admitted talents', and because he 'has taken the leading part in our diplomatic transactions with Persia', Henry Ellis, who was the obvious choice, was to be sent to Persia on a special mission from the Crown.[1]

IV

By co-operating with Russia, and by using principally British soldiers and money to place Mahomet Mirza on the throne of Persia, the British had prevented a Persian version of the treaty of Unkiar Skelessi, if there had ever been any danger of one: they had not yet prevented a Persian version of the convention of St. Petersburg, nor found a way to guard against the effects on the security of British India of the treaty of Turkmanchay, when Persia, in the opinion of James Fraser, 'may be said, I fear, virtually to have lost her independence'.[2] After 1834 this was likely to be more rather than less so, because Mahomet Shah had never seen a demonstration of Britain's power, whereas he had fled before the Russian army at the battle of Gunjah. The board of control had hoped to deal with this problem before the succession crisis, by the changes they had proposed in the treaty of Teheran. Because of Britain's need to stabilize the frontiers of Persia, and to justify claims to equal interest in Persia and equal sway over Persian policy as Russia, as soon as the crisis was over, these changes became more necessary. That their purpose was negative, because ideally both states were to leave Persia alone, except when preventing aggressive foreign policies, made the issue no less urgent. Unfortunately, owing to his quarrels with the Persian government, Campbell had proved unable to revise the terms of the treaty; he was hardly likely to succeed after McNeill had left. All they had done between them was to prevent the appointment of a Persian envoy to London, who would have demanded large sums in arrears of subsidy.

At the beginning of April 1834, Campbell, who had just

---

[1] Bligh to Palmerston, no. 110, 26 Nov. 1834, F.O. 65/214; Ellenborough to sc, 20 Dec. 1834, I.O. E/2/38.

[2] Fraser's *Winter's Journey*, ii. 506.

received his instructions, ignoring the advice of Henry Ellis to make the negotiations look as little as possible like new demands, told Abul Hassan Khan, the Persian foreign minister, that he was empowered to conclude a new commercial treaty. The minister replied, that although the shah was willing, as the trade to be regulated passed through Azerbaijan, the negotiations must await the return of Mahomet Mirza's chief minister from Khorassan. Campbell attributed the postponement, therefore, to the faction at the imperial court who were trying to persuade the shah to delegate to Mahomet Mirza everything delegated to his father, including responsibility for Persia's foreign policy, as a preliminary to his being named heir apparent.[1]

When in June Henry Ellis learnt what was happening, he was both puzzled and displeased: Campbell had done just what he had been told not to do. The commercial negotiations were more likely to be contentious than the political, because the British were asking for trade concessions. Ellis had hoped that, were the amendments to the political treaty settled first, even if the Persians had not been satisfied, they might have interpreted the revisions as an attempt to protect the integrity and independence of Persia, and, had they made new demands, Campbell could have bargained them against the immediate nomination of an heir apparent.[2]

Nothing more was done until September, when Campbell sent home the draft of a commercial treaty based on the terms agreed with Abbas Mirza the previous year. Mahomet Mirza and his minister were in favour of the treaty, as Abbas Mirza had been, but the shah was not, because he had been offered nothing to equal the customs revenue which would be earned by the government of Azerbaijan. Campbell was equally unenthusiastic. A commercial treaty would not help Britain through the succession crisis, and, given the chaotic conditions in Persia, encouraging merchants to travel there, who could not be protected, would be a 'serious and unwarrantable responsibility'. 'I cannot conceal from your Lordship', Campbell told Palmerston, 'my opinion that no beneficial result could possibly spring from the conclusion of a treaty to our commercial interests, at a moment when the spirit

---

[1] Encls. in Campbell to Palmerston, no. 1, 9 Apr. 1834, F.O. 60/34; same to McNaghten, 9 Apr. 1834, I.O. India/SP/1, 24 June 1834, no. 9.

[2] 'Memorandum [by H. Ellis] on the Recent Despatches from Persia', 5 June 1834, F.O. 60/35.

and strength of this government are in a visible course of decline.'[1] The British in the near east were as usual running fast and getting nowhere. The expansion of trade was meant to bring order to Persia, so making the treaty of Teheran unnecessary. Campbell was now saying that a closer political connection would be needed to improve the terms of trade, and that trade would not lead to prosperity and tranquillity, because one depended on the other.

The board of control could not understand why. Despite the setback in 1831, the number of packages imported through Trebizond for Persia had risen from 7,000 in 1830 to nearly 10,000 in 1833, and to over 11,500 in 1834. In 1835 the number was to rise to nearly 20,000, despite the refusal of the Turks to copy the European practice of charging only $\frac{1}{2}$ per cent in transit duties.[2] More important to the British, who saw the increased export of cotton goods as the best way to win the Great Game in Asia, cottons accounted for 90 per cent of all European imports into Trebizond, and 80 per cent of them were British. Here, according the James Brant, was a chance to develop an east–west trade-route to match the north–south route Alexander Burnes had visualized from the Indus towards Bokhara. In 1832 the Russians had extended their customs barriers to Georgia, and introduced vexatious restrictions upon trade at the mouth of the Danube. Overland through Georgia, or down the Danube and across the Black Sea, were the traditional routes taken by European goods bound for Persia. By 1834 Brant had again become confident that the British could undercut them by shipping straight to Trebizond.

In September, when Campbell was blighting hopes of trade, Brant encouraged them, but his condition was the same. A British consul must be posted at Erzerum, because the convention of St. Petersburg had moved the Russian frontier to within twelve miles of the caravan route to Persia; unless the British were seen to be watching closely, it could easily be closed. Except for this

[1] Campbell to Palmerston, no. 2, 18 Sept. 1834, same to Backhouse, nos. 3–4, 17 Sept. 1834, F.O. 60/34.

[2] 'Report [by H. Suter] on the Trade of Trebizond for the Year 1835', in Suter to Palmerston, no. 12, 31 Dec. 1835, F.O. 78/265; 'Memorandum [by C. H. Burgess] on the Communications and Relations between Great Britain and Persia', 5 Sept. 1835, in Backhouse to Lack, 14 Jan. 1836, B.T. 1/316. The figures for the trade were published by C. Issawi, 'The Tabriz–Trabzon Trade, 1830–1900: Rise and Decline of a Route', *International Journal of Middle East Studies*, i (1971), 18–27. They are not very satisfactory for the early period.

political problem, Brant claimed travel in eastern Turkey to be 'free and easy', and Palmerston chose to believe him.[1] So did the board of trade, who in November gave up their opposition to the posting of a consul at Erzerum, because it 'would be highly advantageous to the public service'.[2] James Fraser, who had had a dreadful journey through Anatolia to Azerbaijan the previous winter, knew better. Although the Turks had temporarily pacified the Kurds around Diabekir and Erzerum, expecting them to stay quiet would be naive: 'in such a country firmans from sultan or pasha are but waste paper'.[3]

Whether conditions were too disturbed to make a commercial treaty worth bothering about was not the only cause of difficulty in revising the treaty of Teheran. The negotiations were also entangled with the issue of Anglo-Afghan relations. The purpose of removing article nine was to prevent this; instead the expedition of Shah Shuja to Kandahar caused great resentment against Britain in Persia. The Persians assumed that the government of India had supplied Shah Shuja with men as well as money, which 'was unfriendly to Persia', who in memory of Nadir Shah laid claim to Kandahar.[4] Campbell could not convince them that they were mistaken, that the British would not oppose Persia in Afghanistan. This is not surprising, as it was not true.

One can understand why the Persians should have wished to postpone the revision of the treaty of Teheran, because the British were offering little; it is hard to see why Campbell was equally reticent. The aim of the negotiation was just what he denied, to show both the Kajars and the Russians that the British were determined to maintain Persia as a buffer state, but also to delineate her eastern frontier by separating Anglo-Persian from Anglo-Afghan relations. Until the Persians agreed to remove article nine, Herat could not be treated by the British as part of Afghanistan, nor as the western boundary of the Indian political system. Were Persia permitted to capture Herat, and to put forward claims to Kandahar and Kabul, the political frontier of British India would be pushed back beyond the Hindu Kush.

---

[1] 'Remarks [by J. Brant] on the Trade of Erzerum', in Brant to Palmerston, no. 2, 10 Sept. 1834, with minute of Palmerston, 14 Nov. 1834, F.O. 78/241.

[2] Lack to Shee, 17 Nov. 1834, B.T. 3/25, p. 354.

[3] Fraser, *Winter's Journey*, i. 257.

[4] Encls. 1–2 in Campbell to sc, 23 Sept. 1834, I.O. Persia/51.

The negotiations again broke down when they were resumed in the winter of 1834; Campbell again did what he had been told not to do. Even Charles Grant, who believed that British trade reformed, had been persuaded that in Persia it was preferable to hold back Russia, by denying her the opportunity to interfere, rather than to demand similar opportunities for Britain; that it was therefore preferable not to demand the right to post consuls anywhere in Persia, just because the Russians had it, in order to help the Persians in their struggle since 1828 to prevent the Russians from acting on it. Instead in March 1835 Campbell demanded equal rights for Britain, which caused a crisis when the Persians immediately refused. This 'singular and ungrateful' conduct, concluded Campbell, 'indicates as much fear of England as of Russia'. In fact the Persians had merely taken the British at their word. Having been told so often that the two states had complementary interests, and that Britain would never threaten the independence of Persia, the Persians assumed, as the British had always assumed about them, that they need offer no inducement, because the British would be bound to fight Russia on their behalf.

The Persians, Campbell said,[1]

believe that the interests of Great Britain are so intimately allied with those of Persia that she cannot separate herself from the policy she has hitherto pursued, and [s]he is impressed with the idea that no other resource is left to England but to support Persia at almost any cost, and that no other country but Persia could be made a barrier between Russia and our eastern provinces.

Campbell blamed this on the new shah's chief minister (although it was precisely what he himself had argued), previously thought by everyone including Campbell to be the only honest man in Persia, but who was now accused of being a Russian puppet. When he was assassinated in June, and at least a suspicion exists that Campbell had encouraged the shah to have him killed, Campbell hoped to do better in the negotiations. Again he failed.

The Kajars, tutored for so long by Malcolm, Macdonald, and Campbell, had joined the Bombay School of Indian defence, and had learned their lesson better than had been expected. Because, even if the Russians captured Khiva, they could not invade India

[1] Campbell to Palmerston, no. 2, 12 Mar. 1835, F.O. 60/38.

without first subduing Persia to guard their flank, Persia remained the best place beyond the North-West Frontier at which the British could hold them back. The Persian Connection had always been expressed symbolically. The British had hoped that their recent expression of interest would help them to disentangle themselves from the embarrassment of close relations with Persia, and finally to separate the European and Indian political systems. In 1835 the Persian mission was returned from the East India Company to the Crown, because the Persian Connection, 'more connected with European politics and negotiations than with Indian . . . can be better controlled and directed from this country'.[1] The British had finally tried to correct Canning's mistake. They were too late. Persia, used to fifteen years of neglect, interpreted four years of attention to mean that 'England is determined to preserve her alliance at all costs and support her at all risks'.[2]

Ellis's experiences in Persia in 1835 supported the arguments he had been making since his previous visit in 1814. The Persian Connection must be broken, and Persia treated only as a buffer state, where Britain in future would match Russian influence by threats as often as by inducements.

I really believe [said] Ellis that Persia can never be of much use to us in contributing to the protection of our Indian empire, and I am quite sure that in the event of war between England and Russia, she would be more likely to act against than with us, and I came to the conclusion that we must look nearer to India for defensive alliances.[3]

This meant that the British must defend India by seeking in Afghanistan the paramount influence they had failed to keep up in Persia, and could not expect to keep up as soon as they had to compete against Russia. Ideally this could be managed by expanding Britain's trade through Sind and Afghanistan to Bokhara. If trade could end the unrest, particularly by ending the slave trade, Khiva and Bokhara might copy Afghanistan, and be turned under British supervision into the stable and territorial states they must become, were they to act as a buffer zone between the Russians in

---

[1] 'Memorandum on the Reasons why the Persian Mission was Transferred from the Company to the Crown', 9 May 1850, F.O. 60/214.

[2] Memorandums by Campbell, encls. 4–5 in Ellis to Palmerston, no. 8, 6 Oct. 1835, F.O. 60/37.

[3] Ellis to Palmerston, private, 15 Jan. 1836, Broadlands MSS. GC/EL/41.

the Caucasus and the British in Afghanistan, and were the Russians to be prevented from expanding eastwards from the Caspian.

This was to be an extension of the buffer zone in Turkey and Persia, between the Russians in the Black Sea and the Caspian and the British in the Mediterranean and the Persian Gulf. Nothing would be gained by returning the Persian mission to the foreign office, unless Persia could be separated from the Indian political system. The British purpose in revising the treaty of Teheran had been to draw the frontier between European and Asiatic politics in Khorassan, by persuading Persia to agree that the Afghans were to control Herat. Were Persia, aided by Russia, to capture Herat, the stability of British India would be permanently in jeopardy, because Russia might 'proclaim a crusade against British India, in which she would be joined by all the warlike restless tribes that formed the overwhelming force of Timur'.[1] Britain could not allow the Kajars to capture Herat, once they were bound by treaty to permit the Russians to accompany them.

The probable effects of the capture by Persia of Herat were not some distant speculation, as liberal historians like J. L. Morison, who mocked Englishmen for worrying about how to defend British India, have often implied. By the terms of the treaty of Turkmanchay, if Persia captured Herat, and Russia could develop her trade with Khorassan, she was entitled to post at Herat a consul with a staff of ten. As distinguishing between commercial and political activities had long been proved impossible in central Asia, the Russians at Herat would have been far better placed to influence Afghan politics than the British at Teheran or Ludhiana. At the least, the buffer zone between the European and Indian political systems would have been extended eastwards to Quetta and Peshawar, and the political frontier of British India pushed back to the Indus.

Unless the British, by the annexation of the Punjab and Sind, could turn the Indus into the military, as well as the political, frontier of British India, they would be forced to defend India by counter-action in Europe, in circumstances likely to make such a policy ineffective. The gravest danger to the stability of British India, as everyone from Ellenborough to Sir Charles Metcalfe, from Lord William Bentinck to Charles Grant, and including

[1] Minute of Bentinck, 13 Mar. 1835, I.O. India/MP/35/12, 13 Mar. 1835, no. 11.

Henry Ellis who taught Palmerston, understood, was not the threat of Russian invasion. Russia had no need to invade India: if she could create unrest along the North-West Frontier, or amongst Britain's Indian allies, she would have succeeded where Napoleon failed, because the effect of this lever over British policy would be to carry Russia one step farther towards the creation of a European empire. On the Great Game in Asia, the best British substitute for the Persian Connection, might depend not only the stability of British India but the balance of power in Europe.

XI

Conclusion: The Rules of the Game

> Whose game was empires, and whose stakes were thrones?
> Whose table earth—whose dice were human bones?
>
> BYRON,
> *The Age of Bronze*

THE EASTERN QUESTION (or what should be done with Turkey) and the Great Game in Asia (or how should the British defend India) were two of the great diplomatic puzzles of the nineteenth century, which baffled British statesmen and diplomatists then, and have baffled military and diplomatic historians ever since. The experience of the British between 1828 and 1834 convinced them that if they could solve one they could solve both: historians often forget that one cannot be studied without the other. Two connections between them were obvious. If it could be done anywhere, the best place for a sea power to attack Russia was the Black Sea; the best way to limit Russian expansion was to treat Turkey and Persia as a buffer between the European and Indian political systems. Between 1798 and 1907, whether to prevent France from offering Turkey and Persia to Russia in return for recognition of a French empire in Europe, for which Wellesley and Castlereagh fought to destroy the treaty of Tilsit, to prevent Russia from acting as if she were invulnerable, for which Palmerston and Clarendon fought the Crimean War, or to prevent Austria and Russia from partitioning the Balkans, for which Disraeli and Salisbury manoeuvred patiently and successfully during the Great Eastern Crisis and at the congress of Berlin, on the integrity and independence of Turkey and Persia rested both the security of British India and the European balance of power.

To the British, the integrity of Turkey and Persia meant by 1834 that the two states were to be territories, marked on a map in 1829, and recognized by Russia in the treaties of Turkmanchay and Adrianople. This device, although useful, was not sufficient. The frontiers of Turkey suited neither the Russians in the Caucasus, nor Mahomet Ali, dreaming of independence. After the capture of Erivan and Nakitchevan, which controlled the routes from the Caucasus to Azerbaijan and Irak, the Russians were content with the frontier between the Caucasus and Persia. The key to the security of British India was the location of Persia's unsettled eastern frontier, which the British wanted to be drawn to the west of Herat. If British India were to be secure, Herat must not become part of Persia.

Had Herat been annexed by Persia, Afghanistan would have become part of the buffer zone between the European and Indian political systems, in which the British always had difficulty matching Russia's influence; the political frontier of British India would have been pushed back to the Khyber Pass; and the British would have been barred from Turkestan, which they planned to turn into an extension of the Indian political system, before Russia could extend into it the European system. Britain's greatest difficulty, in creating a buffer zone, and in limiting the expansion of Russia in the near east, was in countering her claim, that as a neighbour of Turkey in Europe and Asia, and of Persia in Asia, she had a greater interest in what happened there than Britain. As soon as the role played by Turkey and Persia in the European balance of power was recognized by the British, they tried to extend to the near east one principle of the concert of Europe, that the concerns of any great power were the concern of all, and that all great powers must subordinate individual ambition to the general need for peace, in order not to destroy the balance of equilibrium.

The British would have preferred to draw a frontier between the European and Indian political systems; they settled for a buffer zone, only when they realized that the frontier would have to be drawn so far east as to endanger them. While the British had ignored the connection between European and Indian politics, the Russians had pushed the frontier between them eastwards from Georgia during the Napoleonic Wars, to the Mahometan Khanates after the treaty of Gulistan, to Khorassan after the treaty of Turkmanchay, and threatened, were Herat captured by Persia, to push it beyond the Khyber Pass. The British, who assumed that Persia attacked Herat at the suggestion of Russia, could not permit Persia to be turned into a Russian protectorate, as long as Afghanistan was divided into four weak and sometimes warring principalities, and Turkestan was divided between oasis states, whose nomadic populations were to be settled before the Russians advanced eastwards from the Caspian towards Khiva. The British, who, by subordinating during the Napoleonic Wars and after the needs of Indian defence to the balance of power in Europe, had missed their chance to defend India in Persia, were determined after 1828 not to repeat their mistake in Afghanistan. If they could not turn Persia into a protectorate, Afghanistan must be turned into one.

Although a buffer zone was Britain's second choice to a frontier between the European and Indian political systems, the need to create and maintain it explains much of Britain's policy in the near east between 1828 and 1834. Not until Mahomet Ali invaded Anatolia after the battle of the Beylan Pass did he threaten the sultan's European function, the control of the Straits. His Asiatic function had been threatened earlier, as soon as the board of control decided, however wrongly, that the Egyptian occupation of Syria would lead to the invasion of Baghdad and the creation of an Arab state, temporarily powerful but permanently unstable. The British did not have to choose which of these interests to defend, or were too slow to do so, because the Russian protectorate over Turkey, established by the treaty of Unkiar Skelessi, was equally threatening to both. The British dilemma in 1833 was not whether to believe that Russia's policy was peaceful, but how to convince her that it would have to be, because Britain knew how to hold her back. The British had to decide not only where and how to defend British India, but how and where to bring pressure against Russia.

As soon as the British decided that the difficulty of defending British India might leave them exposed to Russian pressure in Europe, they had to beware of choosing between their European and Asiatic interests. They knew that ignoring Europe was not an answer: neither tories nor whigs would have agreed with A. J. P. Taylor's claim, that 'we have been most secure when we kept out of Europe'.[1] He meant, of course, but it would not have suited his argument to say so, that Britain was most secure when able to keep out of Europe; her ability depended not on policy but power, and her power depended partly upon India. The British could not curb Russia in Europe until they had discovered how to defend British India. The British never did discover, nor did they curb

[1] A. J. P. Taylor, 'The Road to Ruin', *Sunday Express*, 13 July 1971.

the power of Russia, except twice temporarily, in the Crimea and at the congress of Berlin, when they did both at once, thanks to Count Buol the first time and Prince Bismarck the second. The British knew that a peripheral state depends upon the performance of its allies; unfortunately, when Austria and Germany refused to serve, Persia and Afghanistan were a poor substitute.

British agents in the near east were naturally anxious to make their activities important. To them they seemed so. Often of humble birth, they were spellbound by the age and grandeur of the East. Despite this, they were confident that given the right opportunity they could make their mark; half the near east was the responsibility of the East India Company, whose employees had gone out to India with this in mind. Their harassed and forgetful superiors saw only that they must learn strange names and grapple, if only momentarily, with rulers and places of which they had never heard and in whom they took no interest. Most Englishmen assumed that the less attention paid to local conditions the more sensible the policy. In the near east knowledge was not needed for understanding; Britain's security depended upon the self-confident exercise of power. This did not mean that all British initiatives were likely to succeed; only that attempting to mould policy to local conditions which Englishmen could not understand was likely to fail.

Between 1828 and 1834, the British, taught by Lord Ellenborough and Henry Ellis, learnt that the best way to curb Russia in the near east, while ignoring local conditions, was to seek stability. This was not to be confused with order. Canning had always objected to a policy in south America based upon trying to preserve order, because it would entangle Britain in the internal affairs of other states; Ellis argued that in the near east it would lead instead to collisions. He objected to a connection with Persia based on the power of Abbas Mirza, to one with Baghdad based on the power of Daud, and to one with Egypt based on the power of Mahomet Ali. Whereas their power was transitory so might not outlive them, and supporting them might invite France or Russia to support their rivals, the sultan and the shah were heads of states which could survive. Whether their states were strong or orderly did not matter to Britain, as long as their frontiers were settled and the great powers would agree not to interfere in their internal affairs. Because Britain had no interest in the near east except to keep out others, she had to avoid interfering there herself, except as far as was necessary to restrain them.

This lesson was learned only after embarrassments in Turkey and Persia had shown that trying to outbid Russia for influence was likely to fail, and the rule applied only in the half of the near east belonging to the European political system, in which, as a peripheral and naval power with a comparatively stable social and political structure, Britain was secure against the effects of all changes in the balance of power short of the creation of a European empire. Beyond the North-West Frontier of British India, the British had to create states in central Asia able to forestall the expansion of Russia towards Khiva, because, as a foreign élite ruling a varied and often discontented population, they were exposed in Asia to the dangers besetting the Hapsburg Monarchy in Europe, and had to assume that disorder was contagious and must quickly be suppressed. Since the landing of Bonaparte in Egypt in 1798, the British had decided that India must be defended as far away and as cheaply as possible.[1]

To decide where was easy, to decide how and by whom was difficult. The ideal, because the cheapest, means was trade. Between 1828 and 1834 Utopian utilitarians, who tried hard to seize control of Britain's policy in central Asia, were confident that Britain's goods would export her values. Robinson and Gallagher explained that 'the British political arm had first to break open each area to trade before the technique of control through collaborating classes could operate, and this, in official thinking, was necessary work for diplomats with gunboats in the offing'.[2] This explanation needs to be turned around. Platt countered that British merchants demanded less;[3] the utilitarians demanded more. Trade was to go before and as a substitute for politics, and they aimed not at collaboration but social revolution. The demands of trade would lead to security for property and the fruits of hard work, the only basis for political stability and social order. British India could be most easily and cheaply defended, if Turcomans, Afghans, and Indians, were turned quickly into copies of Englishmen.

---

[1] G. J. Alder, 'Britain and the Defence of India—The Origins of the Problem, 1798–1815', *Journal of Asian History*, vi (1972), 16–17.

[2] Robinson and Gallagher, *Africa and the Victorians*, pp. 5–6.

[3] Platt, 'Further Objections', p. 85.

The Great Game in Asia was not only a plan for action beyond the North-West Frontier, it also depended upon a decision as to where the frontier should be. After pointing out the difficulties of finding satisfactory frontiers, John S. Galbraith concluded, that regardless of the character of the governor-general, the expansion of British India continued almost without interruption throughout the first half of the nineteenth century.[1] The years when Lord William Bentinck governed British India must be seen as one interruption. Under the influence of the utilitarians' most determined opponent in defence policy, Sir Charles Metcalfe, Bentinck pursued a policy of conscious territorial restraint, hoping to establish beyond the North-West Frontier a balance of power between the Punjab, Afghanistan, and Sind, based, as the British conceived the balance of power in Europe, and hoped to create a similar balance in Turkey and Persia, upon respect for the territorial integrity of other states, symbolized by general recognition of their frontiers. The attempt failed, because the Indus states would respect one another only out of fear of the British. If the British were to connect themselves with the states beyond their North-West Frontier, they had to accept the role of paramount power.

Utilitarianism and evangelicalism were the most seductive and influential modes of thought in early nineteenth-century Britain. Underlying their Utopian vision was a realistic calculation of power; or an acknowledgement that any other defence policy for British India would force the British realistically to calculate their power. The simplest and apparently most sensible way to defend British India would have been to defeat a European invader at the border of Turkey and Persia, somewhere between Mosul and Tabriz. This was once planned, in 1808, and failed disastrously when tried in the First World War. Unfortunately, sending a British army to the near east was bound to prove embarrassingly expensive; might embarrass Britain's relations with the states who were to be the battleground; and, however useful during the Napoleonic Wars against a French invasion from Poland, could not prevent the Russians' marching from Khiva up the Oxus or from Astarabad to Herat. Fighting in the near east defeated its own object. A temporary and military measure intended to repel

[1] Galbraith, 'The "Turbulent Frontier"', p. 155.

actual invasion, it could contribute to the tranquillity of British India, neither by preventing threats of invasion, nor by matching Russian political influence in Turkey and Persia.

The Indian Army were not meant to fight, certainly not to fight Europeans; should they have had to, they were not expected to win. Their proper function was to exist. At their most useful they were a police force, perhaps not even that; rather a splendid symbol. They triumphed like the British navy by keeping in being, but their task was harder. The navy at Jutland, for example, had only to avoid defeat: victory in battle was not asked of them. The Indian Army had to avoid going into battle. Having to fight would itself signify that they had failed to overawe.

Had the British fought in the near east to defend India, they would have acted as a continental state; whereas they always hoped to reproduce in Asia their privileged peripheral position in Europe. The British sought continuously an ally to defend India on their behalf. During the Napoleonic Wars the British hoped the Turks would drive Bonaparte from Egypt, that the Russians would prevent his making use of his alliance with Persia.[1] Against Russia after 1829 the choice appeared more difficult: Persia and Afghanistan were not Russia, not even Turkey. Therefore the British tried not to choose between them. They treated the near-eastern states as Newcastle and Chatham had treated the states of Europe: all of them were expected to form a grand alliance against any state named by the British as a threat to the balance of power. The last such alliance was the Baghdad Pact. This policy appeared to satisfy every British requirement. An actual invasion, could their allies defeat it, would be defeated far away; the British, supplying arms and ammunition, or a subsidy in an emergency, should be able to limit their expenses; and a permanent connection should help to ensure the permanence of British influence.

These advantages were vitiated by the apparent drawback that the near-eastern states were all at odds with one another. The British had to act as if they would always be willing to subordinate their differences in order to co-operate with Britain. However foolish, this assumption was equally shrewd. Any other basis for co-operation would have entangled the British in unsolvable local

[1] For a general discussion of the period before 1828 see E. Ingram, 'The Rules of the Game: A Commentary upon the Defence of British India, 1798–1829', *Journal of Imperial and Commonwealth History*, iii (1974–5), 257–79.

quarrels, of no interest to them, and which would not otherwise have affected them. The British interest in the near east was sometimes European, sometimes imperial, but never local. Quarrels between near-eastern states could be ignored by the British, only until they demanded stability in the area; as soon as they visualized a near-eastern balance of power matching the balance of power in Europe, as a balance between frontiers drawn on maps, local quarrels had to cease. Unfortunately, the near-eastern kingdoms were not territorial states. The British had to persuade them to act as if they were, and to persuade European states to treat them as they would one another.

Because of the difficulty, either of sending a British army to fight in the near east, or of relying upon an ally, three methods were considered by which the British might both maintain sufficient influence to ensure stability, and, should it prove necessary, defeat a European invasion. The first, which descended into the Punjab School of Indian defence, followers of John Lawrence's principle of 'masterly inactivity', implied that the North-West Frontier should be defended at the frontier. This was actually a political not a military calculation: the British could ignore developments in the near-eastern states, because none of them was strong enough to cause unrest in British India, whereas any European state strong enough to try was too far away. One of the obstacles would be the quarrels between the near-eastern states. Attacking British India would be as difficult as defending it, because obtaining the help of one state along the route was a guarantee of the enmity of the next.

Even the most alarmed Englishmen never doubted that a British army sent out to India would defeat a European invasion, but planning to fight at the North-West Frontier would do nothing, either to curb the expansion of Russia, to match Russian influence in the near-eastern states, or to guard British India from its unsettling effects. The success of such a policy depended on the utilitarians' and evangelicals' Utopian belief that, given a little time, Indians would grow content with British rule and eager to prevent its overthrow. Conservative imperialists, for example Sir John Malcolm, who had no such illusions, had nevertheless an alternative method of preventing European invasion and curbing the expansion of Russia, free from both the complexities of local politics and the need to fight at the North-West Frontier. This, as

Wolseley later argued in opposition to Roberts, meant attacking Russia in Europe: the Great Game in Asia should be treated when necessary as part of the European balance of power. Wolseley talked of attacking Russia all over the world, but by the 1880s it was difficult to imagine where he could mean; unless he meant in alliance with Germany, which was one reason why the Germans in the 1890s would not agree to an alliance. Earlier Wolseley's meaning would have been obvious, in the Black Sea. In the Crimean War, as far as Palmerston was responsible for defining British policy, it was free for once from its usual dilemma: restoring the balance of power in Europe itself increased the security of British India.

If the British were to stop short of a major European war, for which they would need an ally, trying to defend British India by threatening to retaliate in Europe was likely, as the Dardanelles Expedition had proved in 1807, and as Wellington and Aberdeen if not Palmerston understood, to reveal the limits of sea power. The British found an Asiatic alternative, or frequently hoped that they had found it, in an island fortress in the Persian Gulf. Ideally, this would have prevented any potentially threatening European influence in the near east, by providing a safe market for merchants from Persia, Arabia, and Baghdad, and a method by which British manufactures might be reintroduced into the area. From a fortress in the Persian Gulf, the British could also have exerted equivalent pressure to Russia against the near-eastern states, and when necessary intervened by force. That the governors of the southern provinces of Persia and the Turkish governors of Baghdad would be most susceptible to British influence, and could be used to influence their superiors at Teheran and Constantinople, became an accepted principle of British policy. Although the results were not always equal to British expectations, the attractions of the policy were obvious: it seemed to offer a cheap method of preventing the Russians' marching from Astarabad to Herat.

The British never built this fortress: none of the islands was habitable, and the shah of Persia, except on the occasion in 1813 when he seemed willing to turn Persia into a British protectorate, would not agree. Between 1828 and 1834 a variation of the policy was the British obsession with steamers. Steamers on the Indus, based on a fortress at Bukkur, or a connection with the amirs of

Sind, were to block the Bolan Pass and the Khyber Pass; more important, they were to curb the expansion of Russia and the political upheaval expected to follow, by ferrying British manufactures towards Afghanistan and Bokhara. Similarly, steamers on the Euphrates were to defend Mahmud II against the Egyptians and Russians, by preventing his needing to invoke the treaty of Unkiar Skelessi. Because steamers seemed to provide a method by which naval power could be exercised far inland, the British debated between 1828 and 1834 what should be expected of them and how they should be used.

As soon as the defence of British India was transformed by the treaties of Turkmanchay and Adrianople from a military into a political problem, not how to defend India from invasion but how to curb the expansion of Russia, the British had to try to maintain stability in the near east, without having to maintain order. Rejuvenation, as it used to be called, meant one of two types of reform; social revolution meant to turn Indian and near-eastern states into copies of liberal Britain, or military and diplomatic assistance meant to buttress existing political and social systems. The two usually became entwined and handicapped each other. If the social revolution were to be brought about by trade, trade would have meanwhile to be protected. To provide British protection would belie the object of obtaining security cheaply and without effort; to ask the rulers of near-eastern states to protect trade was to ask them to protect the instrument of their own destruction. The amirs of Sind so stoutly resisted the British demand to open the Indus to British ships, because they knew they could not protect British trade. Trying to govern Sind, not merely rule it, would provoke tribal warfare, the disorder the British wanted the amirs to prevent, and would lead to further British intervention.

The situation was the same in Turkey during the First Mahomet Ali Crisis. In 1832 Palmerston, guided by Stratford Canning, who like members of the secretariat at Bombay applied abstract principles, and did not need to ask questions about local conditions because he knew the answers, aimed at social revolution in Turkey. Mahmud II signed the treaty of Unkiar Skelessi partly because British demands for better government seemed likely to endanger his regime as much as the Egyptian victories. Only the terms of the treaty made Palmerston realize that Britain could not hope to turn

Turkey into a protectorate and must be satisfied with a buffer. The British answer to the famous change in Russian policy, from planning to partition Turkey to maintaining her as a protectorate, was internationally agreed frontiers, followed by such administrative changes as might buttress the existing political system. The expansion of British trade was to be encouraged, not because the values built into British manufactures were contagious, but to increase the revenue of the near-eastern states. Platt may be right to argue that British merchants knew that trade in the near east could not be expanded, because the British who had goods to sell could find little to buy; the government knew that, however marginal, the trade must be encouraged, because its function was to increase security not profit.

In the seven years between 1828 and 1834 this change took place in British policy in Persia as well as Turkey. Protectorates could be set up only in areas out of reach of Russia, and only then at the risk of frontier wars. Since Mountstuart Elphinstone's mission to Shah Shuja at Peshawar in 1808, the British had known that a connection with Afghanistan would lead to war with the Sikhs or Sind. By 1834 they were offered an alternative but equally uncomfortable choice, that led to two disastrous invasions of Afghanistan. If the security of British India were to depend on curbing the territorial expansion and political influence of Russia in the near east, by the creation of a buffer zone between the European and Indian political systems, it would have to be extended into Turkestan, to prevent the expansion of Russia towards Khiva, and thence south-eastwards along the Oxus towards Afghanistan. This meant expanding trade to bring about social revolution, because, until Khiva and Bokhara had been persuaded to end the slave trade, and preferably to replace nomadic by settled habits, Russia would be given opportunities, and might be compelled, to intervene, and could not be expected to treat Turkestan, like Turkey and Persia, as a recognized territory, nor to agree that a Russian advance on Khiva would affect a vital British interest.

By 1834 it was clear to the British, that should Khiva fall to Russia and Herat to Persia, the buffer zone between the European and Indian political systems would have been extended, by the incorporation of Afghanistan, so far east as to be of little use, and that the policy demanding restraint in Persia and Turkey, in an attempt to impose similar restraint on Russia, demanded bold initiatives in Afghanistan and Turkestan, were the British to be able to restrain Russia in the future. The difference in method is obvious and absolute, and reflected the equally obvious and absolute difference between Britain's European role as a peripheral and naval power, and her Asiatic role as a continental and military power. In central Asia, where Russia could not be expected to recognize the common threat of her own expansion, stability depended on a balance not of equilibrium but tension: each state pursuing its own aims would be held back only by the power of others. A fact of geography, that the British had a frontier to defend, and a fact of politics, that they could find no one to defend it for them, were the origins of the Great Game in Asia.

These were the aims and the rules of the Great Game in Asia. To play by them was impossible, because they were contradictory, but the game itself was odd. The object was not to win; but not to lose. The British lost eventually, but not for a long time, and gracefully. Meanwhile, throughout the nineteenth century, with the confidence born of right reasoning and equal ignorance of the facts, countless young Englishmen scoured the near east to find proof of Russian activities and explain how they might be stopped. As they learnt more, they grew hesitant, but between 1828 and 1834 they were at their most bold, ambitious, and self-confident. Admire their achievement; do not puzzle about whence it came. Empires are built by the slightly mad.

Bibliography

MANUSCRIPT SOURCES

I OFFICIAL CORRESPONDENCE

A. *India Office Library, India Office Records*

(i) *Home Correspondence*

I.O. E/2/29–50	Letters from the Board of Control to the East India Company
I.O. E/2/51–4	Appendix to Letters from the Board of Control to the East India Company
I.O. F/1/1–7	Minutes of the Board of Control
I.O. F/2/1–20	Letter Books of the Board of Control
I.O. E/2/1–27	Letters from the East India Company to Board of Control
I.O. E/2/55–57	Correspondence between the Court of Directors and the Board of Control
I.O. L/PS/3/1	Secret Committee Miscellany Book
I.O. L/PS/3/117–84	Political General Correspondence

(ii) *Outgoing Correspondence*

I.O. L/PS/5/537–82	Board of Control's Drafts of Secret Letters and Despatches
I.O. L/PS/6/237–46	Political Letters to Bengal
I.O. L/PS/6/248–70	Political Letters to India
I.O. L/PS/6/411–90	Political Letters to Bombay

(iii) *Incoming Correspondence*

I.O. G/29/–	Factory Records (Persia and Persian Gulf)
I.O. Persia/–	Secret Letters from Persia [not yet numbered in L/PS/9]
I.O. L/PS/5/1–18	Secret Letters from Bengal
I.O. L/PS/5/80–125	Enclosures to Secret Letters from Bengal
I.O. L/PS/5/20–63	Secret Letters from India
I.O. L/PS/5/126–76	Enclosures to Secret Letters from India
I.O. L/PS/5/321–58	Secret Letters to Bombay
I.O. L/PS/5/363–509	Enclosures to Secret Letters from Bombay
I.O. L/PS/6/16–46	Political Letters from Bengal
I.O. L/PS/6/49–82	Political Letters from India

| I.O. L/PS/6/169–218 | Political Letters from Bombay |
| I.O. L/E/3/– | Revenue Letters from Bengal |

(iv) *India Correspondence*

I.O. Bengal/SPC/–	Bengal Secret and Political Consultations
I.O. India/SP/–	India Secret Proceedings
I.O. India/MP/–	India Military Proceedings
I.O. Bombay/SP/–	Bombay Secret Proceedings
I.O. Bombay/SPP/–	Bombay Secret and Political Proceedings
I.O. Bombay/PP/–	Bombay Political Proceedings

(v) *Miscellaneous Correspondence*

| I.O. H/– | Home Miscellaneous Series |
| I.O. L/MAR/C/– | Marine Miscellaneous Series |

B *Public Record Office*

(i) *Board of Trade Records*

B.T. 1/–	(In Letters)
B.T. 2/–	(Foreign Office Correspondence)
B.T. 3/–	(Out Letters)

(ii) *Foreign Office Records*

F.O. 7/–	(Austria)
F.O. 27/–	(France)
F.O. 60/–	(Persia)
F.O. 65/–	(Russia)
F.O. 78/–	(Turkey)
F.O. 93/–	(Protocols of Treaties)
F.O. 97/–	(Supplementary Correspondence—Turkey)
F.O. 181/–	(Russian Embassy and Consular)
F.O. 248/–	(Persian Embassy and Consular)

(iii) *War Office Records*

| W.O. 1/– | (In Letters) |

II Private Papers

(i) *British Library*

Aberdeen Papers	Add. MSS. 43039–358
Auckland Papers	Add. MSS. 37689–718
Heytesbury Papers	Add. MSS. 41511–66
Holland House Manuscripts	Add. MSS. 51318–2254
Morier Papers	Add. MSS. 33839–44
Palmerston Papers	Add. MSS. 48417–589
Wellesley Papers	Add. MSS. 37274–318
Windham Papers	Add. MSS. 37842–95

(ii) *Public Record Office*

Aston Papers	F.O. 355/–
Colchester Papers	P.R.O. 30/9/–
Ellenborough Papers	P.R.O. 30/12/–
Granville Papers	P.R.O. 30/29/–
Pottinger Papers	F.O. 705/–
Stratford Canning Papers	F.O. 352/–

(iii) *India Office Library*

Broughton Papers	I.O. H/835–62
Campbell Papers	MSS. Eur. D/556
Cleveland Public Library Manuscripts	Film. MSS. 759–80
Duke University Manuscripts	Film. MSS. 2408
Malcolm Papers	I.O. H/733–7
Willock Papers	MSS. Eur. D/527

(iv) *Bodleian Library*

Russell of Swallowfield Papers

(v) *Historical Manuscripts Commission*

Broadlands Manuscripts

(vi) *National Library of Scotland*

Minto Papers

(vii) *National Library of Wales*

Kentchurch Court Manuscripts

(viii) *University of Edinburgh Library*

Macdonald Kinneir of Sanda Papers   E.U.L. MSS. Dk/2/–

(ix) *University of Nottingham Library*

Portland Papers

(x) *Department of Paleography and Diplomatic in the University of Durham*

Grey of Howick Papers

PRINTED SOURCES

I OFFICIAL PUBLICATIONS AND WORKS OF REFERENCE

Parliamentary Debates
Parliamentary Papers
AITCHISON, SIR C. U., ed., *A Collection of Treaties, Engagements,*

and Sanads relating to India and Neighbouring Countries (Calcutta, 1862).

HUREWITZ, J. C., ed., *Diplomacy in the Near and Middle East: A Documentary Record, 1535–1914* (2 vols., Princeton, 1965).

II DOCUMENTS, CORRESPONDENCE, AND MEMOIRS

ADAIR, SIR ROBERT, *Negotiations for the Peace of the Dardanelles in 1808–1809* (2 vols., London, 1845).

ARBUTHNOT, MRS., *The Journal of Mrs. Arbuthnot, 1820–1832*, ed. F. Bamford and duke of Wellington (London, 1950).

AVON, ANTHONY EDEN, 1ST EARL OF, *The Memoirs of the Rt. Hon. Sir Anthony Eden: Full Circle* (London, 1960).

BENEVENTO, CHARLES MAURICE DE TALLEYRAND-PERIGORD, PRINCE OF, *Mémoires complets et authentiques de Charles Maurice de Talleyrand, prince de Bénévent*, ed. A. F. de Bacourt (5 vols., Paris, 1967).

——, *Ambassade de Talleyrand à Londres, 1830–31*, ed. G. Pallain (New York, 1973).

BENTHAM, JEREMY, *The Works of Jeremy Bentham*, ed. J. Bowring (11 vols., London, 1838–43).

BROUGHTON, JOHN CAM HOBHOUSE, 1ST BARON, *Recollections of a Long Life*, ed. Lady Dorchester (6 vols., London, 1909–11).

ELLENBOROUGH, EDWARD LAW, 1ST EARL OF, *A Political Diary, 1828–1830*, ed. Lord Colchester (2 vols., London, 1881).

FREYGANG, WILHELM VON, *Letters from the Caucasus and Georgia* (London, 1832).

GREVILLE, CHARLES, *The Greville Memoirs: A Journal of the Reigns of King George IV, King William IV, and Queen Victoria*, ed. H. Reeve (8 vols., London, 1888).

HISTORICAL MANUSCRIPTS COMMISSION: *Report on the Manuscripts of J. B. Fortescue, Esq., Preserved at Dropmore* (10 vols., London, 1892–1929).

JACQUEMONT, VICTOR, *Correspondance de Victor Jacquemont . . . pendant son voyage dans l'Inde (1828–1832)* (2 vols., 4th edit., Paris, 1846).

LONDONDERRY, ROBERT STEWART, 1ST MARQUESS OF, *The Memoranda and Correspondence of Robert Stewart, Viscount Castlereagh*, ed. marquess of Londonderry (12 vols., London, 1848–54).

MACAULAY, T. B., 1st Baron, *Letters of Thomas Babington Macaulay*, ed. T. Pinney (vols. 1–2, Cambridge, 1974).

MELVILLE, HENRY DUNDAS, 1ST VISCOUNT, *Two Views of British India: The Private Correspondence of Mr. Dundas and Lord Wellesley, 1798–1801*, ed. Edward Ingram (Bath, 1970).

METCALFE, CHARLES METCALFE, 1ST BARON, *Selections from the Papers of Lord Metcalfe*, ed. Sir J. W. Kaye (London, 1855).

METTERNICH-WINNEBURG, CLEMENS, PRINCE OF, *Mémoires, documents et écrits divers laissé par le prince de Metternich*, ed. Prince Richard Metternich (8 vols., Paris, 1880–4).

NEUMANN, PHILIP VON, BARON, *The Diary of Philip von Neumann, 1819–1850*, ed. E. Beresford Chancellor (2 vols., London, 1928).

NESSELRODE, KARL ROBERT, COUNT OF, *Lettres et papiers du chancelier comte de Nesselrode, 1760–1850* (11 vols., Paris, 1904–12).

SWIFT, JONATHAN, *The Prose Works of Jonathan Swift*, ed. H. Davis (14 vols., Oxford, 1939–74).

WELLINGTON, ARTHUR WELLESLEY, 1ST DUKE OF, *Despatches, Correspondence, and Memoranda of Field-Marshal Arthur, Duke of Wellington*, ed. duke of Wellington (8 vols., London, 1867–78).

WILSON, THE RT. REVD. DANIEL, BISHOP OF CALCUTTA, *Bishop Wilson's Journal Letters*, ed. D. Wilson (London, 1863).

III TRAVELLERS' TALES AND POLITICAL PAMPHLETS

BARKER, JOHN, *Syria and Egypt during the Last Five Sultans of Turkey: Being Experiences during Fifty Years of Mr. Consul-General Barker*, ed. E. B. B. Barker (2 vols., London, 1876).

BURNES, SIR ALEXANDER, *Travels into Bokhara; Being an Account of a Journey from India to Kabul, Tartary, and Persia; also a Narrative of a Voyage on the Indus . . . in the Years 1831, 1832, and 1833* (3 vols., London, 1834).

BURNES, DR. JAMES, *Narrative of a Visit to the Court . . . of the Ameers of Sind* (Bombay, 1829).

CHESNEY, F. R., *Narrative of the Euphrates Expedition . . . during the Years 1835, 1836, and 1837* (London, 1868).

CONOLLY, ARTHUR, *Journey to the North of India, Overland from England through Russia, Persia and Afghanistan* (London, 1834).

CURZON, G. N., *Persia and the Persian Question* (2 vols., London, 1892).

FRASER, JAMES BAILLIE, *Narrative of a Journey into Khorassan in the Years 1821 and 1822* (London, 1825).

——, *Travels and Adventures in the Persian Provinces on the Southern Banks of the Caspian Sea* (London, 1826).

——, *A Winter's Journey from Constantinople to Teheran, with Travels through Various Parts of Persia* (2 vols., London, 1838).

——, *Travels in Koordistan, Mesopotamia, etc.* (2 vols., London, 1840).

GAMBA, J. F., *Voyage dans la Russie méridionale, et particulièrement dans les provinces situées au delà du Caucase, fait depuis 1820 jusqu'en 1824* (Paris, 1826).

GROVES, A. N., *Journal . . . during a Journey from London to Baghdad . . . also . . . of Some Months Residence at Baghdad* (London, 1831).
——, *Journal of a Residence at Baghdad during the Years 1830 and 1831* (London, 1832).

HOGG, E., *Visit to Alexandria, Damascus, and Jerusalem, during the Successful Campaign of Ibrahim Pasha* (London, 1835).

JACQUEMONT, VICTOR, *État Politique et social de L'Inde du nord en 1830: Extraits de son journal de voyage* (Paris, 1933).
——, *État politique et social de l'Inde du sud en 1832: Extraits de son journal de voyage* (Paris, 1934).

LACY EVANS, G. DE, *On the Designs of Russia* (London, 1828).
——, *On the Practicability of an Invasion of India* (London, 1829).

MACDONALD KINNEIR, JOHN, *A Geographical Memoir of the Persian Empire* (London, 1813).
——, *Journey through Asia Minor, Armenia and Kurdistan in . . . 1813 and 1814* (London, 1818).

MCNEILL, JOHN, *Progress and Present Position of Russia in the East* (London, 1836).

MASSON, CHARLES, *Narrative of Various Journeys* (4 vols., London, 1842–3).

MEYENDORFF, BARON GEORG VON, *Voyage d'Orenbourg à Bokhara fait en 1820* (Paris, 1826).

MONTEITH, WILLIAM, *Kars and Erzerum: With the Campaign of Prince Paskevich in 1828 and 1829* (London, 1856).

MORLEY, LORD, *Recollections* (2 vols., London, 1917).

MOURAVIEV, COUNT N. N., *Voyage en Turcomanie et à Khiva fait en 1819 et 1820* (Paris, 1823).

POTTINGER, HENRY, *Travels in Beloochistan and Sind* (London, 1816).

RAWLINSON, SIR HENRY, *England and Russia in the East* (London, 1875).

ROBERTS, CAPT. E., *Embassy to the Eastern Courts of Cochin-China, Siam, and Muscat . . . during the Years 1832, -3, -4* (New York, 1837).

STOCQUELER, J. H., *Fifteen Months Pilgrimage* (London, 1832).

TREVELYAN, C. E., *On the Education of the People of India* (London, 1838).

URQUHART, DAVID, *Turkey and its Resources* (London, 1833).
——, *Diplomatic Transactions in Central Asia, 1834–39* (London, 1841).

WADE, C. M., *A Narrative of Services, Military and Political, 1801–1844* (Ryde, 1847).

WOLFF, REVD. JOSEPH, *Travels and Adventures* (London, 1861).

IV MONOGRAPHS AND GENERAL WORKS

AFSHAR, MAHMUD, *La Politique européene en Perse* (Berlin, 1921).

ALDER, G. J., 'The Key to India?: Britain and the Herat Problem, 1830–1863', *Middle Eastern Studies*, x (1974), 186–209.

——, 'Britain and the Defence of India—The Origins of the Problem, 1798–1815', *Journal of Asian History*, vi (1972), 14–44.

ALEXANDER, C. M., *Baghdad in Bygone Days* (London, 1928).

ALGAR, H., *Religion and State in Iran, 1785–1906* (Berkeley/Los Angeles, 1969).

AMIN, A. A., *British Interests in the Persian Gulf* (Leiden, 1967).

ANDERSON, M. S., *Britain's Discovery of Russia, 1553–1815* (London, 1958).

——, *The Eastern Question, 1774–1923: A Study in International Relations* (London, 1966).

——, 'Eighteenth-Century Theories of Balance of Power', *Studies in Diplomatic History: Essays in Memory of David Bayne Horn*, eds. R. Hatton and M. S. Anderson (London, 1970), pp. 182–98.

AVERY, P., *Modern Iran* (Cambridge, 1967).

——, 'An Enquiry into the Outbreak of the Second Russo-Persian War, 1826–28', *Iran and Islam: Essays in Memory of the Late Vladimir Minorsky*, ed. C. E. Bosworth (Edinburgh, 1971), pp. 17–45.

BAKER, R. L., 'Palmerston and the Treaty of Unkiar Skelessi', *English Historical Review*, xliii (1928), 83–9.

BAKSHI, S. R., *British Diplomacy and Administration in India, 1807–1813* (New Delhi, 1970).

BARTLETT, C. J., *Great Britain and Sea Power, 1815–1853* (Oxford, 1965).

BADDELEY, J. F., *The Russian Conquest of the Caucasus* (London, 1908).

BAILEY, F. E., 'The Economics of British Foreign Policy, 1825–1850', *Journal of Modern History*, xii (1940), 449–84.

——, *British Policy and the Turkish Reform Movement: A Study in Anglo-Turkish Relations, 1826–1853* (Cambridge, Mass., 1942).

BALLHATCHETT, K., 'The Home Government and Bentinck's Educational Policy', *Historical Journal*, x (1952), 225–9.

——, *Social Policy and Social Change in Western India, 1817–1830* (London, 1957).

BEARCE, G. D., 'Lord William Bentinck: The Application of Liberalism to India', *Journal of Modern History*, xxviii (1956), 234–46.

——, *British Attitudes Towards India, 1783–1858* (London, 1961).

BELL, H. C. F., *Lord Palmerston* (2 vols., London, 1936).

BILGRAMI, A. H., *Afghanistan and British India, 1793–1907* (New Delhi, 1972).

BOLSOVER, G. H., 'Lord Ponsonby and the Eastern Question (1833–1839)', *Slavonic Review*, xiii (1934–5), 98–118.

——, 'Palmerston, Metternich, and the Eastern Question in 1834', *English Historical Review*, li (1936), 237–56.

——, 'David Urquhart and the Eastern Question in 1833–37', *Journal of Modern History*, viii (1936), 444–67.

——, 'Nicholas I and the Partition of Turkey', *Slavonic Review*, xxvii (1948–9), 115–45.

BOULGER, D. C., *Lord William Bentinck* (Oxford, 1892).

BOURNE, KENNETH, *The Foreign Policy of Victorian England, 1830–1902* (Oxford, 1970).

BRAUN, PETER C. M. S., *Die Verteidigung Indiens, 1800–1907: Das Problem des Vorwärtsstrategie* (Cologne, 1968).

BULWER, SIR H. L., *The Life of Henry John Temple, Viscount Palmerston* (3 vols., London, 1870–4).

CASSELS, NANCY G., 'Bentinck: Humanitarian and Imperialist—the Abolition of Suttee', *Journal of British Studies*, v (1965–6), 77–87.

CHAUDHURI, K. N., 'India's Foreign Trade and the Cessation of the East India Company's Trading Activities, 1828–1840', *Economic History Review*, 2nd series, xix (1966), 345–63.

CHOKSEY, R. D., *Mountstuart Elphinstone: The Indian Years, 1796–1827* (Bombay, 1971).

CLIVE, J., *Macaulay: The Shaping of an Historian* (New York, 1973).

CRAWLEY, C. W., 'Anglo-Russian Relations, 1815–40', *Cambridge Historical Journal*, iii (1929), 47–73.

——, *The Question of Greek Independence: A Study of British Policy in the Near East, 1821–1833* (London, 1930).

CUNNINGHAM, ALLAN, '"Dragomania": The Dragomans of the British Embassy in Turkey', *St. Anthony's Papers* (1961), 81–100.

——, 'The Oczakov Debate', *Middle Eastern Studies*, i (1964–5), 209–37.

CURTISS, JOHN S., *The Russian Army under Nicholas I, 1825–1855* (Durham, N.C., 1965).

DAVIS, H. W. C., 'The Great Game in Asia, 1800–1844', *Proceedings of the British Academy*, xii (1926), 179–226.

DODWELL, H. H., *The Founder of Modern Egypt* (Cambridge, 1931).

EDWARDES, MICHAEL, *Playing the Great Game: A Victorian Cold War* (London, 1975).

ENTNER, M. L., *Russo-Persian Commercial Relations, 1828–1914* (Gainesville, 1965).

FASAI, HASAN-E, *History of Persia under Qajar Rule; from the Persian of Farsnama-ye Naseri*, trans. H. Busse (New York, 1972).

FRASER-TYTLER, SIR W. K., *Afghanistan: A Study* (London, 1950).

FURBER, HOLDEN, 'The Overland Route to India in the Seventeenth and Eighteenth Centuries', *Journal of Indian History*, xxix (1951)ʼ 105–21.

GALBRAITH, JOHN S., 'The "Turbulent Frontier", as a Factor in British Expansion', *Comparative Studies in Society and History*, ii (1959–60), 150–68.

GALLAGHER, J., and ROBINSON, R., 'The Imperialism of Free Trade', *Economic History Review*, 2nd series, vi (1953–4), 1–15.

GHORBAL, S., *The Beginnings of the Egyptian Question and the Rise of Mehemet Ali* (London, 1928).

GLEASON, J. H., *The Genesis of Russophobia in Great Britain: A Study in the Interaction of Policy and Opinion* (Cambridge, Mass., 1950).

GLEIG, G. R., *Life of Major General Sir Thomas Munro, Bart.* (2 vols., London, 1830).

GOPAL, SURENDRA, 'Reaching for the Oxus: A Study of Central Asian Politics in the First Half of the Nineteenth Century', *Journal of Indian History*, Golden Jubilee Volume (1973), 745–60.

GORIANOV, S. M., *Le Bospore et les Dardanelles* (Paris, 1910).

GRENVILLE, J. A. S., *Lord Salisbury and Foreign Policy: The Close of the Nineteenth Century* (London, 1964).

HARDEN, EVELYN J., 'Griboedev and the Willock Affair', *Slavic Review*, xxx (1971), 74–91.

HASRAT, B. J., *Anglo-Sikh Relations, 1799–1849* (Hoshiapur, 1968).

HILLIKER, J. F., 'Charles Edward Trevelyan as an Educational Reformer in India', *Canadian Journal of History*, ix (1974), 275–92.

HINDE, WENDY, *George Canning* (London, 1973).

HINSLEY, F. H., *Power and the Pursuit of Peace: Theory and Practice in the History of Relations between States* (Cambridge, 1963).

HOSKINS, H. L., *British Routes to India* (London, 1928).

HUTTENBACK, R. A., *British Relations with Sind, 1799–1843* (Berkeley/Los Angeles, 1962).

INGRAM, EDWARD, 'The Defence of British India', *Journal of Indian History*, xlviii (1970), 565–83, xlix (1971), 57–78, Golden Jubilee Volume (1973), 595–622.

——, 'An Aspiring Buffer State: Anglo-Persian Relations in the Third Coalition 1804–1807', *Historical Journal*, xvi (1973), 509–33.

——, 'A Preview of the Great Game in Asia, 1798–1801', *Middle Eastern Studies*, ix (1973), 3–18, 157–74, 296–314, x (1974), 15–35.

——, 'The Defence of India, 1874–1914: A Strategic Dilemma', *Militärgeschichtliche Mitteilungen* (1974), 215–24.

——, 'The Rules of the Game: A Commentary on the Defence of British India, 1798–1829', *Journal of Imperial and Commonwealth History*, iii (1974–5), 257–79.

ISSAWI, CHARLES, 'The Tabriz-Trabzon Trade, 1830–1900: Rise

and Decline of a Route', *International Journal of Middle East Studies*, i (1971), 18–27.

——, 'British Trade and the Rise of Beirut, 1830–1860', *International Journal of Middle East Studies*, viii (1977), 91–101.

JOHNSTON, H. J. M., *British Emigration Policy, 1815–1830* (Oxford, 1972).

KAYE, SIR J. W., *Life and Correspondence of Henry St. George Tucker* (London, 1854).

——, *Life and Correspondence of Major-General Sir John Malcolm* (2 vols., London, 1856).

——, *Life and Correspondence of Charles, Lord Metcalfe* (2 vols., London, 1858).

——, *Lives of Indian Officers* (London, 1904).

KELLY, J. B., *Britain and the Persian Gulf, 1795–1880* (Oxford, 1968).

KIMCHE, D., 'The Opening of the Red Sea to European Ships in the Late Eighteenth Century', *Middle Eastern Studies*, viii (1972), 63–71.

KISSINGER, H. A., *A World Restored: The Politics of Conservatism in a Revolutionary Age* (Universal Library Edition, New York, 1964).

LAMBTON, A. K. S., 'Persian Society under the Kajars', *Central Asian Journal*, xlviii (1961), 123–39.

LANE-POOLE, STANLEY, *Life of General F. R. Chesney, by his Wife and Daughter* (London, 1885).

——, *Life of the Rt. Hon. Stratford Canning, Viscount Stratford de Redcliffe* (2 vols., London, 1888).

LANG, D. M., *The Last Years of the Georgian Monarchy, 1658–1832* (New York, 1957).

LEWIS, BERNARD, *The Emergence of Modern Turkey* (London, 1961).

LONGFORD, ELIZABETH, *Wellington: Pillar of State* (London, 1972).

LONGRIGG, H. S., *Four Centuries of Modern Iraq* (Oxford, 1925).

LOWE, C. J., *The Reluctant Imperialists: British Foreign Policy, 1878–1902* (2 vols., 1967).

MACDONAGH, O., 'The Anti-Imperialism of Free Trade', *Economic History Review*, 2nd series, 14 (1961–2), 489–501.

MANNONI, O., *Prospero and Caliban: The Psychology of Colonization* (New York, 1956).

MARLOWE, JOHN, *Anglo-Egyptian Relations, 1880–1953* (London, 1954).

MARSTON, T., *Britain's Imperial Role in the Red Sea Area, 1800–1878* (Hamden, Conn., 1961).

Memoir of the Rt. Hon. Sir John McNeill, G.C.B., and of his Second Wife Elizabeth Wilson, by their grand-daughter (London, 1910).

MEREDITH, COLIN, 'Early Qajar Administration: An Analysis of its Development and Functions', *Iranian Studies*, iv (1971), 59–84.

MILLS, H., *Peacock: His Circle and his Age* (Cambridge, 1969).

MITCHELL, H., *The Whigs in Opposition, 1815–1830* (Oxford, 1967).

MOHAN LAL, *Life of the Amir Dost Mahomet Khan* (2 vols., London, 1846).

MONROE, ELIZABETH, *Britain's Moment in the Middle East, 1914–1956* (London, 1963).

MOORE, R. J., 'Imperialism and "Free Trade" Policy in India, 1853–4', *Economic History Review*, 2nd series, xvii (1964–5), 135–45.

MORISON, J. L., 'From Alexander Burnes to Frederick Roberts: A Survey of Imperial Frontier Policy', *Proceedings of the British Academy*, xxii (1936), 177–206.

MOSELY, P. E., *Russian Diplomacy and the Opening of the Eastern Question in 1838 and 1839* (Cambridge, Mass., 1934).

NEW, CHESTER W., *Lord Durham: A Biography of John George Lambton, First Earl of Durham* (Oxford, 1929).

NIGHTINGALE, PAMELA, *Trade and Empire in Western India, 1784–1806* (Cambridge, 1970).

NORRIS, J. A., *The First Afghan War, 1838–1842* (Cambridge, 1967).

PAKRAVAN, EMINEH, *Abbas Mirza* (Teheran, 1958).

PANIGRAHI, D. N., *Charles Metcalfe in India: Ideas and Administration, 1806–1835* (Delhi, 1968).

PARKER, R. A. C., 'Britain, France, and Scandinavia, 1939–40', *History*, lxi (1976), 369–87.

PHILIPS, C. H., *The East India Company, 1784–1834* (2nd edit., Manchester, 1961).

PLATT, D. C. M., *Finance, Trade, and Politics in British Foreign Policy, 1815–1914* (Oxford, 1968).

——, 'The Imperialism of Free Trade: Some Reservations', *Economic History Review*, 2nd series, xxi (1968), 296–306.

——, 'Further Objections to an "Imperialism of Free Trade", 1830–60', *Economic History Review*, 2nd series, xxvi (1973), 77–91.

PRINSEP, HENRY T., *Origin of the Sikh Power in the Punjab and the Political Life of Maharaja Runjeet Singh* (Calcutta, 1834).

PURYEAR, V. J., *International Economics and Diplomacy in the Near East: A Study of British Commercial Policy in the Levant, 1834–1853* (Palo Alto, 1935).

——, *France and the Levant (from the Bourbon Restoration to the Peace of Kutayah)* (Berkeley/Los Angeles, 1941).

——, *Napoleon and the Dardanelles* (Berkeley/Los Angeles, 1951).

RAWLINSON, G., *A Memoir of Major-General Sir Henry Creswicke Rawlinson* (London, 1898).

REID, STUART J., *Life and Letters of the First Earl of Durham* (2 vols., London, 1906).

RIDLEY, JASPER, *Lord Palmerston* (London, 1970).

ROBINSON, GERTRUDE, *David Urquhart: Some Chapters in the Life of a Victorian Knight-Errant of Justice and Liberty* (Oxford, 1920).

ROBINSON, R., and GALLAGHER, J., *Africa and the Victorians: The Official Mind of Imperialism* (London, 1962).

RODKEY, F. S., 'Lord Palmerston and the Rejuvenation of Turkey, 1830–1841', *Journal of Modern History*, i (1929), 570–93, ii (1930), 193–225.

——, 'The Views of Palmerston and Metternich on the Eastern Question in 1834', *English Historical Review*, xlv (1930), 627–40.

——, 'The Attempts of Briggs and Co. to Guide British Policy in the Levant in the Interest of Mahomet Ali', *Journal of Modern History*, v (1933), 324–51.

ROSSELLI, J., *Lord William Bentinck: The Making of a Liberal Imperialist* (London, 1974).

——, 'Lord William Bentinck and his Age', *Bengal: Past and Present*, xciv (1975), 68–88.

SEMMEL, BERNARD, *The Rise of Free Trade Imperialism: Classical Political Economy, The Empire of Free Trade, and Imperialism, 1750–1850* (Cambridge, 1970).

SETON-WATSON, R. W., *Britain in Europe, 1789–1914: A Survey of Foreign Policy* (Cambridge, 1945).

SHAW, A. G. L., ed., *Great Britain and the Colonies, 1815–1865* (London, 1970).

SINGH, KHUSHWANT, *Ranjit Singh* (London, 1962).

——, *A History of the Sikhs* (2 vols., Princeton, 1963).

SOUTHGATE, DONALD, *The Most English Minister: The Policies and Politics of Palmerston* (London, 1966).

SPEAR, PERCEVAL, 'Bentinck and Education', *Cambridge Historical Journal*, v (1938), 78–101.

STOKES, ERIC, *The English Utilitarians and India* (Oxford, 1963).

SWAIN, J. E., *The Struggle for the Control of the Mediterranean Prior to 1848: A Study in Anglo-French Relations* (Philadelphia, 1933).

TEMPERLEY, H. W. V., *England and the Near East: The Crimea* (London, 1936).

——, *The Foreign Policy of Canning* (2nd edit., London, 1966).

THOMPSON, E., *The Life of Charles, Lord Metcalfe* (London, 1937).

THORNTON, A. P., *The Imperial Idea and its Enemies: A Study in British Power* (London, 1959).

TRESSE, R., 'L'Installation de premier consul d'Angleterre à Damas, 1830–1834', *Revue d'histoire des colonies françaises*, xxiv (1936), 359–80.

TREVELYAN, SIR G. O., *The Life and Letters of Lord Macaulay* ('Silver Library' Edition, London, 1908).

VARMA, BIRENDRA, *English East India Company and the Afghans, 1757–1800* (Calcutta, 1968).

VERETÉ, MAYIR, 'Palmerston and the Levant Crisis, 1832', *Journal of Modern History*, xxiv (1952), 143–51.

WARD, J. T., *Sir James Graham* (London, 1967).

WATSON, R. E., *A History of Persia; from the Beginning of the Nineteenth Century to the Year 1858* (London, 1866).

WEBSTER, SIR CHARLES, *The Foreign Policy of Castlereagh* (2 vols., London, 1925–31).

——, 'Palmerston, Metternich, and the European System, 1830–41', *Proceedings of the British Academy*, xx (1934), 125–58.

——, 'Urquhart, Ponsonby, and Palmerston', *English Historical Review*, lxii (1947), 327–51.

——, *The Foreign Policy of Palmerston, 1830–1841* (2 vols., London, 1951).

WRIGHT, H. R. C., *East Indian Economic Problems in the Age of Cornwallis and Raffles* (London, 1961).

YAPP, M. E., 'The Control of the Persian Mission 1822–1836', *University of Birmingham Historical Journal*, vii (1959–60), 162–79.

ZIADEH, N. A., *Damascus under the Mamluks* (Norman, 1964).

UNPUBLISHED WORKS

ADAMIYAT, F., 'The Diplomatic Relations of Persia with Britain, Turkey and Russia, 1815–30' (Ph.D., London, 1949).

BARRETT, C. L., 'Lord William Bentinck in Bengal, 1828–1835' (D. Phil., Oxon., 1953–4).

HERLIHY, P. A. M., 'Russian Grain and Mediterranean Markets, 1774–1861' (Ph.D., Pennsylvania, 1963).

KAPADIA, E. R., 'The Diplomatic Career of Sir Claude Wade: A Study of British Relations with the Sikhs and Afghans, July 1823 to March 1840' (M.A., London, 1938).

KHAN, M. G. I., 'British Policy in Iraq, 1828–43' (Ph.D., London, 1967).

KOURY, G. J. 'The Province of Damascus, 1783–1832' (Ph.D., Michigan, 1970).

MEREDITH, C., 'The Qajar Response to Russia's Military Challenge, 1804–28' (Ph.D., Princeton, 1973).

MIDDLETON, C. R., 'The Administration of British Foreign Policy, 1782–1846' (Ph.D., Duke, 1969).

STRONG, J. W., 'Russian Relations with Khiva, Bokhara, and Kokand, 1800–1858' (Ph.D., Harvard, 1964).

WADE, J. E., 'Persia: Britain's Pawn in India's Defence, 1797–1841' (Ph.D., Georgia, 1968).

YAPP, M. E., 'British Policy in Central Asia, 1830–43' (Ph.D., London, 1959).

Index